MW00622210

THE CALIFORNIA FIELD
A T L A S

THE CALIFORNIA FIELD
A T L A S

———— Written and Illustrated ————
by Obi Kaufmann

Heyday
Berkeley, California

The publisher is grateful to the Moore Family Foundation
for their generous support of this project.

Library of Congress Cataloging-in-Publication Data

Names: Kaufmann, Obi, author, illustrator, cartographer. } Kaufmann, William,
copyright holder.
Title: The California field atlas / written and illustrated by Obi Kaufmann.
Description: Berkeley, California : Heyday, 2017. } "2017 by William
Kaufmann."
Identifiers: LCCN 2017017241 } ISBN 9781597144025 (pbk.)
Subjects: LCSH: Natural areas--California--Maps. } Natural
areas--California--Pictorial works. } National parks and
reserves--California--Pictorial works. } LCGFT: Atlases. } Pictorial maps.
Classification: LCC G1526.G3 K3 2017 } DDC 557.94022/3--dc23
LC record available at https://lccn.loc.gov/2017017241

Cover Art: Obi Kaufmann
Cover Design: Ashley Ingram
Interior Design and Typesetting: Obi Kaufmann and Ashley Ingram

Orders, inquiries, and correspondence should be addressed to:
    Heyday
    P.O. Box 9145, Berkeley, CA 94709
    (510) 549-3564, Fax (510) 549-1889
    www.heydaybooks.com

Printed in China by Imago

10 9 8 7 6 5 4

For Alli

coastal Redwood
Sequoia sempervirens

1: *The California Field Atlas* presumes that every natural feature of California is alive and deserves an emancipated rebirth from the old human paradigms of utility and extraction without reciprocation and gratitude.

2: *The Field Atlas* is a manual of geographic literacy, with both a scientific agenda and an artistic one—one is not political and one is.

Contents

Coulter pine
Pinus coulteri

09. The Counties

Sierra Nevada Bighorn
Ovis canadensis sierrae

California condor
Gymnogyps californianus

Author's Introduction to Reading and Enjoying
The California Field Atlas

This is a love story.

California is the land where I was born and where, having spent a happy life walking through its forests and sleeping out under its stars, I hope to someday die, far off trail under some unnamed sequoia. My spirit is of this place, and to sing of its living spirit is to sing the most interesting song I've ever heard. Although I understand California's puzzle-like personality as well as I have ever understood anything, I still feel like a novice—an infatuated child, a lost and humble beggar asking for its natural wisdom. I want to hold the whole of California in my hand, like a diamond or a spinning top; I want to coax this single piece of the universe into opening up its secrets. By writing this book, I seek to participate in the wild reimagining of this place, past the scars inflicted over the past 200 years, to reveal a story about what has always been here and what will remain long after our human residency here is through. I am a poet and a painter, and my work is based on a mode of naturalist interpretation that builds from hard science to focus the inner lens of truth. With the publication of *The California Field Atlas*, I present a new portfolio of invented geography that balances ecology and aesthetics as driving and orienting forces.

I have been working on this book my whole life. Many of these maps were sketched ten years ago on scraps of paper and have changed little since, while some have gone through ten versions in the last six weeks. The editing process has been as challenging as the drafting process, as how the material is presented is at least as valuable as the raw information itself. Each map is a puzzle, but a puzzle meant to be read more than solved. Sit with each map for a moment before you begin to digest the layout and take in the pattern of the information. I started this project dreaming of presenting California in a compendium of symbols and names—a delivery system of geographic knowledge tuned to such a high and efficient frequency that the transmission of knowledge becomes effortless and the information can be absorbed, more than interpreted. I have always imagined that, with the right lexicon, the map itself might be immediately appreciable, like a rose or a painting.

Every hand-painted map in this book is a story, alas only partially told. Every map presents the veneer of a deeper narrative, complete only in its own understanding of itself, in its own scale and on its own terms. Some of the maps, like poems or short stories, are content to not fully explain themselves. The rhythm to their visual information necessarily affords some modicum of deviation, a barely perceptible margin of subjectivity. The secret to reading these maps is unlocked by the cipher of the icons. The most important road into this labyrinth of geographic language is this book's comprising eleven symbols. Study the key and the puzzle pieces will begin to come together. The relevance of each piece of topography is revealed in its juxtaposition with the other pieces, such that skimming each map reveals—via color, shape, and composition—a number of truths even without the use of a single word.

What California character do I describe here? Map after map piled up in my frenzied quest to peer more deeply into this land's great, beautiful being. Major highways appeared as ghostly red lines, and urban centers became faded red dots beside resplendent green waves of marching forests. The California I describe knows less of humanity in both the past and the future. Those human Californians who wish to continue their blessed residency here will be blessed with vision beyond the  entrepreneurial crush and exist such that all activity aims to create a resource surplus, working to expand nature's inclusive glory and finding this to be the only true kind of wealth.

As you make your way through *The California Field Atlas* you will encounter the results of both editorial choices and stylistic choices. While my greatest challenge has been tackling both of these choices with attention to consistency, I have let the whole thing breathe with a great, soft margin of artful life. The book is replete with un-dotted and un-crossed letters, ghostly lines that hint at the deeper meanings of certain locales and redundant navigation tools that all revolve around the same piece of knowledge. These choices were made intentionally: to reflect a larger creative aesthetic, a song of topography that transcends any books of maps that precede this one.

The issue that cartographers wrestle with above all others is the potentially very thorny issue of *scale*. Most of us who look at maps online are now used to the convention of the scrolling zoom-in, zoom-out feature that translates geographic scale conveniently. In book form, an analog medium, we must invent new contrivances to make consistent the presentation of vastly different and often competing levels of perception, measurement, and narrative. On a human level, *scale* is addressed in the maps of *The California Field Atlas* as sublimated by the use of symbols. A campground bears the same icon as a military base, and a tiny, backcountry group of buildings that can barely be called a community, let alone a town, is notated with the same symbol as a major urban center. This device of symbols is necessary for the equivocation of geographic knowledge, and it is presented in the same way across the entire state to reflect a homogenization of scale. I use the same map icons to serve a larger purpose: to suggest how each map, employing its own themes, dovetails into the greater sensibility, the greater story. By simplifying and standardizing the legend, I am able to make use of an economy of scale that enables every map to either live on its own or be in conversation with any other map, thus presenting an easily digested, unified vision.

The California Field Atlas is organized into ten chapters that move through time, element by element, in a reimagining of California as a heroic capsule, beholden to not much outside of itself that is complete and eternal. Human beings make few incursions into these maps, and those they do make seem transitory or even ineffectual in light of California's broader presence. That being said, this is a book of maps composed in the early 21st century, when the systems of human ecology seem to have infiltrated every natural system except perhaps in the deepest reaches of backcountry wilderness. Issues like the damming of rivers, man-made climate change, and what tomorrow may bring are addressed throughout the book at multiple junctures. However, with the exception of chapter 9, which is based on the largely arbitrary political overlay that makes up California's 58 counties, humanity is a second thought.

I make more reference to major walking trails in this book than I do to roads. Trails tell a different story in that they are often designed to follow ridgelines or to penetrate deep wilderness, unlike a concrete monstrosity useful only for the automobile. The chapters are divided by elemental theme and not by adjacent geography, so one map might follow another that depicts an area several hundred miles away.

I have organized and oriented the maps to conform to a small set of rules. Each map is designated by a four-digit number that indexes the information it presents. You might notice that there is no compass rose, nor are cardinal direction identifiers used in the book. For convenience and standardization, north is the top of the book; in each map, the declination deviance might fall upward of ten degrees. I believe that this margin is forgivable, because it does not alter the quality of the inherent, elemental information provided in any one map. It is also important to remember that each of these maps is an expressive painting and not to get too bogged down with the meaning behind aesthetic choices, such as the use of a particular color for a particular map. My palette was chosen largely from an intuitive place, from my many decades of walking California, and it was designed to convey an abstract spectrum between warm and cold, forested and barren, urban and rural, low and high, and a thousand other polarities open to personal interpretation. Throughout the book, you will find portraits of critters, flowers, or other wild features of the local landscape. I am a wildlife painter; this is my background, vocation, and passion. I have chosen each creature as a kind of totem protector of the region it represents. I see a pantheon of biodiversity on display and an almost topographic relevance in the well-rendered animal, as if the aesthetic truth in form between the portrait and the map are philosophical equivalents, and whatever the reference might be, meaning resonates in the transmitted beauty.

After you have acquainted yourself with the chapter structure of *The California Field Atlas*, the flow of the maps within each chapter, and the mode of information conveyed in each map, then the poetry of the book will be available to you. You can sit with the words. The names are the heart of the power in the geography. A map can be an invitation, an invitation to wield power over a place, to understand its systems and to be counted among its people. The power of geographic literacy is rewarding in its own right, but it is essential to being known as being from any certain place. *The California Field Atlas* is ultimately a map to some intrinsic part in the identity of every Californian: an invitation to those from here to understand what "here" actually is, and for those not from here to maybe understand what being a Californian actually means. This book offers a great unburdening of ignorance and empowers all of California's native and adopted children with a useful mythology, a tool belt to help them unlock their own place within California. This book is not full of road maps, and it won't help you if you are lost in the woods. It comes with a different set of guarantees and assurances, in that it plainly lays out the entirety of the state as a single, integrative being composed of living patterns and ancient processes. The book describes California's core systems of geography, ecology, and topography and shows how those individual systems conspire together to become greater than the sum of their parts.

Welcome to My World:
Notes on Enjoying *The California Field Atlas*

1. Is this a book you sit down with and read? Probably not, unless you are a very special type of person. Each map is designed as a puzzle that, unlocked, reveals something specific, unique, and beautifully integral about each place.

2. These are hand-painted maps. Don't get frustrated by a smudge here or a drip there; these maps live in an expressive world and, given that most were painted outside in the places they depict, that's okay.

3. There are wildlife paintings throughout the book that may or may not be directly related to the subject at hand but generally make geographical sense; you aren't going to see a seal in the desert, but you might find a hummingbird around some flowers or an elk wandering in the redwoods.

4. Each chapter has a different character. Each chapter has its own voice, with its own motifs, icons, and internal patterns of consistency. For example, the mountains of their own chapter are treated as the subjects of portraits in round paintings, and the desert chapter is dirty, smudged with charcoal.

5. The wildlife paintings capture the spirit of the subject as much as its shape and form; you can trust the plumage colors of birds to be pretty accurate, but don't trust red trees or a purple coyote. The paintings contain only limited field-guide-type information.

6. This is my story of California. Although I am a native of California, I'm not Native Californian. I wanted to include tribal maps and traditions and a number of other features of the Native Californian world, but, ultimately, that's another book and not my story.

7. I have hiked, camped, sweated, slept, dreamed, and continue to adventure in all of these places, but this is not that story. This is not a collection of war stories. This is for you. *The California Field Atlas* is a catalog of an eternal face, a book written across the whole realm of California itself. The effort of all these maps cumulates in a great democratization of the geography; the hinterlands get as much attention as the big showstoppers, like Yosemite and the redwoods.

8. I wanted a book that had everything in one place: maps, statistics, and natural history. I didn't want to write an academic field guide, a book of road maps, or a general book of trivia. I wanted to write an essential handbook. I realize that despite all my efforts to create the ultimate compendium, *The California Field Atlas* has my filter on it, and I am a painter and poet, so the book operates through that lens.

Lastly, a warning: I'm not afraid of presenting any false information. I have double-checked and cited my sources over a lifetime of research. What I am afraid of is presenting a too-rosy, greenwashed picture of the natural systems of California. As stewards of this land, we are largely doing a poor job, and perhaps I should have done more to warn of the threats our state faces on an environmental level. I am at peace with what I hope is an uplifting tone throughout the book because that is the feeling I get when I experience California's extensive nature, its biodiversity, its fathomless living networks. I am confident that those networks will survive us and our imposed ecology, and I am happy to introduce you to those networks as I know them to be.

Obi Kaufmann
Oakland, California
2017

00.01 The Ages of the Earth

Era	Period	Epoch	Millions of years ago
Cenozoic	Quaternary	Holocene	
		Pleistocene	0.2
		Pliocene	2-3
	Tertiary	Miocene	5
		Oligocene	24
		Eocene	37
		Paleocene	53-54
Mesozoic	Cretaceous		65
	Jurassic		145
	Triassic		210
Paleozoic	Permian		245
	Carboniferous	Pennsylvanian	280
		Mississippian	
	Devonian		380
	Silurian		410
	Ordovician		435
	Cambrian		500
	Ediacaran		570
Precambrian	Proterozoic		700
			4,600

one square mile

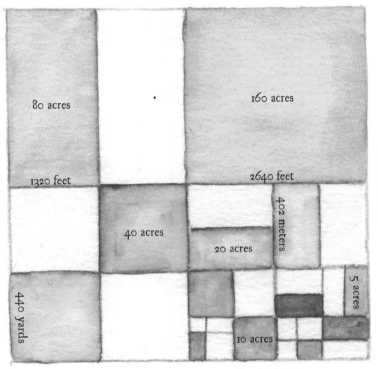

American Football Field
53 yards x 120 yards = 1.32 acres

1000 acres = 1.56 square miles
1000 square miles = 640,000 acres
1 acre = 43,560 square feet
1 mile = 5280 feet = 1.61 kilometer

Named Peak; mountain; named hill; named knoll

Mountain Range; mountain pass; ridgeline; secondary peak; point

Main River; fresh water; primary water feature; waterfall; spring

Tributary; aqueduct; secondary water feature

Lake; body of water; ocean feature; slough; dry lake

Landmark; area of special interest; wildlife area; county border; island

Wilderness; federal wilderness area; natural site; nature preserve

Trail; named trail; road; highway

Park; public land; national forest

Town; city; urban area; backcountry crossroads; ghost town

Camp; campground; fort; military base; ranch; reservation; installation; dam; man-made ruin; historical landmark

00.04 A Note on Binomial Nomenclature

There is a lot of magic in the naming of things. It is my contention that the more we know about nature's secrets, the more we can enjoy it. Simply being able to call the elements of nature by their proper names helps us to experience them and allows their beauty to unfold, both intellectually and emotionally. The common names of animal and plant species are easy to remember, but they don't mean much scientifically. Officially, each species has two names in Latin, which together are considered their universal scientific name. The first part of the name indicates the genus and the second part indicates the specific epithet. Sound the names out loud and get to know them, and the patterns of form and life stories begin to emerge on an ecological level. When talking about a species, refer to its genus, or genera name, and don't worry about learning the second word—the epithet—unless necessary. For example, *Calocedrus decurrens* is the name of the incense cedar, which is also called the Sierra cedar, and which is not actually a true cedar (genus *Cedrus*) at all. *Calocedrus* is the only species of its genus in California, so it both limits confusion by avoiding the generalized common name and is taxonomically accurate to call the tree *Calocedrus* (which translates, conveniently enough, to California cedar).

01. UNFOLDING CALIFORNIA

Short faced bear
Arctodus simus

Map 01.01 Walking California

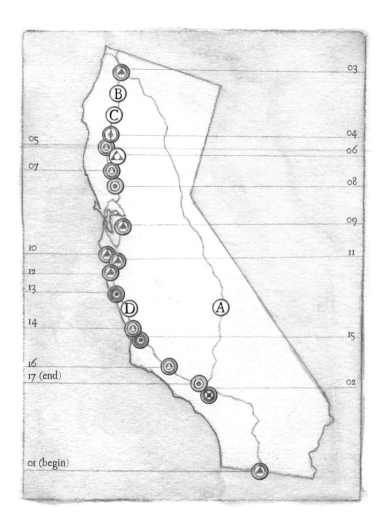

A. The Pacific Crest Trail
B. The Bigfoot Trail
C. The Monument Trail
D. The Condor Trail

01. Campo, the start of the Pacific Crest Trail
02. Agua Dulce
03. The northern crest of the Big Foot Trail
04. Yolla Bolly, the end of the Big Foot Trail
05. Mendocino National Forest
06. Snow Mountain
07. Berryessa Snow Mountain National Monument
08. Lake Berryessa
09. Bay Area Ridge Trail
10. Skyline Boulevard
11. Skyline-to-the-Sea Trail
12. Highway 1
13. Big Sur
14. Los Padres National Forest, northern
15. San Luis Obispo
16. Los Padres National Forest, southern
17. Lake Piru

The California Field Atlas arose from a pedestrian ethic. As you move through the wilderness at a walking pace, nature reveals itself to you, not unlike the way a book does. Just as books require literacy, nature requires a level of conceptual symbol reading and narrative comprehension. California is home to some of the most well-maintained trails that lead through some of the most exquisite landscape the world has to offer. Indeed, these paths not only offer the most navigable passage to California's ecological treasure, but also are certainly among the longest-lasting of all the manufactured infrastructure that humanity has ever conceived; long after our concrete jungles have returned to the dust from which they were built, generations of the distant future will need only trim some shrubs and clear some trees to find the marble staircases of the Condor Trail, or the High Sierra paths through the foxtail pine forests of the John Muir Trail.

California is home to several major wilderness trails that draw a circle around the entire state. In about seven months, you could circumambulate the whole thing. You would start in April at the Mexico border and traverse the 1,699 miles north along the Sierra Crest to the Oregon border. You'd reach the northernmost point of the Bigfoot Trail somewhere in the last half of July. Walking south now, you would make it to south Yolla Bolly sometime in mid-August; you would be hot, but you would stay at 7,000 feet in elevation, where there is plenty of naturally occurring water. Then you would traverse the Mendocino National Forest on forest service roads until you reached Snow Mountain and the Berryessa Snow Mountain National Monument. In a few years, this is when you would be able to join the Monument Trail.

The Monument Trail does not yet exist—it is currently being built—so as you descend through the national monument you would need to again follow forest service roads until you reached the Bay Area Rim Trail. It would now be mid-September, and the cool ocean breeze off the San Francisco Bay would be as refreshing as it is beautiful. The Condor Trail doesn't officially start until Big Sur, so you would most likely follow

Skyline Boulevard across the Santa Cruz Mountains, cut down the Skyline-to-the-Sea Trail at Big Basin State Park, and walk Highway 1 to Big Sur.

It would now be early October, and hopefully there are no late summer wildfires in the Santa Lucias to delay you as you descend through the coastal crest of Monterey County. The Condor Trail unites the Northern and the Southern Los Padres National Forests with only a break in the route through private land in San Luis Obispo. From here, the first part of November would see you on your way to Lake Piru, the end of the Condor Trail in the Angeles National Forest, only 17 miles from Agua Dulce.

Map 01.02 The Pacific Crest Trail in California

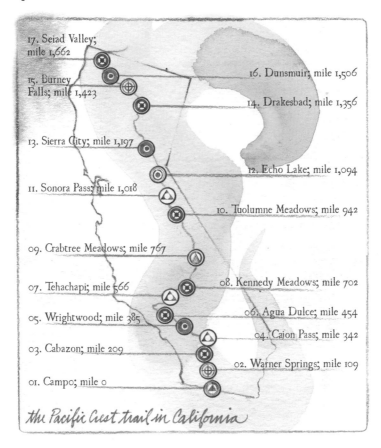

17. Seiad Valley; mile 1,662

15. Burney Falls; mile 1,423

16. Dunsmuir; mile 1,506

14. Drakesbad; mile 1,356

13. Sierra City; mile 1,197

12. Echo Lake; mile 1,094

11. Sonora Pass; mile 1,018

10. Tuolumne Meadows; mile 942

09. Crabtree Meadows; mile 767

07. Tehachapi; mile 566

08. Kennedy Meadows; mile 702

05. Wrightwood; mile 385

06. Agua Dulce; mile 454

04. Cajon Pass; mile 342

03. Cabazon; mile 209

02. Warner Springs; mile 109

01. Campo; mile 0

the Pacific Crest trail in California

The Pacific Crest Trail is a walking highway for humanity to regain and re-member itself, its place, and its purpose; even if you never have a chance yourself to through-hike this most famous of California's trails, let your imagination be filled by its high mountain wonder, taste the same cold wind as the eagles, and dream under the oldest trees on the planet.

The Pacific Crest Trail begins in Mexico and ends in Canada; in California, the marked locations are accompanied by the noted walking mileage.

Map 01.03 The John Muir Trail

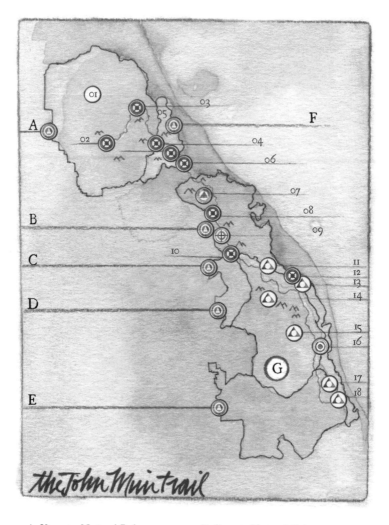

A. Yosemite National Park
B. John Muir Wilderness
C. Kaiser Wilderness
D. Jennie Lakes Wilderness

E. Sequoia National Park
F. Ansel Adams Wilderness
G. Kings Canyon National Park

20 miles

01.03

This trail is the most important for any self-respecting lover of California to experience. The John Muir Trail follows the same footpath as the Pacific Crest Trail across the spine of California's High Sierra for nearly 160 miles, almost entirely above 8,000 feet in elevation; a good portion of it sits higher than 10,000 feet. The route will take you through the three main national parks in the Sierra Nevada: Yosemite, Kings Canyon, and Sequoia. Plan on it taking a bit less than a month to walk, and don't rush it; do it in July when the wildflowers hit and watch heaven unfold.

01. Yosemite National Park
02. Happy Isles
03. Tuolumne Meadows
04. Donahue Pass
05. Garnet Lake Footbridge
06. Red's Meadow
07. Duck Pass Trail
08. Silver Pass
09. Mono Creek
10. Selden Pass
11. Mount Darwin
12. Muir Pass; Middle Palisade
13. Mather Pass; Split Mountain
14. Mount Goddard
15. Taboose Pass; Triple Divide Peak
16. Dollar Lake
17. Forester Pass; Mount Tyndall
18. Whitney Summit

Rae Lakes, High Sierra

Map 01.04 The Bigfoot Trail

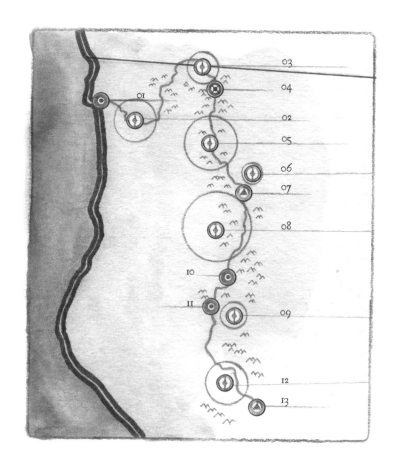

50 miles

01.04

For both the amateur and the professional ecologist, the Bigfoot Trail is probably the most interesting and beautiful in California. The 360-mile trail makes its way through some of the most biodiverse forest in the world. There is no other place in California where you can find more species of trees, flowers, mammals, or birds.

01. Crescent City
02. Siskiyou Wilderness
03. Red Buttes Wilderness
04. Seiad Valley
05. Marble Mountain Wilderness
06. Russian Wilderness
07. Pacific Crest Trail merger
08. Trinity Alps Wilderness
09. Chanchelulla Wilderness
10. Junction City
11. Hayfork
12. Yolla Bolly–Middle Eel Wilderness
13. Ides Cove trailhead

Grizzly falls
Trinity alps

Map 01.05 The Bay Area Rim Trail

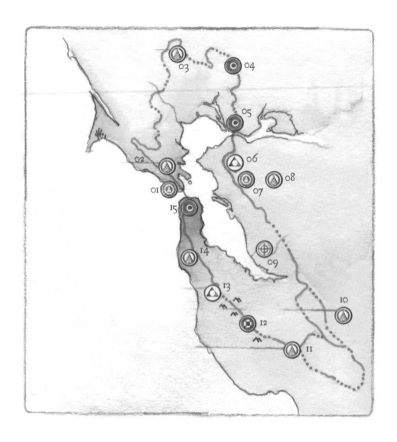

20 miles

01.05

The greatest estuary in America, the San Francisco Bay is traced with an elegant line that is the walking path of the Bay Area Rim Trail. The trail is an excellent way to get in deep with the coast redwood, both as a type of forest ecosystem and a complex organism in itself. In San Mateo and Marin Counties you will find old-growth examples of ancient redwoods, and in Alameda County, you will pass through the ghost of some the most magnificent forests the world has ever known. In Redwood Regional Park, for example, there is a stump that measures 35 feet in diameter. Today, the largest trees in Humboldt County measure a mere 20 feet.

At this point the trail remains incomplete, as indicated by the dashed lines.

01. Muir Woods National Monument
02. Mount Tamalpais
03. Sugarloaf
04. Napa
05. Benicia
06. San Pablo Ridge
07. Redwood Regional Park
08. Alameda Creek
09. Mount Hamilton
10. Mount Umunhum
11. Castle Rock
12. Redwood Preserves
13. Montara Mountain
14. San Francisco
15. Golden Gate Bridge

the Bay area Rim Trail

Map 01.06 The Condor Trail

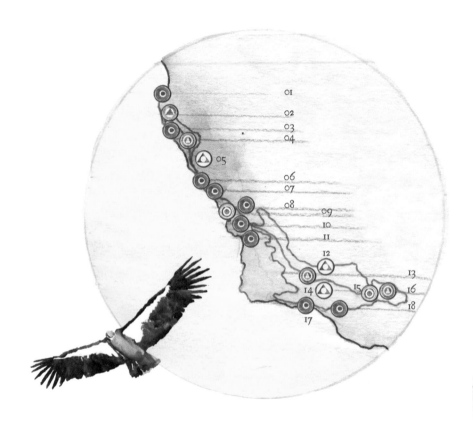

80 miles

01.06

The Condor Trail is a new route on some old trails; many networks of pathways were built here in the 1930s through what would become the San Rafael and Dick Smith Federal Wilderness Areas. Today, there are restored passageways through dense belts of wildflowers, rattlesnakes, black bears, trout ponds, and many other hidden wonders of the Central Coast backcountry. Because of the Condor Trail, for the first time in modern history hikers are able to walk on public land all the way from Los Angeles to Monterey.

01. Monterey
02. Bottchers Gap Trailhead
03. Big Sur
04. Los Padres National Forest
05. Santa Lucia Peak
06. San Simeon
07. Cambria
08. Atascadero
09. Morro Bay
10. San Luis Obispo
11. Pismo Beach
12. Sierra Madre Mountains
13. San Rafael Wilderness
14. San Rafael Mountains
15. Lake Piru
16. Angeles National Forest
17. Santa Barbara
18. Ojai

Sisquoc River, Condor Trail

Map 01.07 Mapping California

The political entity that is California comprises a total land surface of 158,706 square miles. California is about 800 miles (1,288 kilometers) long, with a coastline approximately 840 miles (1,352 kilometers) long. At its most distant points, California is 250 miles (402 kilometers) wide.

On a global network of latitude and longitude designations, California exists at the defined coordinates 36.7783° N, 119.4179° W. That means it is just about 37° north of the equator and 119° west of the prime meridian in England.

Map 01.08 The Nature of California

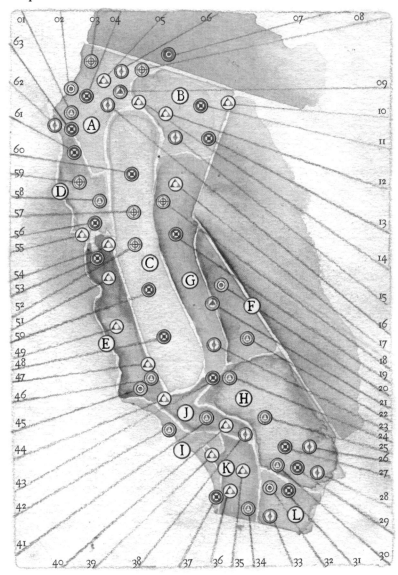

California is a patchwork of dynamic eco-states and bio-republics whose seams are defined by large geomorphic expanses, soil, and watercourses. To understand the bioregions of California is to understand the story of how California works and how it is assembled. Keep this map of key features and references in your proverbial back pocket as you make your way through this compendium; it may help you get your bearings.

A. Northwest California: A land of endless rivers and mountains where the tallest trees in the world reign over a forest of unparalleled diversity and impenetrable wilderness; a bioregion of rare plants, trees, and animals that extends from Redding, up over the Trinity Alps and into Oregon; home to many of California great rivers including the Klamath, the Eel, the Smith, and the Trinity.

B. Northeast California: As part of a mountain range that extends north all the way into Washington State, Shasta, Lassen and several dozen mountains made of lava and volcanic glass dot the primeval landscape of the Modoc Plateau. Ishi Wilderness: a pocket of primal and pristine landscape between the Sacramento Valley and Mount Lassen.

C. The Central Valley: The San Joaquin River Valley, together with the Sacramento River Valley to the north, forms the Central Valley. This large area of land formed by the two rivers exists on the Pacific Flyway, which extends from Alaska to South America—an immeasurably important migration corridor for millions of birds.

D. The Northern Coast: In this region, rare wildflowers bloom near the shores of California's oldest lake, Clear Lake, while tule elk roam scrublands above redwood forests. Diablo Range: rising to just about 3,500 feet, Mount Diablo in the East Bay Area is the northernmost peak in a series of valley peaks that extend south to define the southern

Central Coast mountain ranges. Mount Tamalpais and the forests to the north of San Francisco are ecosystems defined by fire; the closed-cone pines including bishop, knobcone, and Mendocino are fire adapted and fire dependent. These so-called fire forests skirt ancient redwood stands and vast tracts of coastal prairie.

E. The Central Coast: Up from Big Sur, the coastal mountains in this region are once again home to recovering populations of the endangered California condor, and to the Santa Lucia fir, the rarest fir tree in the world. North of the Sierra Madre, the vast Carrizo Plain extends to the Temblor Range, a place of grand silence that floods with beauty each spring as it buries itself in a brief wildflower bloom, covering the region for hundreds of square miles in a rainbow of prismatic colors.

F. The Great Basin Desert: Just west of the state of Nevada sits Mono Lake; the lake provides food for a continent's worth of birds migrating both south and

north. Tucked under the towering cliffs of the east slope of the Sierra Nevada and just north of the most ancient forests in the world, the bristlecone pine forests, Mono Lake lends its eerie beauty to a mysterious lost world.

G. The Sierra Nevada: America's longest contiguous mountain range, the importance of the Sierra Nevada over all facets of California's natural character can not be understated. Extending for over 400 miles, the granite mountain range has isolated the California Floristic Province, indicated on the map by the red line, for 150 million years. Lake Tahoe: few corners of the globe compete with Lake Tahoe for its grandiose beauty, ethereal landscape, sparkling blue water and alpine tranquility. The Yuba River: three branches of this cold and beautiful river braid through the northern Sierra Nevada, defining the rugged characters of both its environment and the people who call these mountains home. The Mother Lode: When gold was found in Coloma in the middle of the 19th century, California was immediately and permanently changed. The Gold Highway, Highway 49, traces a surface line above the massive monolith of subterranean quartz that Gold Rush-era miners immediately began to rip apart when looking for the gold of the Mother Lode.

H. The High Desert: Now connected to the San Bernardino Mountains by the Sand to Snow National Monument, this federally protected terrain offers hundreds of square miles where wild populations of bighorn sheep can roam. Amargosa River: Now a trickle of its ancient self, the river traces the border of California and Nevada. Receding to a subterranean run under Death Valley, the Amargosa is still a necessary piece of this desolate ecological paradise.

I. The South Coast: Rising from the coast over the city of Santa Barbara, the sandstone peaks of these coastal mountains gleam pink and orange in the sunset over the Pacific. Behind the mountainous shield, the Sisquoc River provides sanctuary for 300,000 acres of black bear country underneath shady oak trees that seem at home next to cactus and yucca.

J. The Tranverse Ranges: From the San Gabriel Mountains down to the San Bernardinos, it was only until about 100 years ago that this was the land of the California grizzly bear.

K. The Peninsular Mountains: Deep in the Cleveland National Forest, Palomar chaparral harbors many rare populations of plants. Northeast of San Diego, these mountains, which include the Santa Anas, run down to the beach where arguably the rarest pine tree in the world, the Torrey pine, still thrives in a few isolated stands.

L. The Low Desert: As California's largest state park, Anza Borrego is home to many delicate ecologies and sublime landscapes. It is at Anza Borrego that California sees the westernmost reach of the Colorado Desert, which extends east all the way to the Gulf of Mexico.

Map 01.09 Miocene California

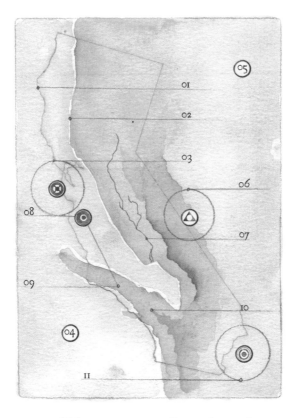

Ten million years ago, California was still putting itself together. The Farallon Plate was still keeping the San Andreas Fault from closing Proto-California like a kind of zipper. The Farallon Plate has now been completely subducted by the Pacific Plate and the North American Plate.

01. Present-day coastline
02. Miocene-age coastline
03. Farallon Plate
04. Pacific Plate
05. North American Plate
06. Sierra Nevada
07. Central Valley
08. Present-day Salinas
09. Miocene-age Salinas
10. Transverse Ranges
11. Gulf of California

Map 01.10 The Late Pleistocene

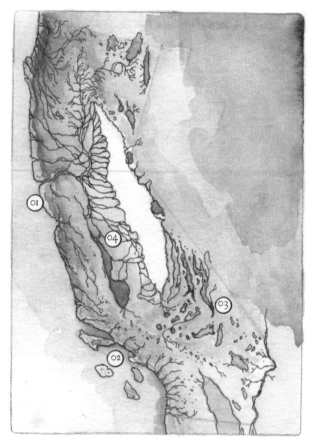

Nothing stays the same in California for very long; imagine how different the region was only 18,000 years ago. At the peak of the great Pleistocene ice age, when most of North America was under a shelf of ice a mile thick, the Sierra Nevada was completely locked in a frozen stasis. So much fresh water was locked in ice globally that the sea level was more than 350 feet lower than it is today.

01. Pleistocene coastline
02. Channel Islands
    connected to the mainland
03. The flooded California desert
04. The Central Valley,
    nearly a lake itself

Columbian mammoth
Mammuthus columbi

The Pleistocene was a time of giants, of megafauna. Dire wolves, giant sloths, cat-like saber-toothed beasts (*Smilodon*), and a whole menagerie of giant creatures lived in California. Walk the prairie at Point Reyes and imagine the coastline 20 miles out. This was the habitat of the Columbian mammoth (*Mammuthus columbi*)—our local, less woolly species—along with the Anza Borrego camel (*Gigantocamelus spatula*), the largest camel, at nine feet tall at the shoulder, to have ever lived.

California camel
Camelops hesternus

Map 01.11 A Patchwork of Ancient Stones

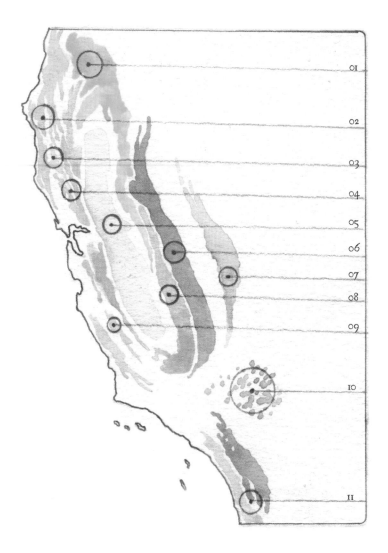

The tangle of geology that is California is decipherable, as remnants of ancient landforms are strewn all over the state. The following key features best demonstrate the age and nature of the California puzzle and are listed along with the geologic age when they experienced their principal formation and when that formation occurred.

01. Modoc Plateau (Miocene epoch, 25 million years ago)
02. Klamath Terrane (Jurassic period, 155 million years ago)
03. Paleogene Franciscan (Cretaceous period, 70 million years ago)
04. Franciscan Complex (Cretaceous period, 70 million years ago)
05. Forearc Strata (Jurassic period, 165 million years ago)
06. Sierra Nevada Batholith (Mesozoic era, 200 million years ago)
07. White Mountain Fold (Triassic period, 250 million years ago)
08. Sierra Slope Uplift (Cretaceous period, 135 million years ago)
09. Salinian Block (Mesozoic era, 200 million years ago)
10. Mojave High Desert (Cretaceous period, 85 million years ago)
11. Santiago Volcanic Arc (Cretaceous period, 135 million years ago)

Map 01.12 The Most Precious Gift

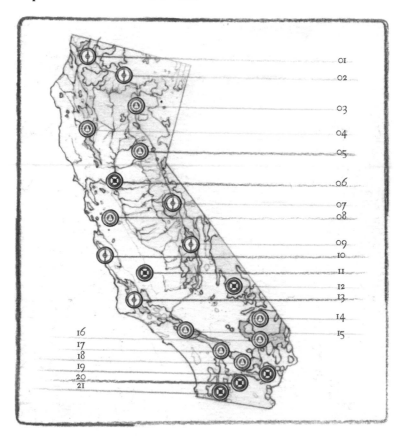

Life has always been crowded in California. Everyone has always wanted to live here, and that is because everyone thrives here. Living in California, we are given the most beautiful gift and the most sacred responsibility. We have a moral imperative to act as kind stewards to the natural and wild systems that struggle to sustain themselves in this time of extinction. Everywhere in California you

find deep systems of living networks that are struggling to survive.

The first step in conservation is land inventory analysis, asking ourselves what land is there to conserve? When considering what a progressive model of conservation might be, what a holistic view of conserving the natural world might entail, we should consider a synthesis of land areas, rather than an analysis: a bringing together rather than a pulling apart. When we recognize that preserving only a piece of nature is not really preserving nature at all, we can begin to plan for the conservation for the whole of this precious gift.

The following are ecosystems of special concern, threatened in various degrees:

(a) by air pollution
(b) by resource depletion
(c) by habitat loss
(d) by climate change
(e) by mismanagement

01. Critically dense conifer forest,
    Russian Wilderness (d)
02. Mount Shasta montane,
    Shasta Wilderness (d)
03. Cascade glacial ecotone,
    Mount Lassen National Park (d)
04. Endangered floral pasture,
    Berryessa Snow Mountain
    National Monument (c)
05. Yuba cedar ridgeline,
    Tahoe National Forest (e)

06. Delta wetlands,
    Yolo Wildlife Refuge (b)
07. High Sierra habitat,
    Emigrant Wilderness (a)
08. Coyote-oak forest,
    Henry Coe State Park (c)
09. Foxtail pine timberline forest,
    John Muir Wilderness (d)
10. Santa Lucia fir,
    Ventana Wilderness (d)
11. Tule elk habitat, Kern National
    Wildlife Refuge;
    Tule Elk State Reserve (b)
12. Desert riparian, Amargosa Canyon
    Dumont Dunes
    Natural Area (c)
13. Big Cone Douglas fir coastal forest,
    San Rafael Wilderness;
    Santa Lucia Wilderness (d)
14. Desert dunes and tortoise habitat,
    Mojave National Preserve (c)
15. Mountain lion rewilding corridor,
    San Gabriel Mountains
    National Monument (c)
16. High Desert scrub, Mojave Trail
    National Monument (d)
17. Big Horn Rewilding Corridor,
    Sand to Snow
    National Monument (c)
18. Joshua tree forest habitat,
    Joshua Tree National Park (d)
19. Mojave desert lily,
    Desert Lily Preserve (c)
20. Migratory bird desert habitat,
    Wister Waterfowl
    Management Area (c)
21. California palm, McCain Valley
    National Cooperative Wildlife
    Management Area (d)

Humanity has been thriving as stewards to the land in California for at least the past 15,000 years. *The California Field Atlas* is preoccupied with asking what kind of stewardship our contemporary society presents and what sustainability for another fifteen thousand years might look like.

02. OF EARTH & MOUNTAINS

eagle peak
(Warner Mountains)

Map 02.01 The Dance of Mountain Provinces

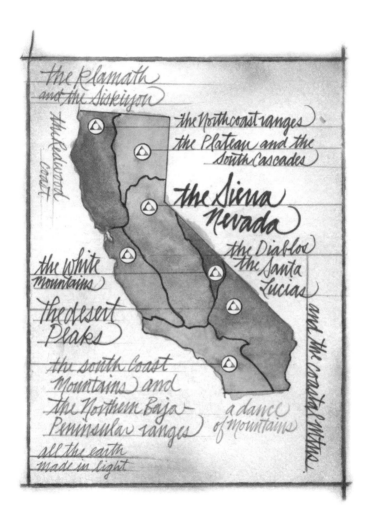

the Klamath
and the Siskiyou

the North coast ranges

the Plateau and the
south Cascades

the Sierra
Nevada

the Redwood
coast

the Diablos
the Santa
Lucias

the white
mountains

The desert
Peaks

the south Coast
Mountains and
the Northern Baja
Peninsular ranges

a dance
of mountains

and the coastal entire

all the earth
made in light

As the fabric of the Earth's crust, floating on its molten mantle, pushes California's mountains around like so many piles of sand, the state's rugged topography is revealed as a temporary layout. Mountains rise, fall, and dance to a geologic rhythm that forever informs every ecological system that manages to gain a foothold. Presently, the mountain provinces of California are most easily categorized into seven main groups: the North Coast Ranges, the Plateau and the South Cascades, the Sierra Nevada, the Central Coast Mountains, the South Coast Mountains, the Desert Peaks, and the Mountains of the Great Basin.

The North Coast Ranges extend from the Siskiyou Mountains, which cross the Oregon border, down to the San Francisco Bay. Often, the North, Central, and South Coast Ranges are lumped together and oversimplified as the Coast Ranges.

The Plateau and South Cascades refer to the two volcanic peaks of Shasta and Lassen, the southernmost extent of the Cascades Mountain Range, which extends north all the way to Canada. The Plateau is shorthand for the Modoc Plateau, a volcanic highland isolated from the rest of California by the volcanoes of the South Cascades. The Plateau extends east from Shasta and, for our purposes, includes the Warner Mountains, just west of the Nevada border.

The Sierra Nevada is the longest contiguous mountain range in America, excluding Alaska. In this map, the Sierra appear to swallow the Great Central Valley, which is not pictured.
The Central Coast Mountains are chiefly defined by the Diablos and Santa Lucias and also include the Santa Marias.

The South Coast Mountains include what are often called the Transverse Ranges and, to the south of Los Angeles, the Peninsular Ranges, which extend up from Mexico and Baja California. The Transverse and Peninsular Ranges are presented here combined as a single arc of the South Coast Mountains, an elegant ridgeline that runs from Santa Barbara around the basin of Los Angeles and down to cross the border at the Tecate Divide, southwest of Anza Borrego State Park. This classification makes sense if the nonvisible fault lines are disregarded and a continuous line is traced along the mountain peaks from the Los Padres National Forest down to the Cleveland National Forest.

The Desert Peaks encompass all the mountain ranges of the Sonoran and the Mojave Deserts. The Little San Bernardino Mountains on the western border of Joshua Tree National Park dip down from the Mojave (or High) Desert to the Salton Basin and the Sonoran (or Low) Desert and are generally accepted as the line between the two desert regions.
The Mountains of the Great Basin extend deep into Nevada and run down the spine of California to form the Inyo and the White Ranges. By this classification of mountain provinces, the mountains of Death Valley National Park are divided between the Mountains of the Great Basin and the Desert Peaks. This differentiation is a largely botanical, as the creosote bush (*Larrea tridentate*), the plant that rules the Mojave, ends its northernmost distribution around here.

Map 02.02 Rock Regions

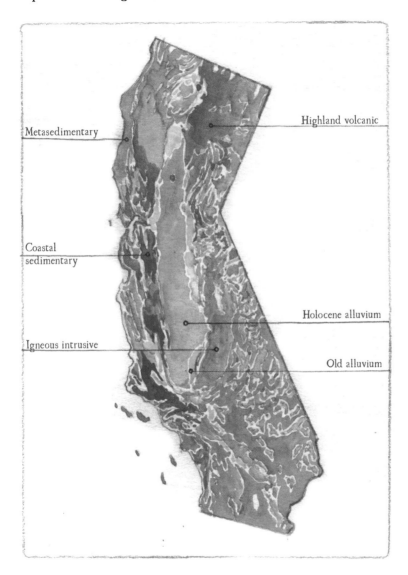

Metasedimentary

Highland volcanic

Coastal
sedimentary

Holocene alluvium

Igneous intrusive

Old alluvium

In high school geology, you probably learned about the three main types of rock: igneous (formed from cooled magma), sedimentary (deposited by a river or wind), and metamorphic (altered by pressure and heat). We can draw broad lines that describe how this combination plays out in six different ways and better understand not only how but when the stones that make up California attained their present configuration. This map is not a study of soil; soil is the upper layer of Earth in which plants grow. Rather, this is a generalized study of the original makeup of the bedrock of California as a grand mosaic of geologic history.

Highland Volcanic: The Modoc Plateau and the northern Sierra Nevada are covered mainly by stone types that can claim eruptions from the volcanoes of the South Cascades as their origin. These types of stones are characterized by being very rich in nutrients, and they hold water well because of their ash content.

Metasedimentary: The North Coast is geologically composed of rocks different from nearly every other part of California. The reason for this may be more climatological than geological: glaciers have only ever formed in a few high mountain peaks in northwestern California, and this has led to only a slow accumulation of river-brought sediment down through thin valleys.

Coastal Sedimentary: As the coastal mountains, formed when tectonic activity along the edge of California was different in character than it is today, continue to be washed away over the course of centuries, the buildup of sedimentary rock occurs.

Holocene Alluvium: With the Sacramento and the San Joaquin Rivers having constantly fed the soil of the Central Valley for many thousands of years, it stands to reason that this great agricultural region is made up mostly of recently deposited alluvium. Alluvium is a general term for all the material deposited by a river or by other method of erosion. Across the Mojave Desert you can see massive alluvial fans, geologic formations that splay out for miles from every canyon mouth, ancient granite mountains turning to dust.

Old Alluvium: The Central Valley is lined with alluvial deposits much older than the younger rock types brought down by the Sierra over the past 100,000 years or so. Eventually, this alluvial stone will transform into a layer of pure sedimentary stone.

Igneous Intrusive: The most uniquely Californian rock type is the kind that makes up the Sierra Nevada, the largest granite deposit in the world. Intrusive rocks are igneous rocks that form from crystallized magma beneath the Earth's surface. California's granite formed in a cavity the size of Nevada, deep underground, and was uplifted by tectonic forces over 200 million years ago. Some geologists believe that the Sierra Batholith, as it is called, may still be rising.

Map 02.03 How California Moves

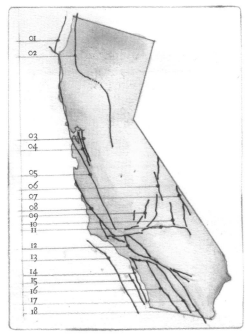

California's Major Tectonic Faultlines

A   B   C

Earthquake Commonality and Severity: A. High threat B. Middle threat C. Low threat

California's Fault Lines

01. Mendocino Feature
02. South Fork Mountain Fault and Mother Lode
03. Calaveras
04. Hayward
05. San Andreas
06. Sierra Nevada
07. Death Valley
08. Nacimiento
09. Kern Canyon
10. Panamint Valley
11. Garlock
12. San Gabriel
13. Palos Verdes
14. Coronado Bank
15. San Diego Trough
16. Whittier-Elsinore
17. San Jacinto
18. San Andreas

Map 02.04 The Mountains of California

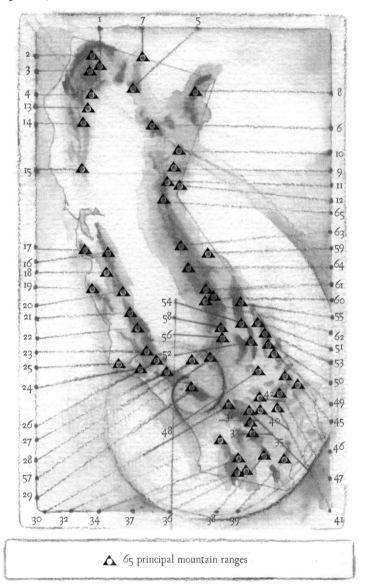

△ 65 principal mountain ranges

There are thousands of mountains in California and hundreds of mountain ranges. The smallest range that is still discrete is probably the Sutter Buttes, which pop up out of the Sacramento Valley like a mushroom in a field: obvious and bold. The longest range is the Sierra Nevada, which is described as a single range but, in fact, contains well over 100 named ridgelines and lineage cells. The trait that links all the ranges of the Sierra Nevada (it is always called the Sierra, never the Sierras) is the common, underlying bedrock of granite. Two hundred million years of ice and uplift have carved, scraped, and polished the Sierra Nevada to such dramatic effect that it looks today as if the mountains have been hewn with clumsy, giant shovels, deliberately and with great force. The coastal mountains across the Central Valley express a greater variety of character than the tall Sierra: from the deep river valleys that cut through the forested slopes of the Klamath Mountains, down through the chaparral and oak-covered squat mountains of the San Francisco Bay Area, across the dotted landscape of ancient dead volcanoes of the Diablo Range and the Santa Lucias. If the Shasta and Lassen volcanoes represent a northern bookend to the story of California's mountains, the southern analogy would be the big guardians San Gorgonio and San Jacinto, who stand over the inland valley, announcing a massive shift in climate and ecology.

This map depicts California's principal ranges, along with each range's highest peak and its elevation:

01. Marble Mountains, Black Marble Mountain (7,442 feet)
02. Siskiyou Mountains, Preston Peak (7,309 feet)
03. Salmon Mountains, Mary Blaine Mountain (6,747 feet)
04. Trinity Alps, Thompson Peak (9,002 feet)
05. Mount Shasta (14,162 feet)
06. Mount Lassen (10, 457 feet)
07. Southern Cascade Mountains
08. Warner Mountains, Eagle Peak (9,892 feet)
09. Diamond Mountains, Adams Peak (8,197 feet)
10. Skedaddle Mountains, Hot Springs Peak (7,860 feet)
11. Bald Mountain Range, Babbitt Peak (8,760 feet)
12. Carson Range, Slide Mountain (9,698 feet)
13. Yolla Bolly Mountains, South Yolla Bolly (8,092 feet)
14. East Snow Mountain (7,056 feet)
15. Mayacamas Mountains, Cobb Mountain (4,720 feet)
16. Diablo Range, Mount Isabel (4,230 feet)
17. Santa Cruz Mountains, Loma Prieta (3,806 feet)
18. Gabilan Range, Mount Johnson (3,465 feet)
19. Santa Lucia Range, Junipero Serra Peak (5,862 feet)
20. Joaquin Ridge, San Benito Mountain (5,241 feet)
21. Temblor Range, Temblor Summit (3,250 feet)
22. La Panza Range, Machesna Mountain (4,063 feet)
23. Sierra Madre Mountains, Peak Mountain (5,843 feet)
24. San Rafael Mountains, Big Pine Mountain (6,828 feet)

25. Santa Ynez Mountains, Divide Peak (4,707 feet)
26. Caliente Range, Caliente Mountain (5,106 feet)
27. San Emigdio Mountains, Mount Pinos (8,831 feet)
28. Tehachapi Mountains, Double Mountain (7,981 feet)
29. San Gabriel Mountains, Mount San Antonio, aka Old Baldy (10,064 feet)
30. San Bernardino Mountains, San Gorgonio (,11,502 feet)
31. San Jacinto Mountains, San Jacinto (10,804 feet)
32. Santa Ana Mountains, Santiago Peak (5,687 feet)
33. Santa Rosa Mountains, Santa Rosa Mountain (8,046 feet)
34. Aquanga Mountains, Palomar Mountain (6,140 feet)
35. Little San Bernardino Mountains, Quail Mountain (5,813 feet)
36. Vallecito Mountains, Whale Peak (5,349 feet)
37. Laguna Mountains, Monument Peak (6,271 feet)
38. Chocolate Mountains, Mount Barrow (2,475 feet)
39. Palo Verde Mountains, Palo Verde Peak (1,795 feet)
40. Bullion Mountains, Hidalgo Mountain (4,435 feet)
41. Turtle Mountains, Bolson Peak (4,231 feet)
42. Bristol Mountains, McGorman Peak (3,225 feet)
43. Old Woman Mountains, Mercury Mountain (3,720 feet)
44. Chemehuevi Mountains, Chemehuevi Peak (3,694 feet)
45. Castle Mountains, Hart Peak (5,543 feet)
46. New York Mountains, Caruthers Peak (7,532 feet)
47. Providence Mountains, Fountain Peak (6,996 feet)
48. Owlshead Mountains, Sugarloaf Peak (4,820 feet)
49. Clark Mountain Range, Clark Mountain (7,292 feet)
50. Kingston Range, Kingston Peak (7,323 feet)
51. Amargosa Range, Funeral Peak (6,384 feet)
52. Panamint Range, Telescope Peak (11,049 feet)
53. Funeral Mountains, Pyramid Peak (6,703 feet)
54. Inyo Mountains, Waucoba Mountain (11,123 feet)
55. White Mountains, White Mountain Peak (14,246 feet)
56. Whitney Portal, Mount Whitney (14,494 feet)
57. Greenhorn Mountains, Tobias Peak (8,284 feet)
58. Great Western Divide
59. Sweetwater Mountains, Mount Patterson (11,673 feet)
60. Ritter Range, Mount Ritter (13,140 feet)
61. Cathedral Range, Mount Lyell (13,114 feet)
62. Clark Range, Merced Peak (11,726 feet)
63. The Dardanelles, Dardanelles Cone (9,524 feet)
64. Yosemite Valley, Tuolumne Peak (10,845 feet)
65. Crystal Range, Pyramid Peak (9,983 feet)

Map 02.05 Ancient Sierra Fault Formations

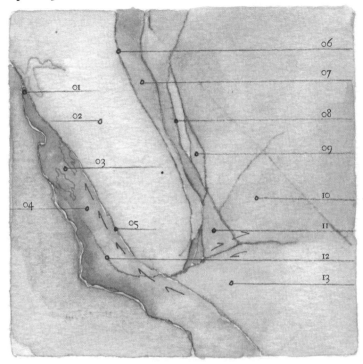

100 miles

02.05

Over 200 million years ago, the great Sierra Batholith rose like a wedge from the Miocene ocean to produce the first glimpse of modern California. Since then, the granite of the Sierra has rearranged itself—moving and transforming, riding transverse faults for hundreds of miles, and creating distinct geologic zones. These zones spread out over the southern Sierra Nevada like a quilt of broken earth, never content to sit still and threatening to shift again at any moment. Geologists employ a bevy of technical jargon to describe the mechanics of the systems that paint a picture of how California was assembled.

01. Present-Day San Francisco

02. Great Valley Forearc Basin: A forearc is defined in geology as the region between a deep oceanic trench and an uplifted volcanic arc.

03. Salinian Pendants: A pendant is a projecting mass of rock that is surrounded by an igneous intrusion, such as a batholith or a block. The Salinian Pendants are broken pieces of the Sierra Nevada that migrated up the San Andreas Fault with the Salinian Block.

04. Salinian Block: A block, or a fault block, is a very large, uniform mass of rock, sometimes hundreds of miles long, created by localized tectonic stress. The Salinian Block is a massive chunk of the Sierra Batholith that migrated all the way to near the Salinian Valley.

05. San Andreas Fault: The famous transverse fault, the San Andreas Fault acts as a conveyor belt, moving all the earth to its west (the Pacific Plate) north, while all the earth to its east (the North American Plate) fractures and breaks at the stress. The San Andreas Fault is a sliding vein of rock that defines the geologic landscape of California as much as any mountain could.

06. Foothills Suture: A geologic suture is where individual geologic terranes join together but are not stressed and do not move in the same way that faults do, although sutures are generally surrounded by fault zones.

07. Sierra City Mélange: A geographic mélange is a metamorphic rock formation created from the scraping of a downward-moving tectonic plate against a batholith or other substrate, in a subduction zone, as this area was 200 million years ago.

08. Snow Lake Terrane: A terrane is a geological entity that is defined on all sides by faults and has its own distinctive stratigraphy, structure, and geological history.

09. Inyo Passive Margin: A passive margin is a shelf that defines the boundary between the continental batholith and the ancient oceanic shelf. The Inyo Passive Margin is the geologic boundary east of the Sierra Crest, including Owens and Bishop Valleys.

10. Death Valley Terrane: This mass of fragmented tectonic activity includes the Funeral and the Panamint Ranges, which exhibit distinct metamorphic rocks fundamentally different from those found north in the Great Basin Ranges.

11. El Paso Terrane: This rugged geologic shelf runs up the east slope of the southern Sierra Nevada and, most notably, includes Red Rock State Park.

12. Garlock Fault: This is California's longest east–west running fault line and is responsible for creating the Transverse Ranges of the San Gabriels and the Tehachapis.

13. Roberts Mountains Allochthon: An allochthon in structural geology is a large block of rock that has been moved from its original site of formation, usually by what is called low-angle thrust faulting, which is not subduction or transverse movement. The Roberts Mountains Allochthon is defined by the present-day Antelope Valley.

Map 02.06 Mountains of the Sierra Nevada

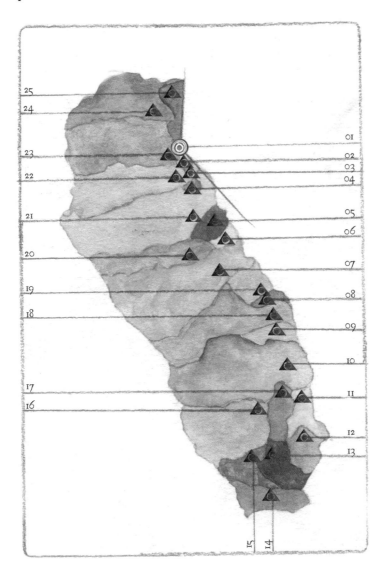

An uplifted single piece of granite, the Sierra Nevada slopes gradually west, down to the San Joaquin Valley, and on its east slope, drops down suddenly 14,000 feet to the Great Basin. Its eroded glacial valleys and peaks, full of light and character, are exemplified across two dozen peaks. This map of mountain cells is divided into what have been called "lineage groups," which are named for a specific region's highest peak within boundaries drawn by key saddles and watersheds. A single range may have dozens of mountain cells, which may in turn have several lineage groups. Much like a map of watersheds, the mountain-cell perspective is a cartographic convenience for analyzing patterns across the larger range.

In this map, the most prominent Sierra peaks are noted, along with their elevations and associated mountain cells.

01. Lake Tahoe
02. Freel Peak (10,881 feet), Stan Lake Mountain
03. Hawkins Peak (10,024 feet), Humboldt-Toiyabe National Forest
04. Highland Peak (10,935 feet), Ebbetts Pass
05. Tower Peak (11,755 feet), North Yosemite Rim
06. Twin Peaks (12,323 feet), Hoover Wilderness
07. Mount Ritter (13,140 feet), Ritter Range
08. Mount Darwin (13,830 feet), Goddard Divide
09. Mount Pinchot (13,495 feet), South Fork Kings River
10. Mount Whitney (14,494 feet), Sequoia National Park
11. Olancha Peak (12,123 feet), South Sierra Wilderness
12. Owens Peak (8,453 feet), Owens Peak Wilderness
13. Piute Peak (8,417 feet), Piute Mountains
14. Double Mountain (7,981 feet), Tejon Ranch
15. Breckenridge Mountain (7,548 feet), Hobo Ridge
16. Slate Mountain (9,302 feet), Giant Sequoia Mountains
17. Kern Peak (11,510 feet), Golden Trout Wilderness
18. North Palisade (14,242 feet), Inconsolable Range
19. Mount Humphreys (13,986 feet), John Muir Wilderness
20. Mount Hoffman (10,850 feet), South Ridge Hetch Hetchy
21. Leavitt Peak (11,569 feet), Emigrant Wilderness
22. Round Top (10,063 feet), Mokelumne Wilderness
23. Pyramid Peak (9,983 feet), Desolation Wilderness
24. Mount Lola (9,143 feet), Donner Mountains
25. Babbitt Peak (8,760 feet), Bald Mountain Range

A Timeline for the Formation of the Sierra Nevada

01. 550 million years ago (the early Cambrian period): The oldest rocks in Yosemite are formed.

02. 200 million years ago (the Mesozoic era): The great granite batholith of the Sierra Nevada is created when the Farallon Plate slips under the North American Plate.

03. 65 to 45 million years ago (the middle Cenozoic era): The ancestral Sierra Nevada become severely eroded into low-lying mountains.

04. 40 million years ago (the Eocene epoch): The mountains begin their uplift and start to resemble their present selves.

05. 5 million years ago (the Pliocene era): Multiple eras of deep glaciation begin to work their magic.

06. 1 million years ago (the Sherwin): The most extensive and longest-lived glacier period documented in the Sierra begins, lasting 300,000 years and shaping the Yosemite Valley with a parade of earth-moving glaciers called the Sherwin series.

Coyote
Canis latrans

Yosemite Valley

Map 02.07 The High Sierra

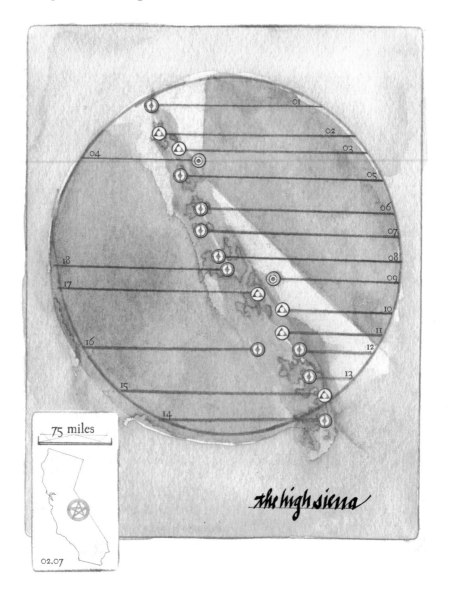

75 miles

the high sierra

02.07

The family of exposed granite peaks between 7,000 and 14,000 feet called the High Sierra forms a chain of vertebrae down the spine of the Sierra Nevada. The name High Sierra applies to a rocky region of land above the timberline in the alpine zone. Isolated by glaciation, the High Sierra is a world to itself that extends for about 225 miles, from north of Yosemite (although pieces of the High Sierra exist all the way into Plumas County) south to Cottonwood Pass; it is consistently about 20 miles wide. Elevations in the High Sierra range from 7,100 feet (Bald Eagle Mountain, Bucks Lake Wilderness) to over 14,000 feet (Mount Whitney, John Muir Wilderness).

Mount Ritter

Map 02.08 The Big Peaks

- the Mammoth Crest
- tom's Place
- A mount Morgan 13,005'
- A Red Slate 13,163'
- the Mono Divide
- A Mt. Stan 12835'
- A Mt. Abbot 13,715'
- A Basin Mountain 13,240'
- • Bishop
- the Pinnacles
- A Merriam Peak 13,103
- A Mt. Humphreys 13,986'
- A Mt. Goethe 13,264'
- • Big Pine
- A Mt. Darwin 13,830'
- A Mt. Powell 13,361'
- Bishop Pass
- A Mt. Agassiz 13,891'
- A North Palisade 14,242'
- A Split Mountain 14,058'
- A Mount Pinchot 13,495'
- John Muir Wilderness
- A Diamond Peak 13,126'
- A Mount Keith 13,977'
- A Mt. Williamson 14,375'
- A Mt. Russell 14,086'
- A Mt. Whitney 14,494'
- A Mt. Langley 14,042'
- A Cirque Peak 12,900'

the Sierra Crest

5 miles

02.08

Mount Whitney is the highest point in the lower 48 states. The Sierra Nevada rises out of the High Desert with an elevation increase of 14,000 feet in less than 100 miles. These mountains continue to rise due to the massive Sierra granite batholith cracking caused by tectonic forces pushing up against the southern edge of the mountains.

Northern flicker
Colaptes auratus

Map 02.09 Mount Whitney

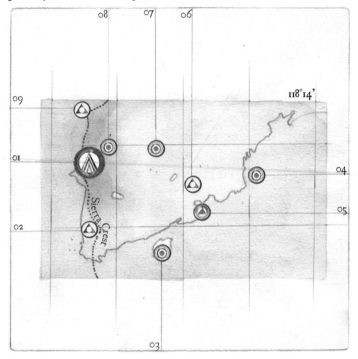

Because it is the tallest peak in the lower 48, Mount Whitney is a political marker for a number of land designation borders. The mountain is on the boundary between Inyo and Tulare Counties, and it resides only 84.6 miles northwest of the lowest point in North America, at Badwater in Death Valley National Park, which lies at 279 feet below sea level. Mount Whitney's west slope is in Sequoia National Park and its east slope is in Inyo National Forest. The mountain's summit is the southern end of the John Muir Trail, which winds down 212 miles from Yosemite Valley.

The route to the summit of Mount Whitney is up the Mount Whitney Trail, which starts at Whitney Portal, at an elevation of 8,360 feet. The hike is 22 miles round-trip with over 6,000 feet of elevation gain. It regularly takes two days of hard hiking to summit the peak.

01. Mount Whitney (14,505 feet)
02. Mount Muir (14,018 feet)
03. Consultation Lake
04. Mirror Lake
05. Mount Whitney Trail
06. Thor Peak (12,306 feet)
07. Upper Boy Scout Lake
08. Iceberg Lake
09. Mount Russell (14,094 feet)

1 mile

Mount Whitney
king of California Mountains

02.09

Map 02.10 Mount Humphreys

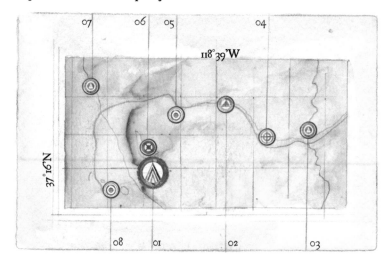

At just a hair under 14,000 feet, Mount Humphreys remains the tallest peak in its corner of Inyo National Forest, overlooking the city of Bishop. With the Humpreys Basin of lakes to the west and Lake Sabrina to the southeast, Mount Humphreys, inside a beautiful corner of the John Muir Wilderness, is a beacon of beauty and adventure.

Despite its prominence over Bishop Valley, the northern climbing route up Mount Humphreys is a lonely trail. Not many climbers and hikers take the summer route mainly because the peak doesn't reach 14,000 feet and therefore doesn't carry the prestige of the taller peaks. A strange thing, given the unique position of the peak over the Bishop Valley with the best vantage of the White Mountains to the east and the whole of the Whitney Crest to the south.

01. Mount Humphreys (13,986 feet)
02. Humphreys Route
03. John Muir Wilderness boundary
04. McGee Creek
05. Langley Reservoir
06. Humphreys Glacier
07. Inyo National Forest boundary
08. Humphreys Lakes

1 mile

02.10

mount Humphrys
Jewel over Bishop Valley

Map 02.11 Pyramid Peak

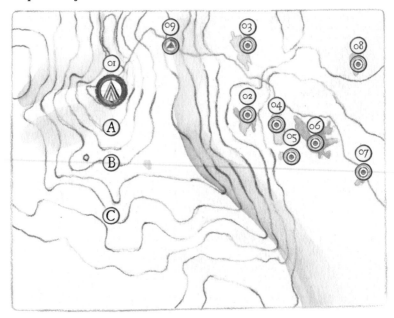

For many, Pyramid Peak is the apex of beauty in the High Sierra. Being the highest point in the Desolation Wilderness, Pyramid Peak can be seen as the predominant peak from as far south as the Mokelumne Wilderness. The moun-tain range that Pyramid Peak rises from is called the Crystal Range, and it is named this for a reason. At dawn on any given winter's day, with a fresh jacket of snow, the bright pink light catches the granite facets that compose the mountain's face and throws a scintillating spray of prismatic light for miles in all directions.

01. Pyramid Peak (9,883 feet)
02. Gefo Lake
03. Pyramid Lake
04. Toem Lake
05. Osma Lake
06. Ropi Lake
07. Pitt Lake
08. Desolation Lake
09. Summit Trail

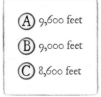

Ⓐ 9,600 feet
Ⓑ 9,000 feet
Ⓒ 8,600 feet

1/2 mile

02.11

Pyramid Peak
Glaciers over the Desolation

Map 02.12 Mountains of the North Coast Ranges

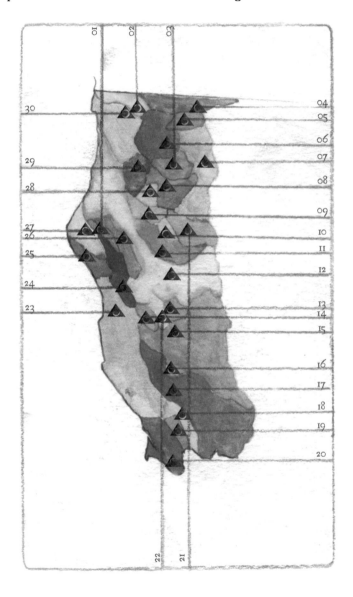

65 miles

02.12

These roadless expanses of twisting river valleys through dark forests of towering trees have been described by the ecologist David Rains Wallace (1983) as a "knot" and by the poet Gary Snyder (1995) as "without end"—both apt descriptions of a topography that includes some of California's most powerful rivers and remote mountains.

In this map, the most prominent North Coast peaks are noted, along with their elevations and associated mountain cells.

01. Grasshopper Mountain (3,379 feet), Humboldt Redwoods State Park
02. Preston Peak (7,309 feet), Siskiyou Mountains
03. Russian Peak (8,196 feet), Russian Wilderness
04. Cottonwood Peak (6,607 feet), Ash Creek
05. Indian Creek Baldy (6,275 feet), Plumbug Creek
06. Boulder Creek (8,299 feet), Marble Mountains

07. Mount Eddy (9,025 feet), Eddy Mountains
08. Thompson Peak (9,002 feet), Trinity Alps
09. Hayfork Bally (6,277 feet), Hayfork Divide
10. Chanchelulla Peak (6,399 feet), Chanchelulla Wilderness
11. North Yolla Bolly (7,863 feet), Yolla Bolly–Middle Eel Wilderness
12. South Yolla Bolly (8,092 feet), Mendocino National Forest
13. Black Butte (7,448 feet), Black Butte River
14. Big Signal Peak (6,175 feet), Sanhedrin Wilderness
15. Snow Mountain (7,056 feet), Snow Mountain Wilderness
16. Mount Konocti (4,299 feet), Lake County
17. Cobb Mountain (4,720 feet), Mayacamas Mountains
18. Mount Hood (2,730 feet), Hood Mountain Regional Park
19. Sonoma Mountain (2,295 feet), Sonoma Mountains
20. Mount Tamalpais (2,571 feet), Mount Tamalpais State Park
21. Bully Choop Mountain (6,974 feet), Trinity Mountains
22. Hull Mountain (6,873 feet), Berryessa Snow Mountain National Monument
23. Cahto Peak (4,233 feet), Mendocino County
24. Iron Peak (4,485 feet), Rattlesnake Ridge
25. King Peak (4,087 feet), King Range Wilderness
26. Black Lassic (5,916 feet), Mount Lassics Wilderness
27. Mount Pierce (3,185 feet), Bear River Ridge
28. Thurston Peaks (7,309 feet), Limestone Ridge
29. Salmon Mountain (6,956 feet), Salmon Mountains
30. Bear Basin Butte (5,292 feet), Siskiyou Wilderness

Map 02.13 Landforms of the Northwest

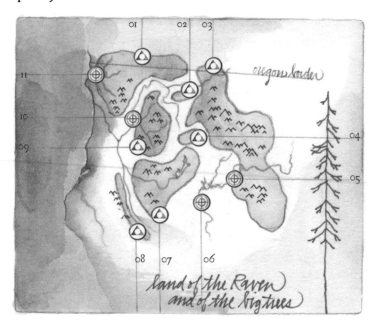

Deciphering the tangle of mountains and rivers that compose California's northwest corner can be a daunting task. Tracing the lines of the major rivers (the Klamath, the Trinity, and the Eel) and how they outline the major mountain units (the Siskiyou, the Klamath, and the Cascades) is the best way to start to piece together the great green puzzle.

01. Siskiyou Mountains
02. Scott Bar Mountains
03. Cascade Mountains
04. Scott Mountains
05. Pit River
06. Sacramento River
07. Trinity Alps and the Trinity River
08. South Fork Mountains and the south fork of the Eel River
09. Salmon Mountains, Marble Mountains, and the Salmon River
10. Klamath River
11. Smith River

35 miles

02.13

Map 02.14 Boulder Peak

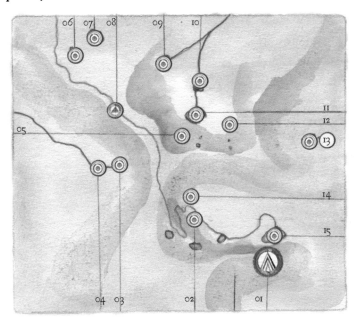

The highest point in the Marble Mountains wilderness, Boulder Peak rises above a necklace of sapphire lakes that dot the untouched landscape. There are no roads that lead here, and because of the area's remoteness, a determined hiker can imagine that the mountain is all their own on any given summer day. The marble quality of the black rock comes from metamorphic rock made from a half-mile-thick layer of fossilized seashells from when this uplifted range lay at the bottom of the ancient Pacific.

1 mile

02.14

01. Boulder Peak (6,968 feet)
02. Upper Mumbo Lake
03. Mumbo Lake
04. Mumbo Basin
05. Upper Cliff Lake
06. Upper Gumboot Lake
07. Gumboot Lake
08. Pacific Crest Trail
09. Cedar Lake
10. Lower Cliff Lake
11. Middle Cliff Lake
12. Terrace Lake
13. Devil's Pocket Lake
14. Upper Seven Lake
15. Echo Lake

Boulder Peak
Backcountry mountain lakes

Map 02.15 Bear Mountain

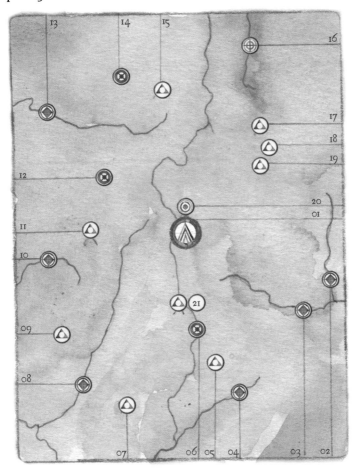

Bear Mountain, nestled into the Siskiyou Mountains, confidently boasts the richest biodiversity and biomass per forest acre anywhere in the world. When in these unglaciated mountains, which have preserved a primordial mix of life, each step is a step back in time. A network of ancient vitality still holds despite 100 million years of climatic and environmental upheaval.

01. Bear Mountain (6,415 feet)
02. Ten Mile Creek
03. Clear Creek
04. North Fork Dillon Creek
05. Kelsey Range
06. Siskiyou-Del Norte County border and Six Rivers–Klamath National Forest border
07. Baldy Peak (6,775 feet)
08. South fork of the Smith River
09. Blue Ridge
10. Jones Creek
11. Hurdy Gurdy Butte (4,717 feet)
12. Bear Basin Butte Botanical Area
13. Siskiyou fork of the Smith River
14. Broken Rib Mountain Botanical Area
15. Rib Mountain (5,824 feet)
16. Illinois River
17. El Capitan (6,827 feet)
18. Copper Mountain (6,355 feet)
19. Preston Peak (7,309 feet)
20. Devil's Punchbowl

8 miles

02.15

Bigleafmaple
(acer macrophyllum)

Bear Mountain
Biodiversity haven

Map 02.16 Mount Tamalpais

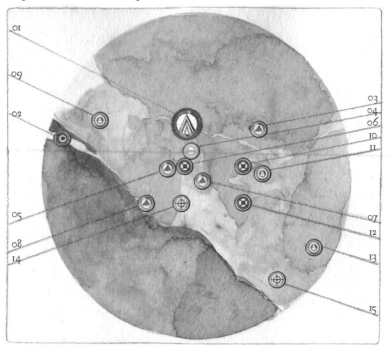

The highest peak in the Marin Hills is known to locals as Mount Tam. It looms over San Francisco, harbors groves of old-growth coast redwoods among numerous other pockets of dynamic wilderness, and is protected by a patchwork of national, state, and local land designations. Mount Tamalpais State Park, Muir Woods National Monument, Golden Gate National Seashore, and the Marin Municipal Water District all share in the protection of the mountain.

01. Mount Tamalpais, East Peak (2,571 feet)
02. Bolinas Lagoon
03. Panoramic Highway
04. Pantoll Ranger Station
05. Dipsea Trail
06. Coyote Ridge
07. Coastal View Trail
08. Highway 1
09. Mount Tamalpais State Park
10. Cathedral Grove
11. Muir Woods National Monument
12. Kent Canyon
13. Golden Gate National Recreation Area
14. Lone Tree Creek
15. Redwood Creek

2.5 miles

Mount Tamalpais
Crown of the Bay

02.16

Map 02.17 Mountains of the Modoc Plateau and the South Cascades

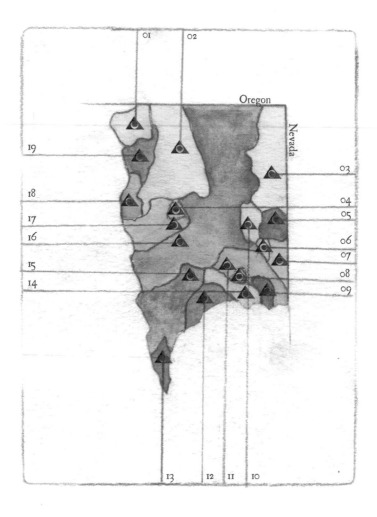

100 miles

02.17

The Warner Mountains define the northeast edge of California and shield the Modoc Plateau from the Great Basin desert to the east. The Columbia Plateau extends from Washington and Idaho down to touch Northern California's Modoc Plateau only across Goose Lake. To the east, the Basin and Range ecosystem, one of the four deserts in the United States, is defined by no watercourse that leads to the sea; rather, all find their terminus in the Nevada wilderness.

This mountain cell complex includes the southernmost volcanoes of the Cascade Range, which extends up into Canada. Defined by lonely, steep volcanoes, the Cascades in California are best defined by Mount Shasta and Mount Lassen, two volcanoes that are not part of the Sierra Nevada.

In this map, the most prominent volcanic peaks of the southern Cascade Range are noted, along with their elevations and associated mountain cells.

01. Willow Creek Mountain (7,830 feet), Little Shasta Mountains
02. Mount Hoffman (7,913 feet), Glass Mountains
03. Eagle Peak (9,892 feet), Warner Mountains
04. Burney Mountain (7,863 feet), Hat Creek Mountains
05. Observation Peak (7,964 feet), Madeline Plains Mountains
06. Shaffer Mountain (6,735 feet), Litchfield Mountains
07. Hat Springs Peak (7,680 feet), Skedaddle Mountains
08. Kettle Rock (7,820 feet), Taylorsville Mountains
09. Dixie Mountain (8,327 feet), Dixie Mountains
10. Fredonyer Peak (7,943 feet), Eagle Lake Mountains
11. Keddie Peak (7,499 feet), Keddie Ridge Mountains
12. Bald Eagle Mountain (7,183 feet), Bucks Lake Wilderness
13. South Buttes (2,117 feet), Sutter Buttes
14. Mount Ingalls (8,360 feet), Grizzly Ridge Mountains
15. Butt Mountain (7,866 feet), Coon Hollow Mountains
16. Lassen Peak (10,457 feet), Lassen Volcanic National Park
17. Crater Peak (8,683 feet), Thousand Lakes Wilderness
18. Tombstone Mountain (5,613 feet), McCloud River Mountains
19. Mount Shasta (14,162 feet), Mount Shasta

Map 02.18 Mount Shasta

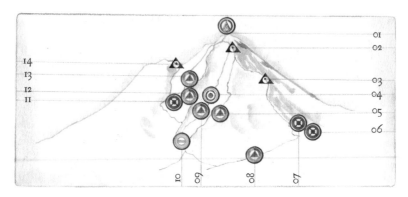

Mount Shasta is huge by every measure. It is the second-highest peak in the Cascade Range and the fifth-highest peak in California. Commanding universal respect due to its size and potential destructive power as an active volcano, Mount Shasta is often referred to by locals as Papa Shasta.

This map is a bit different than other maps in this chapter; the map depicts the southwest face of the mountain and the most frequently used routes to scale the large volcano's summit. There are no easy routes up the mountain; most climbers agree that when the weather holds, Avalanche Gulch is the least technical way out.

01. Summit (14,179 feet)
02. Thumb Rock (12,923 feet)
03. Shastarama (11,135 feet), Sargents Ridge Route
04. Lake Helen (10,400 feet)
05. Green Butte Ridge
06. Panther Meadows
07. Old Ski Bowl (7,800 feet)

08. Everitt Memorial Highway
09. Avalanche Gulch
10. Horse Camp (7,880 feet)
11. Hidden Valley
12. Casaval Ridge
13. West Face
14. Shastina (12,330 feet), Cascade Gulch

1.5 miles

02.18

Mount Shasta
Sleeping Giant

Map 02.19 Lassen Peak

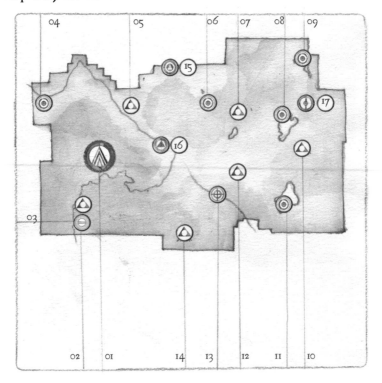

Mount Lassen, which last erupted in 1917, is the largest "dome" volcano in the world. It is the southernmost volcano in the Cascade volcanic arc, which extends north all the way to Canada. Lassen Volcanic National Park, demarcated above, comprises 167 square miles of land alive with hydrothermal sites and forest that has been tortured and sculpted by hundreds of thousands of years of boiling earth and fire.

01. Lassen Peak (10,457 feet)
02. Diamond Peak (7,968 feet)
03. Kohm Yah-mah-nee Visitor Center
04. Manzanita Lake
05. Raker Peak (7,483 feet)
06. Cluster Lakes
07. Fairfield Peak (7,272 feet)
08. Snag Lake
09. Butte Lake
10. Mount Hoffman (7,883 feet)
11. Juniper Lake
12. Crater Butte (7,267 feet)
13. Kings Creek
14. Sifford Mountain (7,408 feet)

5 miles

02.19

Mount Lassen
the southern-most Volcano

Map 02.20 Mountains of the Central Coast Ranges

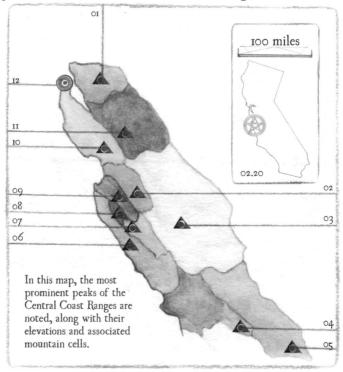

In this map, the most prominent peaks of the Central Coast Ranges are noted, along with their elevations and associated mountain cells.

Two 100-mile mountain ranges dominate the folded earth of California's Pacific coast. The Diablos extend down from the East Bay to the Gabilans. Across from the Salinas Valley, the Santa Lucias run from Monterey down to the Sierra Madres, east of Santa Maria.

01. Mount Diablo (3,849 feet), Diablo Mountains
02. Mount Johnson (3,465 feet), Gabilan Range
03. San Benito Mountain (5,241 feet), Joaquin Ridge
04. Caliente Mountains (5,106 feet), Caliente Mountains
05. Mount Pinos (8,831 feet), San Emigdio Mountains
06. Cone Peak (5,155 feet), Ventana Wilderness
07. Junipero Serra Peak (5,862 feet), Santa Lucia Mountains
08. South Ventana Cone (4,965 feet), Ventana Mountains
09. Palo Escrito Peak (4,467 feet), Sierra de Salinas
10. Loma Prieta (3,806 feet), Santa Cruz Mountains
11. Mount Isabel (4,230 feet), Diablo Mountains
12. San Francisco

Map 02.21 The Peaks of the Bay Area

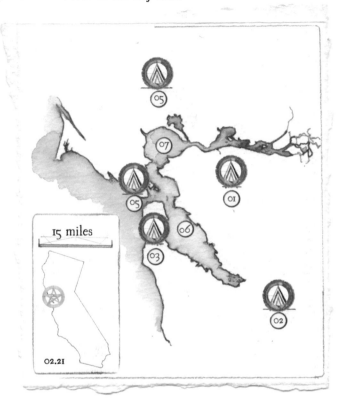

It is the mountains that define the shape of California's largest estuary, the San Francisco Bay. In the narrow strait between Mount Tamalpais and the San Francisco Peninsula—crowned by Montara Mountain, a relatively low peak that rises at the western edge of the Santa Cruz Mountains—the Golden Gate Bridge stands.

01. Mount Diablo (3,849 feet), Contra Costa County
02. Mount Hamilton (4,216 feet), Santa Clara County
03. Montara Mountain (1,898 feet), San Mateo County
04. Mount Tamalpais (2,574 feet), Marin County
05. Mount Saint Helena (4,341 feet), Lake County
06. San Francisco Bay
07. San Pablo Bay

Map 02.22 Mount Diablo

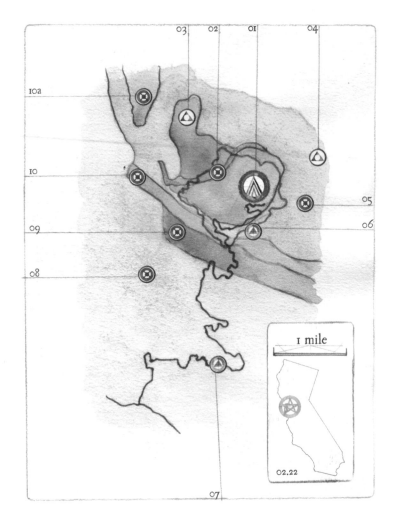

1 mile

02.22

Mount Diablo, the northernmost peak in the Diablo Range, rose from the surrounding land through a geological phenomenon called uplift. A much older piece of rock pushed its way up through much younger strata. The mosaic of stones near the peak are almost 20 million years older than the stones and soil on the valley floor, nearly 4,000 feet below.

There are many curious facets to the grander story of Mount Diablo: its wildflower bloom, its oak tree gardens, its mountain lion populations, its Native Californian mythology as the birthplace of humanity, its history as a meridian site as designated by the early pioneers of the Bay Area. Among these facets, the geology of the mountain is perhaps its most unique feature. No other mountain in California shares its history in how it mechanically and tectonically gained regional prominence.

Ophiolite is the name for the Mesozoic rocks that formed on the ancient seabed that now surrounds the peak of the mountain. Serpentinite is a rock frequently found in association with ophiolite. While the stones that make up Mount Diablo are very old, the mountain itself only began rising a mere ten million years ago. Most geologists agree that although the old faults that began the process of Mount Diablo's rise are gone, a single thrust fault remains that continues to push the peak skyward at a the rate of a few millimeters a year.

01. Mount Diablo Peak (3,484 feet)
02. Serpentine
03. Eagle Peak, surrounded by the Mount Diablo Ophiolite formation
04. North Peak
05. Great Valley geologic groupings
06. Summit Trail
07. South Gate Road
08. Mio-Pliocene formations that surround Diablo
09. Miocene formations
10. & 10a. Eocene formations

Steller's Jay
Cyanocitta Stelleri

Mount Diablo
Geological anomaly

Map 02.23 The Diablo Mountains

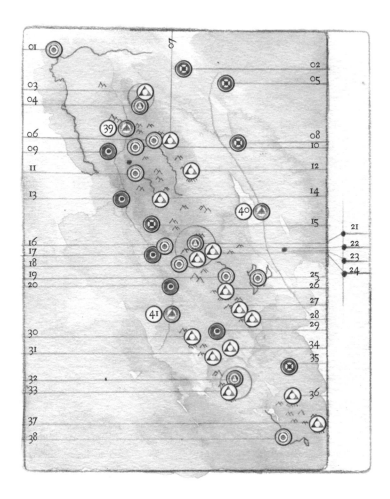

27 miles

02.23

The historically rich Diablo Mountains are home to the Calle Real, the missionary road that defined 18th-century California. More than 10,000 people lived here at the time of conquest.

The Diablo Range is the coastal mountain network that stretches from Mount Diablo in the north to San Benito Mountain, 120 miles to the south. The average elevation across the range is about 3,000 feet. The tallest peaks in the range complex rise to over 5,000 feet. The oak-laden plateaus across this, the longest of California's Coast Ranges, are usually at about 2,500 feet. The hills surrounding the mostly isolated peaks rise to about 1,000 feet at most.

01. San Francisco Bay and San Pablo Bay
02. Contra Costa County
03. Mount Diablo Peak (3,484 feet)
04. Mount Diablo State Park
05. San Joaquin County
06. Lake del Valle State Recreation Area
07. Cedar Mountain (3,675 feet)
08. Stanislaus County
09. Fremont
10. San Antonio Reservoir
11. Calaveras Reservoir
12. Red Mountain (3,680 feet)
13. San Jose
14. Mount Hamilton (4,213 feet)
15. Santa Clara County
16. Anderson Lake
17. Morgan Hill
18. Coyote Lake County Park
19. Pacheco Lake
20. Gilroy
21. Henry Coe State Park
22. Burra Burra Peak (2,287 feet)
23. Merced County
24. Wilson Peak (2,651 feet)
25. San Luis Reservoir
26. Pacheco Peak (2,770 feet)
27. Lavedga Peak (3,801 feet)
28. Reinoso Peak (3,472 feet)
29. Mission San Juan Bautista
30. Fremont Peak (3,171 feet)
31. Mount Johnson (3,465 feet)
32. Pinnacles National Park
33. North Chalone Peak (3,304 feet)
34. Cerro Bonito (3,992 feet)
35. Clear Creek Management Area
36. Bucks Peak (4,153 feet)
37. San Benito Peak (5,241 feet)
38. Hernandez Reservoir
39. Interstate 680
40. Interstate 5
41. Interstate 101

Coyote
Canis latrans

Map 02.24 San Benito Peak

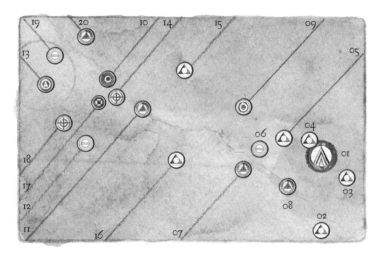

Pine and incense cedar forests protect the endemic San Benito evening primrose. The San Benito Mountain Research Area, within the Clear Creek Management Area, has been closed for over ten years due to potential health hazards from the asbestos mines that existed there in the 20th century. In that time of isolation, the local ecologies have found sanctuary and the numbers of coyotes, eagles, deer, and mountain lions have grown; finding traces of each species in surrounding areas is not uncommon.

01. San Benito Peak, (5,267 feet)
02. Condon Peak (4,970 feet)
03. Santa Rita Peak (5,165 feet)
04. San Carlos Peak (4,845 feet)
05. Sampson Peak (4,663 feet)
06. Oak Flat Campground
07. Clear Creek Road
08. Los Gatos Creek Road
09. Hernandez Reservoir
10. San Benito

11. Bitterwater Road
12. Sans Topo Ranch
13. Pinnacles National Park
14. San Benito River
15. Griswold Hills
16. Mustang Ridge
17. San Andreas Fault Zone
18. Chalome Creek
19. Bear Valley Ranch
20. Highway 25

6 miles

02.24

San Benito Peak
Coyote playground

Map 02.25 Pacheco Peak

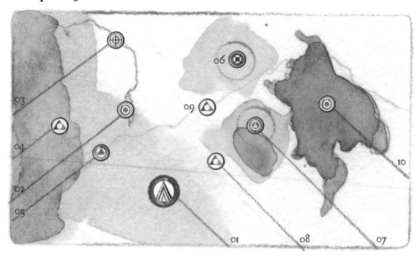

The 7,000-acre Pacheco State Park is home to Pacheco Peak, and perhaps the more famous Pacheco Pass, which straddles the rocky oak woodland above the massive San Luis Reservoir. John Muir came through the Pacheco Pass on his first walking trip to the Sierra Nevada in the 1860s. Pacheco Pass is where California's high-speed rail line will cross the Diablo Mountains from the Central Valley. Cottonwood Creek Wildlife Area is home to approximately 6,300 acres of excellent Central Valley habitat, harboring populations of wild pigs, black-tailed deer, gray fox, long-tailed weasels, and dozens of species of birds.

01. Pacheco Peak (2,770 feet)
02. Pacheco Lake (472 feet)
03. North Fork, Pacheco Creek
04. Gulnac Peak (2,276 feet)

05. Highway 152, aka Pacheco Pass Highway
06. Cottonwood Creek Wildlife Area
07. Pacheco State Park
08. Spike's Peak (1,927 feet)
09. Pacheco Pass
10. San Luis Reservoir

6 miles

02.25

Pacheco Peak
Passage to the Valley

Map 02.26 The Santa Lucia Mountains

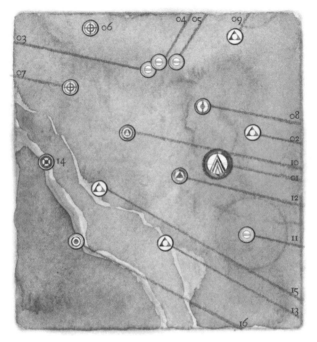

To the west of the Diablos, the Santa Lucia Mountains extend from Monterey down the coast to San Luis Obispo. The Santa Lucia Mountains are home to some of the rarest conifer trees in the world, including the Santa Lucia fir and the bigcone Douglas fir. Santa Lucia Peak, at 5,862 feet, is the largest peak in California's Coastal Mountains, and was recently renamed Junipero Serra Peak in honor of the founder of California's 18th century Spanish Mission complex.

The Santa Lucia Mountains reach right up to and follow a path down the rugged Central Coast along Highway 1, south of Big Sur. The hot springs of Esalen hang

out over the precipitous cliff underneath Cone Peak, which rises straight up from the sea to 5,155 feet.

01. Santa Lucia Peak (5,862 feet)
02. Pinyon Peak (5,264 feet)
03. Arroyo Seco Guard Station
04. Arroyo Seco Group Camp
05. Arroyo Seco Campground
06. Tassajara Creek
07. Lost Valley Creek
08. Ventana Wilderness
09. Arroyo Seco Road
10. Santa Lucia Memorial Park
11. Fort Hunter Liggett
12. Milpitas Road
13. Cone Peak (5,155 feet)
14. Esalen Institute

8 miles

Santa Lucia Peak
a throne for condors

02.26

Map 02.27 Mountains of the South Coast Ranges

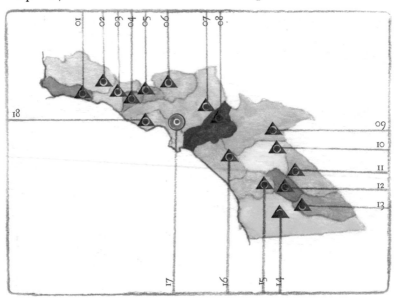

As the Pacific Plate slides past the North American Plate, carrying Los Angeles northward to San Francisco, the Baja Peninsula folds the southland into two major mountain regions: the Peninsular Ranges, which move from Mexico into the Los Angeles Basin, parallel to the Pacific coast, and the Transverse Ranges, which run perpendicular to every other major mountain range in the state. The three major Transverse Ranges are the Santa Ynez, the San Gabriel, and the San Bernardino Mountains. The major Peninsular Ranges are the Santa Anas, the Santa Rosas, and San Jacinto Peak.

In this map, the most prominent peaks of the Central Coast Ranges are noted, along with their elevations and associated mountain cells.

100 miles

02.27

01. Santa Ynez Peak (4,298 feet), Santa Ynez Mountains
02. Big Pine Mountain (6,828 feet), San Rafael Mountains
03. Reyes Peak (7,510 feet), Pine Mountain
04. Hines Peak (6,704 feet), Topatopa Mountain
05. Alamo Mountain (7,367 feet), Sespe Wilderness
06. Burnt Peak (5,788 feet), Angeles Mountains
07. Mount Baden-Powell (9,399 feet), San Gabriel Mountains
08. Mount San Antonio, aka Old Baldy (10,064 feet), Cucamonga
    Wilderness, San Gabriel Mountains
09. San Gorgonio (11,502 feet), San Bernardino Mountains
10. San Jacinto (10,804 feet), San Jacinto Mountains
11. Toro Peak (8,716 feet), Santa Rosa Mountains
12. Hot Springs Mountain (6,533 feet), Los Coyotes Reservation
13. Whale Peak (5,349 feet), Vallecito Mountains
14. Cuyamaca Peak (6,512 feet), Cuyamaca Rancho State Park
15. Palomar Mountain (6,140 feet), Aguana Mountain
16. Santiago Peak (5,687 feet), Old Saddleback, Santa Ana Mountains
17. Los Angeles
18. Castro Peak (2,824 feet), Santa Monica Mountains

Song sparrow
Melospiza melodia

Vermillion flycatcher
Pyrocephalus rubinus

Map 02.28 Mount Piños

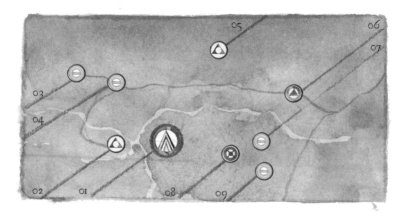

Mount Piños in the Los Padres National Forest, on the boundary between Ventura and Kern Counties, is the highest point in Ventura County and the highest point of the Transverse Ranges west of Tejon Pass.

The mountain's broad peak is capped in forests that are high enough to resemble the Sierra Nevada as much as any conifer forest in the Coast Ranges. The mountain supports large networks of wildlife that notably include five species of owls and significant black bear populations. The area is known for black nighttime skies and is excellent for stargazing. The most popular summer site for late-night sessions under the stars is the parking area at Chula Vista, two miles east of the peak.

01. Mount Piños (8,831 feet)
02. Cerro Noroeste (8,286 feet)
03. Toad Spring Camp
04. Mil Potrero Camp
05. San Emigdio Mountain (7,492 feet)
06. Mil Potrero Highway
07. McGill Camp
08. Chula Vista
09. Mount Piños Camp

3 miles

02.28

Mount Piños
Pines and flowers

Map 02.29 The East San Gabriel Mountains

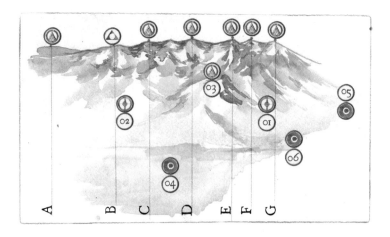

Mount San Antonio's peaks dominate the northward view of the Los Angeles Basin skyline. More commonly called Mount Baldy, Mount San Antonio is the highest of the network of peaks that cluster here in the San Gabriel Mountains. It is the highest point in the San Gabriel Mountains National Monument. This chain of designed wilderness areas has no roads and has become excellent bear habitat. Grizzly bears were common here as recently as 100 years ago. Black bears did not live here until 1933, when the forest service relocated eleven problematic bears from Yosemite Valley.

This map depicts a view of the San Gabriels facing east from the San Jose Hills south of West Covina.

A. Mount Baden-Powell (9,399 feet)
B. Blue Ridge
C. Pine Mountain (9,648 feet)
D. Mount San Antonio,
   aka Old Baldy (10,064 feet)

E. Telegraph Peak (8,985 feet)
F. Ontario Peak (8,896 feet)
G. Cucamonga Peak (8,859 feet)

01. Cucamonga Wilderness (13,007 acres)
02. Sheep Mountain Wilderness (41,883 acres)
03. Johnstone Peak (3,178 feet)
04. Glendora
05. San Antonio Heights
06. San Dimas

5 miles

02.29

Map 02.30 The Many Peaks of San Gorgonio

2 miles

02.30

The highest mountain in Southern California, Mount Gorgonio lies just a few miles north of another peak that tops out over 11,000 feet: San Jacinto. Together, the two peaks represent a gate of sorts that defines the eastern end of the Transverse Ranges. This is where the Low Desert meets the High Desert above Coachella Valley.

01. San Gorgonio Mountain (11,502 feet)
02. Galena Peak (9,324 feet)
03. Little San Gorgonio Peak (9,133 feet)
04. San Bernardino Peak (10,864 feet)
05. San Bernardino East Peak (10,691 feet)
06. Charlton Peak (10,806 feet)
07. Dobbs Peak (10,495 feet)
08. Poopout Hill (7,840 feet)
09. Shields Peak (10,680 feet)
10. Anderson Peak (10,840 feet)
11. Ginnell Mountain (10,284 feet)
12. Lake Peak (10,161 feet)
13. Jepson Peak (11,205 feet)

Map 02.31 San Jacinto and the Santa Rosa Mountains

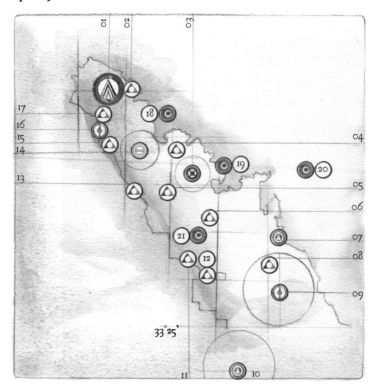

Over the tiny community of Pinyon, you can stand on the edge of the one road in town and see to the north the giant bowl of the San Jacinto ridgeline as it circles around for 30 miles in both directions. As you do, the long, gray peaks of Santa Rosa Mountain and Toro Peak loom behind you. This remote island in the sky, above the Low Desert to both the east and the west, is paradise to the kings of this wilderness: the coyote and the bighorn sheep who rule over their terrain of white sage, yucca, and

8 miles

02.31

stands of mixed-conifer forests that were left here long ago when the world was different, among the now-desiccated mountain-scape rich with life perfectly adapted to it.

These two sister ranges extend for approximately 60 miles from the San Bernardino Mountains southeast to Anza Borrego State Park. The wildlife found in these mountains has been defined by climate since the Pleistocene. These forests, which include sizable populations of fir and pine, California black oak, and even Coulter pine, are all relic ecosystems left isolated in their heights as the low-lying desert that surrounds them warmed in modern days.

01. San Jacinto Peak (10,804 feet)
02. Desert Angel Peak (2,356 feet)
03. Santa Rosa Mountains State Game Refuge
04. Murray Hill (2,200 feet)
05. Bald Mountain (4,454 feet)
06. Asbestos Mountain (5,265 feet)
07. Santa Rosa and San Jacinto National Monument boundary
08. Martinez Mountain (6,548 feet)
09. Santa Rosa Mountains Wilderness (78,576 acres)
10. Anza Borrego State Park
11. Santa Rosa Mountain (8,046 feet)
12. Toro Peak (8,716 feet)
13. Palm View Peak (7,160 feet)
14. Agua Caliente Indian Reservation
15. Tahquitz Peak (8,846 feet)
16. San Jacinto Wilderness (32,186 acres)
17. Marion Mountain (10,362 feet)

Little willow flycatcher
Empidonax traillii brewsterii

Map 02.32 Palomar Mountain

Palomar Mountain evolves as you rise through the strata of its forests. Because of its exposure to the sea, the top of the mountain receives almost 30 inches of rain a year, classifying it as down-right temperate, which is unique for the otherwise arid San Diego County. Up in Palomar Mountain State Park, a thick understory of ferns blanket the ground under the mixed-conifer forest—a testament to this enjoyed precipitation.

The most culturally famous feature on the mountain is the Palomar Observatory.

The mountain's summit is two miles east of the observatory and not accessible by road.

01. Palomar Mountain (6,140 feet)
02. Palomar Mountain State Park border
03. Doane Creek
04. Cedar Grove Group Camp
05. Azalea Creek
06. Boucher Lookout
07. Doane Valley Natural Reserve
08. Doane Valley Campground
09. Doane Pond
10. Doane Valley Reservoir
11. Park headquarters

2 miles

Palomar Mountain
Observations into the Wild

02.32

Map 02.33 Mountains of the Desert

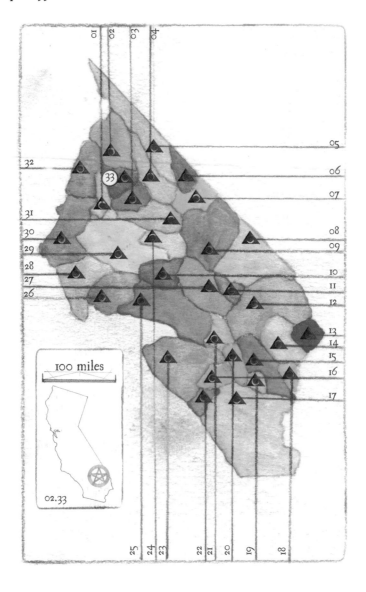

From Death Valley down to the Salton Sea, the Mojave Desert ramps down into the Colorado Desert. From the High Desert plateau of Joshua Tree across the juniper woodlands of the New York Mountains and down to the Colorado River, the mountain ranges that define this landscape are a great, dry labyrinth of creosote bush and Joshua tree that skirt tall, snow-covered peaks—sky islands for remnant stands of mountain trees.

In this map, the most prominent desert peaks are noted, along with their elevations and associated mountain cells.

01. Straw Peak (5,578 feet), Slate Range
02. Telescope Peak (11,049 feet), Panamint Range
03. Brown Mountain (5,125 feet), Long Valley Mountains
04. Funeral Peak (6,384 feet), Black Mountains
05. Pyramid Peak (6,703 feet), Funeral Mountains
06. Nopah Peak (1,946 feet), Nopah Range Wilderness
07. Kingston Peak (7,323 feet), Kingston Range
08. New York (7,532 feet), New York Mountains
09. Clark Mountain (7,929 feet), Clark Mountain Range
10. Sleeping Beauty (3,980 feet), Cady Mountains
11. Fountain Peak (6,996 feet), Providence Mountains
12. Mercury Mountain (3,720 feet), Old Woman Mountains Wilderness
13. Savahia Peak (2,695 feet), Whipple Mountains
14. Bolson Peak (4,231 feet), Turtle Mountains Wilderness
15. Hidalgo Mountain (4,435 feet), Bullion Mountains
16. Monument Mountain (4,834 feet), Cottonwood Mountains
17. Black Butte (4,504 feet), Chuckwalla Mountains
18. Black Hill (1,225 feet), Big Maria Mountains
19. Palo Verde Peak (1,795 feet), Palo Verde Mountains Wilderness
20. Aqua Peak (4,416 feet), Coxcomb Mountains, Joshua Tree National Park
21. Lead Mountain (2,891 feet), Sheephole Mountains
22. Mount Barrow (2,475 feet), Chocolate Mountains
23. Quail Mountain (5,813 feet), Little San Bernardino Mountains, Joshua Tree National Park
24. Alvord Peak (3,456 feet), Tiefort Mountains
25. Argos Mountain (4,488 feet), Rodman Mountains
26. East Ord Mountain (6,068 feet), Ord Mountains
27. Granite Peak (6,762 feet), Granite Mountains
28. Quartzite Mountain (4,532 feet), Shadow Mountains, Antelope Valley
29. Eagle Crags (5,512 feet), Pilot Knob Mountains, China Lake
30. Red Mountain (5,261 feet), Rand Mountains
31. Turquoise Mountain (4,511 feet), Avawatz Mountains
32. Maturango Peak (8,839 feet), Argus Range
33. Manly Peak (7,196 feet), Manly Peak Wilderness

Map 02.34 Clark Mountain

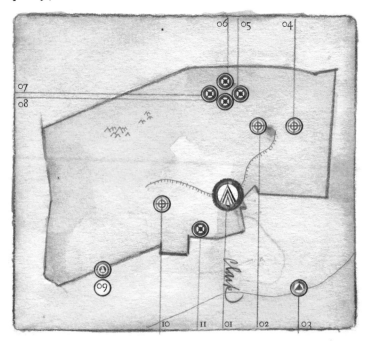

In the 19th century, after the Gold Rush in the north, many trains of men and mules came to Clark Mountain and dug deep holes to extract a sizable amount of gold and silver. The mountain towers over a stop on Interstate 15 called Mountain Pass, and it is the highest point in the Mojave National Preserve and, in fact, in all the Mojave Desert ranges. Like many peaks in the greater Mojave area, Clark Mountain harbors conifer forests near its peak; most unusually, the white fir *(Abies concolor)* is found here in its southernmost location. Clark Mountain is the north-ernmost reach of the Mojave National Preserve and is separated from the main park by Interstate 15.

01. Clark Mountain (7,929 feet)
02. Greens Well
03. Mountain Pass
04. Stonewell Mine
05. Little Bullock Mine
06. Beatrice Mine
07. Alley Mine
08. Whitfield Spring
09. Mojave National Preserve border
10. Parchika Spring
11. Copper World Mine

2 miles

Clarke Mountain
desert forests over the Mojave

02.34

Map 02.35 Telescope Peak

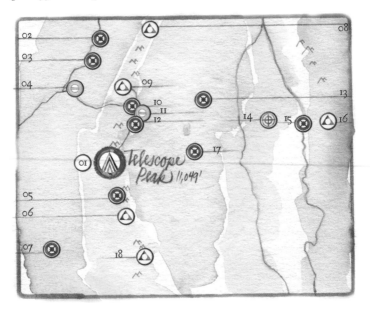

Telescope Peak is the mountain heart of Death Valley National Park, as well as its highest point. From its summit, also the highest point of the Panamint Range, the viewshed extends for over 100 miles in all directions. Telescope Peak boasts the greatest vertical rise above local terrain of any mountain in the contiguous United States, rising more than two vertical miles over Badwater, just a couple of linear miles away. In the old forests near its peak, rare pines including limber (*Pinus flexilis*), and a species of bristlecone pine (*Pinus longaeva*) wait out long, dry seasons high above the hottest environment in North America.

01. Telescope Peak (11,049 feet)
02. Eureka Mine
03. Nemo Canyon
04. Wildrose Campground
05. Panamint City (ghost town)
06. Sentinel Peak (9,636 feet)
07. Ballarat (ghost town)
08. Aguereberry Point (6,433 feet)
09. Wildrose Peak (9,064 feet)
10. Charcoal kilns
11. Thorndike Camp
12. Mahogany Flat
13. Death Valley Canyon
14. Shorty's Well
15. Badwater (282 feet below sea level)
16. Dante's View (5,475 feet)
17. Eagle Borax Works
18. Porter Ridge

9 miles

telescope peak
snow in the furnace

02.35

Map 02.36 Mountains of the Great Basin in California

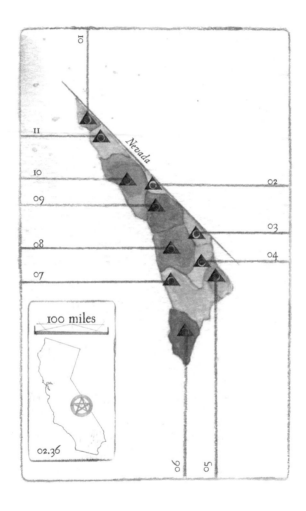

The Great Basin, one of North America's great deserts, spills over the Nevada border into California on the state's easternmost edge. These mountains, made up of two principal ranges—the Inyo and the White—are greener than the mountains of the Mojave to the south and drier than the Sierra Nevada to the west.

In this map, the most prominent Great Basin peaks are noted, along with their elevations and associated mountain cells.

01. Mount Patterson (11,673 feet), Sweetwater Mountains
02. Mount Dubois (13,559 feet), Boundary Peak Wilderness, Northern White Mountains
03. Last Chance Mountain (8,456 feet), Sylvania Wilderness, Last Chance Range
04. Dry Mountain (8,674 feet), Last Chance Range, Death Valley National Park
05. Tin Mountain (8,953 feet), Cottonwood Mountains, Death Valley National Park
06. Coso Peak (8,160 feet), Upper Centennial Flat, Coso Range Wilderness
07. Mount Inyo (11,107 feet), Inyo Mountains Wilderness
08. Waucoba Mountain (11,123 feet), Whippoorwill Flat Research Natural Area, Inyo Mountains
09. White Mountain Peak (14,246 feet), Ancient Bristlecone Pine Forest, White Mountains
10. Glass Mountain (11,123 feet), Sentinel Meadow Research National Area, Glass Mountain Ridge, Inyo National Forest
11. Potato Peak (10,236 feet), Bodie Hills, Geiger Grade

coyote
Canis latrans

Map 02.37 White Mountain Peak

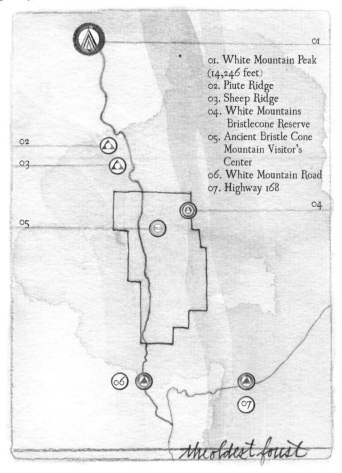

01. White Mountain Peak
(14,246 feet)
02. Piute Ridge
03. Sheep Ridge
04. White Mountains
Bristlecone Reserve
05. Ancient Bristle Cone
Mountain Visitor's
Center
06. White Mountain Road
07. Highway 168

the oldest forest

The White Mountains are home to what may be not only the oldest trees in the world, but also the oldest single living organisms in the world: the bristlecone pines. Up on their precipitous slopes along the north face of White Mountain ridge, they have counted at least 5,000 long years of life. There are populations of bristlecones in eastern Nevada as well, but nowhere other than at White Mountain Peak has a grove of these ancient trees been able to find such perfect conditions—some alchemical mix of altitude, aridity, and soil type able to sustain these long-lived plants through an unparalleled march of terrestrial longevity.

6 miles

white Mountain Peak
ancient living forests

02.37

03. OF WATER & RIVERS

Kern River Golden trout
Oncorhynchus aquabonita

Churning, falling, cascading, bending, funneling, coursing, cutting, running, jetting, spurting, gushing, and rushing: the rivers, streams, and creeks of California run courses as dramatic and as varied as the topography they claim as their own.

This chapter presents a portfolio of maps that describe various aspects of California's waterscape. First is a series that describes California's freshwater riverscape regions (map 03.01 through map 03.05). Second is a series that outlines human interaction with that riverscape through constructed features including dams, reservoirs, aqueducts, and canals (map 03.06 through map 03.10); this section includes a map of Tulare Lake as an example of human engineering influencing the native waterscape. Third is a series of watercourse maps that describe 24 major natural rivers and a few adjacent features that are ecologically unique, including Lake Tahoe, the San Francisco Bay, the Monterey Peninsula, and the Los Angeles Aqueduct (map 03.11 through map 03.32). Fourth is a series of maps dedicated to the isolated Channel Islands of Southern California (map 03.33 through map 03.36) and the unique systems they support.

As described above, the third part of this chapter, the watercourses (map 03.11 through map 03.32), is organized by geographic region from north to south. The first group of watercourse maps begins in the northeastern corner of California (map 03.11, Pit River) and ends at the southern tip of

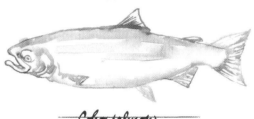

Coho salmon
Oncorhynchus kisutch

the Sierra Nevada (map 03.20, Kern River). These ten maps appear in order as they form a descending ladder down the eastern half of the state. A map of Lake Tahoe, the jewel of alpine California, closes this section.

The next group of watercourse begins in the northwestern corner of California (map 03.22, Klamath River) and ends with the coastal watersheds of Orange County (map 03.29, Santa Ana River).

The final grouping of watercourses describes how water is moved in California's deserts (map 03.30 through map 03.32) by the flow of the Mojave River and the Colorado. The Los Angeles Aqueduct (map 03.31) is included here, as it has fundamentally altered the local waterscape and has become part of the story of the desert.

Map 03.01 The Unleashed Waterscape

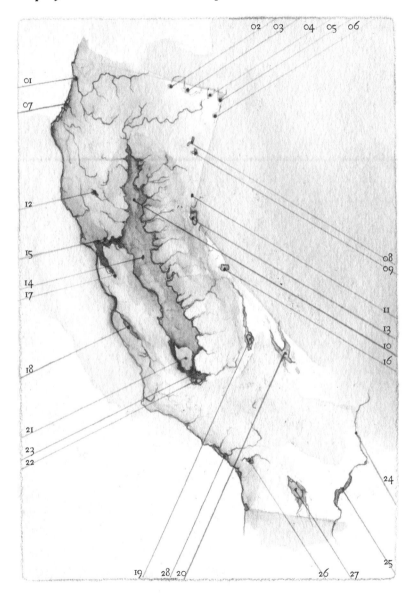

Without dams, aqueducts, farms, and diversions, California's lush, riparian blueprint is revealed as a vast network of sheltered wetlands, vast marsh fields, coastal salt prairies, rich vernal pools, and long, unbroken alkaline basins. Teeming with fecund life, this primitive and pristine model supports enormous ecosystems of a paradise restored. This map is an imaginative diagram, based on historical sources, of what a post-dam California might look like.

01. Klamath Lake and wetlands
02. Tule Lake
03. Lost River wetlands
04. Goose Lakes
05. Surprise Valley Lakes
06. Washoe Lake System
07. Humboldt Bay
08. Eagle Lake
09. Honey Lake
10. Freshwater marshes of
     the Upper Sacramento
11. Sierra Valley riparian meadows
12. Clear Lake
13. Lake Tahoe Basin
14. San Joaquin River freshwater basin
15. Coastal brackish wetlands
16. Mono Lake
17. South Bay salt reaches
18. Salinas wetlands
19. Owens River system
20. Amargosa alkali lake system
21. Tulare Lake
22. Buena Vista Lake
23. Kern Lake
24. Colorado River
25. Chemehuevi riparian desert forest
26. Lake Elsinore
27. Salton Sink
28. Coastal salt marshes

Black-necked stilt
Himantopus mexicanus

Map 03.02 The Riverscape

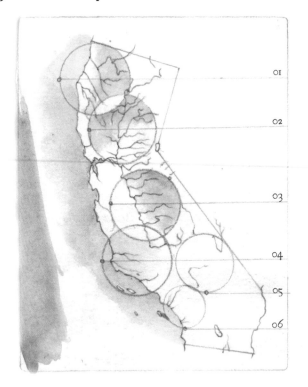

01. The North Coast River Systems
02. The Sacramento River and its tributaries
03. The San Joaquin River and its tributaries
04. Central Coast (Salinas to Santa Ana)
05. Mojave Desert (Mojave to Amargosa)
06. South Coast (Los Angeles to San Diego)

North of the Transverse Mountains, the riverscape comprises four main hydrological regions, which are responsible for 93 percent of the state's naturally flowing water. Within these four regions, approximately 90 major rivers claim nearly 250,000 miles of running water. Many of these ancient rivers, with origins in the Sierra Nevada, lie in mysterious volcanic mountain tangles. Others directly reach the sea and hold the home waters to historical runs of steelhead and Pacific salmon, with their seemingly infinite capacity to remember and navigate their way back to their place of birth to spawn. Whatever their source and habitat, the rivers represent living veins for the larger entity of California and sustain all life here in the land of fire forests, sage mountains, and ranges of light.

Black oyster catcher
Haematopus bachmani

Belted kingfisher
Megaceryle alcyon

American Coot
Fulica american

Map 03.03 The Rivers of California

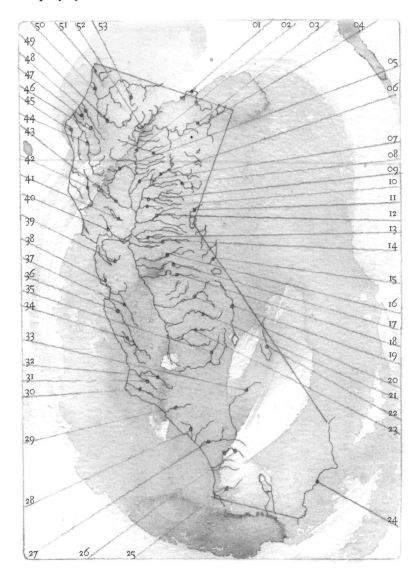

Every river has its own character. Not only that, but every stretch of every river has its own unique signature of delivery based on geology, climate, and biologic interference, whether by humans, animals, or plants. On an ecological level, what makes ecosystems work is a chicken-and-egg question: if the river informs the forest with the water it needs, which informs the climate with the carbon store it needs, which informs the river with the precipitation it needs, where does the process begin?

Osprey
Pandion haliaetus

10. Bear River
11. Truckee River
12. American River
13. Cosumnes River
14. Mokelumne River
15. Walker River
16. Stanislaus River
17. Tuolumne River
18. Merced River
19. Owens River
20. San Joaquin River
21. Kings River
22. Amargosa River
23. Tule River
24. Colorado River
25. San Diego River
26. San Jacinto River
27. Santa Ana River
28. Los Angeles River
29. Santa Clara River
30. Santa Ynez River
31. Sisquoc River
32. Cuyama River
33. Mojave River
34. Nacimiento River
35. Kern River
36. Salinas River
37. San Benito River
38. San Lorenzo River
39. Alameda Creek
40. Napa River
41. Putah Creek
42. Russian River
43. Cache Creek
44. Eel River
45. Mattole River
46. Van Duzen River
47. Elk River
48. Mad River
49. Trinity River
50. Klamath River
51. Smith River
52. McCloud River
53. Scott River

01. Lost River
02. Sacramento River
03. Pit River
04. Antelope Creek
05. Stony Creek
06. North fork of the Feather River
07. Butte Creek
08. Middle fork of the Feather River
09. Yuba River

Map 03.04 The Watersheds of California

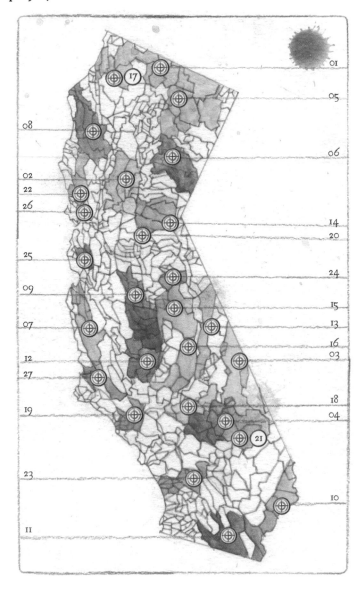

The two largest watersheds in California are the Sacramento and the San Joaquin. The two rivers that feed these watersheds separately gather the water of 25 major rivers and funnel them together to form North America's largest estuary, the San Francisco Bay Delta. To understand the arterial function of the Sacramento and the San Joaquin River networks is to understand the source of California's ecological fecundity.

tule perch
Hysterocarpus traskii

Ranking California's 27 largest (of 190) watershed networks by land area, based on the data offered by the California State Department of Conservation, offers insight into how all water ecologies are connected. A watershed is an area of land, a basin defined by a ridge that separates waters flowing to different rivers. This map could be expanded into a diagram describing the flow of water into several thousand creek-bed tributaries around the state. The list is organized not by water volume, but by sheer acreage. Some of the largest watersheds, like the Amargosa and the Mojave, contain some of the smallest amounts of water.

This list of watersheds describes the generalized geography, whether political, regional, or ecological.

01. Klamath River; Oregon state border
02. Sacramento River; Colusa and Tehama Basin
03. Amargosa River; Nevada state border
04. Mojave River; San Bernardino Mountains
05. Pit River; Modoc and Shasta Counties
06. Feather River; northern Sierra Nevada
07. Salinas River; central Coast Mountains
08. Eel River; coast redwood forests
09. San Joaquin River; the Central Valley
10. Colorado River; the Arizona border
11. Alamo River; the Imperial Valley and the Salton Sea
12. Tulare Sink; the southern Central Valley
13. Owens River; Owens Lake
14. Yuba River; northern Sierra Nevada
15. San Joaquin River; central Sierra Nevada
16. Kern River; southern Sierra Nevada
17. Trinity River; tributary of the Klamath River
18. Rock River; the Antelope Valley
19. Santa Clara River; Ventura County
20. American River; central Sierra Nevada
21. Cadiz Valley; Mojave Trails National Monument
22. Russian River; Mendocino and Sonoma Counties
23. Santa Ana River; Santa Ana Mountains
24. Merced River; central Sierra Nevada
25. Coyote Creek; South San Francisco Bay
26. Petaluma River; the wetlands of the North Bay
27. Santa Maria River; Sierra Madre Mountains

Map 03.05 Hot Springs of California

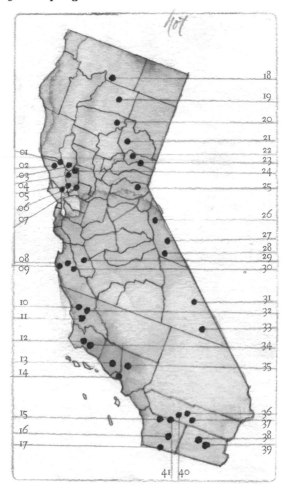

Beneath the thin veneer of the Earth's outer crust, a tectonic machine grinds and broils, forever fragmenting California's cracked surface. The same factor responsible for California's many earthquakes is also responsible for its many hot springs: the dynamic nature of the Earth itself. It just so happens that, often, this geothermal energy heats up a surface pool of water to just the right temperature for humans to be able to enjoy recreationally.

01. Vichy Springs
02. Orr Hot Springs
03. Soda Baths
04. Harbin Hot Springs
05. White Sulphur Springs
06. Sonoma Mission Inn
07. Dr. Wilkinson's Hot Springs
08. Sykes Hot Springs
09. Esalen Institute
10. Avila Hot Springs
11. Las Cruces Hot Springs
12. Gaviota Springs
13. Big Caliente Springs
14. Beverly Hot Springs
15. Murrieta Hot Springs
16. Agua Caliente Springs Park
17. Jacumba Hot Springs Spa
18. Stewart Mineral Springs
19. Big Bend Hot Springs
20. Drakesbed Guest Ranch
21. Campbell Hot Springs

22. Woody's Feather River Hot Springs
23. Sierra Hot Springs
24. Wilbur Hot Springs
25. Grover Hot Springs
26. Buckeye Hot Springs
27. Hot Creek
28. Mono Hot Springs
29. Little Caliente
30. Tassajara Buddhist Meditation Center
31. Furnace Creek Inn
32. Sycamore Mineral Springs
33. Tecopa County Hot Springs
34. Glen Ivy Hot Spring
35. Wheeler Hot Spring
36. Desert Hot Springs Spa
37. Two Bunch Palms
38. Fountain of Youth Spa
39. Bashfords Hot Mineral Spa
40. Sam's Family Spa
41. Spa Hotel and Mineral Springs

Great blue heron
Ardea herodias

Map 03.06 Dams of California

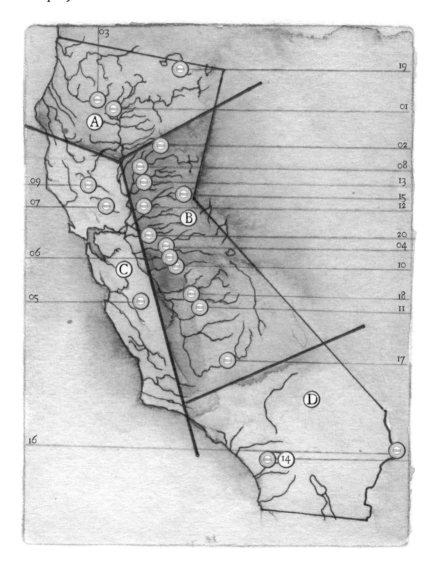

The amount of water held by a reservoir resource is measured in acre-feet. An acre-foot is the volume of one acre of surface area to a depth of one foot. When planning for water usage across the state, California estimates one acre-foot of water to be the annual usage of a suburban family household. One acre-foot per year is equivalent to 893 gallons per day. The following is an analysis of the total percentage of water storage (reservoir space) divided among four regions across California.

A. Northern water
9.2 million acre-feet of water storage
11 percent of California's total water storage

B. Sierra Nevada water
44.8 million acre-feet of water storage
54 percent of California's total water storage

C. Coastal Mountains water
16 million acre-feet of water storage
19 percent of California's total water storage

D. Southland water
12.8 million acre-feet of water storage
15 percent of California's total water storage

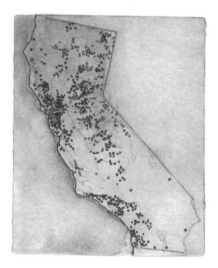

Some 1,400 named dams crowd the valleys and choke the rivers of the Golden State. There are no fully wild major rivers left. Only by the federal protection of a wild and scenic rivers designation do small stretches of free water still rage. The ecological stranglehold that dams represent on wild rivers cannot be overstated. Although human ecology of the 20th century owes a lot of its success to the water resources that dams make available, the California of the 21st century and beyond needs new modes of water delivery and distribution. We have invested too much in an outdated, unethical model of water storage, energy production, and flood prevention. The toll dams take on the natural world is unsustainable and will begin to adversely affect human ecology as agriculture begins to suffer, wildlife continues to disappear, and societal tensions rise.

01. Shasta Dam (Sacramento River) formed Lake Shasta, which can hold 4.55 million acre-feet.

02. Oroville Dam (Feather River) formed Lake Oroville, which can hold 3.54 million acre-feet.

03. Trinity Dam (Trinity River) formed Trinity Lake, which can hold 2.45 million acre-feet.

04. New Melones Dam (Stanislaus River) formed New Melones Lake, which can hold 2.40 million-acre feet.

05. San Luis Dam (off-stream reservoir) formed San Luis Reservoir, which can hold 2.04 million acre-feet.

06. New Don Pedro Dam (Tuolumne River) formed Don Pedro Lake, which can hold 2.03 million acre-feet.

07. Monticello Dam (Putah River) formed Lake Berryessa, which can hold 1.60 million acre-feet.

08. Canyon Dam (Feather River) formed Lake Almanor, which can hold 1.31 million acre-feet.

09. Cache Creek Dam (Cache Creek) is on Clear Lake, with a usable storage capacity of 1.16 million acre-feet.

10. New Exchequer Dam (Merced River) formed Lake McClure, which can hold 1.03 million acre-feet.

11. Pine Flat Dam (Kings River) formed Pine Flat Lake, which can hold 1.00 million acre-feet.

12. Folsom Dam (American River) formed Folsom Lake, which can hold 0.98 million acre-feet.

13. New Bullards Bar Dam (North Yuba River) formed New Bullards Bar Reservoir, which can hold 0.97 million acre-feet.

14. Diamond Valley Dam (off-stream reservoir) formed Diamond Valley Lake, which can hold 0.80 million acre-feet.

15. Lake Tahoe Dam (Truckee River) is on Lake Tahoe, with a usable storage capacity of 0.73 million acre-feet.

16. Parker Dam (Colorado River) formed Lake Havasu, which can hold 0.65 million acre-feet.

17. Isabella Dam (Kern River) formed Lake Isabella, which can hold 0.57 million acre-feet.

18. Friant Dam (San Joaquin River) formed Millerton Lake, which can hold 0.52 million acre-feet.

19. Clear Lake Dam (Lost River) formed Clear Lake, which can hold 0.45 million acre-feet.

20. Camanche Dam (Mokelumne River) formed Camanche Reservoir, which can hold 0.42 million acre-feet.

fawn lily
Erythronium pusaterii

Map 03.07 California's Aqueducts

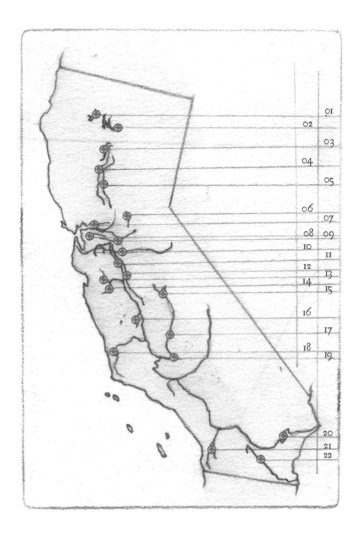

The transport of water around California is one of the great engineering wonders of the world. The thousands of miles of canals and aqueducts are grander than even the ancient aqueduct systems designed during the Roman Empire. Whether or not they will enjoy the useful longevity of the Roman aqueducts is another matter altogether. California's interconnected water system serves over 30 million people, irrigates more than 5 million acres of farmland, and manages over 40 million acre-feet of water per year. As climate change begins to change the way water business is being done, and as the human population of California increases, political tensions arise over how best to allot the limited hydrological resources in this historically arid region.

01. Trinity Lake
02. Shasta Lake
03. Corning Canal
04. Tehama–Colusa Canal
05. Glen–Colusa Canal
06. Folsom South Canal
07. North Bay Aqueduct
08. Contra Costa Canal
09. Mokelumne Canal
10. Hetch Hetchy Aqueduct
11. California Aqueduct
12. Delta–Mendota Canal
13. Santa Clara Conduit
14. Hollister Conduit
15. Millerton Lake
16. Coalinga Canal
17. Friant–Kern Canal
18. Cachuma Canal
19. Cross Valley Canal
20. Colorado River Aqueduct
21. San Diego Aqueduct
22. Coachella Canal

white sturgeon
Acipenser transmontanus

Map 03.08 The Sacramento River and Its Tributaries

San Pablo Bay

Sacramento River

The deep greens and golden browns of the Sacramento River paint a thick swath of color down the meridian of California's northern Central Valley. With tributaries that branch into the most remote corners of Northern California, the Sacramento River is, by any measure, the largest river in the whole state.

85 miles

03.08

The Sacramento River runs for over 440 miles and the greater Sacramento River watershed sprawls for nearly 30,000 square miles. Despite being heavily dammed, diverted, and reduced, the Sacramento River still maintains salmon runs and supports bird populations in the millions.

01. McCloud River
02. Pit River
03. Sacramento River
04. Shasta Lake
05. Hat Creek
06. Clear Creek
07. Cottonwood Creek
08. Battle Creek
09. South fork of Cottonwood Creek
10. Lake Almanor
11. Thomes Creek
12. East branch of the Feather River
13. North fork of the Feather River
14. Stony Creek
15. Middle fork of the Feather River
16. Lake Oroville
17. Butte Creek
18. Cache Creek
19. Yuba River
20. Clear Lake
21. Main branch of the Feather River
22. Bear River
23. Putah Creek
24. American River

Ruddy duck
Oxyura jamaicensis

Map 03.09 The San Joaquin River and Its Tributaries

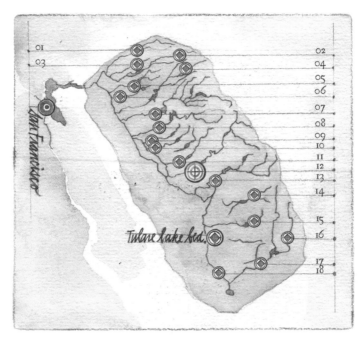

All the snowmelt of the southern Sierra Nevada floods down to join the San Joaquin River on its determined path toward its delta mouth. The San Joaquin River runs for over 360 miles, although its course has been severely altered in the 20th century. The headwaters of the San Joaquin River are high in the Sierra, pressed against the crest that defines Yosemite National Park. The wild, mountain San Joaquin River runs along the border of Madera and Fresno Counties before it enters a staircase of dams into the Central Valley. The San Joaquin River Valley is historical habitat for great populations of spawning salmon and, set along the Pacific Flyway, is home to ever-diminishing populations of migratory birds. Today, the volume of the river's flow is dramatically reduced, putting a dire toll on all natural systems that depend on it.

85 miles

03.09

Common green darner
Anax junius

Map 03.10 Tulare Lake

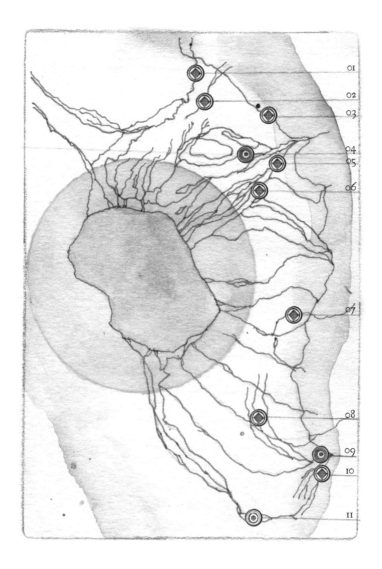

01
02
03
04
05
06
07
08
09
10
11

38 miles

03.10

Only 150 years ago, large herds of tule elk roamed through the thick tule reed on the shores of California's freshwater inland sea. The dry lakebed that was Tulare Lake was, until very recently, the largest lake west of the Mississippi. According to historical records from the mid-19th century, the lake would occasionally overflow into the San Joaquin watershed, but for the most part it was—and is—part of an endorheic water system: a closed water basin that holds all of its captured water and allows no outflow to other external bodies of water. By the end of the 19th century, Tulare Lake had been diverted so much that it was destroyed. In years when there is enough rain, portions of the lakebed rise and the ghost of the Tulare lives. With active stewardship and by significantly altering agricultural water strategy, the lake might one day return.

01. Kings River and the Fresno Slough
02. Cottonwood Creek
03. Friant Kern Canal
04. Visalia
05. Elk Bayou on the Tule River
06. Woodville wetlands
07. White Water River
08. Calloway Canals
09. Bakersfield
10. Stine and Buena Vista Canals
11. Lake Webb and the Buena Vista Lake Bed

Raccoon
procyon lotor

Map 03.11 The Pit River and Its Tributaries

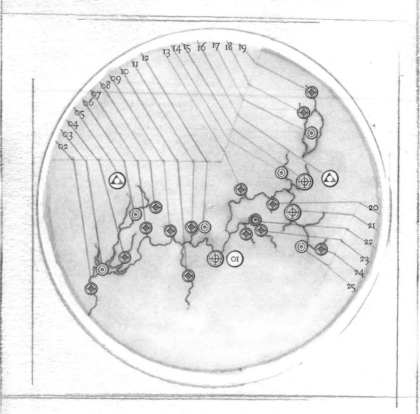

Most rivers in Northern California dry out in the hot summer, but the Pit River—fed by enormous watersheds and a strong spring system through the dense, volcanic soil of the Modoc Plateau—is swollen year-round. The Pit River has two forks that meet near the town of Alturas. The river is the longest tributary of the Sacramento River and supplies a majority of the water for Shasta Dam. In the last 30 miles of its historical course, it is swallowed by Shasta Lake.

Length: 210 miles
Watershed: 3,400 square miles
Headwaters: North fork near Davis Creek, south of Goose Lake; south fork near Buck Mountain, Warner Mountains
Mouth: Shasta Lake

75 miles

03.11

01. Pit River
02. Sacrament River
03. Shasta Lake
04. Squaw Creek
05. Mount Shasta (14,162 feet)
06. McCloud Lake
07. Kosk Creek
08. Angel Creek
09. Clark Creek
10. Hat Creek
11. Fall River
12. Big Lake
13. Turner Creek
14. Big Sage Reservoir
15. North fork of the Pit River
16. Bald Mountain (8,270 feet)
17. Goose Lake
18. Drews Creek
19. Thomas Creek
20. Canyon Creek
21. South fork of the Pit River
22. Adin
23. Ash Creek
24. Cedar Creek
25. Moon Lake

Antelope
Antilocapra americana

Map 03.12 The Feather River

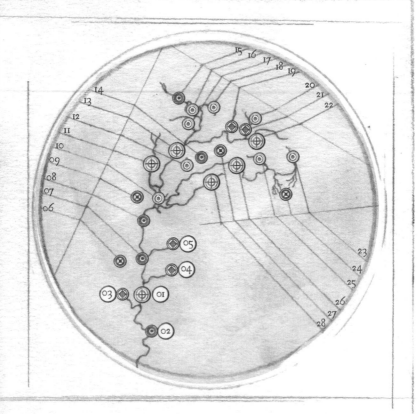

The Feather River collects its water from two of California's major mountain ranges: the volcanic peaks of Mount Lassen in the South Cascades, and the alpine meadows of Sierra Valley in the northern Sierra Nevada. Despite the Feather's geographically disparate origins, it is the region's mightiest river. The largest by volume of all tributaries of the Sacramento River, the Feather River has four major branches that join at Lake Oroville. It finally joins the Sacramento after picking up the Yuba and the Bear Rivers at the base of Sutter County.

Length: 70 miles
Watershed: 6,000 square miles
Headwaters: North fork, Lassen Peak; middle fork, Sierra Valley; south fork, Southern Plumas County; west branch, Butte County
Mouth: Sacramento River, near Fremont Weir Wildlife Area

20 miles

03.12

01. Feather River
02. Sacramento
03. Sacramento River
04. Bear River
05. Yuba River
06. Sutter County
07. Yuba City
08. Oroville
09. Butte County
10. Lake Oroville
11. West branch of the Feather River
12. Bucks Lake
13. North fork of the Feather River
14. Quincy
15. Chester
16. Lake Almanor
17. Butt Valley Reservoir
18. Mountain Meadows Reservoir
19. Lights Creek
20. Antelope Lake
21. Indian Creek
22. East branch of the Feather River
23. Frenchman Lake
24. Sierra Valley
25. Lake Davis
26. Middle fork of the Feather River
27. Plumas County
28. South fork of the Feather River

Black bear
Ursus americanus

Map 03.13 The Yuba River

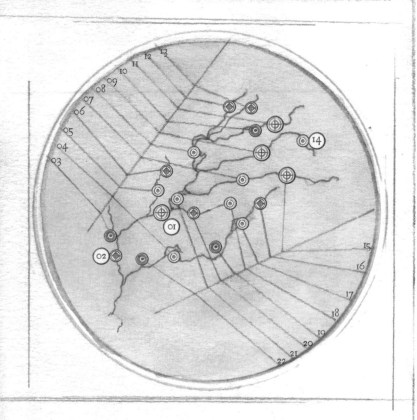

The rugged Yuba River dances down over a course crowded with broken granite boulders, feeding fragrant cedar forests and frenzied trout ponds. The Yuba River is the main tributary of the Feather River. Its three forks—north, south, and middle—run west from the crest of the Sierra. The main stem of the Yuba is the length of the river that develops from the confluence of the north and middle Yuba.

Length: 61 miles
Watershed: 1,400 square miles
Headwaters: North fork near Yuba Pass,
Nevada County; middle fork near Jackson
Meadows and Moscove Meadow; south
fork near Donner Pass, Soda Springs
Mouth: Feather River, near Yuba City

5 miles

03.13

01. Yuba River
02. Feather River
03. Yuba City
04. Camp Far West
    Reservoir
05. Collins Lake
06. Dry Creek
07. Lake Spaulding

08. New Bullards Bar Reservoir
09. Middle fork of the Yuba River
10. Downieville
11. North fork of the Yuba River
12. Slate Creek
13. Canyon Creek
14. Jackson Meadows Reservoir
15. South fork of the Yuba River
16. Bear River
17. Rollins Reservoir
18. Scotts Flat Reservoir
19. Grass Valley
20. Deer Creek
21. Englebright Lake
22. Wheatland

Golden stone shuck
(Calineuria californica)

Map 03.14 The American River

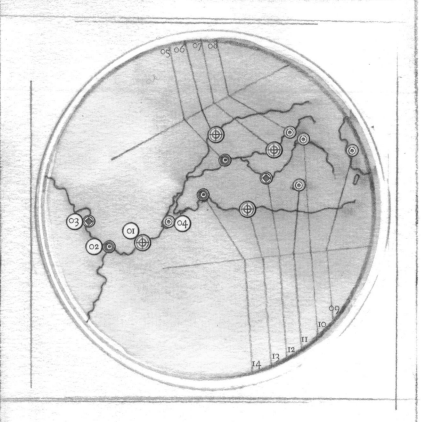

A bubbling froth of white water before Folsom Dam finally calms it, the savage American River has three forks that converge at Folsom Lake. From the Folsom Dam it runs placidly for 32 miles along the Jedediah Smith Memorial Trail into the city of Sacramento.

Length: 120 miles
Watershed: 287 square miles
Headwaters: North fork near
Granite Chief, Squaw Valley; middle fork
two miles from the source of the north
fork, near Emigrant Pass; south fork
near Echo Summit, El Dorado County
Mouth: Sacramento River, near Old
Sacramento

01. American River
02. Sacramento
03. Sacramento River
04. Folsom Lake
05. Forest Hill
06. North fork of the American River
07. Middle fork of the American River
08. French Meadows Reservoir
09. Lake Tahoe
10. Hell Hole Reservoir
11. Union Valley Reservoir
12. Rubicon River
13. South fork of the American River
14. Coloma

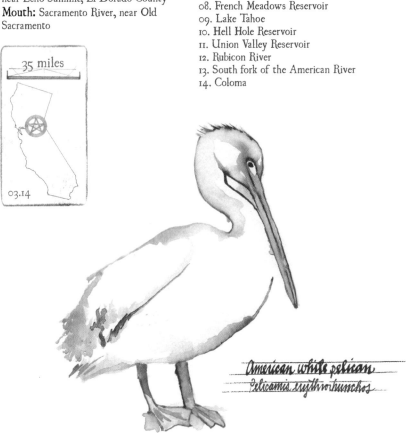

35 miles

03.14

American white pelican
Pelicanus erythrorhynchos

Map 03.15 The Cosumnes River and the Mokelumne River

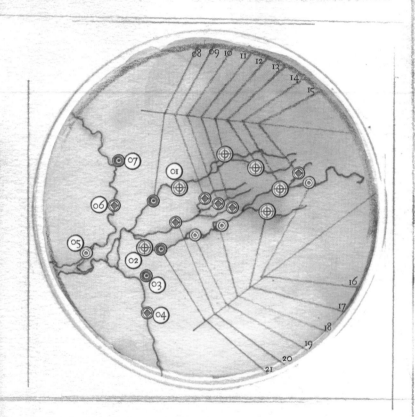

The Cosumnes (pronounced Cah-SOOM-niss) River and the Mokelumne (pronounced Moe-KELL-oom-ee) River run parallel to each other, south of the American River and north of the Stanislaus River. The Cosumnes does not have any major dams and although it has been diverted and polluted, salmon reintroduction is planned at the Cosumnes River Preserve. The Cosumnes is the largest tributary of the Mokelumne, which is divided into the Upper Mokelumne, above Pardee Reservoir in Calaveras County, and the Lower Mokelumne.

Cosumnes River
Length: 50 miles
Watershed: 1,200 square miles
Headwaters: Middle fork near Leak Spring Hill, El Dorado County
Mouth: Mokelumne River, near Thornton

20 miles

03.15

Mokelumne River
Length: 95 miles
Watershed: 2,140 square miles
Headwaters: Near Tryon Peak, southeast of Ebbetts Pass
Mouth: San Joaquin River, near Bradford Island

01. Cosumnes River
02. Mokelumne River
03. Stockton
04. San Joaquin River
05. Sacramento–San Joaquin River Delta
06. Sacramento River
07. Sacramento
08. Elk Grove
09. South fork of Dry Creek
10. Sutter Creek
11. Jackson Creek
12. North fork of the Cosumnes River
13. South fork of the Cosumnes River
14. North fork of the Mokelumne River
15. Bear River
16. Salt Springs Reservoir
17. South fork of the Mokelumne River
18. Pardee Reservoir
19. Camanche Reservoir
20. Dry Creek
21. Lodi

Chain fern
Woodwardia fimbriata

Map 03.16 The Stanislaus River

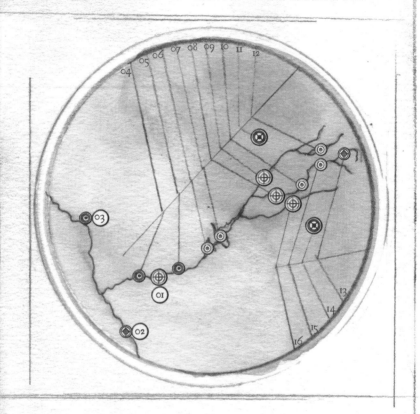

Running from the Emigrant Wilderness and passing through the heart of the Calaveras Sequoia Groves, the north fork of the Stanislaus River meets the south fork near the town of Arnold before it drops into the Central Valley. The Stanislaus River is an extensively dammed river that runs along the border between Calaveras and Tuolumne Counties. Four reservoirs in the Sierra Nevada and two major reservoirs in the Central Valley now minimize its flow into the San Joaquin River.

Length: 96 miles
Watershed: 1,075 square miles
Headwaters: Near Leavitt Peak,
Sonora Pass
Mouth: San Joaquin River,
near Caswell Park

01. Stanislaus River
02. San Joaquin River
03. Stockton
04. Ripon
05. Oakdale
06. Tulloch Reservoir
07. New Melones Lake
08. Middle fork of the Stanislaus River
09. North fork of the Stanislaus River
10. Beardsley Lake
11. Calaveras County
12. Splicer Reservoir
13. Clark fork of the Stanislaus River
14. Tuolumne County
15. Donnell Lake
16. South fork of the Stanislaus River

30 miles

03.16

Valley oak
Quercus lobata

Map 03.17 The Tuolumne River

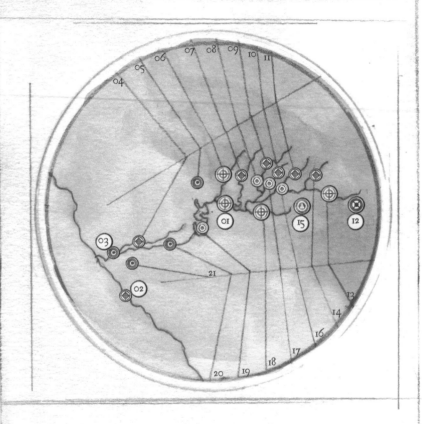

The Tuolumne River begins its journey to the Central Valley across the northern half of Yosemite National Park. There, it is quickly stopped by the Hetch Hetchy Reservoir, which supplies the drinking water for the city of San Francisco. Hetch Hetchy Valley is now underwater, although for millions of years it was the geological twin of Yosemite Valley, and, should everyone agree that the dam is outdated and ripe for removal, it will be again.

Length: 148 miles
Watershed: 2,000 square miles
Headwaters: Near Tuolumne Meadows, Yosemite National Park
Mouth: San Joaquin River, near Modesto

25 miles

03.17

01. Tuolumne River
02. San Joaquin River
03. Modesto
04. Dry Creek
05. Sonora
06. North fork of the Tuolumne River
07. Clavey River

08. Cherry Lake
09. Cherry Creek
10. Eleanor Creek
11. Falls Creek
12. Tuolumne Meadows
13. Tuolumne River
14. Piute Creek
15. Yosemite National Park
16. Hetch Hetchy Reservoir
17. Eleanor Creek
18. South fork of the Tuolumne River
19. Lake Don Pedro
20. Waterford
21. Turlock

The Tuolumne River, Yosemite

Map 03.18 The Merced River and the San Joaquin River

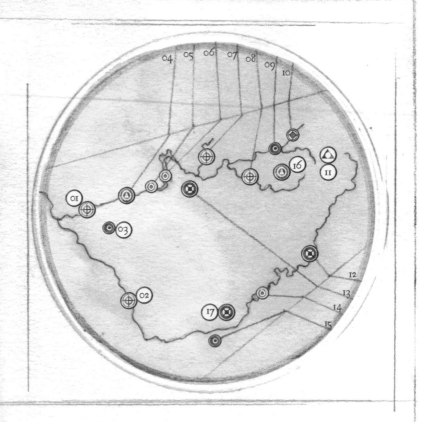

The Merced River traces a meandering path through Yosemite Valley. In the past 100 years, the river has been diverted enough that no living salmon runs remain. A restoration project was recently launched, and a fish hatchery has been developed to restore the ecology.

Length: 145 miles
Watershed: 1,725 square miles
Headwaters: The Clark Range,
Yosemite National Park
Mouth: San Joaquin River,
near Hills Ferry

22 miles

03.18

01. Merced River
02. San Joaquin River
03. Merced
04. McConnell State
    Recreation Area
05. Lake McSwain
06. Lake McClure

07. North fork of the Merced River
08. South fork of the Merced River
09. Yosemite Village
10. Tenaya Creek
11. Clark Mountains
12. Geographic center of California
13. Mariposa County
14. Millerton Lake
15. Fresno
16. Yosemite National Park
17. Madera County

Red-bellied newt
Taricha rivularis

Map 03.19 The Kings River

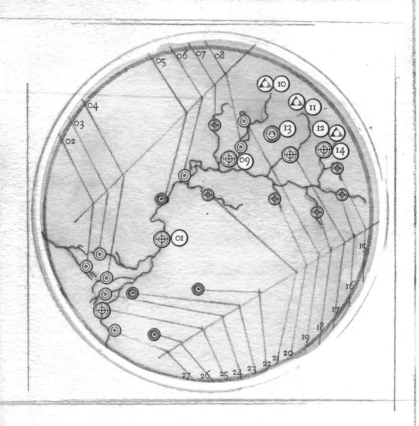

The Kings River comes roaring through the narrow canyons inside the national park that bears its name to spread wide over a massive alluvial fan in the Central Valley. Until the mid-19th century, the Kings River fed the Tulare Lake region; now it is diverted enough so that no water makes it that far.

Length: 125 miles
Watershed: 1,600 square miles
Headwaters: Middle fork near Goddard Divide, Kings Canyon National Park
Mouth: Divides under Pine Flat Dam to Tulare, some to San Joaquin

18 miles

03.19

01. Kings River
02. Fresno Slough
03. Murphy Slough
04. North fork of the Kings Slough
05. Centerville
06. Pine Flat Reservoir
07. Dinkey Creek
08. Wishon Reservoir

09. North fork of the Kings River
10. Red Mountain (11,951 feet)
11. North Palisade (14,242 feet)
12. Mount Pinchot (13,495 feet)
13. Kings Canyon National Park
14. South fork of the Kings River
15. Wood Creek
16. Bubbs Creek
17. Middle fork of the Kings River
18. Roaring Creek
19. Courtright Reservoir
20. Boulder Creek
21. Mill Creek
22. Visalia
23. Hanford
24. Clarks fork of the Kings Slough
25. South fork of the Kings Slough
26. Corcoran
27. Tulare Lake Bed

Western rattlesnake
Crotalus organus

Map 03.20 The Kern River

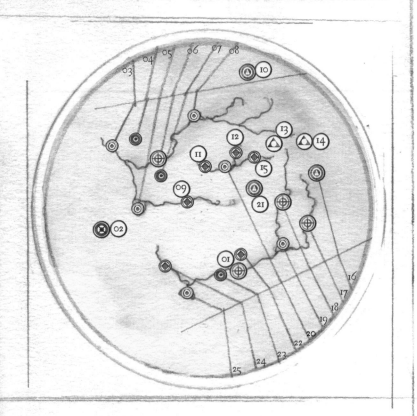

The Kern River is the southern bookend of the Sierra Nevada snowmelt rivers and the southernmost of the rivers that flow from the east to the west coming down from the mountains; most notably, the Kern River drains Mount Whitney itself. The Kern River used to empty into the now-dry Buena Vista Lake; now it is almost entirely diverted.

Length: 164 miles
Watershed: 3,600 square miles
Headwaters: North fork at
Mount Whitney
Mouth: Buena Vista Lake Bed

21 miles

03.20

01. Kern River
02. San Joaquin Valley
03. Fresno Slough
04. Fresno
05. Tulare Lake Bed
06. Kings River
07. Visalia
08. Pine Flat Reservoir
09. Tule River

10. Kings Canyon National Park
11. Kaweah River
12. North fork of the Kaweah River
13. Great Western Divide
14. Mount Whitney (14,494 feet)
15. East fork of the Kaweah River
16. Sequoia National Park
17. South fork of the Kern River
18. Kern Canyon
19. Isabella Lake
20. Lake Kaweah
21. Giant Sequoia National Monument
22. Poso Creek
23. Bakersfield
24. Kern River Flood Channel
25. Buena Vista Lake Bed

Tule
Schoenoplectus acutus

Map 03.21 Lake Tahoe

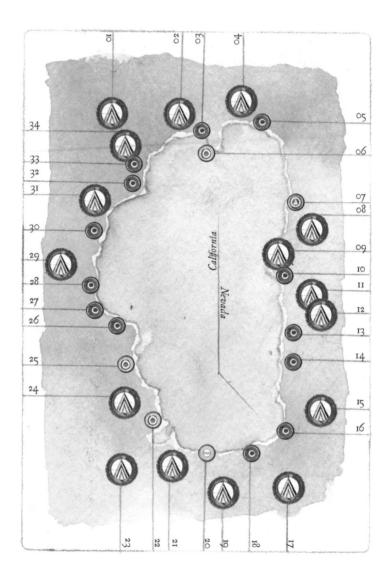

Lake Tahoe is so ancient, so beautiful, and so perfectly situated in its mountain basin that it is hard to imagine a time in the Earth's history when it didn't exist. Sapphire water under a mirroring sky shelter and feed old-growth sugar pine groves that line the lake where glittering peaks rise up in a circle, as if in welcome counsel to those seeking their sage advice. The Lake Tahoe basin is well populated with humans; to escape the growing urban net, traverse the Tahoe Rim Trail in the summer and find all the peaks here listed.

5 miles

03.21

01. Mount Pluto (8,612 feet)
02. Martis Peak (8,742 feet)
03. Kings Beach
04. Rose Knob Peak (9,710 feet)
05. Incline Village
06. Crystal Bay
07. Lake Tahoe Nevada State Park
08. Marlette Peak (8,780 feet)
09. Captain Pomin Rock (7,538 feet)
10. Glen Brook
11. South Camp Peak (8,866 feet)
12. Genoa Peak (9,150 feet)
13. Lake Ridge
14. Skyland
15. Daggett Pass (7,334 feet)
16. Stateline
17. Monument Peak (10,067 feet)
18. South Lake Tahoe
19. Tahoe Mountain (7,249 feet)
20. Camp Richardson
21. Fallen Leaf Lake
22. Emerald Bay
23. Mount Tallac (9,735 feet)
24. Rubicon Peak (9,183 feet)
25. Meeks Bay
26. Tahoma
27. Homewood
28. Tahoe Pines
29. Scott Peak (9,829 feet)
30. Tahoe City
31. Truckee River Valley
32. Dollar Point
33. Carnelian Bay
34. Mount Watson (8,424 feet)

Lake Tahoe

Map 03.22 The Klamath River

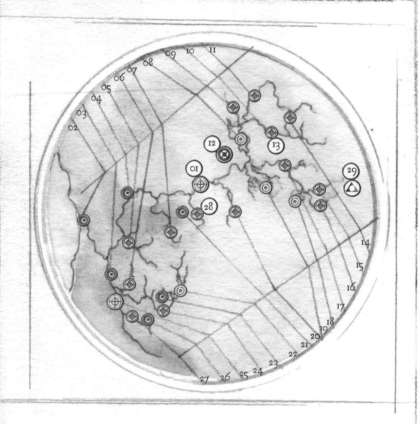

The Klamath River draws a huge S shape from east to west across the Oregon and California border into the hard tangle of mountains that is the Klamath–Siskiyou region. The Klamath is the main artery of a net of major tributaries that still harbor viable populations of wild salmon who see this convoluted landscape not as a maze, but merely as home.

Length: 260 miles
Watershed: 16,000 square miles
Headwaters: Upper Klamath Lake, Oregon
Mouth: The town of Klamath, Del Norte County

32 miles

03.22

01. Klamath River
02. Klamath
03. Willow Creek
04. Happy Camp
05. Salmon River
06. New River
07. Scott River
08. Upper Klamath Lake
09. Woods Creek
10. Sprague River
11. Williamson River
12. Oregon state border
13. Sprague River
14. Sycah River
15. Willow Creek
16. Boles River
17. Lost River
18. Clear Lake
19. Tule Lake
20. Butte Creek
21. Yreka
22. Trinity Lake
23. Weaverville
24. Main fork of the Trinity River
25. South fork of the Klamath River
26. Hayfork
27. Hayfork Creek
28. Shasta River
29. Blue Mountain (5,740 feet)

american fisher
Martes pennanti

149

Map 03.23 The Eel River

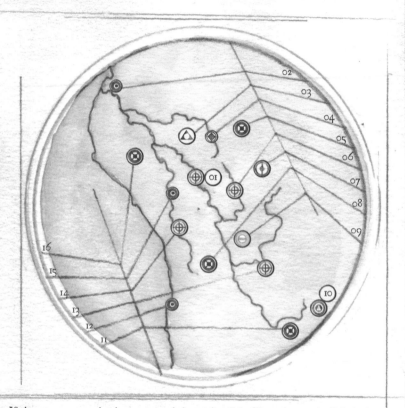

If there is one river that begins to rival the might of the Klamath, it is the Eel. And that is not just because of the Eel's long length, its water-carrying capacity, or its ability to attract tributaries, but also because of its ferociousness. The Eel River exists in a geologically active area and landslides are common, adding to the threat of flooding by channeling huge amounts of water through narrow gorges.

The Eel River has been spared the ecological destruction of major dams in its lower reaches by its legal designation as a wild and scenic river, although grazing and logging continue to affect its ecology.

Length: 200 miles
Watershed: 3,700 square miles
Headwaters: Mendocino County,
near Berryessa Snow Mountain
National Monument
Mouth: Humboldt Bay, near Eureka

27 miles

03.23

01. Eel River
02. Fortuna
03. Charles Mountain
(4,225 feet)
04. Van Duzen River
05. Trinity County
06. North fork of the
Eel River

07. Yolla Bolly–Middle Eel Wilderness
08. Mendocino County
09. Round Valley Reservation
10. Berryessa Snow Mountain National
Monument
11. Lake County
12. Fort Bragg
13. Middle fork of the Eel River
14. South fork of the Eel River
15. Garberville
16. Humboldt County

coho salmon
Oncorhynchus kisutch

Map 03.24 The Russian River

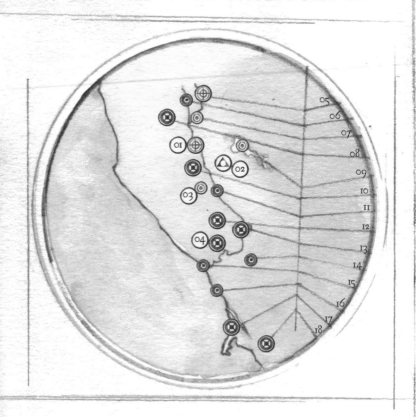

Unusually for a Northern California river, the Russian River begins its march to the sea from Mendocino County southward before it banks to the west. The nutrient-rich, deep green soup of the Russian River feeds a valley full of both ancient redwoods and contemporary vineyards on its lazy, winding course.

Length: 110 miles
Watershed: 1,490 square miles
Headwaters: Just north of Redwood Valley near the Laughlin Range
Mouth: Sonoma Coast, near Jenner

27 miles

03.24

01. Russian River
02. Mayacamas Mountains
03. Lake Sonoma
04. Armstrong Redwoods Preserve
05. East branch of the Russian River
06. Redwood Valley
07. Lake Mendocino
08. Mendocino County
09. Clear Lake
10. Anderson Valley
11. Healdsburg
12. Sonoma County
13. Russian River Valley
14. Santa Rosa
15. Jenner
16. Bodega Bay
17. Point Reyes
18. Marin County

Valley elderberry longhorn beetle
Desmocerus californicus

153

Map 03.25 The San Francisco Bay

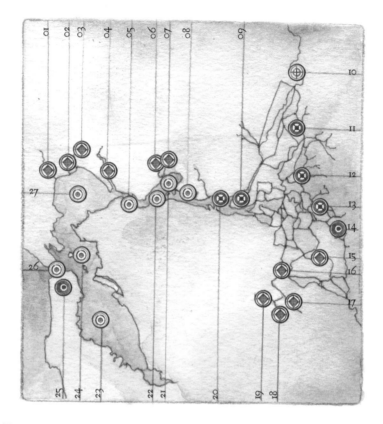

The prosperity that the Bay Area is afforded, both ecologically and culturally, comes from the dance of fresh and salt water across this very sensitive system. An estuary is a coastal body of water with a free connection to the open sea, where fresh water mixes with sea water, and San Francisco Bay is North America's largest estuary. Through the huge machine that is the natural state of the San Francisco Bay, all the waters of all the rivers of the Sierra Nevada and beyond flow together. Mixing with the incoming tide through the Golden Gate, vast wetlands breathe and support an arrayed mosaic of endemic life patterns, forms, and systems.

19 miles

03.25

01. Novato Creek
02. Petaluma River
03. Sonoma Creek
04. Napa River
05. Carquinez Strait
06. Suisun Creek
07. Suisun Slough
08. Honker Bay
09. Sherman Island
10. Sacramento River
11. Stone Lakes National
    Wildlife Area

12. White Slough Wildlife Area
13. San Joaquin River
14. Stockton
15. Middle River
16. Clifton Court Forebay
17. Delta Mendota Canal
18. California Aqueduct
19. South Bay Aqueduct
20. Lower Sherman Island Wildlife Area
21. Grizzly Bay
22. Suisun Bay
23. San Francisco Bay
24. Central Bay
25. San Francisco
26. Golden Gate
27. San Pablo Bay

Ridgeway's clapper
Rallus obsoletus

Map 03.26 The Monterey Peninsula

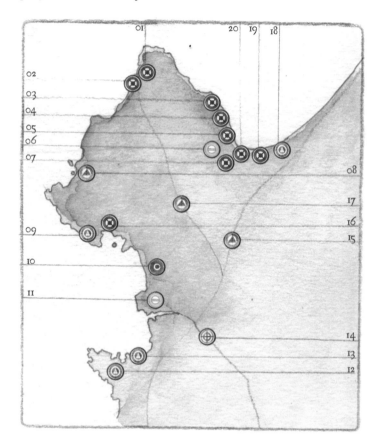

Out in this dreamlike forest that is the famous 17-Mile Drive from Pacific Grove to Pebble Beach, cypress and pine are sculpted by the hard Pacific wind to form intricately woven and protective spaces where a grand portfolio of endemic species thrive. It is here that the Monterey pine and the Monterey cypress found their original, native home before being appropriated as the world's most popular suburban topiaries.

2 miles

03.26

Monterey cypress forest

Map 03.27 The Salinas River

Old habitat for steelhead, Chinook salmon, and golden beaver, the Salinas watershed supports the most fertile agricultural landscape outside of the Central Valley. Much of the Salinas River runs underground and replenishes hidden aquifers.

Length: 170 miles
Watershed: 4,160 square miles
Headwaters: North end of the La Panza Mountains
Mouth: Monterey Bay, Salinas River National Wildlife Refuge

19 miles

03.27

01. Salinas River
02. Marina
03. Soledad
04. Arroyo Seco
05. King City
06. San Lorenzo Creek
07. Paso Robles
08. Huerhuero Creek
09. Cholame Creek
10. Strandon
11. San Juan Creek
12. Santa Margarita Lake
13. Indian Creek
14. Atascadero
15. Lake Nacimiento
16. Lake San Antonio
17. San Ardo Oil Field
18. Nacimiento River
19. San Antonio River
20. Big Sur
21. Santa Lucia Mountains

California Buckeye Butterfly
Junio coenia

Map 03.28 The Los Angeles River

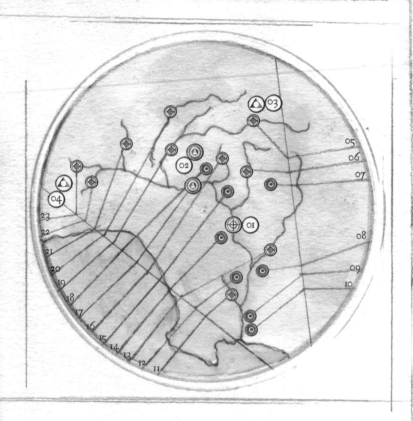

Early in the 20th century, devastating floods destroyed much of the Los Angeles River flood basin. In response, the city imprisoned the entire metropolitan Los Angeles River in a concrete channel. By 1940, no native species of fish had survived the internment. A plan has been put forward to restore many hundreds of acres of natural habitat, for the intelligent emancipation of the river and ultimately for ecosystem-wide reconstruction.

Length: 45 miles
Watershed: 827 square miles
Headwaters: Bell Creek and Arroyo Calabasas, two streams in Canoga Park
Mouth: Long Beach, Los Angeles County

19 miles

03.28

01. Los Angeles River
02. San Gabriel National Monument
03. San Gabriel Mountains
04. Santa Monica Mountains
05. Big Tujunga Creek
06. Arroyo Seco
07. Pasadena
08. Downey
09. Lakewood
10. Long Beach
11. Compton Creek
12. Compton
13. Rio Hondo
14. Los Angeles
15. Glendale
16. Verdugo Wash
17. Griffith Park
18. Burbank
19. Tujunga Wash
20. Pacoima Wash
21. Aliso Creek
22. Arroyo Calabasas
23. Bell Creek

California fan Palm
Washingtonia filifera

Map 03.29 The Santa Ana River

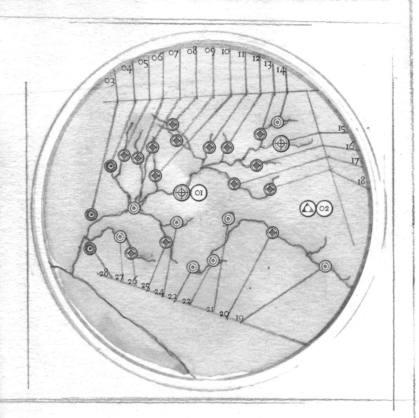

Many parts of the Santa Ana River are often dry and only occasionally accept the challenge of a long, tough course to the sea. From the alpine peaks of the San Bernardino Mountains, what little water the river can gather pushes down through miles of hot chaparral and then, aided by nearly 50 tributaries, crawls through the arid coastal plains to be delivered to the Pacific. The Santa Ana River is the longest in Southern California.

Length: 96 miles
Watershed: 2,650 square miles
Headwaters: Coon Creek,
San Bernardino Mountains
Mouth: Huntington Beach

16 miles

03.29

01. Santa Ana River
02. San Jacinto Peak
(10,804 feet)
03. Anaheim
04. Pomona
05. San Antonio Creek
06. Cucamonga Creek
07. Deer Creek
08. Cajon Wash
09. Lytle Creek
10. Day Creek

11. Warm Creek
12. City Creek
13. Bear Creek
14. Big Bear Lake
15. Santa Ana River
16. Mill Creek
17. San Timoteo Creek
18. Yucaipa Creek
19. Lake Hemet
20. San Jacinto River
21. Lake Perris
22. Canyon Lake
23. Lake Elsinore
24. Lake Mathews
25. Temescal Creek
26. Irvine Lake
27. Santiago Creek
28. Santa Ana

Red tail hawk
Buteo jamaicensis

Map 03.30 The Mojave River

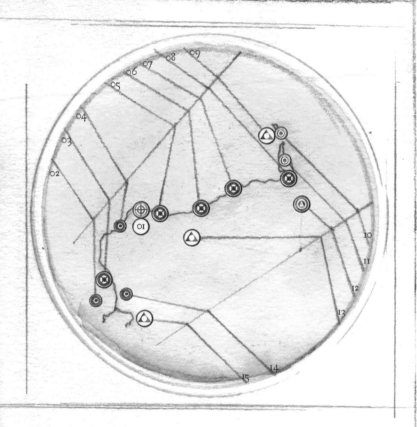

For most of the year, the Mojave River is hidden. Retreating underground only to rise in a few protected canyons, the Mojave, like most of the residents who live in ecosystems supported by its waters, is a survivor. For all of its apparent desolation, if you stand chest high among the reeds of Afton Canyon, deep in Mojave Trails National Monument, on a cool spring evening and listen to the frogs sing to the sunset, you'll forget what all the survival fuss is about.

Length: 110 miles (intermittent)
Watershed: 4,600 square miles
Headwaters: Delamar Mountain
(8,535 feet), San Bernardino Mountains
Mouth: Mojave River Wash, Mojave
National Preserve

05. Mojave Valley
06. Coyote Dry Lake
07. Afton Canyon
08. Devil's Playground
09. Soda Mountain
10. Silver Dry Lake
11. Soda Dry Lake
12. Mojave Trails National Monument
13. Cady Mountains
14. Apple Valley
15. Butler Peak (8,539 feet)

24 miles

03.30

01. Mojave River
02. Hesperia
03. Victor Valley
04. Barstow

our lord's candle yucca
Hesperoyucca whipplei

Map 03.31 The Los Angeles Aqueduct

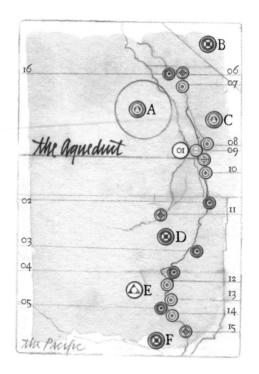

the Aqueduct

the Pacific

largemouth bass
Micropterus salmoides

27 miles

03.31

The question about how to get water to the people of Los Angeles has always been vexing for city planners. The Los Angeles Aqueduct is the machine by which Los Angeles irrigated its exaggerated desert plain in the first decades of the 20th century to become the second-largest metropolis in North America. The ever-thirsting city built a second aqueduct in the middle of the century to take a deeper drink of the Owens Valley and the Mono Lake Basin. Before Los Angeles could drink Mono Lake, the aqueduct was regulated to maintain the level of the lake at the minimum that the existing ecosystem would require to survive. Because of this, today only about 50 percent of the capacity of the aqueduct is allocated to Los Angeles and the rest is kept in Mono and Inyo Counties.

As you come over from Death Valley, the pale dust bowl of Owens Lake stands out like a shimmering bowl of bones in the wavering heat against the backdrop of the Sierra Nevada. The Owens River system, now desiccated by the aqueduct, stands as a victim to the urban thirst of the faraway city. The problem never went away, and water sustainability for Los Angeles is potentially the biggest obstacle for the city's long-term habitability.

A. Sequoia National Forest
B. Nevada
C. Death Valley
D. Mojave Desert
E. San Bernardino Mountains
F. Los Angeles Basin

01. Los Angeles Aqueduct
02. Indian Wells
03. Mojave
04. Neenach
05. Saugus
06. Owens River
07. Tinemaha Reservoir
08. Owens Lake
09. Cottonwood Power House
10. Hoiwee Reservoirs
11. Kern River
12. Elizabeth Lake
13. Dry Canyon Reservoir
14. Fernando Reservoir
15. The Los Angeles River
16. Bishop

Map 03.32 The Colorado River

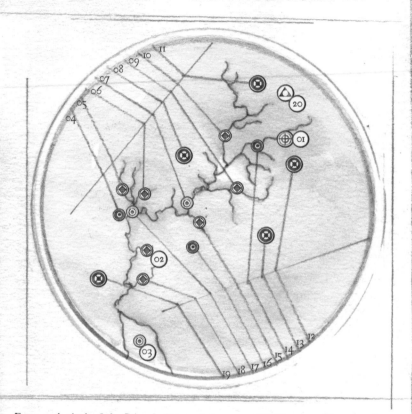

Few people think of the Colorado River as being part of California, and for most of its course through seven states and eleven national parks, it isn't. Dropping down into the river valley from the hot grays and ruddy browns of the Colorado Desert in California to the pale greens and deep blues of the strong river is always a shock. The border of Arizona could not be more clearly rendered: a broad line of Utah state water on its way to Mexico, passing through a borderland, artificially swollen by a series of dams, giving the illusion that there is more water here than there actually is as it is siphoned for human usage. There are many illusions in the desert, and the idea that this water will actually make it to the sea is one. In truth, every drop of the Colorado River is so regulated and spent at this point in its journey that it is a wonder that, even in the wettest years, any bit of it makes it to the Baja Gulf at all. The Colorado must be so disappointed by the denouement of its grand journey in the sands of the Sonoran Desert.

120 miles

03.32

Length: 1,450 miles
Watershed: 300,000 square miles
Headwaters: La Poudre Pass, Southern Rocky Mountains, Colorado
Mouth: Gulf of California, Mexico

01. Colorado River
02. Bill Williams River
03. Gulf of California
04. Las Vegas
05. White River
06. Virgin River
07. Lake Powell
08. Utah
09. San Juan River
10. Green River
11. Colorado
12. New Mexico
13. Arizona
14. Grand Junction
15. Little Colorado River
16. Phoenix
17. Lake Mead
18. Gila River
19. California
20. La Poudre Pass

Raven
Corvus corax

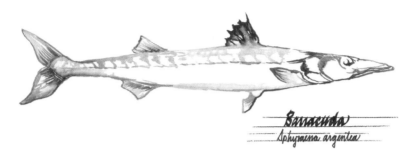

Barracuda
Sphyraena argentea

the islands of california

Standing on the beach in Goleta, just north of Santa Barbara, you will get tar on your feet from the natural seepage as you watch the sun set over the black islands on the horizon. On this small length of the Pacific between the mainland and the islands, over the past several hundred thousand years, a number of plants and animals have developed into their own distinct species, including the island fox, pine, goat, lizard, salamander, and skunk.

There are eight principal islands in the archipelago: from north to south, San Miguel, Santa Rosa, Santa Cruz, Anacapa, Santa Barbara, Santa Catalina, San Nicolas, and San Clemente. The largest island is Santa Cruz, at 97 square miles, and the two smallest are Anacapa and Santa Barbara, which are just about one square mile apiece.

channel island fox
Urocyon littoralis

Map 03.33 California's Channel Islands

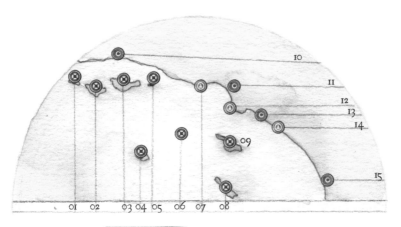

01. San Miguel Island
02. Santa Rosa Island
03. Santa Cruz Island
04. San Nicolas Island
05. Anacapa Island
06. Santa Barbara Island
07. Point Dume
08. San Clemente Island
09. Santa Catalina Island
10. Santa Barbara
11. Los Angeles
12. Point Vicente
13. Long Beach
14. Dana Point
15. La Jolla

vermillion rockfish
sebastes miniatus

Map 03.34 Anacapa Islands

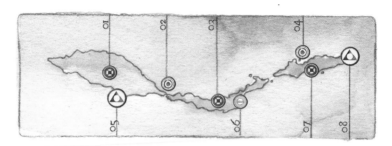

The Anacapa Islands comprise three islets, which collectively span five miles. Anacapa is the closest of the Channel Islands to the mainland; its name comes from the Chumash word Anyapah, which was the original name of Santa Cruz Island.

01. West Anacapa
02. Frenchy's Cove
03. Middle Anacapa
04. Cathedral Cove
05. Cat Rock
06. East Fish Camp
07. East Anacapa
08. Arch Rock

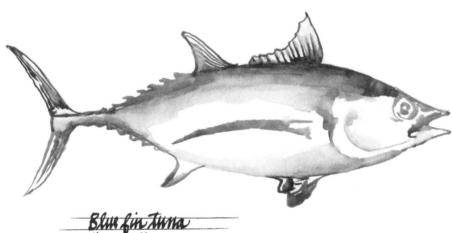

Blue fin tuna
thunnus thynnus

Map 03.35 Santa Barbara Island

Arch Point

Santa Barbara Island is approximately one square mile and is topped by two steep-sloped peaks. Signal Peak is 635 feet tall and is circled by 5.5 miles of trails. The island night lizard, a threatened species, makes Santa Barbara Island its home and lives among the giant coreopsis, a species of sunflower.

01. Webster Point
02. Shag Rock
03. Archor Point Loop Trail
04. Signal Peak Loop Trail
05. Sutil Island
06. Elephant Seal Cove Trail

Gray whale
Eschrichtius robustus

Map 03.36 Santa Catalina Island

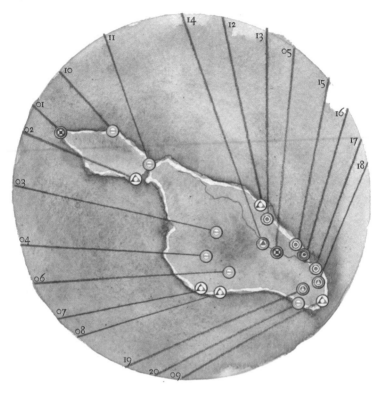

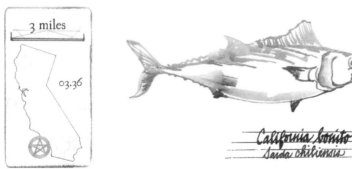

3 miles

03.36

California bonito
Sarda chiliensis

This rocky 22-mile-long island is the most developed by humans of all the Channel Islands. Some 4,000 people live on Santa Catalina, which is within the boundaries of Los Angeles County. The Catalina Island Conservancy protects 45,000 acres, or 90 percent, of the island as a wildlife sanctuary. Endemic flora includes the Catalina manzanita, mahogany, dudleya, bedstraw, and ironwood.

01. Lands End
02. Lobster Point
03. Airport in the Sky
04. Rancho Escondido
05. Toyon Junction
06. Middle Ranch
07. China Point
08. Salsa Verde Point
09. Seal Rocks
10. Parsons Landing
11. Two Harbors Campground
12. Long Point
13. White Cove
14. Old Stage Road
15. Hamilton Cove
16. Avalon
17. Avalon Bay
18. Crescent Beach
19. Bird Park
20. Hermit Gulch Campground

Anna's hummingbird
Calypte anna

04. OF FIRE
& FORESTS

Red fir
Abies magnifica

It is not only water in California that brings life to the forests, but also fire. Fire is the great equalizer that draws the lines, thins the fat, frees the space, opens the seeds, moves the land, and calls the wildflowers. The trees themselves, having worked out their relationship with fire over several hundred million years, respond with a whole toolbox of evolutionary resources to not only adapt, but to thrive and perhaps even become dependent on moments of extreme heat to survive and propagate. The closed-cone pine forests of the coast won't open their tightly bound seed cones until temperatures soar, as in the presence of direct flame. The redwoods of the coastal canyons are able to make roots come out of the middle of their trunks when fire-related landslides suddenly move the surface level of the soil 50 feet higher than it was moments before. The white fir forests of the Sierra Nevada would crowd themselves out of their own habitat with diseased saplings were it not for a good cleansing by wildfire. Fire lets the forests breathe by clearing massive acreage of young trees that would otherwise choke the shaded habitat created by the elder trees. To wonder at the creative powers of fire, look no further than a wildflower meadow the year after an inferno has moved through and watch an ocean of colorful wildflowers spring from the blackened ground, now able to enjoy their time in the sun.

Douglas fir cone

California is a dancing machine of forest ecosystems that best operates in a fine balance between dualities that include fire and water, aridity and hydration, soil and erosion, climatic consistency and variation, and the push and pull between native and invasive plants and animals. Maintaining this balance is what determines the type and amount of fuel, or biomass, and thus the intensity and periodic occurrence of wildfire, also called the fire regime. All forests, woodlands, and grasslands have a fire regime. Grasslands like to burn often, some as often as every year. Forest and woodlands like to burn too, but less often; fire regimes can vary between zero and more than 200 years. Many factors have recently thrown the ancient balance of fire regimes across California out of alignment, including plant invasion and fire-suppression strategies to protect housing developments in regions with known fire regimes. A well-balanced forest naturally burns with a fire regime that ignites with calendrical precision.

It is easy to map a coastline, a river, or even a mountain; it is an entirely different matter to map a forest. Forests, woodlands, prairies, and grasslands are living systems that expand and retreat, fail to delineate themselves as singular pieces of geography,

live oak acorns

and resist easy classification. Everywhere across California, there are forests. Forests of all varieties: from the oak-dotted Central Valley along the rugged coast into the hottest reaches of the deserts, and of course up and over the High Sierra crest. There are forests alive in the rocky barrens where there is no soil at all but only the compact remains of ancient trees carpeting granite peaks, those first pioneering specimens having somehow figured out how to grow amid the original, extreme austerity.

There are old-growth forests that are thousands of years old, and second-growth forests that were planted after the Gold Rush. There are even forests without trees and only woody tangles of shrubbery so tall that it forms an overhead canopy. But no matter the type, all California forests have a relationship to fire that, in many cases, is at least as creative as it is destructive.

California oak

mountain hemlock
tsuga mertensiana

Map 04.01 Managing California

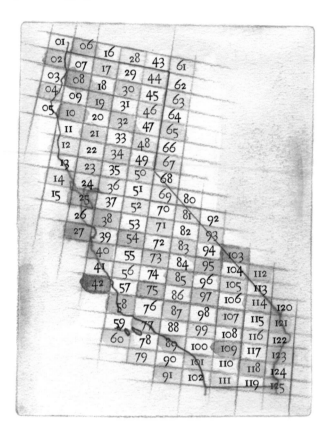

Of all the bureaucratic maps in this book, this one's cellular elegance makes it the most appealing; the geography of California is laid out in convenient rectangles presenting a form of organization that is digestible and necessary for a statewide agency that requires the kind of simplistic, quick-reference view this map provides. The culture that made and uses this map has a very specific agenda, which is based on the response to emergency as a way of life. The homogeneity of the map template assumes an equivocal relationship to every corner of the state. The California Land Management grid is a tool used by the U.S. Forest Service, the Bureau of Land Management, and the California Department of Forestry and Fire Protection (CAL FIRE) to map wildland management campaigns across California's varied geography.

01. Gold Beach
02. Crescent City
03. Orick
04. Eureka
05. Cape Mendocino
06. Grants Pass
07. Happy Camp
08. Hoopa
09. Hayfork
10. Garberville
11. Covelo
12. Ukiah
13. Point Arena
14. Bodega Bay
15. Farallon Islands
16. Medford
17. Yreka
18. Mount Shasta
19. Redding
20. Red Bluff
21. Willows
22. Lakeport
23. Healdsburg
24. Napa
25. San Francisco
26. Palo Alto
27. Santa Cruz
28. Klamath Falls
29. Tule Lake
30. McArthur
31. Burney
32. Lake Almanor
33. Chico
34. Yuba
35. Sacramento
36. Lodi
37. Stockton
38. San Jose
39. Monterey
40. Point Sur
41. Cambria
42. Point Estero
43. Lake View
44. Cedarville

45. Alturas
46. Eagle Lake
47. Susanville
48. Portola
49. Truckee
50. Placerville
51. San Andreas
52. Oakdale
53. Merced
54. Mendoza
55. Coalinga
56. Paso Robles
57. San Luis Obispo
58. Santa Maria
59. Point Conception
60. Santa Rosa Island
61. Adel
62. Vya
63. High Rock Canyon
64. Gerlach
65. Kumiva Peak
66. Reno
67. Carson City
68. Smith Valley
69. Bridgeport
70. Yosemite Valley
71. Shaver Lake
72. Fresno
73. Visalia
74. Delano
75. Taft
76. Cuyama
77. Santa Barbara
78. Laguna Harbor
79. San Nicolas Island
80. Excelsior Mountains
81. Benton Range
82. Bishop
83. Mount Whitney
84. Three Rivers
85. Isabella Lake
86. Tehachapi
87. Lancaster
88. Los Angeles

89. Long Beach
90. Santa Catalina Island
91. San Clemente Island
92. Goldfield
93. Last Chance Range
94. Saline Valley
95. Darwin Hills
96. Ridgecrest
97. Cuddleback Lake
98. Victorville
99. San Bernardino
100. Santa Ana
101. Oceanside
102. San Diego
103. Beatty
104. Death Valley Junction
105. Owlshead Mountains
106. Soda Mountains
107. Newberry Springs
108. Bear Lake
109. Palm Springs
110. Borrego Valley
111. El Cajon
112. Las Vegas
113. Mesquite Lake
114. Ivanpah
115. Amboy
116. Sheephole Mountains
117. Eagle Mountains
118. Salton Sea
119. El Centro
120. Davis Dam
121. Needles
122. Parker
123. Blythe
124. Trigo Mountains
125. Yuma

Map 04.02 Mapping the Fire Regime

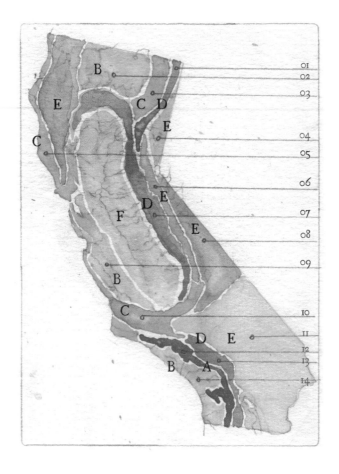

The fire regime consists of the pattern, frequency, and intensity of wildfire in any specific area. The fire regime is based on fuel type, fuel load, and fuel density. Fire intensity is measured on a spectrum from low severity to mixed severity to—most devastating—replacement severity. A replacement severity fire means that the fire burns with such ferocity that it might wholly destroy the existing ecosystem and break the chain of succession.

A. Fire Regime Group 1:

0- to 35-year frequency; low to mixed severity; affects perennial grassland and nonwoody prairie with significant populations of grasses that live more than two years, common traits in many native grasses.

B. Fire Regime Group 2:

0- to 35-year frequency; replacement severity; affects annual grassland and nonwoody prairie with significant populations of grasses that die annually and, in several cases, need annual fire to propagate, common traits in many invasive grasses.

C. Fire Regime Group 3:

35- to 200-year frequency; low to mixed severity; affects shrublands and woody chaparral that exhibit many fire-adaptive and fire-dependent traits including root-stem regrowth and cone pollination based on extreme temperatures, as in closed-cone pines.

D. Fire Regime Group 4:

35- to 200-year frequency; replacement severity; affects lower montane forests of the Sierra Nevada and Coast Ranges.

E. Fire Regime Group 5:

200+-year frequency; any severity; affects the Mojave Desert, the upper montane forests of the Sierra Nevada, and the damp redwood forests of the Coast Ranges.

F. Fire Regime Group 6:

altered natural landscape; agricultural land; no existing wildfire regime

01. Warner Range and North Plumas (D)
02. Shasta Valley (B)
03. Modoc Plateau and Lassen (C)
04. Honey Lake Great Basin (E)
05. North Coast oak woodland (C)
06. High Sierra (E)
07. Sierra Nevada low montane (D)
08. Mono Basin desert (E)
09. Coast Range chaparral and rangelands (B)
10. Coast woodlands and chaparral (C)
11. Mojave and Colorado Desert (E)
12. South Coast Mountains grassland (A)
13. San Bernardino and Santa Rosa Mountains montane (D)
14. South Coast grassland (B)

Map 04.03 Annual Wildfires per Watershed

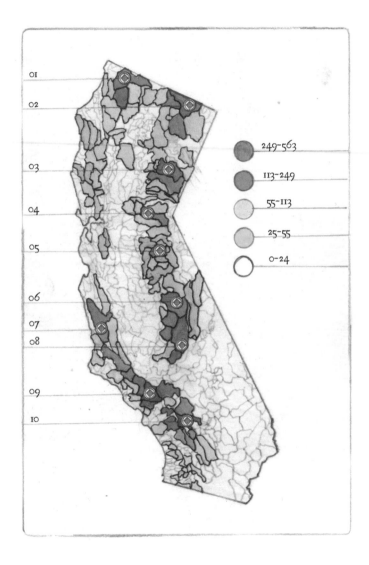

249-563

113-249

55-113

25-55

0-24

A watershed, or area of land defined by elevated features, begins to tell the story of how that specific area drains itself of water. This is a good place to start taking averages and mapping fire return intervals.

This map shows the average annual wildfires in the ten most fire-prone watersheds from 2005 to 2015.

01. Klamath River, Siskiyou County
02. Lost River, Modoc and Siskiyou County
03. North fork of the Feather River, Plumas County
04. Middle fork of the American River, Placer County
05. Stanislaus River, Calaveras County
06. San Joaquin River headwaters, Fresno County
07. Salinas River and Nacimiento River, Monterey County
08. Kern River headwaters, Tulare County
09. Santa Clara River headwaters, Ventura County
10. Santa Ana River headwaters, Los Angeles County

coastal sagebrush
Artemisia californica

Map 04.04 The Fire Threat and the Chaparral

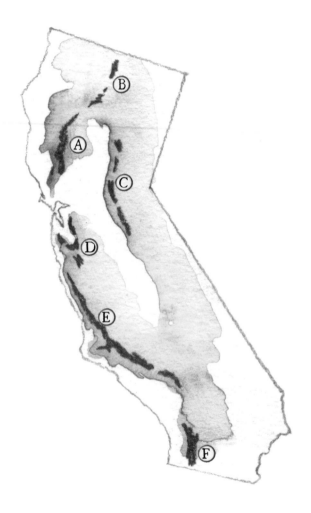

Inside the areas detailed by the black pencil marks are California's largest concentrations of the chaparral vegetation type. The gradated nature of this map gives the general impression of where the most massive wildfires usually occur and what damage they can do to human communities, from a very saturated red color along the coast, where the fires can be very intense and destructive, to the pale hues of the outlying, less-inhabited areas that are given more of a chance to remain established under a more natural regime with less of a threat to property.

A. The chaparral of the Berryessa Snow Mountain National Monument in Lake, Glenn, and Colusa Counties holds some of the largest chamise stands in the state.

B. The chaparral of Shasta Valley in Siskiyou County begins to mix with sagebrush steppe grasslands.

C. The chaparral of Eastern Central Valley is thickest from Plumas County down to Calaveras County, but continues down to Tulare County, forming a continuous ring of chaparral around the entire Central Valley.

D. The chaparral of the Diablo Mountains, from Contra Costa to San Benito Counties, is a carpet of sage and juniper; woody shrub forests here withstand long, hot summers year after desiccating year.

E. The chaparral of the Central Coast bridges the Northern and the South Los Padres National Forests.

F. The chaparral of the Peninsular Ranges of San Diego County represents an arid ecology where the plant mix often juxtaposes shrub conifer and desert succulent.

In the Mediterranean climate of California, one vegetation type above all others means fire: chaparral. A community of twisting hardwood shrubs that blanket the foothills at the edges of the valley grasslands, chaparral attains maturity about 15 years after a fire, when it is more able to resist the overly destructive aspects of the fire regime. Areas of old chaparral, containing many species of manzanita that are both fire dependent and fire adaptive, experience the most intense fires California has to offer with what is surely the botanical equivalent of joy.

The typified wild ecosystem of the Mediterranean climate has produced this type of plant community around the rim of the Great Valley and down the Coast Ranges. Cool, wet winters and hot, dry summers dictate the patterns of how these woody shrubs mix under the oak and pine.

Chamise (*Adenostoma fasciculatum*)
Manzanita (*Arctostaphylos* sp)
Ceanothus (*Ceonothus* sp)
Gray pine (*Pinus sabiniana*)
Buckeye (*Aesculus calífornica*)
Blue oak (*Quercus douglasii*)
Valley oak (*Quercus lobata*)

Map 04.05 Fire Severity

The language of California is fire, and the vocabulary that makes up this language is predictable, decipherable, and episodic. Fire regimes have characteristics based on seasonality, fire-return interval, size, spatial complexity, intensity, severity, and fire type. Fire-adapted and fire-dependent plant species rule the California Floristic Province, and always will. As fire sweeps through a healthy forest (not one suffering from overgrowth due to modern fire suppression policies), the ground fuel is spent, making way for wildflowers; because healthy forests regularly burn, big trees, with their thickly barked bases and minimal, low-hanging branches, recover quickly. Only when limb fuel, carried by overgrowth to the canopy, is too abundant does the fire balance of the backcountry become unbalanced. This map depicts contemporary patterns of the most intense wildfire sites over the past fifty years.

Map 04.06 Carbon Stores

Forests are carbon stores, and they become carbon sinks when they increase in density or area. A carbon sink is a natural or artificial reservoir that accumulates and stores some carbon dioxide. The process by which carbon sinks remove carbon dioxide from the atmosphere is known as carbon sequestration. Wildfire and deforestation release absorbed carbon back into the atmosphere. Coast redwood forests contain more carbon than any other ecosystem in the world; three acres of redwood forest contains the carbon equivalent of the annual emissions of greenhouse gases by 500 Americans.

The dark portions of this map represent the density of forest cover and carbon sequestration across California, where it is measured at the threshold of one million parts per acre, and thus recognized as a working carbon sink.

Map 04.07 California's Floral Biogeography

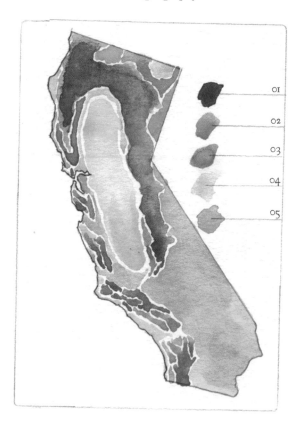

A floral biogeographic zone is a large yet distinct region of plant communities that have coevolved into a unique and localized system. Every aspect of accurately categorizing the floral biogeographic zones of California presents challenges. Every map, every zone can be opened further, explored more, and turned into ten more maps. Floral biogeographic zones are incredibly complex systems in which soil type, exposure, elevation, climate, precipitation, air quality, fire, endemic versus invasive pressures, livestock, and human development all conspire to present a living mosaic that thwarts all but the broadest analysis. Despite the exasperating complexities, if you walk these backcountry trails enough, elegant templates of plant distribution can be drawn and patterns of widespread botanical distribution are revealed. Each named biogeographic zone is one biogeographic zone type. The biogeographic zone types in California are:

01. Forest: A system of trees, both deciduous and coniferous, with a closed canopy in both lower and upper montane localities.

02. Woodland: A low-density forest with limited shade and an understory of herbaceous shrubs; characterized by chaparral and oak.

03. Scrubland: A plant community with only shrubs or short, woody plants; coastal sage scrub.

04. Prairie: A temperate grassland that may or may not contain shrubs; this kind of biogeography defines the Central Valley.

05. Desert: A composite of zone types across the Mojave and the Colorado Deserts in California that includes desert dry wash, desert riparian, desert saltbrush scrub, and desert shadscale scrub.

The list maps of biogeographic zones, organized by plant base, are collections of between six and twelve plant species that collectively represent how floral relationships are localized. The plant species listed are not necessarily keystone plant species in any given ecosystem, but they are all endemic.

Foxtail pine
Pinus balfouriana

Map 04.08 The Forests of the Klamath

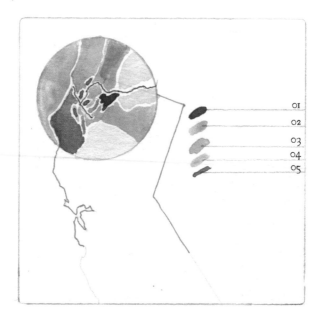

01
02
03
04
05

The steep river valleys of the Klamath–Siskiyou region is an ancient hotbed of biodiversity and has a staggeringly rich collection of forests to prove it. The plants found here are at least as varied as in any zone of the California Floristic Province.

Sugar pine (*Pinus lambertiana*)
Ponderosa pine (*Pinus ponderosa*)
White fir (*Abies concolor*)
Tanoak (*Lithocarpus densiflora*)
Canyon live oak (*Quercus chrysolepis*)
Chinquapin (*Chrysolepis chrysophylla*)
Port Orford cedar (*Chamaecyparis lawsoniana*)
Western white pine (*Pinus monticola*)
Incense cedar (*Calocedrus decurrens*)
Jeffrey pine (*Pinus jeffreyi*)
Knobcone pine (*Pinus attenuata*)
Sitka spruce (*Picea sitchensis*)
Western Hemlock (*Tsuga heterophylla*)

Five basic biogeographical regions make up the forests and woodlands of the Klamath-Siskiyou region. This land of seemingly infinite diversity eludes simple categorization, and for every type noted below, an exception seems pending.

o1. **Serpentine Siskiyous:** At 1,500 to 4,500 feet of elevation, this montane chaparral region features mixed conifers, including Jeffrey pine and Douglas fir.

o2. **Inland Siskiyous:** At 1,000 to 8,000 feet of elevation, this region features multilayered conifers, including broadleaf evergreens and ponderosa pines, and deciduous trees such as black oak and madrone.

o3. **Coastal Siskiyous:** At 600 to 5,300 feet of elevation, this region, with its maritime climate and xeric and udic soils, supports dark forests of redwood, hemlock, spruce, and Port Orford cedar.

o4. **Oak savanna foothills:** At 1,400 to 4,000 feet of elevation, this Mediterranean-climate region is defined by a sparsely closed canopy and features incense cedar, Jeffrey pine, knobcone pine, live oak, and gray pine.

o5. **Klamath River ridges:** At 3,800 to 7,500 feet of elevation, this continental-climate region is characterized by a drought-resistant conifer mix and features extreme conifer biodiversity, exhibiting over a dozen species of conifer, including sugar pine and white fir.

ruby crowned kinglet
Regulus calendula

Map 04.09 The Forests of the North Central Coast

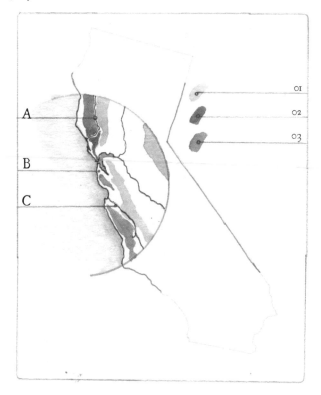

The forest of the Northern Central Coast, south of Klamath and North of San Luis Obispo

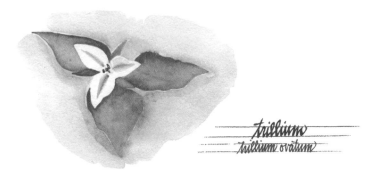

trillium
trillium ovatum

01. **Coastal Conifer dominated forest:**
    Fir, Douglas Fir and Coastal
    Redwood
02. **Inland Oak Woodland** and
    Chaparral
03. **Lower Montane Sierra** Foothills

A. The Russian River
B. The San Francisco Peninsula
C. The Salinas River

The Northern California coastal forest
ecoregion is part of the Pacific temperate
rain forests ecoregion, which extends from
Monterey County north to Alaska. The
Pacific temperate rain forest ecoregion
exists because of a climatological anomaly
that brings storms and fog all year long.
The summers in this ecoregion tend to be
cooler than the winters.

This Northern California coastal forest
contains the tallest trees in the world.
The coast redwood exists in every
habitat of the coastal evergreen forest.
The redwood and Douglas fir forests of
Central and Northern California climb
dark ravines to interact with oaks and
shrub understories that always skirt their
favorite giants.

Douglas fir (*Pseudotsuga menziesii*)
Coast redwood (*Sequoia sempervirens*)
Tanoak (*Notholithocarpus densiflorus*)
Pacific madrone (*Arbutus menziesii*)
California bay laurel
      (*Umbellularia californica*)
Canyon live oak (*Quercus chrysolepis*)
Interior live oak (*Quercus wislizenii*)
Coast live oak (*Quercus agrifolia*)
Black oak (*Quercus kelloggii*)
Oregon oak (*Quercus garryana*)
Bigleaf maple (*Acer macrophyllum*)
Coulter pine (*Pinus coulteri*)
Gray pine (*Pinus sabiniana*)

Bishop pine
Pinus muricata

Map 04.10 The Forests of the South Coast

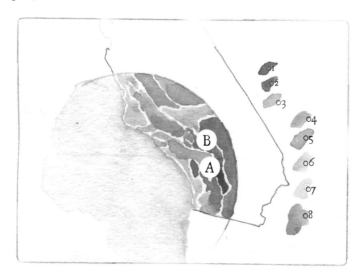

Throughout San Diego County's Cleveland National Forest and up into the Santa Ana Mountains, the forests are susceptible to microclimates that influence their course and distribution. Thick conifer forests tend to grow on the west-facing slopes, whereas the east-facing slopes support more chaparral.

Brown creeper
Certhia americana

Color Key to Vegetation of the South Coast

01. Southern woodland and chaparral dominant
02. Transverse montane forest
03. Central Valley prairie
04. Carrizo scrub
05. South Coast scrub
06. Central Coast scrub
07. El Tejon oak woodland
08. Mojave and Colorado Desert

A. Peninsular Montane Forests

Tanoak (*Notholithocarpus densiflorus*)
Madrone (*Arbutus menziesii*)
Canyon live oak (*Quercus chrysolepis*)
Coast live oak (*Quercus agrifolia*)
California bay laurel (*Umbellularia californica*)
Jeffrey pine (*Pinus jeffreyi*)
Coulter pine (*Pinus coulteri*)
Bigcone Douglas fir (*Pseudotsuga macrocarpa*)

B. Transverse Montane Forests

Exemplified in the San Bernardino and
the San Gabriel Mountains of Los
Angeles County, the transverse montane
chaparral creeps as far north as the Santa
Ynez Mountains and as far south as the
Santa Rosa Mountains.

Scrub oak (*Quercus berberidifolia*)
Chamise (*Adenostoma fasciculatum*)
Manzanita (*Arctostaphylos* sp)
Bigcone Douglas fir (*Pseudotsuga macrocarpa*)
Canyon live oak (*Quercus chrysolepis*)

Monterey cypress
Cupressus macrocarpa

Map 04.11 The Montane Forests of the Sierra Nevada

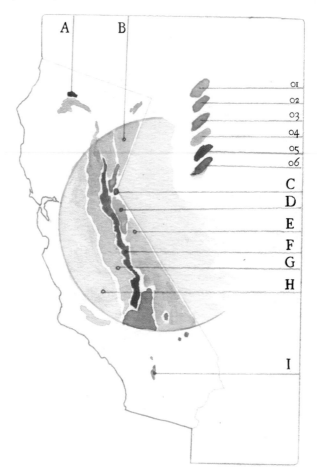

01. Central Valley grassland
02. White Mountains, Great Basin desert
03. Sierra Nevada lower montane
04. Northern Great Basin sagebrush
05. Sierra Nevada upper montane
06. Upper Mojave desert

A. Upper montane outside of the Sierra Nevada: The Trinity Alps and the Marble Mountains both exhibit the same trees as the upper montane in the Sierra Nevada, except for red fir. In the Klamath Mountains, Shasta fir dominates instead of red fir.

B. Northern Great Basin: In Lassen County, desert scrubland spreads out across the arid landscape in the northern rain shadow of the Sierra Nevada.

C. Lake Tahoe: Within the basin of Lake Tahoe, the three forest types include lower montane, upper montane, and Great Basin flora.

D. Mono, Sierra, and Nevada Counties: This lower montane forest is dominated by Jeffrey pine.

E. Volcanic scrublands: From 5,000 feet to 10,000 feet in elevation, the varied Mono Basin rises to the bristlecone forests of the White Mountains, which are blanketed in Great Basin montane forests.

F. The High Sierra: The upper montane is defined by very poor soil and extreme weather.

G. Ponderosa pine belt: The lower montane is dominated by incense cedar and ponderosa pine across the Sierra Foothills and low mountains.

H. The Central Valley: The gentle, oak-dappled hills down from the west slope of the Sierra Nevada cover themselves annually in a brilliant show of vernal wildflowers.

I. Relic stands of alpine trees: On peaks in the transverse and the peninsular ranges as well as in the northern Mojave, there is evidence of widespread forests from the last Ice Age.

The Lower Montane

The indicator species of the lower montane forest is the ponderosa pine. The montane forest rises against the west slopes of the Sierra Nevada across its entire length. In the southern reaches, ponderosa pines can be found at elevations upward of 9,000 feet, and in the north they begin to taper out at about 5,000 feet.

Ponderosa pine (*Pinus ponderosa*)
Jeffrey pine (*Pinus jeffreyi*)
Sugar pine (*Pinus lambertiana*)
Douglas fir (*Pseudotsuga menziesii*)
White fir (*Abies concolor*)
Incense cedar (*Calocedrus decurrens*)
Black oak (*Quercus kelloggii*)
Manzanita (*Arctostaphylos* sp)
Bigleaf maple (*Acer macrophyllum*)

The Upper Montane

The upper montane forest is the forest of the High Sierra. Dramatic glacial landscapes, bereft of much soil, present wind-sculpted forests that twist and turn in a centuries-long dance.

Lodgepole pine (*Pinus contorta*)
Jeffrey pine (*Pinus jeffreyi*)
Western white pine (*Pinus monticola*)
California red fir (*Abies magnifica*)
Sierra juniper (*Juniperus grandis*)
Huckleberry oak (*Quercus vaccinifolia*)
Red heather (*Phyllodoce breweri*)

Map 04.12 California's Scrublands and Prairies

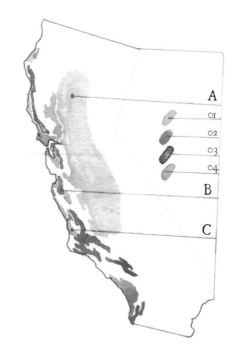

A. Sacramento River Valley
B. Salinas Valley
C. San Luis Obispo

01. Central Coast Prairie

On the bluffs of Point Reyes National
Seashore or south in Andrew Molera
State Park near Big Sur, patchwork collections of native bunchgrasses speak an
ecological language all their own. In the
springtime for a just a few weeks, a parade of colorful iris and lupine graces the
gray-green landscape with bold flashes of
purple and yellow.

California oatgrass (*Danthonia californica*)
California fescue (*Festuca californica*)
Blue bunchgrass (*Festuca idahoensis*)
Leafy reedgrass (*Calamagrostis foliosa*)
Tufted hairgrass (*Deschampsia cespitosa*)
Meadow barley (*Hordeum brachyantherum*)
Bracken fern (*Pteridium aquilinum*)
Douglas iris (*Iris douglasiana*)
Blue dicks (*Dichelostemma capitatum*)
Blue-eyed grass (*Sisyrinchium bellum*)

02. South Coast

During the Pleistocene era, 20,000 years
ago, when the coastline was much farther

to the west than it is today, coastal sage scrub was the food base for mammoths and other megafauna of the day.

California sagebrush (*Artemisia californica*)
Black Sage (*Salvia mellifera*)
White sage (*Salvia apiana*)
California buckwheat (*Eriogonum fasciculatum*)
Coast brittlebush (*Encelia californica*)
Golden yarrow (*Eriophyllum confertifolium*)
Toyon (*Heteromeles arbutifolia*)
Lemonade berry (*Rhus integrifolia*)

03. North Coast Scrub

Coast redwoods like to be close to the ocean, but not too close. They usually stop about a mile from the shore, giving the smaller woody plants a chance at whatever light they can get through the perpetual fog.

Coyote brush (*Baccharis pilularis*)
California yerba santa (*Eriodictyon californicum*)
Coast silk-tassel (*Garrya elliptica*)
Salal (*Gaultheria shallon*)
Yellow bush lupine (*Lupinus arboreus*)

04. Central Valley Prairie

The Central Valley is a shadow of the biogeographic zone it used to be, as only 1 percent of the original grassland remains intact after 200 years of human agriculture.

Purple needlegrass (*Nassella pulchra*)
California poppy (*Eschscholzia californica*)
Owl's clover (*Castilleja exserta*)
Western sycamore (*Platanus racemosa*)
Box elder (*Acer negundo*)
Fremont cottonwood (*Populus fremontii*)
Valley oak (*Quercus lobata*)

Ponderosa pine
Pinus ponderosa

Map 04.13 The Pine Trees of California

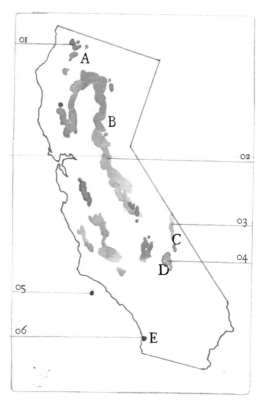

There are 19 species of pine (*Pinus*) tree in California. They range from common mountain species (ponderosa, Jeffrey, sugar, lodgepole) to less common mountain species (northern foxtail, southern foxtail, whitebark, limber, western white) to the desert mountain species (single-leaf pinyon, Parry pine, Colorado pinyon, bristlecone) to foothill species (Coulter, ghost, knobcone), to the rare coastal pine species (Torrey, bishop, shore).

A. Northern foxtail pine distribution range (light blue)
B. Gray pine distribution range (orange)
C. Great Basin bristlecone pine distribution range (blue-green)
D. Southern foxtail pine distribution range (dark green)
E. Torrey pine distribution range (red)

01. The largest stands of northern foxtail pine are in the Marble Mountains.

02. Gray pine traces the foothill rim around the whole Central Valley.

03. The westernmost stand of the Great Basin bristlecone pine is in the White Mountains.

04. The southern foxtail pine exists in large stands in the High Sierra of Kings Canyon National Park.

05. The Torrey pine exists only on the bluffs of the Torrey Pines State Natural Reserve in San Diego County, and its cousin, the Island Torrey pine, a sub-species, exists only on the south side of Santa Rosa Island.

torrey pine
Pinus Torreyana

Map 04.14 A Tale of Two Cedars

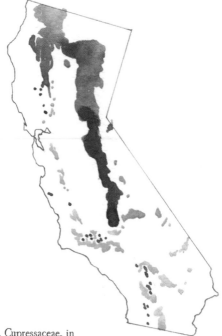

The cedar family, Cupressaceae, in California contains eight types of cypress (Paiute, Tecate, Cuyamaca, Monterey, Mendocino, Baker, McNab, and Sargent), four types of cedar (yellow—*Callitropsis*, incense—*Calocedrus*, Port Orford—*Chamaecyparis*, and western red—*Thuja*), two types of redwood (coast redwood, or *Sequoia sempervirens*, and Sierra redwood, or *Sequoiadendron giganteum*) and five types of juniper (California, common, Sierra, western, and Utah).

In purple on the map, *Calocedrus decurrens* (Sierra cedar) should really be called Siskiyou cedar, as its largest specimens live in the poor soil reaches of the far Northwest.

In yellow on the map, *Juniperus californica* (desert cedar, or California juniper) is at home at high elevations in the Mojave and in the Inyo Mountains of the Great Basin; it is distributed throughout the chaparral belt that rings the Central Valley.

Although the map seems to indicate that they hold separate distribution ranges, especially in the transverse Coast Ranges, in many instances in these areas the two trees grow side by side.

incense cedar
Calocedrus decurrens

California juniper
Juniperus californica

Map 04.15 The Fir Trees of California

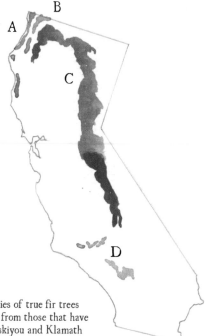

There are eight species of true fir trees (*Abies*) in California, from those that have tiny ranges in the Siskiyou and Klamath Mountains (Pacific silver, subalpine, and Shasta), to those that range over larger ranges in the same mountains (grand, noble), to the Sierra fir trees (white, red), to a single outlier on California's Central Coast (bristlecone).

Fir trees are very good at hybridizing with one another; because of this, accurate identification of species types can be difficult.

A. Grand firs (tan): Extending up into the Pacific Northwest of Oregon and Washington, grand firs are one of the most common true fir trees north of the Siskiyou Mountains.

B. Hybrid firs (green): Fir identification in the Siskiyou and Trinity Mountains can be tricky because, in this zone, grand firs hybridize regularly with white firs.

C. White firs (red): The most common true firs in the Sierra Nevada, white firs are quick to sprout after wildfires, and can thus dominate and quickly overpopulate forest space below 7,000 feet in elevation.

D. Rocky Mountain white firs: A subspecies, Rocky Mountain white firs live in the transverse central range.

Map 04.16 The Oak Gardens

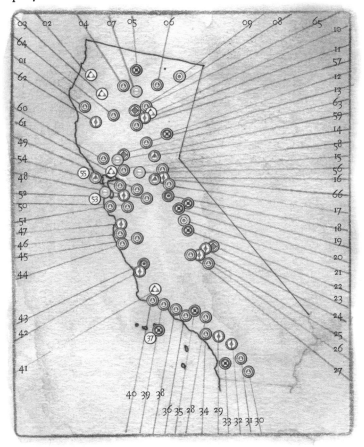

There is hardly a place on the map where Old Man Oak isn't happy in California. There are nine common species of oak tree (genus *Quercus*) in the state, and they all have similar yet varying mechanisms of fitting in with their neighbors. Some grow huge and sprawl over nearly an acre of grassland (valley oaks), some are fine in the snow among alpine conifers (black oaks), some add perennial green to the landscape by keeping their leaves all year long (live oaks), and some can withstand drought-like conditions for extended periods of time in the company of cacti (canyon oaks). Traipse around the whole state, west of the Mojave, and you will never be too far from the secluded and pastoral wisdom of Old Man Oak.

California's Major Oaks

V: Valley oak (Q. *lobata*)
B: Black oak (Q. *kelloggii*)
Bl: Blue oak (Q. *douglassii*)
O: Oregon oak (Q. *garryana*)
Cl: Coast live oak (Q. *agrifolia*)
Il: Interior live oak (Q. *wislizenii*)
C: Canyon oak (Q. *chrysolepis*)
I: Island oak (Q. *tomentella*)
S: Scrub oak (Q. *berberidifolia*)*

* Also often called coastal scrub oak (Q. *dumosa*), leather oak (Q. *durata*), Tucker oak (Q. *john-tuckeri*), or island scrub oak (Q. *pacifica*)

List of Oak Forests
and the Type of Oaks Exhibited

01. Richardson Grove State Park (O, C, B)
02. Schoolhouse Peak, Redwood National Park (O, C, B)
03. Mad Ridge, Oak Grove Campground (O, C)
04. Whiskeytown–Shasta–Trinity National Recreation Area (V, B)
05. Sacramento River Canyon, Shasta Valley (B)
06. McArthur–Burney Falls Memorial State Park (B, O)
07. Tower House (V)
08. Hat Creek Rim (Bl)
09. Quail Spring (B)
10. Finley Butte, Lassen National Forest (Bl)
11. Dye Creek Preserve, Nature Conservancy (Bl)
12. Genesee Valley (B, Il)
13. Bidwell Park, Chico (V)
14. Highway 49, Independence Trail, South Yuba (C, B)
15. Folsom Lake State Recreation Area (Bl)
16. Cosumnes River Preserve (V)
17. Indian Grinding Rock State Historic Park (V, C, B)
18. Twain Harte (Il, C, B)
19. Yosemite Valley (B)
20. Merced River Canyon (C)
21. Bass Lake (Bl, B, V)
22. Squaw Leap, San Joaquin River Gorge (Bl)
23. Middle fork of the Kaweah River (Bl, IL, C, B, V)
24. Kaweah River Reserve (Bl, C, IL)
25. Kaweah Oaks Preserve (V)
26. California Hot Springs, Sequoia National Forest (Bl, Il, B, C)
27. Mooney Grove Park, Visalia (V)
28. Baxton Flats/Seven Oaks, Barton Flats Recreation Area (B, C)
29. Ronald W. Caspers Wilderness Park (Cl)
30. Cuyamaca Rancho State Park (C)
31. Palomar Mountain State Park (C)
32. Wilderness Gardens Preserve (Cl)
33. Los Peñasquitos Canyon Preserve (Cl, S)
34. Crystal Cove State Park (Cl, S)
35. Charlton Flats (C)
36. Leo Carrillo State Beach (Cl)
37. Santa Cruz Island (I, Cl, C)
38. Point Mugu State Park (Cl)
39. Toro Canyon Park (Cl, S)
40. Nojoqui Falls Park (Cl)
41. Figueroa Mountain (V, S, Cl, C)
42. Lake Osos Oaks State Natural Reserve (Cl)
43. Santa Margarita (Cl)
44. Pfeiffer Big Sur State Park (Cl)
45. Pinnacles National Park (Cl, V, Bl)
46. Toro County Park (Cl, V, Il)
47. Elkhorn Slough Reserve (Cl)
48. Caswell Memorial State Park (V)
49. Oak Grove Regional Park (V)
50. Henry W. Coe State Park (V, B, Bl, Cl, C, Il)
51. Castle Rock State Park (Cl, B)
52. Ohlone Regional Wilderness (Bl, Cl)

blue oak
Quercus douglasii

Map 04.17 The California Redwoods

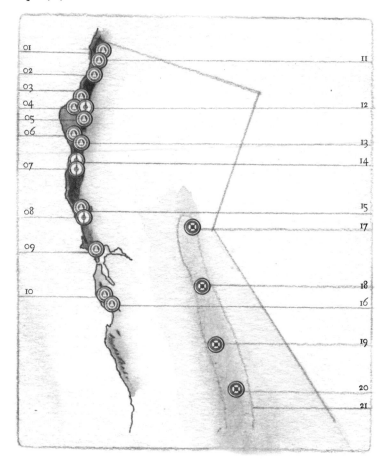

John Muir called the giant sequoia of the Sierra Nevada an immortal tree, as he believed that if it were not for their tremendous weight and shallow roots, sequoias might be able to live forever. Indeed, before the newcomers in the 19th century decided that it was a good idea to start chopping these giants down, the only real cause of their death was that they would eventually grow so large and top-heavy that they would topple in a winter storm. The giant sequoia (*Sequoiadendron giganteum*) is the most massive tree species in the world, and its cousin, the coast redwood (*Sequoia sempervirens*), is the tallest.

Being the tallest tree in the world might not be the most interesting trait of the coast redwood, however. Coast redwoods have a litany of tools at their evolutionary disposal to manage the endeavor of living for 2,000 years. They are fireproof; with its thick suit of deep, insulating bark, the largest tree might survive ten major fires in its life. They make their own weather; the orientation and structure of the needles gathers coastal fog and, in great enough numbers, the grove regulates the microclimate of the forest. They are able to climb; if a landslide occurs in their deep canyon, dramatically altering the soil line, they can sprout roots from any point in their trunk. They can survive being chopped down; to the consternation of many cattle farmers, it is very difficult to transform a redwood grove into a pasture, as the trees will grow up from their roots to form several new saplings. They never rot, making antimicrobial chemicals in their bark that resist fungus and other decomposing agents; a fallen tree might lie on the forest floor for centuries because of this ability.

Old-growth forest has an ecology all its own, very different from second-growth forests on all levels of ecological study. It will take several hundred years for California to remake the old growth that was destroyed over the past 160 years, and who's to say what will be the biotic makeup of the new old growth.

The following are the major coast redwood forests, with approximate old-growth forest area listed in parentheses:

01. Jedediah Smith Redwoods State Park (14 square miles)
02. Prairie Creek Redwoods State Park (16 square miles)
03. Redwood National Park (32 square miles)
04. Grizzly Creek Redwoods State Park (1 square mile)
05. Humboldt Redwoods State Park (26 square miles)
06. Smithe Redwoods State Natural Reserve (contains no old-growth coast redwood forest)
07. Mailliard Redwoods State Natural Reserve (1 square mile)
08. Armstrong Redwoods State Natural Reserve (2 square miles)
09. Muir Woods National Monument (2 square miles)
10. Big Basin Redwoods State Park (7 square miles)
11. Del Norte Coast Redwoods State Park (4 square miles)
12. Headwaters Forest Reserve (2 square miles)
13. Richardson Grove State Park (3 square miles)
14. Montgomery Woods State Natural Reserve (3 square miles)
15. Hendy Woods State Park (0.5 square miles)
16. Henry Cowell Redwoods State Park (1 square mile)

In California, there are approximately 75 existing groves of giant sequoias in four geographical groups; some contain fewer than ten trees, whereas others have more than a hundred. The four geographical groups are:

17. The Placer County Big Trees Grove: North of the Kings River, this is the northernmost group; it contains eight groves: two at Calaveras, three in Yosemite, and three in the Sierra National Forest.

18. The Kings River Big Trees Grove: In the Kings River watershed, which includes Giant Sequoia National Monument, Kings Canyon National Park, and Sequoia National Forest, there are 16 extant groves; the Evans Grove Complex is made up of the Lockwood, the Little Boulder Creek, the Boulder Creek, and the Evans Groves.

19. The Kaweah River Big Trees Grove: The 23 groves in this group are either in Sequoia National Park or in private ownership, with a couple of exceptions in Sequoia National Forest and Kings Canyon National Park.

20. The Tule River and Kern River Big Trees Grove: From Redwood Mountain Grove in the north down to the southernmost big trees at Deer Creek, 23 groves extend across Tulare County from Giant Sequoia National Monument through Sequoia National Park to Mountain Home Demonstration State Forest and into the Tule River Reservation.

21. Distribution range of the giant sequoia.

Giant Sequoia
sequoiadendron giganteum

Map 04.18 The Headwaters Forest Reserve

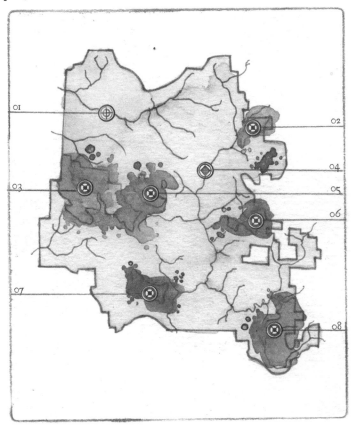

1 mile

04.18

The Headwaters Forest Reserve is a 7,400-acre group of old-growth coast redwood groves managed by the Bureau of Land Management as part of the National Landscape Conservation System. The reserve was established in 1999 after a 15-year battle over the fate of this grove—a keystone moment for the conservation movement in California.

01. North fork of the Elk River
02. All Species Grove
03. Headwaters Grove
04. Lawrence Creek
05. Elkhead Springs Grove
06. Shaw Creek Grove
07. Allen Creek Grove
08. Owl Creek Grove

05. OF WIND & WEATHER

Map 05.01 Contemporary Ecological Zones of California

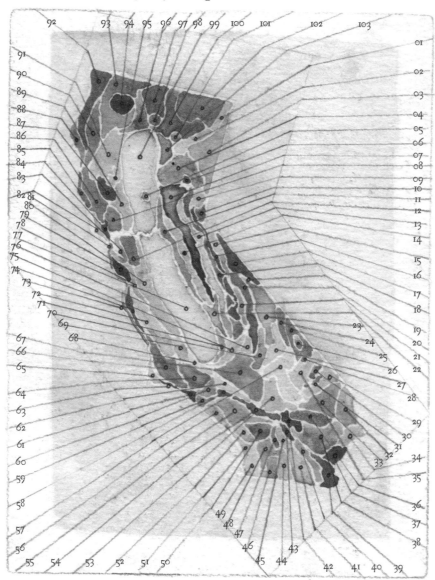

Aridity determines the course of California ecology. The abundance or scarcity of water can make forests march and mountains dissolve, and it can make or break the most clever of human communities. Water, of course, is tempered by an even more powerful force: climate. Everything under the sun is influenced by the sun. Wind, heat, and snow all conspire to maintain a delicate balance. That is, until an X factor is introduced. In our time, that X factor might be produced by the force of global human civilization, recklessly calling the bluff of the most powerful maker of ecosystems.

Whereas an ecosystem is a discrete unit that consists of living and nonliving parts interacting to form a stable system, an ecological zone may contain several dozen ecosystems defined by a larger geographic feature or region. The ecological zones of California are generalized here and accompanied in parentheses by the locales that typify their wild nature. This list is organized as a complete, introductory catalog: each landscape feature forming a link in the narrative chain that is California ecology.

The geographic features across this survey of California's major ecological zones may include mountain ranges (see, e.g., 43, Little San Bernardino Mountains), multiple mountain ranges (93, the Klamath Knot), or mountain cells within larger ranges (21, Mount Whitney crest), watersheds (86, Russian River riparian), river valleys (15, Walker River Valley), forest groves (103, Ishi Wilderness), wetlands (84, San Pablo wetlands), basins (69, Carrizo Plain); or climatic zones of plant-type differentiations (13, sugar pine belt).

01. Desert conifer and sagebrush forests of the Werner Mountains (Cedar Creek Interpretive Trail)

02. Pit River riparian wetlands of Big Valley (Ash Creek Wildlife Area)

03. Nevada high desert of the Madeline Plains (Biscar National Wildlife Area)

04. Volcanic highlands of Eagle Lake (Biz Johnson National Recreation Trail on the Susan River)

05. Isolated peaks over the Sacramento River at the Sutter Buttes (Peace Valley)

06. Sierra Buttes Lakes Basin (Gold Lake)

07. Gold Highway ridges and valleys (Yuba River)

08. Napa River Valley (Skyline Wilderness Park)

09. Sierra Valley (Antelope Valley Wildlife Area)

10. Tahoe Basin (D. L. Bliss State Park)

11. Gold Highway oaklands (Indian Grinding Rock State Historical Park)

12. Sunol creeklands (Ohlone Regional Wilderness)

13. Sugar pine belt (Mokelumne Wilderness)

14. Gray pine chaparral transition (Traverse Creek Botanical Area)

15. Walker River Valley (Pick Meadow Wildlife Area)

16. Alpine High Sierra (Red Lake Wildlife Area)

17. Mono Basin and Range (Mono Basin National Forest Scenic Area)

18. Foxtail pine belt (Kearsarge Pass)

19. White Mountain bristlecone
    (Schulman Grove)
20. Owens Valley lowland
    (Crater Mountain Area of
    Critical Environmental Concern)
21. Mount Whitney crest
    (Whitney Pass)
22. Western Rise of the Sequoia forest
    (General Sherman Tree)
23. Desolation of the Northern
    Death Valley (Saline Valley)
24. Funeral Mountains Wilderness
    (Ash Meadows National
    Wildlife Refuge)
25. Amargosa Canyon
    (Dumont Dunes Natural Area)
26. Kingston Range Wilderness
    (Tecopa Pass)
27. China Lake
    (Avawatz Mountains)
28. Clark Mountain
    (Ivanpah Springs)
29. Bigelow Cholla Gardens Wilderness
    (South Pass)
30. New York Mountains
    (Caruthers Canyon)
31. Providence Mountains
    (Hole in the Wall)
32. Chemehuevi Mountains Wilderness
    (Trampas Wash Trail)
33. Cadiz Dunes Wilderness
    (Amboy)
34. Whipple Mountains Wilderness
    (Copper Basin Reservoir)
35. Cima Dome forests
    (Teutonia Peak)
36. Sheephole Valley Wilderness
    (Sheephole Pass)
37. Big Maria Mountains Wilderness
    (Midland Camp)
38. Joshua Tree Wilderness
    (Pinto Basin)
39. Indian Pass Wilderness
    (Black Mountain)
40. Algodones Dunes
    (Roadrunner Camp)

41. Imperial Valley
    (Salton Sea)
42. Yucca Valley highland
    (Big Morongo Canyon Reserve)
43. Little San Bernardino Mountains
    (Black Rock Canyon)
44. West Salton alluvial slope
    (Yuha Desert)
45. Coachella Valley
    (Whitewater River)
46. Anza Borrego rise
    (Vallecito Mountains)
47. San Jacinto Wilderness
    (Cactus to Clouds Trail)
48. Santa Rosa high forests
    (Spitler Peak Trail)
49. San Ysidro Mountains
    (Hollenbeck Canyon
    Wildlife Area)
50. San Jacinto Badlands
    (Chino Hills State Park)
51. San Clemente Bluffs
    (Crystal Cove State Park)
52. Santa Ana Mountains
    (Santa Rosa Plateau
    Ecological Reserve)
53. South Mojave
    (Lucerne Valley)
54. San Bernardino Mountains
    (Sugarloaf National
    Recreation Trail)
55. Inland Empire
    (Whittier Narrows
    Nature Center)
56. Los Angeles coast
    (Las Tunas State Beach)
57. Mojave River Wash
    (Mojave Narrows
    Regional Park)
58. Magic Mountain Wilderness
    (Dillon Divide Canyon)
59. Santa Monica Mountains
    (Point Mugu State Park)
60. Sespe riparian
    (Sespe Gorge Trail)
61. Santa Clara River mouth
    (Steckel County Park)

62. Tejon chaparral
    (Tejon Pass)
63. Gaviota purple sage coast
    (Gaviota Springs Trail)
64. Chumash Wilderness
    (Mount Pinos)
65. Vandenberg grasslands
    (Barka Slough)
66. Sisquoc riparian
    (Manzana Schoolhouse)
67. West Mojave
    (Antelope Valley)
68. Maricopa oil desert
    (Bitter Creek National
    Wildlife Refuge)
69. Carrizo Plain
    (Wallace Creek Trail)
70. El Paso Mountains
    (Red Rock Canyon State Park)
71. Tehachapi Pass
    (Horse Canyon Area of
    Critical Environmental Concern)
72. Salinas Valley
    (San Lorenzo Regional Park)
73. Big Sur coastal steppe
    (Andrew Molera State Park)
74. Santa Lucia coastal mountains
    (Santa Lucia Memorial Park)
75. South Sierra
    (Isabella Lake)
76. Piute Mountains
    (Inspiration Point
    Botanical Area)
77. San Joaquin River confluences
    (Mendota Wildlife Area)
78. Santa Clara Valley
    (Joseph Grant County Park)
79. Santa Cruz Mountains
    (Big Basin State Park)
80. Inland Diablo Mountains
    (Henry Coe State Park)
81. San Francisco Peninsula fog coast
    (San Bruno Mountain Park)
82. Point Reyes coastal prairie
    (Sky Trail)

83. San Francisco Bay wetlands
    (Coyote Hills Regional Park)
84. San Pablo wetlands
    (San Pablo Bay
    National Wildlife Refuge)
85. Coastal redwood forests
    (Mailliard Redwoods
    State Reserve)
86. Russian River riparian
    (Russian River Valley)
87. Clear Lake Basin
    (Clear Lake State Park)
88. Kings Range
    (Horse Mountain Creek Trail)
89. Tuleyome chaparral
    (Berryessa Snow Mountain
    National Monument)
90. Redwood valleys
    (Headwaters Grove)
91. Yolla Bolly–Middle Eel Wilderness
    (Stuart Gap Trail)
92. Prairie Creek coastal forests
    (Redwood National Park)
93. Klamath Knot
    (Bear Basin Butte)
94. Trinity alpine
    (Canyon Creek Trail)
95. Snow Mountain
    (North Ridge Trail)
96. Shasta–Trinity uplands
    (Cantara Ney Springs
    Wildlife Area)
97. Shasta Valley
    (Shasta Valley Wildlife Area)
98. Mount Shasta
    (Whitney Falls Trail)
99. Sacramento River Valley
    (Sacramento National
    Wildlife Refuge)
100. Glass Mountain lava lands
    (Medicine Lake)
101. Mount Lassen
    (Hat Lake Trail)
102. Modoc Plateau
    (Dutch Flat Wildlife Area)
103. Ishi Wilderness
    (Tehama Wildlife Area)

Map 05.02 The General Climate

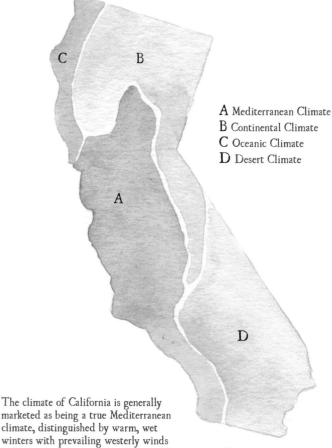

A Mediterranean Climate
B Continental Climate
C Oceanic Climate
D Desert Climate

The climate of California is generally marketed as being a true Mediterranean climate, distinguished by warm, wet winters with prevailing westerly winds and calm, hot, dry summers. This general climate type occurs at similar latitudes around the globe and is also characteristic of Chile, South Africa, and southwestern Australia. California is also influenced by an oceanic climate, a continental climate, and a desert climate. The oceanic climate is typical of the west coasts at the middle latitudes of most continents, and it features warm summers and cool winters, with a relatively narrow annual temperature range. The continental climate features generalized semarid, very hot summers and very cold winters. The desert climate of California has such low levels of precipitation that no wood trees grow. Only scrubland, yuccas, and palm ecosystems thrive in riparian areas.

Map 05.03 The New Climate Model

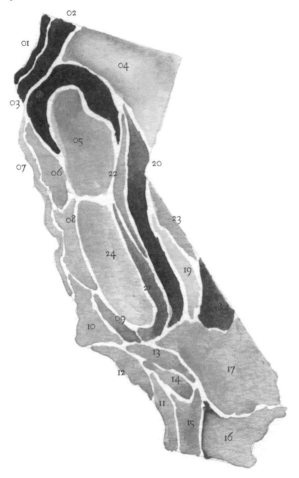

Influenced by the complete list of ecosystems as described in map 05.01 and then overlaid with the climate template described in map 05.02, with specific data points, a new climate model can be drawn. The detailed minimum and maximum temperatures described in the key are based on average daytime highs and lows. Precipitation is measured as an average of yearly rainfall/snowfall.

01. Humboldt coast
January minimum: 40°F
January maximum: 57°F
July minimum: 52°F
July maximum: 54°F
Precipitation: 55 inches

02. Siskiyou rainbelt
January minimum: 35°F
January maximum: 55°F
July minimum: 55°F
July maximum: 95°F
Precipitation: 90 inches

03. Yolla Bolly Range
January minimum: 35°F
January maximum: 55°F
July minimum: 55°F
July maximum: 90°F
Precipitation: 33 inches

04. Modoc Plateau
January minimum: 20°F
January maximum: 45°F
July minimum: 50°F
July maximum: 85°F
Precipitation: 13 inches

05. Sacramento Valley
January minimum: 37°F
January maximum: 55°F
July minimum: 66°F
July maximum: 98°F
Precipitation: 15 inches

06. Napa Ridges and Valleys
January Minimum 35°F
January Maximum 58°F
July Minimum 58°F
July Maximum 82°F
Precipitation 23 inches

07. Northern Central Coast
January minimum: 46°F
January maximum: 57°F
July minimum: 54°F
July maximum: 66°F
Precipitation: 30 inches

08. Inland Coast Ranges
January minimum: 37°F
January maximum: 58°F
July minimum: 67°F
July maximum: 100°F
Precipitation: 19 inches

09. Carrizo dry lands
January minimum: 35°F
January maximum: 68°F
July minimum: 70°F
July maximum: 95°F
Precipitation: 6 inches

10. Southern Central Coast
January minimum: 45°F
January maximum: 72°F
July minimum: 62°F
July maximum: 80°F
Precipitation: 7 inches

11. South Coast
January minimum: 49°F
January maximum: 65°F
July minimum: 65°F
July maximum: 75°F
Precipitation: 7 inches

12. Los Angeles River basin
January minimum: 48°F
January maximum: 68°F
July minimum: 64°F
July maximum: 85°F
Precipitation: 5 inches

13. Transverse Ranges
January minimum: 35°F
January maximum: 60°F
July minimum: 55°F
July maximum: 90°F
Precipitation: 18 inches

14. Inland Empire
January minimum: 43°F
January maximum: 69°F
July minimum: 64°F
July maximum: 95°F
Precipitation: 12 inches

15. Cleveland National Forest
January minimum: 43°F
January maximum: 69°F
July minimum: 72°F
July maximum: 83°F
Precipitation: 12 inches

16. Colorado Desert
January minimum: 43°F
January maximum: 65°F
July minimum: 84°F
July maximum: 105°F
Precipitation: 2 inches

17. Mojave Desert
January minimum: 37°F
January maximum: 60°F
July minimum: 69°F
July maximum: 101°F
Precipitation: 6 inches

18. Death Valley
January minimum: 40°F
January maximum: 67°F
July minimum: 88°F
July maximum: 117°F
Precipitation: 3 inches

19. Owens Valley
January minimum: 23°F
January maximum: 54°F
July minimum: 56°F
July maximum: 95°F
Precipitation: 7 inches

20. Sierra Nevada upper montane forest
January minimum: 16°F
January maximum: 43°F
July minimum: 41°F
July maximum: 81°F
Precipitation: 33 inches

21. Tehachapi Pass
January minimum: 30°F
January maximum: 64°F
July minimum: 59°F
July maximum: 84°F
Precipitation: 10 inches

22. Sierra Nevada low montane forest
January minimum: 27°F
January maximum: 57°F
July minimum: 62°F
July maximum: 91°F
Precipitation: 36 inches

23. Bodie
January minimum: 5°F
January maximum: 40°F
July minimum: 34°F
July maximum: 78°F
Precipitation: 8 inches

24. San Joaquin Valley
January minimum: 38°F
January maximum: 60°F
July minimum: 69°F
July maximum: 100°F
Precipitation: 12 inches

lark sparrow
Chondestes grammacus

pygmy nuthatch
Sitta pygmaea

Map 05.04 Climate Change Indicators

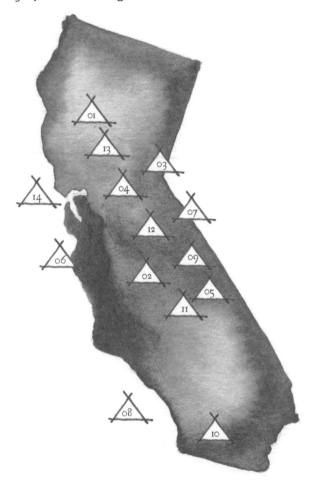

The careful measurement of averages makes for the best science when attempting to decipher the changing global state of our shared climate. By observing the subtle hints and noting the minor clues that point to major challenges, we can put the puzzle pieces together. What we are seeing across the state is an acceleration of natural processes inherent in how California has always worked: namely, nothing is static, nothing is guaranteed.

Here are some the major indicators of climate change that are currently unfolding:

01. Warmer temperatures statewide: Since 1985, the average air temperature at Mount Shasta, Sacramento, and Los Angeles has increased by an annual average of 1.5°F.

02. Winter frost decline in the Central Valley: Instances of winter chill, a necessary constituent in the formation of fruit, have been decreasing steadily since 1950.

03. Freezing level elevation at Lake Tahoe: The measure of altitude by which freezing temperatures are recorded has risen by 500 feet over the past 50 years.

04. Water storage decline in the foothills: Spring runoff captured from the Sierra Nevada has declined by 9 percent in the past century.

05. Mountain glacier shrinkage in the Sierra Crest: The glaciers of the Sierra Nevada have shrunk over 50 percent since 1900, consistent with worldwide glacial melt.

06. Sea level elevation along the coast: The sea level in San Francisco and La Jolla has risen eight and six inches, respectively, over the past 100 years.

07. Mountain lake temperature elevation: The surface water temperature at Lake Tahoe and six other lakes in California and Nevada has risen 10°F in 30 years.

08. South Coast ocean temperature elevation: The coastal ocean surface temperature at La Jolla has increased 1.8°F over the past 100 years.

09. Lower montane forest retreat: The conifer forest of the Sierra Nevada has been steadily retreating upslope over the past 60 years.

10. Santa Rosa Mountains vegetation retreat: The distribution of dominant plant species in the Santa Rosa Mountains has moved upslope by 65 percent over the past 30 years.

11. Earlier butterfly appearance in the Central Valley: Butterflies have been appearing earlier in the spring every year for the past 40 years, indicating drier, warmer weather.

12. Upward movement of small mammals in Yosemite: Small mammals in Yosemite National Park have been occupying habitat at increasingly higher yearly elevations at a rate of a few feet higher in elevation every year for the past 50 years.

13. Decline of Chinook salmon run on the Sacramento: With less food for juveniles to eat before they return up the river to spawn, due to warmer ocean temperatures, the population doing so has crashed since 2004.

14. Reduction of bird populations on the Farallon Islands: The breeding success of the Cassin's auklet and other species has been greatly reduced since 2005, positively correlated with prey abundance in adult foraging grounds due to irregular ocean conditions.

Map 05.05 Precipitation

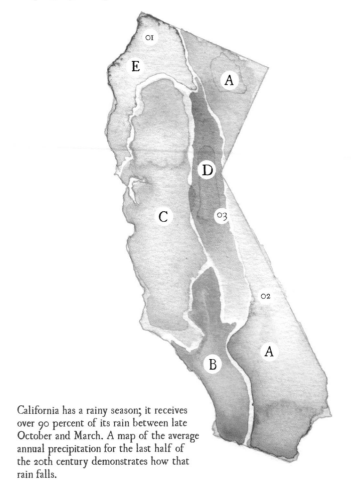

California has a rainy season; it receives over 90 percent of its rain between late October and March. A map of the average annual precipitation for the last half of the 20th century demonstrates how that rain falls.

A. 0 to 10 inches
B. 11 to 30 inches
C. 31 to 60 inches
D. 61 to 80 inches
E. Over 80 inches

01. Gasquet (town): This is the rainiest place in California, with an average rainfall of 95 inches annually.
02. Death Valley: This is the hottest and driest place in North America.
03. Tamarack, Calaveras County: In January 1911, 33 feet of snow fell here, the most ever recorded for a single month in North America.

Map 05.06 Hydrological Regions

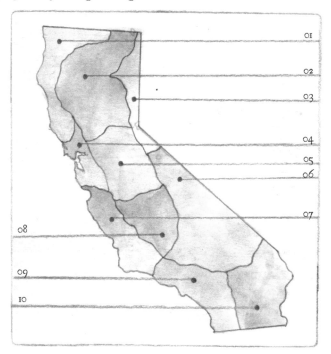

California's ten hydrological regions are essential in our understanding of how water must be transported to sustain human ecology. California receives a total average of 192.2 million acre-feet of rain in any given year. By seeing the percentages of that number, as recorded in each hydrologic region, we can see the ratios that give us a clue to how much rain falls where.

01. North Coast: 55.9 million acre-feet (29 percent)
02. Sacramento River: 52.4 million acre-feet (27 percent)
03. North Lahotan: 6.0 million acre-feet (4 percent)
04. San Francisco Bay: 5.5 million acre-feet (3 percent)
05. San Joaquin Valley: 21.8 million acre-feet (11 percent)
06. South Lahotan: 9.3 million acre-feet (5 percent)
07. Central Coast: 12.3 million acre-feet (6 percent)
08. Tulare Lake: 13.9 million acre-feet (7 percent)
09. South Coast: 10.8 million acre-feet (6 percent)
10. Colorado River: 4.3 million acre-feet (2 percent)

Map 05.07 El Niño

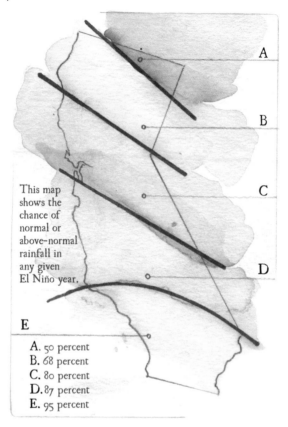

This map shows the chance of normal or above-normal rainfall in any given El Niño year.

A. 50 percent
B. 68 percent
C. 80 percent
D. 87 percent
E. 95 percent

El Niño is an ocean-warming event that occurs off the west coast of South America and, by altering global weather patterns, influences the rain that California receives in what are called El Niño years. El Niño (so called because it often reaches its zenith near Christmas) is known to potentially bring drought-breaking rivers from the sky across California, especially Southern California. El Niño happens every five to fifteen years, and evidence suggests that this ocean-warming pattern has been occurring for the past 15,000 years or so.

Although there is only a weak correlation between El Niño and above-average precipitation across California, Californians have come to hope for it to bring some measure of salvation from drought.

Map 05.08 Snow in the Sierra

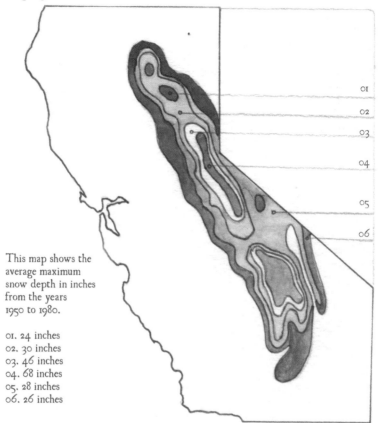

01
02
03
04
05
06

This map shows the
average maximum
snow depth in inches
from the years
1950 to 1980.

01. 24 inches
02. 30 inches
03. 46 inches
04. 68 inches
05. 28 inches
06. 26 inches

Snow depth certainly influences snowpack, the measure of the water bank of modern
human ecology in California; one cubic foot of fallen snow produces about 1.5 cubic
inches of water. The process by which snow becomes water is actually quite complex.
Mountain snowpacks do not melt steadily, varying according to weather, ground
temperature, and exposure to the sun's rays. A snowpack begins to melt when its temperature from top to bottom equalizes at 32°F. Before reaching this isothermal state,
the snowpack has different temperatures at different depths. Ground temperature, air
temperature, and exposure to incoming solar radiation affect how quickly the snowpack
becomes isothermal. South-facing slopes and open areas receive the most solar radiation
and therefore have the highest melt rates.

Map 05.09 Air Basins

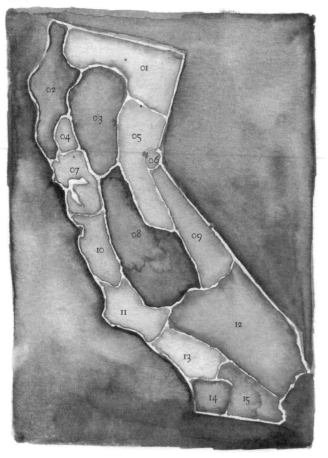

The Environmental Protection Agency has divided the state of California into these 15 labeled regions, or air basins, for the purpose of managing the state's air resources on a regional basis. An air basin generally has similar meteorological and geographic conditions throughout.

01. Northeast Plateau
02. North Coast
03. Sacramento Valley
04. Lake County
05. Mountain Counties

06. Lake Tahoe
07. San Francisco Bay
08. San Joaquin Valley
09. Great Basin Valleys
10. North Central Coast

11. South Central Coast
12. Mojave Desert
13. South Coast
14. San Diego County
15. Salton Sea

Map 05.10 Air Pollution

The counties painted red in this map are ones where levels of pollution fail to fall below unhealthy levels for extended periods in any given year. Three main factors are responsible for unhealthy levels of air pollution in California: direct air pollutants emitted by human activity and industry, the trappings of those pollutants by the wind, and a sunny climate that helps to form and trap ozone as a reaction between human-made pollutants and ultraviolet light.

Indicated counties routinely score a 100 or higher on the Environmental Protection Agency's Air Quality Index, which means that they have measured ground-level atmospheric concentrations of at least 0.14 parts per million for sulfur dioxide and 0.085 parts per million for ozone, qualifying the air in the county as unhealthy.

Map 05.11 Drought

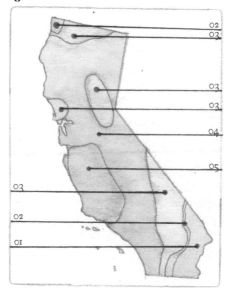

There have been nine major droughts in California since 1900. Each major drought, defined as multiple years with below-average precipitation across the state, lasts an average of three years.

In a land defined by aridity, what meaning is there in the calamitous word *drought?* As California's human population increases and forest habitats are encroached on by modern development, the cresting crisis seems both imminent and perpetual. In an era of increasing dryness, how will the lines be moved so that we aren't living in constant crisis?

This map describes the five levels of drought severity in California—from abnormal dryness to exceptional drought—and the pattern of drought across California's landscape based on the drought that lasted from 2012 through 2016.

05 Exceptional drought
04 Extreme drought
03 Severe drought
02 Moderate drought
01 Abnormal dryness

The continuing drought in California can be attributed to the following factors:

· water infrastructure inadequacy

· deficient water distribution systems

· reservoir capacity reservation, limiting long-term storage

· absence of rain over an extended number of years

· climate change and increasing aridity

· water rights complexity and special interest groups

· large water consumers, especially the cattle industry

Map 05.12 Wind

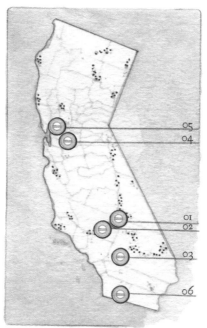

California wind farms collectively have the capacity to generate approximately 12,000 gigawatt-hours of electricity annually, or approximately 5 percent of total usage. California's annual thirst for electricity is currently about 265,000 gigawatt-hours each year.

This map shows the major wind farms in California, with their average operating outputs.

01. Alta Wind Energy Center, Kern County: 1,000 gigawatt-hours per year
02. Tehachapi Pass Wind Farm, Kern County: 700 gigawatt-hours per year
03. San Gorgonio Pass Wind Farm, Riverside County: 600 gigawatt-hours per year
04. Altamont Pass Wind Farm, Alameda County: 600 gigawatt-hours per year
05. Shiloh Wind Power Plant, Solano County: 500 gigawatt-hours per year
06. Ocotillo Wind Energy Project, Imperial County: 300 gigawatt-hours per year

The six largest wind-power stations add a usable 4,000 gigawatt-hours of electricity to California's electrial grid every year. The small black dots on the map indicate clusters of wind farms by county and cumulatively account for approximately 8,000 gigawatt-hours of electrical power.

Map 05.13 Solar Energy

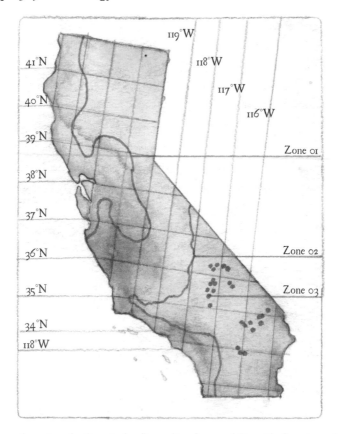

In 2015, the major solar farms in San Bernardino, Inyo, and Riverside Counties—whose general locations are indicated with red dots on the map—accounted for nearly 8 percent of the state's energy requirement. Across the Mojave Desert (zone 3), the sun radiates up to 9 kilowatt-hours per square meter per day. The average California household uses 30 kilowatt-hours of electrical energy per day. If rooftop panels were installed statewide, California has the technical potential to generate nearly three-quarters (75 percent) of its electrical needs.

Zone 01. between 3.0 and 5.0 kWh/m²/Day
Zone 02. between 5.0 and 7.0 kWh/m²/Day
Zone 03. between 7.0 and 9.0 kWh/m²/Day

Map 05.14 The Grid's Energy Sources

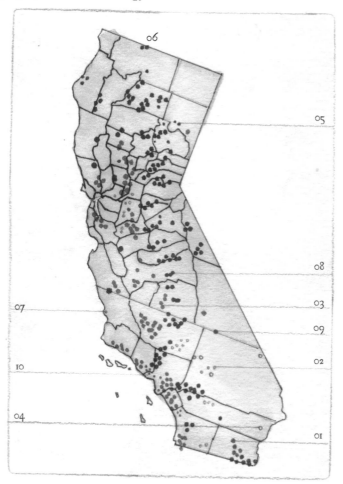

The grid consists of the network of energy resources fed by an array of extraction and production technologies that supply the electricity demands of California's human society. This map shows total electricity sources, expressed as a percentage of California's total energy production.

01. **Natural gas** (42 percent): Burning natural gas on an industrial scale turns turbines to generate electricity. Over 40 natural gas power plants currently operate across California. Of the natural gas burned at these plants, 90 percent is imported from other states. Most of that imported natural gas is extracted by the process of hydraulic fracking, which has revolutionized California's energy grid in the past 20 years but is nonrenewable. While burning natural gas emits 50 percent fewer pollutants than burning coal, greenhouse emissions are still a concern.

Renewable energy (22 percent): By the year 2020, California is required by state law to obtain at least 33 percent of its electricity from renewable sources, not including hydroelectricity. Today, an accounting of the annual percentages of California-produced electrical energy by renewable sources is:

02. **Wind** (5 percent)
03. **Solar** (8 percent)
04. **Geothermal** (5 percent)
05. **Biomass** (4 percent)

06. **Nuclear energy** (9 percent): California has one remaining nuclear power plant: Diablo Canyon in Santa Barbara County, which is to shut down by 2025. At the height of the industry, there were five nuclear power plants, including Diablo Canyon, Rancho Seco, San Onofre, Vallecitos, and Humboldt Bay.

07. **Hydroelectric energy** (7 percent): In big months, California's hydroelectric power-supplying dams can generate close to one-fifth of the state's electricity. Hydroelectric power is not considered a viable renewable energy source in the long term because as water becomes scarcer and the ecological cost grows, it is not worth the destruction such dams cause.

08. **Coal and landfill gas** (14 percent)

09. **Privately generated power sources** (15 percent)

Map 05.15 California at Night

As our ability and appetite to eat at the darkness with our ever-glowing electric lights becomes less and less something we are told we need to concern ourselves with, those of us who prefer the comfort that the delicious black of a wilderness night affords wonder what the long-term cost of such energy expenditure might be. The wise know that that which burns brightest burns shortest, and some quiet, cool darkness might be just what the doctor is ordering.

Map 05.16 California's Vernal Pools

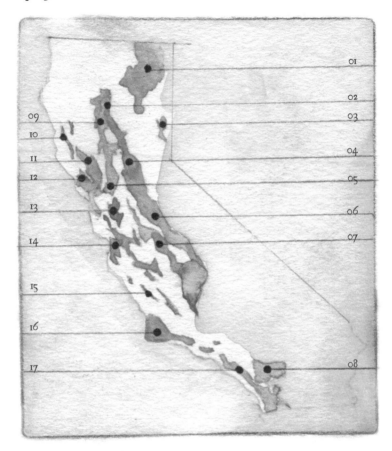

One of the great seasonal phenomena of California, occurring at the climax of the rainy season, is the creation of vernal pools and the parade of wildflowers that follows. A unique kind of temporary wetlands ecosystem, vernal pools host an array of species, from birds to bears. In a restored virgin California waterscape, nearly 30 percent of the state would become vernal pool territory every year from March to May. These regions, as they exist in various stages of vitality and sustainability, are here featured in major clusters as recognized by the California Department of Fish and Wildlife.

Western meadowlark
Sturnella neglecta

Map 05.17 The Wine Regions of Napa Valley

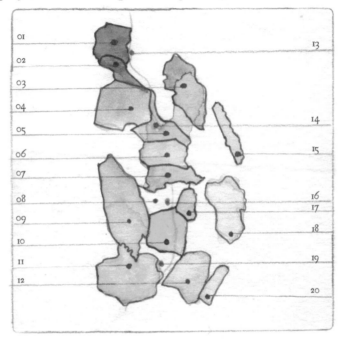

9 miles

05.17

California wine owes its brilliance to the climate of Napa Valley. A climate dryly described in map 05.03 as the Napa ridges and valleys, the Napa Valley is, in fact, a little bit of heaven. The conspiring of weather and earth to produce the world's best wine attracts human pilgrims from across the planet who understand and even revere the humble wine grape.

01. Calistoga
02. Diamond Mountain
03. Howell Mountain
04. Spring Mountain
05. St. Helena
06. Rutherford
07. Oakville
08. Yountville
09. Mount Veeder
10. Oak Knoll
11. Carneros
12. Coombsville
13. Calistoga
14. St. Helena (town)
15. Chiles Valley
16. Yountville
17. Stags Leap district
18. Atlas Peak
19. Napa
20. Wild Horse Valley

Map 05.18 The Tule Fog

Every winter morning, a thick fog—a cold spirit—moves through the Central Valley and settles in its quiet crevasses, searching for the purple needlegrass, the tule reed, and the lost elk. The tule fog is occurring less and less often as machine-minded mankind embeds itself in the ways of a warming world.

06. OF LIFE, DEATH, & THE DESERT

Mojave roadrunner
Geococcyx californianus

A working, living desert is a complicated network of delicate ecosystems. Whereas the casual traveler might dismiss the rugged, even barren landscape as treeless, desolate, and uninviting, the traveler who is drawn to it finds no corner of the place bereft of remarkable biological and botanical strategies laced across ancient patterns of geology and climatology.

The deserts of California exist in the rain shadow of the Sierra Nevada. The geographic structure of the rain shadow not only dictates its arid climate but also sets the region apart from the California Floristic Province, bestowing to the region a character all its own. Because of the desert's geographic isolation, an ecologist might ask if it, while certainly part of the political entity that is California, might be separate from the ecological entity that is California. As it is, you can look to the mountain peaks of the desert and find remnant stands of the same alpine forests that populate the Sierra Nevada, a clue to the long history of a tumultuous climate, demonstrating a push-pull relationship between the deserts and the rest of California.

cactus wren
campylorhynchus brunneicapillus

Map 06.01 The Deserts of California

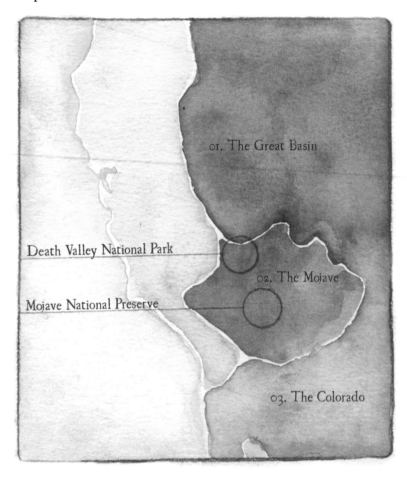

The three desert regions of California are the Great Basin, the Mojave, and the Colorado. The Great Basin Desert extends east from the Sierra Nevada into the state of Nevada. The Mojave Desert, California's quintessential desert, in the rain shadow of the Tehachapi Mountains, is bounded by the San Gabriel and San Bernardino Mountains on its southwestern edge and extends east into Nevada and Arizona. The Colorado, or Low Desert, lies between the Colorado and the Transverse Ranges of San Diego and reaches down into Mexico as part of the larger Sonoran Desert.

Map 06.02 Ancient Lakes of the Mojave

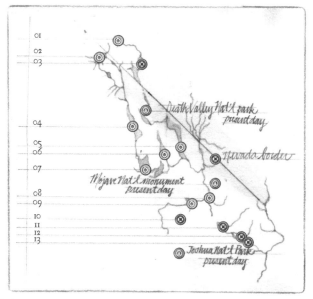

50 miles

06.02

This map portrays the Pleistocene-era lake and river system of the Mojave Desert 100,000 years ago, when water levels were at their highest and riverine connections may have existed between the ancient lakes.

01. Lake Lahontan
02. Lake Russell
03. Columbus Basin
04. Lake Owens

05. Lake Manley
06. Lake Panamint
07. Lake Searles
08. Lake Mojave

09. Lake Manix
10. Lucerne Basin
11. Bristol Basin
12. Cadiz Basin
13. Danby Basin

At the end of the late Pleistocene, a geologic era that began about two million years ago and didn't end until just over 10,000 years ago, the Mojave Desert was radically different in character than it is today: it was both far wetter and far cooler. Forested woodlands, filled with plant species that are now confined to isolated mountaintops, blanketed fecund river basins. Evidently, the ecosystems were so rich in greenery that herbivorous megafauna populations thrived for many tens of thousands of years. That activity decreased only when, about 15,000 years ago, the Mojave River was dammed by seismic events; at this time, the era of the desert lake began as the Mojave and the Amargosa River systems backed up and filled the desert's vast basins.

Map 06.03 A California Desert Overview

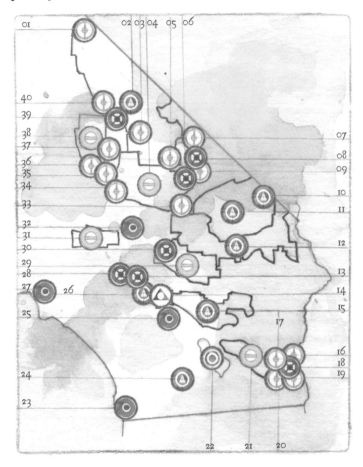

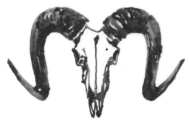

45 miles

06.03

The deserts of California represent a vast tract of ruthless environments that play by their own rules, totally unlike any other part of California.

01. Eureka Wilderness
02. Furnace Creek, Death Valley National Park
03. Manly Peak Wilderness
04. Fort Irwin
05. Ibex Hills Wilderness
06. Sheep Creek Springs
07. Amargosa Wild and Scenic River
08. Dumont Dunes Recreation Area
09. Kingston Range Wilderness
10. Castle Mountains National Monument
11. Mojave National Preserve
12. Mojave Trails National Monument
13. Black Lava Butte Area of Critical Environmental Concern
14. San Gorgonio Peaks
15. Joshua Tree National Park
16. Palo Verde Wilderness
17. Milpitas Wash Wilderness
18. Vinegar Wash Special Management Area
19. Indian Pass Wilderness
20. Buzzards Peak Wilderness
21. Chocolate Mountains Aerial Gunnery Range
22. Salton Sea
23. San Diego
24. Anza Borrego State Park
25. Palm Springs
26. Sand to Snow National Monument
27. Los Angeles
28. Stoddard Valley Recreation Area
29. Twentynine Palms Marine Corps Base
30. Johnson Valley Recreation Area
31. Edwards Air Force Base
32. Barstow
33. Soda Mountains Wilderness
34. Grass Valley Wilderness
35. Golden Valley Wilderness
36. Ridgecrest
37. Great Falls Basin Wilderness
38. China Lake
39. Surprise Canyon Creek Wild and Scenic River
40. Darwin Falls Wilderness

Joshua tree
Yucca brevifolia

Map 06.04 Federal Wilderness Areas of the Desert

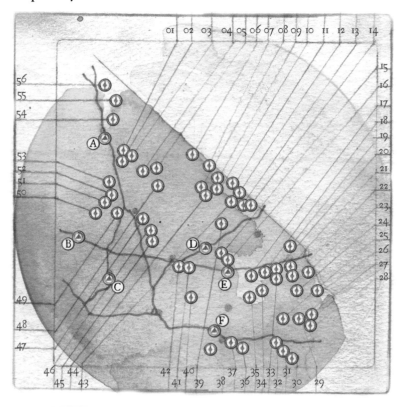

65 miles

06.04

Total: 3.4 million acres
Average wilderness area size: 61,179 acres
Largest wilderness area: Palen/McCoy Wilderness (236,488 acres)
Smallest wilderness area: Saddle Peak Wilderness (1,530 acres)

01. Malpais Mesa (31,906 acres)
02. Coso Range (49,296 acres)
03. Darwin Falls (8,189 acres)
04. Argus Range (65,726 acres)
05. Surprise Canyon (24,433 acres)
06. Funeral Mountains (25,707 acres)
07. Resting Springs (76,312 acres)
08. Ibex (28,822 acres)

09. Nopah Range (106,623 acres)
10. South Nopah Range (17,059 acres)
11. Pahrump (73,726 acres)
12. North Mesquite (28,955 acres)
13. Mesquite (44,804 acres)
14. Stateline (6,964 acres)
15. Kelso Dunes (144,915 acres)
16. Bristol (71,389 acres)
17. Trilobite (37,308 acres)
18. Clipper Mountains (33,843 acres)
19. Dead Mountains (47,158 acres)
20. Piute Mountains (48,080 acres)

30. Palo Verde Mountains (30,605 acres)
31. Little Chuckwalla Mountains (28,052 acres)
32. Chuckwalla Mountains (99,548 acres)
33. Old Woman Mountains (165,170 acres)
34. Sheephole Valley (188,169 acres)
35. Cleghorn Lakes (39,167 acres)
36. Orocopia (51,289 acres)
37. Mecca Hills (26,356 acres)
38. Santa Rosa (78,576 acres)
39. Hollow Hills (22,366 acres)
40. Big Mountain (38,599 acres)
41. Rodman Mountains (34,264 acres)
42. Newberry Mountains (26,102 acres)
43. Kingston (199,739 acres)
44. Saddle Peak Hills (1,530 acres)
45. Black Mountain (20,458 acres)
46. Grass Valley (38,186 acres)
47. Golden Valley (36,536 acres)
48. Manly Peak (12,897 acres)
49. El Paso Mountains (23,679 acres)
50. Bright Star (8,191 acres)
51. Kiavah (86,244 acres)
52. Owens Peak (73,866 acres)
53. Sacatar Trail (50,451 acres)
54. Inyo Mountains (198,874 acres)
55. Sylvania Mountains (18,682 acres)
56. Piper Mountain (72,192 acres)

bighorn sheep
ovis canadensis

21. Bigelow Cholla (14,645 acres)
22. Stepladder Mountains (83,195 acres)
23. Chemehuevi Mountains (85,864 acres)
24. Turtle Mountains (177,309 acres)
25. Palen/McCoy (236,488 acres)
26. Whipple Mountains (76,123 acres)
27. Riverside Mountains (24,004 acres)
28. Big Maria Mountains (45,384 acres)
29. Rice Valley Mountains (41,777 acres)

A. Highway 395
B. Highway 58
C. Highway 14
D. Highway 15
E. Highway 40
F. Highway 10

Map 06.05 Parks and Monuments of the Mojave

20 miles

06.05

01. Mojave National Preserve: This preserve comprises 1.6 million acres between Interstate 15 and Interstate 40. Protected by the National Park System in 1994 under the California Desert Protection Act by the U.S. Congress, it was previously designated as the East Mojave National Scenic Area, under the jurisdiction of the Bureau of Land Management.

02. Mojave Trails National Monument: This monument spans 1.6 million acres, including more than 350,000 acres of previously congressionally designated wilderness. It was designated as a national monument in 2016.

03. Joshua Tree National Park: This park covers a land area of 790,636 acres, of which 429,690 acres is a designated wilderness area. Having been a national monument since 1936, Joshua Tree became a national park in 1994. The park straddles two of California's deserts, as they are divided by ecology: the Mojave to the north and the Colorado to the south.

04. Sand to Snow National Monument: This monument protects 154,000 acres, with the Bureau of Land Management managing 83,000 acres and the U.S. Forest Service managing 71,000 acres. The monument runs from the Coachella Valley up to over 11,000 feet, including San Gorgonio.

Map 06.06 Mojave National Preserve

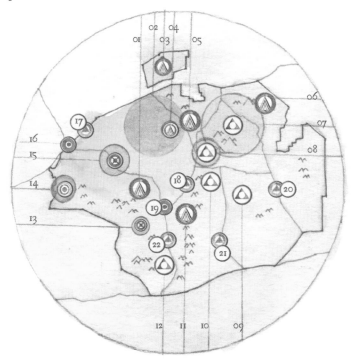

No other region of the California desert rivals the plant diversity found in the Mojave National Preserve. Approximately 2,450 native vascular plant species have been documented in the California desert, representing 38 percent of the native species in the state. Among desert landscapes in North America, nothing touches the preserve's unparalleled diversity and high degree of endemism.

01. Kelso Peak (4,764 feet)
02. Shadow Valley
03. Clark Mountain (7,929 feet)
04. Cima Dome (5,775 feet)
05. Kessler Peak (6,163 feet), Ivanpah Mountains
06. Castle Peak (5,829 feet), New York Mountains
07. Juniper-pinyon forest, New York Mountains
08. Pinto Mountain (6,144 feet), Mid Hills
09. Fenner Valley
10. Columbia Mountains
11. Fountain Peak (6,996 feet)
12. Granite Mountains
13. Kelso Dunes
14. Soda Lake
15. Cinder Cone Lava Beds
16. Baker and the Halloran Springs
17. Highway 15
18. Cima Road
19. Kelso
20. Lanfair Road
21. Essex Road
22. Kelbaker Road

Map 06.07 Mojave Trails National Monument

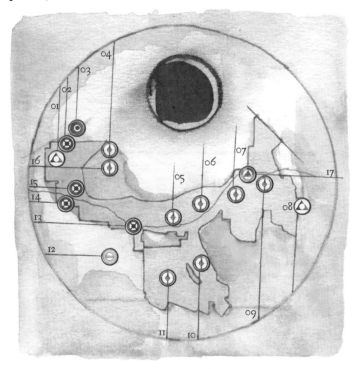

The legislation of the Mojave Trails National Monument emerged from the all-too-often cacophonous discourse of 21st-century American politics. This consolidation of older land designations emerges as a shining beacon exemplifying the potential of federal efforts to focus forward-thinking policy. This 1.6-million-acre (2,500-square-mile) monument does not belong to us, but to our grandchildren.

01. Cady Mountains
02. Afton Canyon
03. Baker
04. Kelso Dunes Wilderness
05. Trilobite Wilderness
06. Clipper Mountain Wilderness
07. Piute Mountains Wilderness
08. Lobeck's Pass
09. Bigelow Cholla Garden Wilderness
10. Cadiz Dunes Wilderness
11. Sheephole Valley Wilderness
12. Twentynine Palms Marine Reserve
13. Amboy Crater
14. Pisgah Crate
15. Sleeping Beauty Valley
16. Bristol Mountains Wilderness
17. Interstate 40

Map 06.08 Joshua Tree National Park

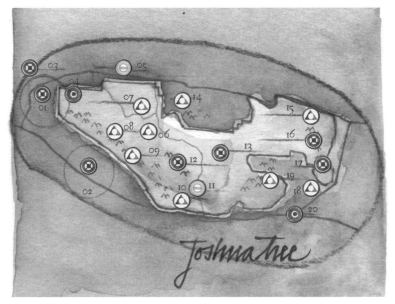

Joshua Tree National Park encompasses habitat exemplifying both the Mojave and the Colorado Deserts. From the pinyon pine–covered uplands of the Little San Bernardino Mountains, and down into the cholla cactus–dotted lowlands of the Pinto Basin, the park's rich ecological portfolio showcases a wide variety of what the California Desert has to offer. The iconic plant that has lent its name to the park, the Joshua tree, can be found in dense stands from the town of Joshua Tree and along the park's northern border. Joshua trees are one of the keystone plants defining the Mojave ecoregion. Joshua trees don't exist in the southern half of the park.

01. Monongo Valley and the Sand to Snow National Monument
02. Coachella Valley
03. Yucca Valley to Pioneertown
04. Joshua Tree
05. Twentynine Palms
06. Hexie Mountains and Lost Horse Valley
07. Queen Mountain (5,677 feet), Joshua Tree Wilderness
08. Keys View
09. Monument Mountain (4,834 feet)
10. Cottonwood Pass (2,800 feet)
11. Cottonwood Visitor's Center
12. Cholla Cactus Garden
13. Pinto Basin
14. Twentynine Palms Mountain (4,562 feet)
15. Aqua Peak (4,416 feet)
16. Pinto Wells
17. Desert Lily Preserve
18. Eagle Mountain (1,280 feet)
19. Eagle Mountains and the Big Wash
20. Desert Center

Map 06.09 Sand to Snow National Monument

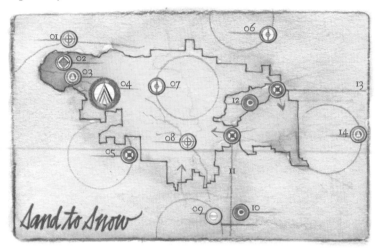

Sand to Snow, designated as a national monument in 2016, is a necessary wildlife corridor up the east face of San Gorgonio, connecting Joshua Tree National Park with the San Gorgonio Wilderness across the Morongo Preserve.

01. Santa Ana River
02. Forsee Creek
03. San Bernardino National Forest
04. San Gorgonio (11,502 feet)

05. Mill Creek Canyon
06. Bighorn Mountain Wilderness
07. San Gorgonio Wilderness
08. South fork of the Whitewater River
09. Morongo Reservation
10. Palm Springs
11. Big Morongo Canyon wildlife corridor
12. Morongo Valley
13. Little San Bernardino Mountains wildlife corridor
14. Joshua Tree National Park

mojave tortoise
gopherus agassizii

Map 06.10 The Amargosa Basin

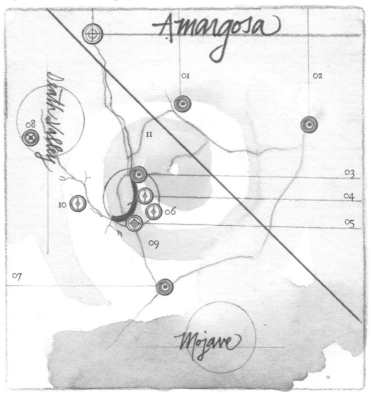

20 miles

06.10

The Amargosa River Basin is a string of jewel-like oases that stretches for 175 miles along the border of California and Nevada. Although most of the Amargosa River flows underground, it supports vast networks of endemic riparian habitats that feed a host of endangered species, including the Devil's Hole pupfish, Amargosa toad, and Ash Meadows gumplant.

01. Pahrump, Nevada
02. Las Vegas, Nevada
03. Tecopa
04. Amargosa Canyon and the
    Dumont Dunes Natural Area
05. Amargosa River
    Wild and Scenic River

06. Amargosa River Area of
    Critical Environmental Concern
07. Baker
08. Badwater Basin
09. Silurian Valley
10. Death Valley Wilderness
11. Highway 178

Map 06.11 The Salton Sea

20 miles

06.11

An ecological disaster, a ghost, an accident: The Salton Sea is only 100 years old, a hypersaline lake maintained by runoff from agricultural irrigation that has no outlets. Because of its location in an area of high evaporation, the lake has been incessantly accumulating soluble salts and insoluble additives its whole life. Once one of the most productive ecosystems in North America, hosting 100 million fish, the Salton Sea is now sick and flounders without a recovery plan.

Gila woodpecker
Melanerpes uropygialis

Map 06.12 The Colorado and Sonoran Deserts

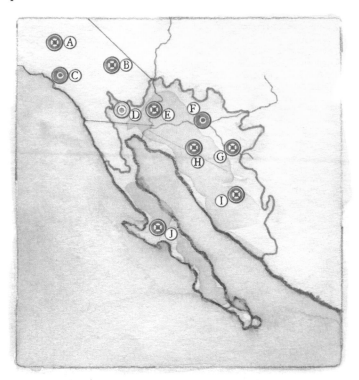

100 miles

06.12

California's Colorado Desert is a small part of the larger Sonoran Desert. It encompasses approximately seven million acres, including the heavily irrigated Coachella and Imperial Valleys. The Colorado Desert is home to many unique terrestrial habitats. Among the yucca and cholla cactus, the desert saltbush, and the sandy soil grasslands, vernal wildflowers bloom in micro-ecoregions that support a surprisingly high level of biodiversity. Higher elevations are dominated by pinyon and juniper forest, with areas of manzanita and even small pockets of Coulter pine.

More than half of the desert's plant species are herbaceous annuals, and timely winter rains feed great fields of early spring wildflowers under the smoketree, ironwood, and palo verde trees. In the Sonoran and Colorado Deserts, populations of mule deer, bobcat, desert kangaroo rat, cactus mouse, black-tailed jackrabbit, Gambel's quail, and red-diamond rattlesnake tough out the harsh climate.

The Colorado Desert is home to precarious numbers of endangered wildlife species, including the flat-tailed horned lizard, Coachella Valley fringe-toed lizard, desert tortoise, prairie falcon, Andrew's dune scarab beetle, peninsular bighorn sheep, and California leaf-nosed bat.

A. California
B. Mojave Desert
C. Los Angeles
D. Salton Basin
E. Colorado Desert
F. Phoenix
G. Arizona
H. Sonoran Desert
I. Mexico
J. Baja California

tarantula
Aphonopelma smithi

Map 06.13 The Kingston Range

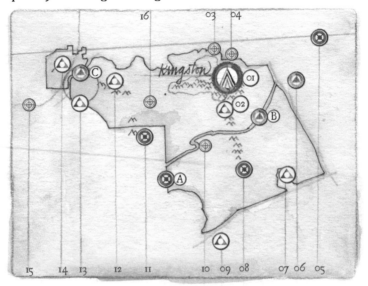

9 miles

06.13

With known habitat for over 500 plant species, the Kingston Range is one of the most botanically rich areas of the desert. In this ecological transition zone, the creosote-dominant Mojave Desert begins to transform into the sagebrush-dominant Great Basin Desert.

01. Kingston Peak (7,323 feet)
02. Kingston Range Ridge
03. Crystal Spring
04. Horse Thief Spring
05. Inyo–San Bernardino county line
06. Excelsior Mine Road
07. Shadow Mountain
08. Kingston Wash
09. Turquoise Mountain
10. Kingston Spring

11. Valjean Valley
12. Dumont Hills
13. Dumont Dunes
14. Sperry Hills
15. Amargosa River
16. Rabbit Holes Spring

A. Border of the Kingston Range Wilderness
B. Kingston Range Road
C. Smith Talc Road

Map 06.14 Castle Mountains National Monument

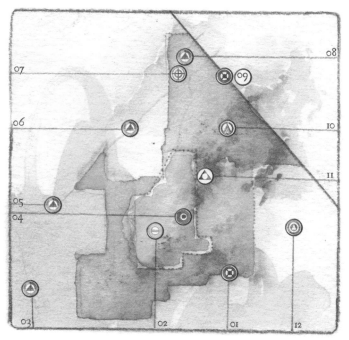

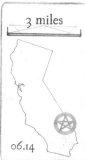

3 miles

06.14

At 21,000 acres, Castle Mountains is the smallest of the Mojave's national parks and monuments. Designated in 2016, it is also one of the newest. This remote landscape of rock formations and limited vegetation is surrounded on three sides by the Mojave National Preserve.

01. National Monument border
02. Historical boundary of the Hart Mining District
03. Ivanpah Road
04. Hart Mine town ruin
05. Castle Mountains Road
06. Mine Hart Road
07. Stagecoach Springs
08. Walking Box Ranch Road
09. Nevada state border
10. Hart Peak (5,543 feet)
11. Castle Peaks
12. Mojave National Preserve

Map 06.15 View of Castle Peaks from Hart Peak

01 02   03   04   05

01. Peak 1
02. Peak 2
03. Peak 2.5
04. Dove Beach Mark
05. North Castle Butte

This map depicts the view of Castle Peaks south from Hart Peak. Castle Mountains National Monument is not currently accessible by any paved roads. Surrounded on three sides by the Mojave National Preserve, it includes a portion of the Lanfair Valley watershed and provides critical habitat for a variety of rare desert flora and fauna.

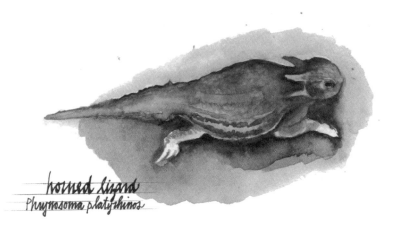

horned lizard
Phrynosoma platyrhinos

chuckwalla
Sauromalus ater

Jackrabbit
Lepus californicus

Map 06.16 Death Valley National Park

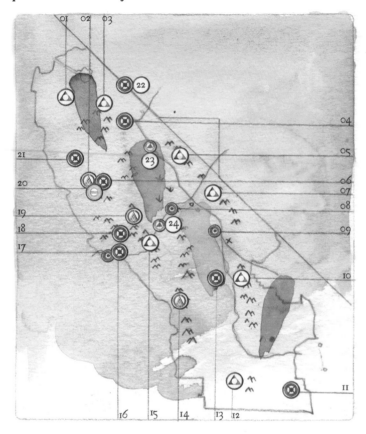

18 miles

06.16

Death Valley is part of the largest national park outside of Alaska. There is nothing dull about this diverse landscape and complex topography, which includes salt flats that harbor tiny populations of desert pupfish, sand dunes that get dusted with colorful coats of spring wildflowers, badlands where bighorn sheep have roamed for 100,000 years, scrub valleys where coyotes and roadrunners thrive, hidden riparian greenery for a host of water-loving creatures you would never expect to see here, colorful mineral deposits over a billion years old, mountains that rival the tallest in California, and basins that dip well below sea level. Almost all of the park—95 percent—is designated federal wilderness area.

01. Saline Range
02. Ubehebe Peak (5,678 feet)
03. Dry Mountain (8,674 feet)
04. Grapevine Ranger Station
05. Grapevine Peak (8,738 feet)
06. Cottonwood Mountains
07. Chloride Cliff (4,760 feet)
08. Stovepipe Wells
09. Furnace Creek
10. Funeral Peak (6,384 feet)
11. Inyo/San Bernardino county line
12. Sugarloaf Peak (4,820 feet)
13. Amargosa River

14. Panamint Range
15. Towne Pass (4,963 feet)
16. Panamint Valley
17. Panamint Springs (1,940 feet)
18. Darwin Plateau
19. Hunter Mountain (7,365 feet)
20. Homestake Camp
21. Saline Valley
22. Nevada State border
23. Mesquite Flat
24. Emigrant Canyon

Pronghorn
Antilocapra americana

Map 06.17 Anza Borrego State Park

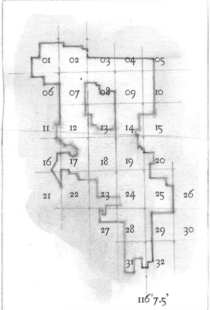

22 miles

06.17

116°7.5'

Sit on one of the miles-wide bajadas in the springtime at the center of the park and watch the low yucca plateau burst stalks ten feet tall, transforming the place into a forest unlike any other on Earth. Anza Borrego, the largest of California's state parks, is a cache of geophysical treasures, including multiple fossil sites, pre-Columbian pictographic rock art sites, bighorn sheep habitats, native desert palm oases, and rare ironwood forests, and it hosts a unique and dramatic seasonal wildflower display.

01. Bucksnort Mountain (5,984 feet)
02. Collins Valley
03. Clark Lake
04. Rabbit Peak (6,640 feet)
05. Desert Shores
06. Hot Springs Mountain (6,533 feet)
07. Borrego Palm Canyon
08. Clark Lake
09. Fonts Point
10. Seventeen Palms
11. Ranchita
12. Tubb Canyon
13. Borrego Sink
14. Borrego Mountain (1,207 feet)
15. Shell Reef
16. Julian
17. Earthquake Valley
18. Whale Peak (5,349 feet)
19. Harper Canyon
20. Lower Borrego Valley
21. Cuyamaca Peak (6,512 feet)
22. Monument Peak (6,271 feet)
23. Aqua Caliente Spring
24. Arroyo Tapiado
25. Coyote Mountains Wilderness
26. Plaster City
27. Carrizo Gorge Wilderness
28. Sweeney Pass
29. Jacumba Mountains Wilderness
30. Painted Gorge
31. Jacumba
32. In-Ko-Pah Gor

Map 06.18 The Great Basin

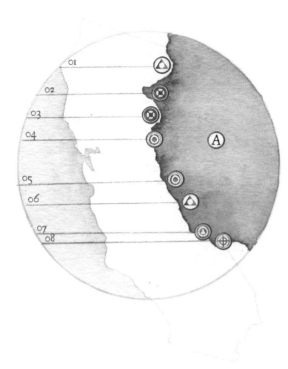

A. The Great Basin Desert, red, and its western border in California

01. The Warner Mountains; Modoc County

02. Madelaine Plains; Lassen County

03. Sierra Valley; Sierra County

04. Lake Tahoe

05. Mono Lake

06. The While Mountains; Inyo County

07. Death Valley National Park

08. Amargosa River

A sharp, cold breeze moves across the sagebrush as you rise out of Mono Valley into the Bodie Hills and winter on the Great Basin Desert. A thick, gray mat of fragrant sagebrush extends in all directions with no relief from the monotonous rhythm. Travel on and you'll see purple mountains on the horizon, or maybe you'll come to the edge of a river canyon on a plateaued mesa; the canyon will most likely be dry. The gray land is reflected by a gray sky that never offers rain, but might bring snow. For all of the Great Basin's desolation, the swelling of a silent poetry resounds, and the imminent weight of vastness before the endless, rolling plain to the east brings a unique sublimation to the permitting heart.

The Great Basin Desert climbs into California at a few points along the state's eastern flank, including Modoc County, Lassen County, Mono County, Inyo County, and the northeastern edge of San Bernardino County. Most of the state of Nevada is in the Great Basin Desert, a region so called because it has no river outlets to the sea.

07. OF WILDLIFE & WILD GARDENS

Douglas iris
Iris douglasiana

In the era of protected parks, in which wildlife is segregated from other populations of perhaps the same species across miles of urban obstacles, we see the need to protect island communities of threatened wildlife. Ecologists refer to these populations as either evolutionarily significant units or distinct population segments. Both are scientific classifications that are useful in the consideration of conservation action. An evolutionarily significant unit is any species, subspecies, geographic race, or population that has an established habitat in a given ecosystem. A distinct population segment may be a tiny but reliably noted occurrence of an endangered species; in fact, it may be a single nesting site, a den, or even a wildflower.

Among biologists, the question of conservation quickly brings up the question: what actually is a species? Surely we can see the morphological difference between a bear and a mountain lion, but what amount of time is needed for subspecies to hybridize enough to be classified as a single species? Or, conversely, when a species is divided, how long does it take before quantifiable observations are enough to classify a new species, or at least a new subspecies? The answers to these questions, like most in ecology, have as many exceptions as they do rules—especially in California, where biologists are contemplating the status of thousands and thousands of wildlife species.

According to *The Jepson Manual: Vascular Plants of California*, 5,862 species of native plants and 1,023 species of foreign plants have been introduced during human colonization in the past 400 years. Regardless of individual species name, the best way to understand plants and their ecology is to learn the plant families. The six most common plant families in California are: Asteraceae (the sunflower family), Poaceae (the grass family), Fabaceae (the pea family), Scrophulariaceae (the figwort family), Brassicaceae (the mustard family), and Cyperaceae (the sedge family).

Northern pintail
Anas acuta

Map 07.01 Endangered Wildlife

Wildlife conservation in the 21st century is a daunting challenge; it often feels hopeless. However, there are legal tools for those who hear the call to help protect sustainable populations of wildlife. The most famous of these legal tools is the federal Endangered Species Act of 1973. In addition to providing a listed designation of both threatened and endangered species of plants and animals, the act states that the government is compelled to assist in the protection of those species and their habitats. The statute is meant to prevent extinction of vulnerable plant and animal species, primarily through development of recovery plans and protection of critical habitat. The enforcement of this law is the responsibility of the U.S. Fish and Wildlife Service and the National Marine Fisheries Service. There have been a number of success stories of recovery that involve endangered species over the past several decades. Here are four.

01. El Segundo blue butterfly: The entire species population was reduced to 1,000 individuals in the 1970s, but it has been saved from extinction by restoration efforts that by 2011 had steadily increased the population at the Airport Dunes to 123,000.

02. Southern sea otter: The population was reduced to 50 in 1914. After being listed under the Endangered Species Act in 1977, the population now stands at 3,000.

03. Peregrine falcon: Yosemite National Park has the highest peregrine falcon nesting density in the world, and now it enjoys habitat statewide; the population was reduced to 324 individuals in 1975 and listed as endangered in 1970; today, there are approximately 3,500 nesting pairs.

04. Humpback whale: In the mid-1960s, only 1,200 individuals swam in the North Pacific. After being listed as endangered in 1970, the population has recovered to more than 22,000 members.

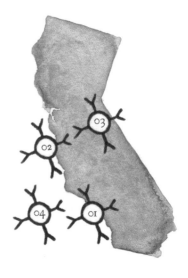

Northern Goshawk
Accipiter gentilis

Map 07.02 California's Endangered Landscapes

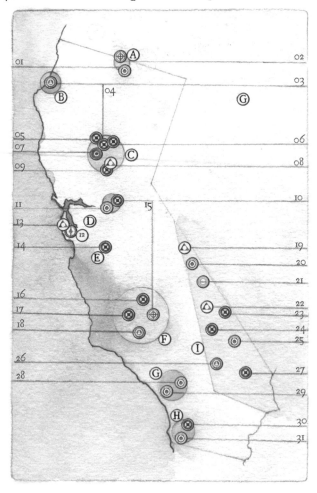

Thirty-one examples over nine bioregions exemplify California's resilient ability to sustain delicate ecosystems despite the ever-encroaching and potentially disastrous pressures of a legion of threats, including but not limited to pollution, human population growth, invasive species, a changing climate, and wildfire regime cycle shift. Despite all of this, these wild gardens remain intact and continue to exhibit ancient, living-network systems that represent an earlier, perhaps more pristine version of California.

Region A:
South Cascades plateau and the
freshwater marshes of the Great Basin

> 01. Tule Lake
> 02. Lower Klamath River Basin

Region B:
North Coast old-growth redwood forest
and the big tree groves in the land of
salmon

> 03. Prairie Creek

Region C:
Sacramento River Valley and the grand
highways of avian migration

> 04. Delevan
> 05. Logandale
> 06. Graylodge and Butte Sink
> 07. Colusa
> 08. Sutter Buttes
> 09. Collins Eddy

Region D:
Riparian forests of the Inland Delta and
the delicate, brackish waterways

> 10. Woodbridge
> 11. The Delta
> 12. Palo Alto Baylands

Region E:
Coastal sage scrub and the rare flowers of
the San Francisco Peninsula

> 13. San Bruno Mountain
> 14. Los Banos Grande Riparian
>   Inland Forest

Region F:
Grasslands of the South Valley and the
elk habitats along the Coast Ranges

> 15. Kern River
> 16. LoKern Plains
> 17. Elkhorn Plains
> 18. Carrizo Plains

Region G:
Southland old growth and the mountains
that remember the grizzly

> 28. Lake Arrowhead
> 29. Upper Newport tidal
>   marshes

Region H:
Sun-swept coastal forest and the rare
pine forests of the peninsular ranges

> 30. Hollenbeck Canyon
> 31. Tijuana Slough

Region I:
The staircase of the desert from the
Colorado up the spine of the Sierra

> 19. Bodie Bluff
> 20. Mono Lake and Basin
> 21. Fish Slough
> 22. Panamint Range
> 23. Stovepipe Wells
> 24. Great Falls Basin
> 25. Tecopa Amargosa Marsh
> 26. Red Rock Canyon
> 27. Kelso Dunes

Map 07.03 Chinook Salmon

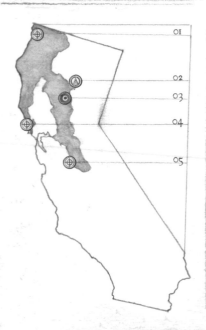

The California runs are the southern-most runs of the Chinook. At least 17 distinct runs of Chinook salmon are recognized in California.

There are fall-run Chinook salmon in coastal streams from Cape Blanco in Oregon south to the Klamath River in Oregon, and finally to the Russian River in California.

The range on this map represents the potential habitat extent of the Chinook salmon across the stream networks of Northern and Central California. Listed below are a few landmarks that delineate the current range.

01. Mouth of the Klamath River
02. Mount Lassen
03. Chico
04. Russian River
05. San Joaquin River

Chinook salmon
Oncorhynchus tshawytscha

Map 07.04 Steelhead Salmon

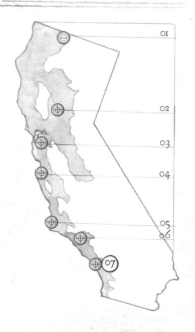

Rainbow trout and steelhead salmon, or steelhead trout, are the same species, but rainbow trout live in fresh water only, whereas steelhead are anadromous. Unlike most salmon, steelhead can survive spawning and can spawn in multiple years.

01. Dam location on the Klamath River representing the contemporary limit to the salmon run inland; the dams on the Klamath are currently scheduled for removal in the next ten years, which will greatly increase steelhead habitat accessibility.
02. Sacramento River Valley
03. Alameda Creek
04. Salinas River
05. Santa Maria River
06. Santa Clara River
07. Santa Ana River

Steelhead salmon
Oncorhynchus mykiss irideus

Map 07.05 Coho Salmon

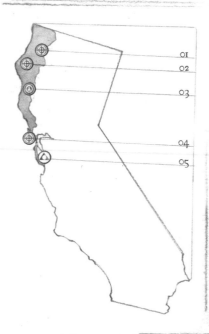

Coho salmon are also called silver salmon. When in the ocean, Coho salmon have silver sides and dark-blue backs; when they return to fresh water to spawn, their jaws and teeth become hooked and they develop bright-red sides and bluish-green and dark spots on their backs. The Coho salmon population in the Northern California region has declined from an estimated 400,000 naturally spawning fish in the 1940s to fewer than 10,000 naturally producing adults today. The range on this map represents the potential habitat extent of the Coho salmon across the stream networks of Northern California.

01. Trinity River
02. Eel River
03. Berryessa Snow Mountain National Monument and the headwaters of the Eel
04. Redwood Creek
05. Santa Cruz Mountains

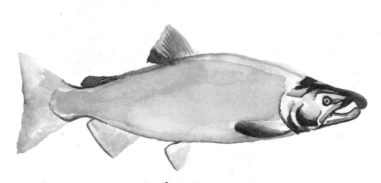

Coho salmon
Oncorhynchus kisutch

Map 07.06 Mountain Lions

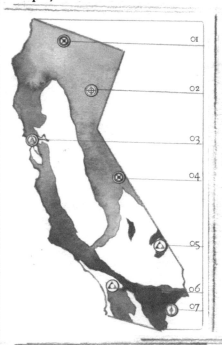

More than half of California is mountain lion habitat. Mountain lions live in many different types of habitat in California, from deserts to humid Coast Range forests, and from sea level to 10,000-foot elevations. They generally will be most abundant in areas with plentiful deer. Estimates of the mountain lion population in California vary between 4,000 and 6,000.

The range on this map represents the habitat extent where mountain lions thrive:

01. Shasta Valley
02. The four forks of the Feather River
03. Mount Tamalpais
04. Mono Valley
05. New York Mountains
06. Santa Ana Mountains
07. Big Maria Wilderness

mountain lion
Puma concolor

Map 07.07 Red Foxes

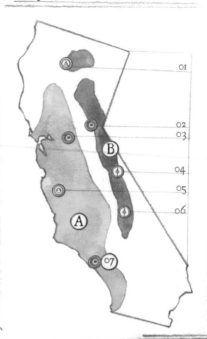

The nonnative red fox is an intruder. Not to be confused with the native Sierra Nevada red fox, a threatened species found only in the Sierra Nevada and Cascade mountain ranges, the European red fox was introduced decades ago for fox hunting and fur farming. Their populations have grown over time and spread throughout the Sacramento Valley to other lowland areas and to the coast.

A. Range of the invasive red fox
B. Range of the native red fox

01. Mount Shasta
02. Nevada City
03. Sacramento
04. Ansel Adams Wilderness
05. Pinnacles National Park
06. Golden Trout Wilderness
07. Los Angeles

red fox
Vulpes vulpes

Map 07.08 Black Bears

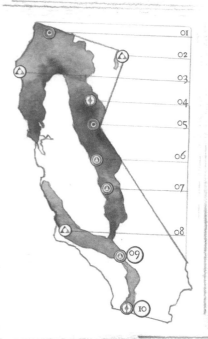

Black bears are distributed throughout much of North America. They are common in California, with an estimated population of about 30,000. They can be found mostly in mountainous areas above 3,000 feet of elevation. Montane hardwood, montane chaparral, and mixed conifer forests sustain large bear populations. Other habitat types, such as valley foothill hardwood, provide seasonally important habitat.

01. Happy Camp
02. Warner Mountains
03. Kings Range
04. Bucks Wilderness
05. Truckee
06. Yosemite National Park
07. Sequoia National Park
08. Sierra Madre Mountains
09. Sand to Snow National Monument
10. Hauser Wilderness

Black bear
Ursus americanus

Map 07.09 Condors

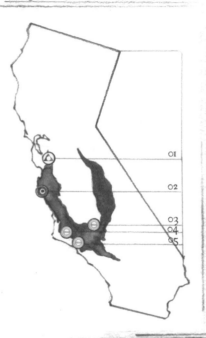

In 1987, all remaining wild California condors—27 individuals in total—were captured in an attempt to save the species. The original group now numbers well over 300, and a reintroduction program has begun across the coastal mountains of Central and Southern California.

This map indicates major reintroduction sites as well as the condor's current potential range, where recent sightings have been recorded.

01. The Diablo Range
02. Big Sur
03. Tejon Ranch
04. Sisquoc Condor Sanctuary
05. Sespe Condor Sanctuary

California condor
Gymnogyps californianus

Map 07.10 Mountain Kingsnakes

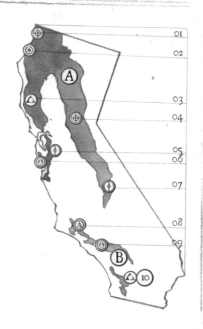

Two different species are developing in an example of isolated populations going through speciation, a common process in the history of California's biodiverse portfolio.

A. Lampropeltis zonata is larger and more aggressive than its southern cousin.

B. Lampropeltis multifasciata is composed of all populations in the Peninsular Ranges and in the Transverse Ranges.

Listed below are areas of known concentrations of both subspecies:
01. Mouth of the Smith River
02. Humboldt Bay
03. Mayacamas Mountains
04. Yuba River Valleys
05. Ohlone Wilderness
06. Big Basin State Park
07. Domeland Wilderness
08. Mount Pinos
09. San Gabriel National Monument
10. Santa Rosa Mountains

mountain kingsnake
Lampropeltis zonata

Map 07.11 Desert Pupfish

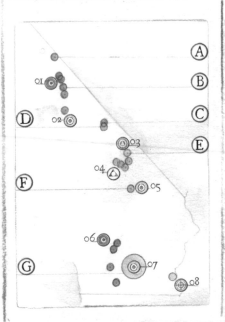

The story of the last stand of the desert pupfish is the story of a tough little fish that does not mind extremes of temperature and salinity. Seven subspecies exist in isolated populations across the Mojave. Now on the brink of extinction, only through aggressive conservation efforts will any of these populations remain in the near future.

01. Bishop
02. Owens Lake (dry lakebed)
03. Death Valley National Park
04. Avawatz Mountains
05. Soda Lake
06. Palm Springs
07. Salton Sea
08. Colorado River

Noted in this map, indicated by differing colors, are the general locations of individual ponds and specific intermittent streams across the California desert where the seven isolated subspecies of pupfish make their homes.

40 miles

07.11

A. Amargosa pupfish (*Cyprinodon nevadensis armargosae*)
B. Owens pupfish (*C. radiosus*)
C. Salt Creek pupfish (*C. salinus*)
D. Cottonball Marsh pupfish (*C. salinus milleri*)
E. Shoshone pupfish (*C. nevadensis shoshone*)
F. Saratoga Springs pupfish (*C. nevadensis nevadensis*)
G. Salton Desert pupfish (*C. macularius*)

desert pupfish
Cyprinodon ssp.

Map 07.12 Tiger Salamanders

California tiger salamanders have survived in vernal pools for millions of years, but now they are on the endangered species list in a rapidly drying state with less and less habitat. There are several distinct populations of California tiger salamanders that may represent different species: the populations in Sonoma County and the one in Santa Barbara County are endangered, and the Central California population is threatened.

A partial list of critical, endangered habitat includes:

01. Dunnigan Creek, Yolo County
02. Jepson Prairie, Sonoma County
03. San Joaquin River, Northern
04. Santa Clara Valley
05. San Joaquin River, Southern
06. Ana Creek, San Benito County
07. Proposed Tiger Salamander
    Sanctuary, Santa Barbara County
08. Petaluma Marsh, Sonoma County

California tiger salamander
Ambystoma californiense

Map 07.13 Kangaroo Rats

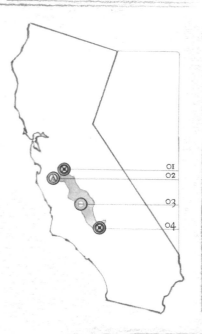

It is hard to find a kangaroo rat on nights when any moon at all shines down on the valley floor. At just four inches long, the largely nocturnal kangaroo rat is the smallest rodent in its genus, and it knows better than to chase seeds in anything but total darkness. Its tail ends with a large tuft of fur and is longer than its head and body combined. Kangaroo rats don't run, but bounce like their namesake, using their tails for balance.

There are only a few habitats left that carry viable populations of kangaroo rats. Known populations still exist only in a few counties of the southern Central Valley, and westward to the crest of the Diablo Mountains.

01. Merced County
02. Pacheco Peak
03. Lemoore Naval Air Station
04. Kern County

San joaquin rat
Dipodymes nitratoides

Map 07.14 Desert Hummingbirds

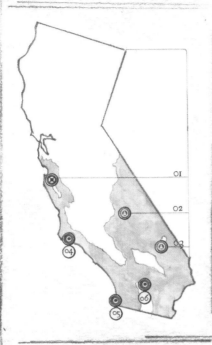

The spring is a very busy time for this diminutive hummingbird. When the first rains hit, the male birds begin their courtship rituals as all members of the species enjoy the nectar-filled flowers that blanket the Mojave and beyond.

On cold nights, despite the desert hummingbird's seemingly endless, frenetic energy, it is able to enter into a torpor in which its heart rate slows and it can conserve some of that sugar-filled energy. The desert hummingbird is also called the purple-throated humming-bird, after a French nobleman.

01. Salinas Valley
02. Red Rock State Park
03. Mojave National Preserve
04. Santa Barbara
05. Palm Springs
06. San Diego

costa's hummingbird
Calypte costae

Map 07.15 Wild Pigs

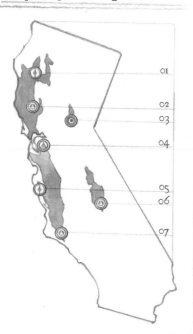

Although wild pigs can be found in 56 of California's 58 counties, this map represents the distribution of significant populations. The pigs arrived here in the early 1700s, when Spanish and Russian settlers used them as livestock, and many escaped and became feral. All experienced travelers to California's backcountry know that if you come across a wild pig, especially a mama pig, you'd better find a tree fast and climb it; this is the only way to be sure to get away from these all-too-often grumpy characters.

01. Yolla Bolly Wilderness
02. Berryessa Snow Mountain National Monument
03. Auburn
04. Mount Diablo
05. Ventana Wilderness
06. Sequoia National Forest
07. Los Padres National Forest

wild pig
Sus scrofa

Map 07.16 Wild Horses

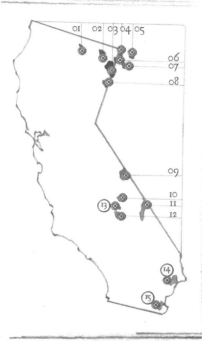

The Bureau of Land Management (BLM) manages wild horses and burros that roam over 9 million acres. The vision is to protect wild horses and burros, while ensuring that their populations are managed to maintain or restore a thriving ecological balance. California's appropriate management level is currently 1,746 horses and 453 burros.

01. Red Rock Lakes
02. Devil's Garden
03. Twin Peaks
04. Carter Reservoir
05. Bitner
06. Nut Mountain
07. Buckhorn
08. Fort Sage
09. Piper Mountain
10. Waucobe-Hunter Mountains
11. Chicago Valley
12. Centennial
13. Lee Flat
14. Chemehuevi
15. Chocolate-Mule Mountains

wild horse
Equus ferus

The six most common plant families in California are:

A. Brassicaceae (the mustard family)
B. Cyperaceae (the sedge family)
C. Asteraceae (the sunflower family)
D. Poaceae (the grass family)
E. Fabaceae (the pea family)
F. Scrophulariaceae (the figwort family)

elegant Brodiaea (Brodiaea elegans)

Wildflowers of Berryessa Snow Mountain National Monument California

Red Ribbons (Clarkia concinna)

California tidy tips

Jimson Weed (Datura wrightii)

Layia platyglossa

Blue oak, Quercus douglasii

Map 07.17 California Floristic Province

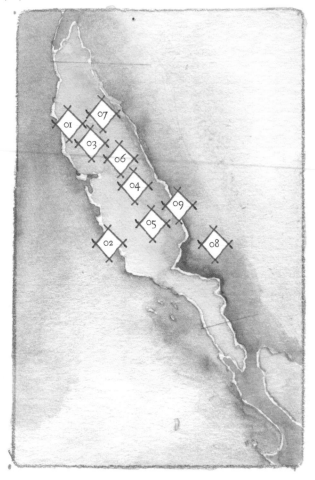

Nearly one-fourth of all plants found in North America north of Mexico, and more than in any other state, grow in California. More than 6,000 species of native flowering plants, conifers, and ferns grow in what is called the California Floristic Province. The province includes the Siskiyou Mountains to the north, so its border slips into the southern extremes of Oregon; to the south, it includes some peninsular species, extending slightly into Mexico. It does not include the Desert Floristic Province of both the Mojave and the Great Basin, which includes botanical patterns that are best developed outside the state.

The nine classifications depicted here describe how the California Floristic Province applies generally to the zonation of vegetation, in both shrubland and forestland across the state.

01. Coastal forest: From south of Big Sur up to the Oregon border, the coastal forest is defined by coast redwood, often with Douglas fir and accompanied by closed-cone pines, most regularly bishop and knobcone pine.

02. Coastal sage scrub: Scrubland along the coast in Northern California often, when mixed with forestland, includes cypress and is dominated by coyote brush. In the south, artemisia and salvia are dominant.

red paintbrush
Castilleja affinis

03. Chaparral: Scrubland that is regulated by a true Mediterranean climate of hot summers and a predictable rainy season, populated mainly by wood shrubs, is California chaparral. These shrubs include juniper, chamise, scrub oak, and manzanita.

04. Great Valley grassland: Over the centuries, the oak-dotted valley prairies and wetlands have been wholly converted to agriculture.

05. Valley woodland forest: Low-elevation forests climb the sides of the valley bowl toward the ridgelines; these forests are made up of many types of conifers, including pines, firs, cedars, and junipers.

06. Montane forest: High-elevation forests are sparse and rocky, with often-isolated populations of rare conifers clinging to granitic mountaintops.

07. Sagebrush scrub: The landscape that dominates the basin and range country of the West. Sagebrush artemisia dominates the dry horizon across many states.

08. Creosote bush scrub: This is the ecotype that defines the Mojave Desert. Creosote bush often lives with Joshua tree in the High Desert and without it in the Low (Colorado) Desert.

09. Pinyon-juniper woodland: The two trees in the this type of desert forest can be found supporting ecosystems as far south as the New York Mountains in the Mojave, and as far north as mountainous slopes near Mono Lake.

Map 07.18 California's Wildflower Gardens

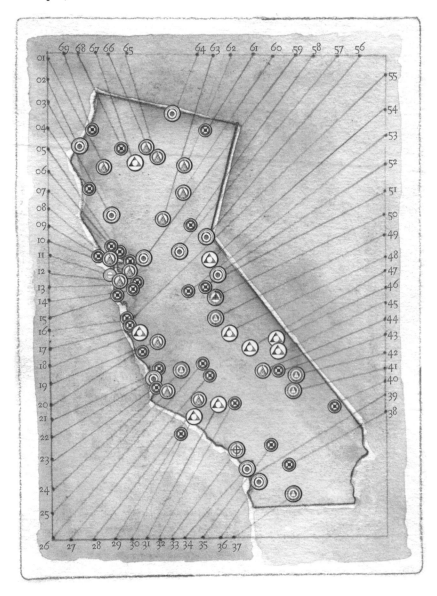

01. Red Mountain
02. Humboldt Bay salt marshes
03. Boggs Lake
04. Pygmy forest of Mendocino
05. Santa Rosa plain
06. Vine Hill barrens
07. Antioch dunes
08. Point Reyes Peninsula
09. Mount Tamalpais
10. Mount Diablo
11. San Francisco Presidio
12. San Bruno Mountain
13. San Antonio Valley
14. Santa Clara Valley
15. Bonny Doon sandhills
16. Monterey Bay dunes
17. Monterey pine-cypress forest
18. Santa Lucia Mountains
19. San Benito Mountain
20. Big Sur sage scrub
21. Arroyo de la Cruz
22. Morro Bay
23. Cuesta Ridge West
24. Carrizo Plain
25. Figueroa Mountain
26. South Valley saltbush scrub
27. Guadalupe-Nipomo dunes
28. Mount Pinos
29. Northern Channel Islands
30. Santa Monica Mountains
31. San Gabriel Mountains
32. Pebble Plains of Big Bear Valley
33. Santa Ana River wash
34. Newport Bay salt marsh
35. Western Riverside County
36. San Diego vernal pools
37. Anza Borrego
38. Santa Rosa Plateau
39. Torrey Pine Forest
40. Eastern Mojave
41. Red Rock Canyon
42. Death and Panamint Valley
43. Owens Valley
44. Owens Peak
45. Inyo Mountains

46. White Mountains
47. Piute Range
48. Red Hills of Tuolumne County
49. Giant Sequoia
50. The John Muir Trail
51. Valley oak forest
52. Winnemucca Lake
53. San Joaquin grasslands
54. Pine Hill
55. Fort Ord
56. Lake Tahoe Basin
57. Sacramento Valley vernal pools
58. Sierra Valley
59. Sacramento River Valley
60. North Table Mountain
61. Modoc Plateau
62. Lassen Peak
63. Sutter Buttes
64. Tule Lake
65. Mount Shasta
66. Mount Eddy
67. Yolla Bolly Mountains
68. Bear Valley
69. The Lanphere-Christensen dunes

alpine shooting star
Dodecatheon alpinum

hummingbird sage
Salvia spathacea

Map 07.19 Wildflower Epicenter Study: The Carrizo Plain

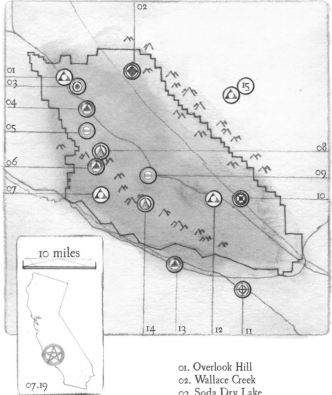

10 miles

07.19

Home to one of California's largest collections of rare plants and flowers, the Carrizo Plain is probably reminiscent of what the Great Central Valley used to be like. During a beautiful spring bloom, a colorful living carpet covers the whole valley and the Carrizo Plain scintillates in a prismatic spray of tiny, happy flowers. John Muir once wrote that in walking across the valley during March, April, and May, one footstep would press about a hundred flowers.

01. Overlook Hill
02. Wallace Creek
03. Soda Dry Lake
04. Soda Lake Road
05. Goodwin Education Center
06. Caliente Ridge Trail
07. Caliente Range
08. Painted Rock (2,321 feet)
09. KCL Ranch campground
10. San Andreas Fault
11. Cuyama River
12. Elkhorn Scarp
13. Highway 166
14. Caliente Mountain (5,106 feet)
15. Temblor Range

Map 07.20 Wildflower Epicenter Study: Mount Figueroa

Beneath the open oak and pine forests near the isolated peak of Mount Figueroa, a fantastic display of spring flowers opens across the warm, wet hillsides. Throughout the spring, the purple of the sky lupine (*Lupinus*) and the contrasting orange of the poppy (*Eschscholzia*) vie for the attention of massive numbers of pollinators. Late March brings out the early bloomers, the shooting stars (*Dodecatheon*); in April and May come the chocolate lilies (*Fritilaria*) and paintbrush (*Castilleja*).

01. Nira Campground
02. Davy Brown Campground
03. Munch Canyon
04. Davy Brown Creek
05. Figueroa Peak (4,528 feet)

06. Figueroa Campground
07. Figueroa Mountain Road
08. Ranger Peak
09. Cachuma Saddle
10. Cachuma Creek

3 miles

Mount Figueroa
Wildflower Peak

07.20

o8. OF PARKS & PROTECTION

John Muir
California's first conservationist

Map 08.01 California's Protected Lands

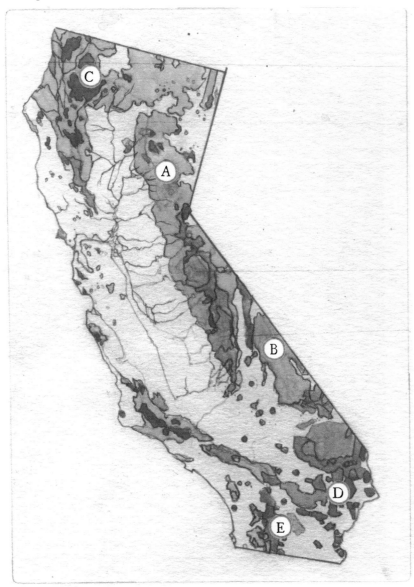

The parks and other protected public lands of California provide an inventory manifest of the rewilding effort. While the industrial character of America, both as an individual and as a concept, was tempered with wilderness and park legislation in the 20th century, the environmentalist in the 21st century wonders if more federal legislation by itself will be enough to fend off the continued threats to land conservation. If the aim is to conserve sufficient habitat to ensure the long-term survival of at least a healthy modicum of California's biodiversity, will these islands of protection, so isolated from other populations across difficult traverses of human society, support the general populations of wildlife enough to accomplish what we need them to? Whatever the case, at this point, we have a rigorous legal network to defend a growing portfolio of protected lands, and understanding the general outline of the park system is a necessary component to being an active wildlife defender in the 21st century.

In the interest of conservation, preservation, resource allocation, or recreation, wild lands in California operate under the management of federal, state, regional, or private agencies. The main categories of land protection include a range of legal designations that carry their own sets of laws for land use.

The categories of natural land protection include national parks, national monuments, federal wilderness areas, state parks, state forests, state game refuges, state game reserves, areas of critical environmental concern, natural research areas, national scenic trails, wildlife areas, wildlife sanctuaries, wildlife preserves, open space preserves, wild and scenic rivers, national conservation areas, national preserves, regional parks, and regional wilderness areas.

Map 08.01 depicts a scaled diagram of designated and protected natural lands in California, color-coded by management agency.

A. National Forest — light green

B. National Monument or Park — orange

C. Federal Wilderness area managed by the forest service — dark green

D. Federal Wilderness area managed by the Bureau of Land Management — red

E. State Parks — pink

Bobcat
Lynx rufus

Map 08.02 Federal Lands in California

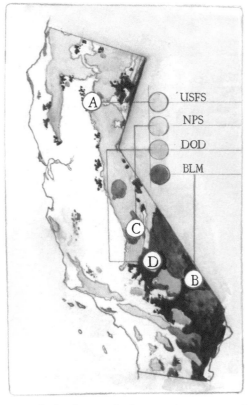

USFS

NPS

DOD

BLM

Federal agencies manage 45 percent of the land in California. The type of land managed by the Forest Service, the Bureau of Land Management, and the National Park Service is called public land, as opposed to private land (which accounts for 55.5 million acres, or 55 percent, of California's total 101 million acres of land).

A. Forest Service land (20.9 million acres, or 20.7 percent): The Forest Service is responsible for managing the national forests, which include the federal wilderness areas in these forests but do not include national or state parks or monuments.

B. Bureau of Land Management land (15.4 million acres, or 15.3 percent): From rangeland to wilderness land, the BLM handles a lot of different land uses, including conservation, recreation, and variance (range land and energy development) designations, and a bunch of land areas legally described as "general public lands."

C. National Park Service land (7.7 million acres, or 7.6 percent): Death Valley, Yosemite, Kings Canyon, Sequoia, Joshua Tree, Mojave, San Gabriel, Sand to Snow, Mojave Trails, and Berryessa Snow Mountain National Monuments are among the huge pieces of California managed by the National Park Service, or in conjunction with the Bureau of Land Management. Together, they represent the largest collection of national parks in the country.

D. Department of Defense land (1.9 million acres, or 1.9 percent): Four branches of the military—the navy, army, marines, and air force—operate large installations in California. Most are in the Mojave Desert, including Fort Irwin, Twentynine Palms, China Lake, Edwards, and the Chocolate Mountains Artillery Range.

Map 08.03 The National Forests

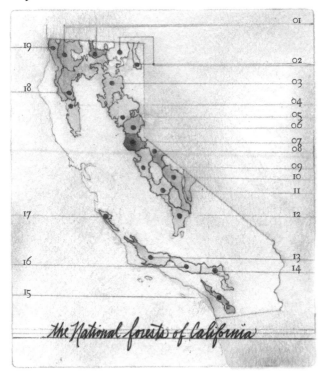

The National forests of California

The mission of the Forest Service is "to sustain the health, diversity, and productivity of the nation's forests and grasslands to meet the needs of present and future generations." The Forest Service manages 19 national forests in California. A national forest is an administrative and not an ecological distinction. It is the job of the Forest Service to monitor, regulate, and balance the resource usage inside the national forests, including the extraction of resources like timber and petrol-based energy; to protect the ecosystems inside living forests; and to provide recreational opportunities.

01. Klamath
02. Modoc
03. Lassen
04. Mendocino
05. Plumas
06. Tahoe
07. El Dorado
08. Toiyabe
09. Stanislaus
10. Inyo

11. Sierra
12. Sequoia
13. Los Padres
    (southern portion)
14. San Bernardino
15. Cleveland
16. San Gabriel
17. Los Padres
    (northern portion)
18. Shasta
19. Six River

Map 08.04 California's Coastal National Monument

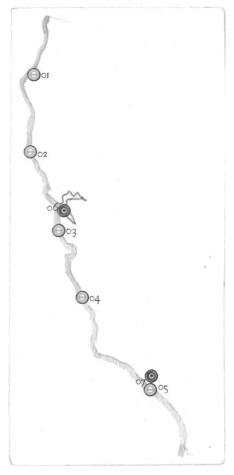

The California Coastal National Monument protects the entire California coast, including all islets, reefs, and rock outcroppings within 12 miles of shore. The California coast is 1,100 miles long, and with an estimated 20,000 outcroppings, the monument protects approximately 2,300 acres of land. There are five access points, called gateways, that offer information to the public about this, the longest and most widely viewed of all national monuments in California: the Trinidad Gateway in Humboldt County, Point Arena Gateway in Mendocino County, Pigeon Point Gateway in Santa Cruz County, Piedras Blancas–San Simeon Gateway in San Luis Obispo County, and Palos Verdes Peninsula Gateway in Los Angeles County.

01. Trinidad Gateway in Humboldt County

02. Point Arena Gateway in Mendocino County

03. Pigeon Point Gateway in Santa Cruz County

04. Piedras Blancas–San Simeon Gateway in San Luis Obispo County

05. Palos Verdes Peninsula Gateway in Los Angeles County

06. San Francisco

07. Los Angeles

Map 08.05 Wild and Scenic Rivers

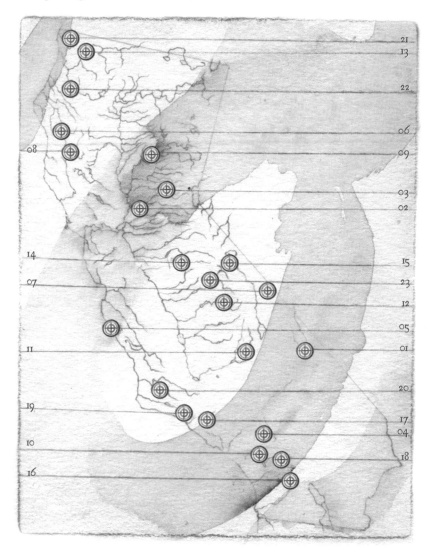

Currently, about 1 percent of California's rivers are designated as wild and scenic. In most cases, only a few miles are given this designation, which preserves the free-flowing nature of rivers, preventing damming, polluting, or any potential disturbing activity in non-federal areas, something the Wilderness Act and other federal designations cannot do.

01. Amargosa River
02. Lower American River
03. North fork of the American River
04. Bautista Creek
05. Big Sur River
06. Black Butte River
07. Cottonwood Creek
08. Eel River
09. Feather River
10. Fuller Mill Creek
11. Kern River
12. Kings River
13. Klamath River
14. Merced River
15. Owens River Headwaters
16. Palm Canyon Creek
17. Piru Creek
18. North fork of the San Jacinto River
19. Sespe Creek
20. Sisquoc River
21. Smith River
22. Trinity River
23. Tuolumne River

sacramento perch
Archoplites interruptus

Cathedral Peak
Yosemite National park

National Monuments versus National Parks

Both national monuments and national parks come into being because of a designation by the president. Theodore Roosevelt's Antiquities Act of 1906 gave the president of the United States the authority to create national monuments from public lands to protect significant natural, cultural, or scientific features. National parks are designated to protect land due to its scenic, inspirational, educational, and recreational value. National monuments are areas that have historical, cultural, or scientific interest. The National Park Service oversees all parks and some monuments. However, the U.S. Forest Service, U.S. Fish and Wildlife Service, National Oceanic and Atmospheric Administration, Department of Defense, and Bureau of Land Management also manage certain monuments, based on their purposes and locations.

Bald eagle
Haliaeetus leucocephalus

Map 08.06 Yosemite National Park

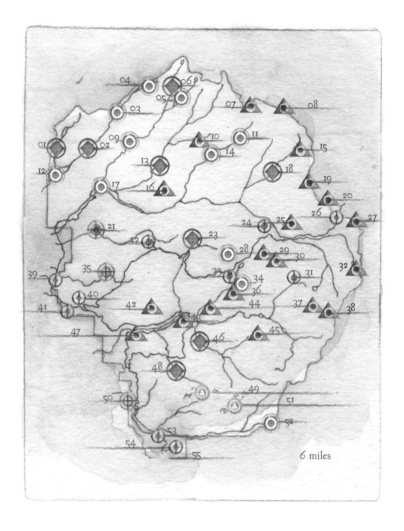

6 miles

6 miles

08.06

Most of the four million people who visit Yosemite every year believe that the seven square miles that make up its granite-walled floor are the majority of what the park has to offer. Those who have spent any amount of time in the paradisiacal backcountry have a much more rewarding, expansive view of the incredible ecological and aesthetic bounty of the land.

The park encompasses 748,000 acres with elevations that range from 2,000 to over 13,000 feet. Yosemite, by any measure, is a revelation of ecological composition and geological wonder. While many tourists have found Yosemite to be the jewel in the crown that are these mountains, those who have studied it at length know that there are actually many Yosemites; dozens of breathtakingly beautiful glacial valleys, filled with light, lay scattered across the entire length of the Sierra Nevada.

01. Kibbie Creek
02. Kendrick Creek
03. Edyth Lake
04. Twin Lakes
05. Tilden Lake
06. Falls Creek
07. Slide Mountain
08. Matterhorn Peak
09. Lake Vernon
10. Piute Mountain
11. Benson Lake
12. Lake Eleanor

13. Rancheria Creek
14. Table Lake
15. Shepherd Crest
16. Rancheria Mountain
17. Hetch Hetchy Reservoir
18. Return Creek
19. Mount Conness
20. Gaylor Peak
21. Middle fork of the Tuolumne River
22. White Wolf
23. Yosemite Creek
24. Little Devils Postpile
25. Lembert Dome
26. Tioga Pass
27. Mount Dana
28. May Lake
29. Cathedral Peak
30. Unicorn Peak
31. Tuolumne Pass
32. Kuna Peak
33. Olmsted Point
34. Tenaya Creek and Lake
35. South fork of the Tuolumne River
36. Clouds Rest
37. Mount Maclure
38. Mount Lyell
39. Oak Flat entrance
40. Tuolumne Grove
41. Merced Grove
42. El Capitan
43. Sentinel Dome
44. Glacier Point
45. Half Dome
46. Illilouette Creek
47. Turtleback Dome
48. Bridalveil Creek
49. Horse Ridge
50. South fork of the Merced River
51. Buena Vista Crest
52. Spotted Lakes
53. Wawona
54. Mariposa Grove
55. South entrance

Map 08.07 Sequoia National Park

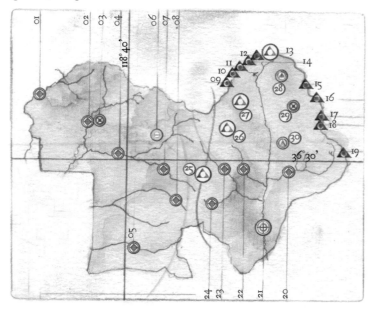

6 miles

08.07

An appreciation of Sequoia National Park could be said to rely on a contemplation of scale. Somewhere between the very large and the very small, the most telling truths of this mysterious wilderness are revealed: the largest trees in the world grow here from seeds inside a cone no larger than a walnut. The big trees themselves, the giant sequoias, are single organisms, but they are so massive that each of them supports an ecosystem of insects, other plants, lichens, birds, and mammals, compelling us to wonder where the individual ends and the community begins. When you gaze up at a sequoia tree, you are also looking back through time for thousands of years; you have an opportunity to consider humanity's impact on the natural world and what respectful stewardship might mean in defense of these grand elders' simple right to continue to live where humanity's decisions to conserve or destroy are becoming ever-more absolute.

01. North fork of the Kaweah River
02. Middle fork of the Kaweah River
03. General Sherman Tree
04. East fork of the Kaweah River
05. South fork of the Kaweah River

06. Bearpaw High Sierra Camp
07. Cliff Creek
08. Mineral Creek arm of
     the Kaweah River
09. Milestone Mountain (13,641 feet)

10. Midway Mountain (13,666 feet)
11. Table Mountain (13,630 feet)
12. Thunder Mountain (13,588 feet)
13. Kings–Kern Divide
14. Mount Jordan (13,344 feet)
15. Mount Barnard (13,990 feet)
16. Tunnabora Peak (13,566 feet)
17. Mount Whitney (14,494 feet)
18. Trail Crest (13,680 feet)
19. Mount Langley (14,042 feet)
20. Rock Creek

21. Kern Canyon and Kern River
22. Chagoopa River
23. Big Arroyo Canyon
24. Soda Creek
25. Great Western Divide
26. Picket Guard Peak (12,302 feet)
27. Kern Point (12,798 feet)
28. John Muir Trail
29. Crabtree Meadow
30. Mount Guyot (12,300 feet)

The view looking southwest from Moro Rock, Sequoia National Park, for approximately 150 miles.

01. Switchback Peak (5,024 feet)
02. Buckeye Hills
03. Milk Ranch Peak (6,250 feet)
04. Ash Peaks Ridge
05. Mitchell Peak (3,574 feet)
06. San Joaquin Valley
07. Temblor Range, Coast Range

Golden crowned kinglet
Regulus satrapa

Map 08.08 Kings Canyon National Park

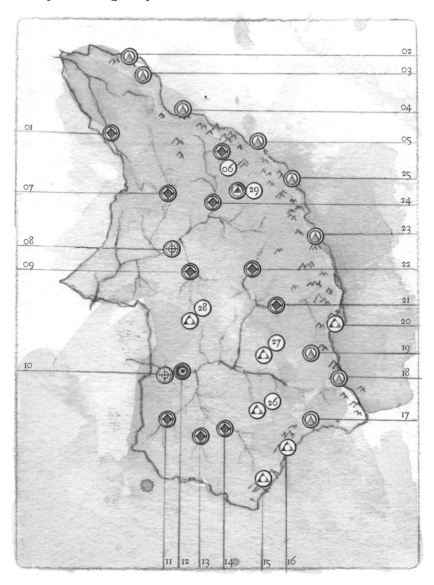

8 miles

08.08

The winding canyon road up the Kings River to Roads End is another in the long list of glacier-carved valleys that compete with Yosemite for top spot as the most immanently beautiful or transcendently sublime. Head up to the high county and marvel at how there is sure no curvilinear shape under heaven that the southern foxtail pine has not been twisted by centuries of wind and snow to become.

01. South fork of the San Joaquin River
02. Mount Goethe (13,264 feet)
03. Mount Darwin (13,830 feet)
04. Bishop Pass and Mount Agassiz (13,891 feet)
05. North Palisade (14,242 feet)
06. Palisade Creek, Pacific Crest Trail
07. Goddard Creek
08. Middle fork of the Kings River
09. Dougherty Creek
10. South fork of the Kings River
11. Sugarloaf Creek
12. Roads End ranger station
13. Ferguson Creek
14. Roaring River
15. Colby Pass (12,000 feet)
16. Thunder Mountain (13,588 feet)
17. Mount Stanford (13,963 feet)
18. Mount Gould (13,005 feet)
19. Mount Clarence King (12,905 feet), above the Sixty Lakes Basin
20. Mount Pinchot (13,495 feet), above the John Muir Trail
21. Woods Creek
22. South fork of the Kings River
23. Mount Pinchot (13,495 feet)
24. Middle fork of the Kings River
25. Split Mountain (14,058 feet)
26. Barton Peak (10,370 feet)
27. Gardiner Pass
28. Monarch Divide
29. Pacific Crest Trail

Clark's nutcracker
Nucifrag columbiana

Map 08.09 Channel Islands National Park

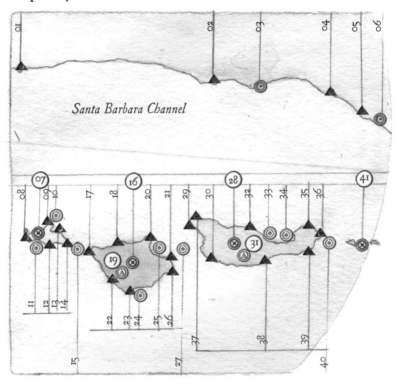

15 miles

08.09

The isolated chain of undeveloped islands federally protected as Channel Islands National Park comprises five of the eight Channel Islands: San Miguel, Santa Rosa, Santa Cruz, Anacapa, and Santa Barbara. The park hosts a wildlife portfolio of 150 documented species of plants and animals that exist only on these five islands and nowhere else in the word.

01. Point Conception
02. Goleta Point
03. Santa Barbara
04. Rincon Point
05. Pitas Point
06. Ventura
07. San Miguel Island

08. Point Bennett
09. Harris Point
10. Cuyler Harbor
11. Tyler Bight
12. Crook Point
13. Prince Island
14. Cardwell Point
15. San Miguel Passage
16. Santa Rosa Island
17. Sandy Point
18. Brockway Point
19. Black Mountain (1,298 feet)
20. Carrington Point
21. Skunk Point
22. Cluster Point
23. South Point
24. Johnsons Lee
25. Bechers Bay
26. East Point
27. Santa Cruz Channel
28. Santa Cruz Island
29. Fraser Point
30. Morse Point
31. Devil's Peak (2,470 feet)
32. Diablo Point
33. Prisoners Harbor
34. Chinese Harbor
35. Scorpion Anchorage
36. San Pedro Point
37. West Point
38. Bowen Point
39. Sandstone Point
40. Anacapa Passage
41. Anacapa Island

Because of the islands' isolation, many species of terrestrial animals here maintain local, endemic populations, most of which are endangered. These species include but are not limited to:

Baja California tree frog
Channel Islands slender salamander
Island deer mouse
Island fence lizard
Island fox
Island night lizard
Island spotted skunk
Santa Cruz Island gopher snake
Side-botched lizard
Southern alligator lizard
Townsend's big-eared bat
Western harvest mouse

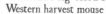

double-crested cormorant
Phalacrocorax auritus

Map 08.10 Federal Wilderness Areas

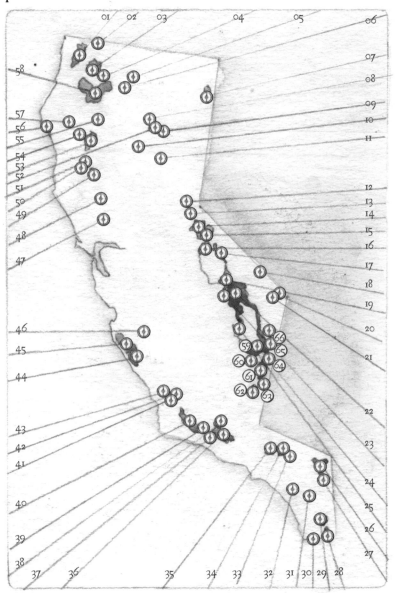

The Wilderness Act, signed into law in 1964, created the National Wilderness Preservation System and recognized wilderness as "an area where the earth and its community of life are untrammeled by man, where man himself is a visitor who does not remain." The act further defined wilderness as "an area of undeveloped federal land retaining its primeval character and influence without permanent improvements or human habitation, which is protected and managed so as to preserve its natural conditions."

Designated wilderness is the highest level of conservation protection for federal lands. Only Congress may designate wilderness or change the status of wilderness areas. Wilderness areas are designated within existing federal public land. Congress has directed four federal land-management agencies—the U.S. Forest Service, the Bureau of Land Management, the U.S. Fish and Wildlife Service, and the National Park Service—to manage wilderness areas so as to preserve and, where possible, to restore their wilderness character. All federal wilderness areas exist within selected portions of national forests, parks, wildlife refuges, and other public lands; the law limits uses to those consistent with the Wilderness Act, which mandates the following:

- the protection of watersheds and clean water sources vital to downstream municipalities and agriculture;
- the protection of habitat supporting diverse wildlife populations, including endangered species;
- the prohibition of logging and oil and gas drilling;
- the prohibition of motorized or mechanical vehicles or equipment and bicycles;
- the allowance of non-invasive scientific research; and
- the allowance of certain grandfathered uses, including resource extraction, grazing, mining, and water, as long as no one area is significantly impacted.

This map describes 58 wilderness areas west and north of the Mojave and Colorado Deserts.

01. Siskiyou	21. Piper Mountain	40. San Rafael
02. Red Buttes	22. John Muir	41. Garcia
03. Marble Mountains	23. Kaiser	42. Machesna Mountain
04. Russian	24. Monarch	43. Santa Lucia
05. Mount Shasta	25. Jennie Lakes	44. Silver Peak
06. Castle Crags	26. San Gorgonio	45. Ventana
07. South Warner	27. San Jacinto	46. Pinnacles
08. Thousand Lakes	28. Hauser	47. Cedar Roughs
09. Caribou	29. Sawtooth Mountains	48. Cache Creek
10. Ishi	30. Otay Mountain	49. Snow Mountain
11. Bucks Lake	31. Aqua Tibia	50. Sanhedrin
12. Granite Chief	32. San Mateo Canyon	51. Yuki
13. Desolation	33. Cucamonga	52. Lassen
14. Mokelumne	34. Sheep Mountain	53. Yolla Bolly–Middle Eel
15. Carson-Iceberg	35. San Gabriel	54. North Fork
16. Emigrant	36. Sespe	55. Chanchelulla
17. Hoover	37. Matilija	56. Kings Range
18. Boundary Peak	38. Chumash	57. Mount Lassic
19. Ansel Adams	39. Dick Smith	58. Trinity Alps
20. Sylvania Mountains		

Map 08.11 King Range Wilderness and National Conservation Area

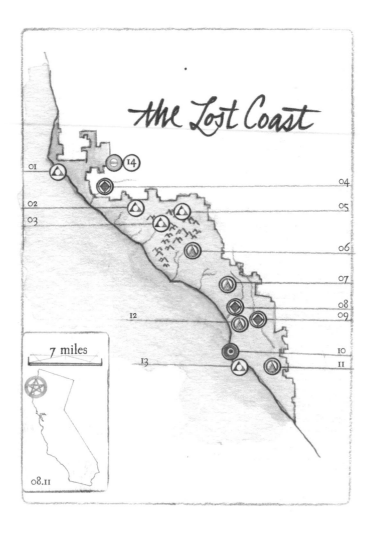

No roads head out to the Lost Coast, the nose of California and America's rugged westernmost point. In 1970, 60,000 acres of this remote coastal mountain range was designated as the King Range National Conservation Area. The rocks and islands just offshore were later incorporated as part of the California Coast National Monument. In 2006, 42,585 acres of the national conservation area was designated as the King Range Wilderness. The California Coastal Trail traces the spine of the range.

01. Punta Gorda
02. Oat Hill (2,392 feet)
03. Telegraph Ridge
04. Cooksie Creek
05. King Ridge
06. King Peak (4,087 feet)
07. Saddle Mountain (3,292 feet)

08. Gitchell Creek
09. Bear Creek
10. Shelter Cove
11. Paradise Summit (2,250 feet)
12. Horse Mountain (1,920 feet)
13. Chemise Mountain (2,598 feet)

Digger bee
anthophora plumipes

yellow headed bumblebee
Bombus vosnesenskii

Map 08.12 Pinnacles National Park

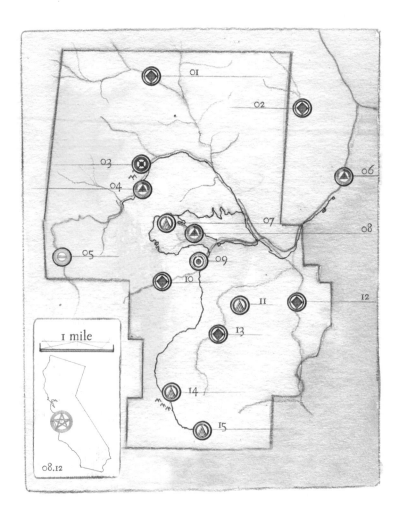

The heart of Pinnacles National Park and Pinnacles Wilderness is a displaced volcanic extrusion that has ridden the ever-moving San Andreas Fault north for almost 200 miles since its formation 23 million years ago. Despite being renowned as California condor habitat, the park is also home to a dizzying cornucopia of wildlife diversity, including 149 bird species, 69 butterfly species, 400 bee species (the greatest diversity of bee species on the planet), and 14 of California's 24 species of bat.

01. North Chalone Creek
02. McCabe Canyon
03. Balconies
04. Balconies Cave Trail
05. Chaparral Trailhead
06. Highway 146
07. Hawkins Peak (2,720 feet)

08. Bear Gulch Trail
09. Bear Gulch Reservoir
10. Bear Creek
11. Mount Defiance (2,657 feet)
12. Chalone Creek
13. Frog Canyon
14. North Chalone Peak (3,304 feet)
15. South Chalone Peak (3,269 feet)

Townsends big-eared bat
Corynorhinus Townsendii

Map 08.13 Berryessa Snow Mountain National Monument

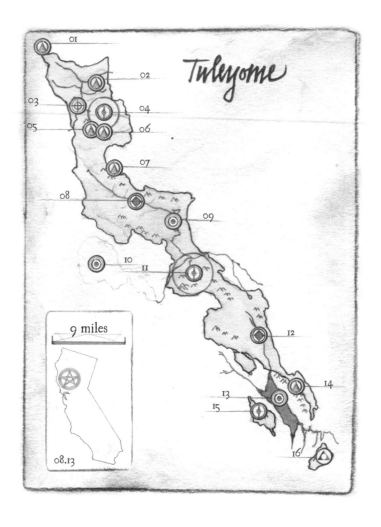

Tuleyome

9 miles

08.13

Northern California's newest national monument comprises 331,000 acres in Napa, Yolo, Solano, Lake, Colusa, Glenn, and Mendocino Counties. The monument forms a jagged line down the heart of the inland North Coast Ranges from the Snow Mountain Wilderness in the north, down across North Fork Canyon and the main fork of Cache Creek, and up Blue Ridge past Berryessa Peak and down into the Putah Creek Valley. This largely unknown and underexplored block of California wildland was designated as a national monument in 2016 to protect its many endangered ecological communities.

01. Bald Mountain (6,740 feet)
02. Saint John Mountain (6,746 feet)
03. Eel River
04. Snow Mountain Wilderness
05. West Snow Mountain (7,038 feet)
06. East Snow Mountain (7,056 feet)
07. Goat Mountain (6,121 feet)
08. North fork of Cache Creek

09. Indian Valley Reservoir
10. Clear Lake
11. Cache Creek
12. Eticuera Creek
13. Lake Berryessa
14. Berryessa Peak (3,057 feet)
15. Cedar Roughs Wilderness
16. Pleasants Ridge

Cedar waxwing
Bombycilla cedrorum

Common yellowthroat
Geothlypis trichas

Map 08.14 Redwood Coastal Parks

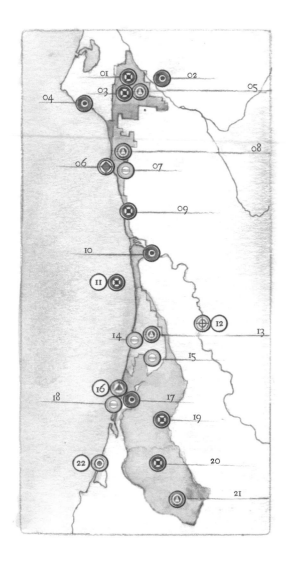

18 miles

08.14

The historically contentious patchwork of resource legislation that governs Redwood State and National Parks is certain to shift around in the next 100 years. The parks are Redwood National Park, Del Norte Coast Redwoods State Park, Jedediah Smith Redwoods State Park, and Prairie Creek Redwoods State Park. The parks total 133,000 acres within Del Norte and Humboldt Counties and collectively protect 45 percent of all remaining old-growth coast redwood forests, totaling at least 39,000 acres.

01. Simpson-Reed Grove
02. Hiouchi
03. Stout Grove
04. Crescent City
05. Redwood National Park
06. Damnation Creek
07. Demartin Camp
08. Del Norte Coast Redwoods State Park
09. Trees of Mystery
10. Klamath
11. Crescent City Marsh Wildlife Area
12. Klamath River
13. Prairie Creek Redwoods State Park Headquarters
14. Gold Beach Camp
15. Elk Prairie Camp
16. Redwood Creek Trail
17. Orick
18. Stone Lagoon Visitor Center
19. Howard Libbey Tree
20. Big Lagoon Wildlife Area
21. Redwood National Park
22. Big Lagoon

King Salmon
Oncorhynchus tshawytscha

Map 08.15 The State Parks

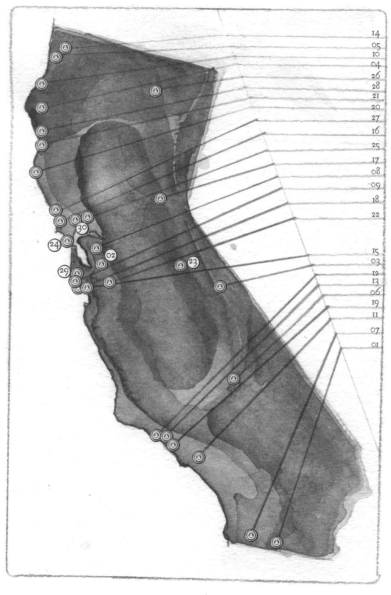

14
05
10
04
26
28
21
20
27
16
25
17
08
09
18
22

15
03
12
13
06
19
11
07
01

The 30 largest state parks are listed here in decreasing order of size, with superlative features noted. This list excludes recreation areas, which are often on reservoirs, and vehicular recreation areas.

Superlative Features
(a) Exceptional geology

(b) Rare botanical ecology

(c) Rural and remote

(d) Crowded with people

(e) Scenic camping

01. Anza Borrego Desert State Park (a)(b)(c)(e)
02. Henry W. Coe State Park (b)(c)(e)
03. Mono Lake Tufa State Natural Park (a)(c)
04. Humboldt Redwoods State Park (b)(d)(e)
05. Del Norte Redwoods State Park (b)
06. Red Rock Canyon State Park (a)(c)(e)
07. Cuyamaca Rancho State Park (b)(c)(e)
08. Mount Diablo State Park (a)(b)(d)(e)
09. Big Basin Redwoods State Park (b)(d)(e)
10. Prairie Creek Redwoods State Park (b)(d)
11. Chino Hills State Park (d)
12. Point Mugu State Park (d)(e)
13. Topanga Canyon State Park (b)
14. Jedediah Smith Redwoods State Park (b)(c)
15. Forest of Nisene Marks State Park (b)(d)
16. Sonoma Coast State Park (c)(e)
17. South Yuba River State Park (a)(d)(e)
18. Wilder Ranch State Park (b)
19. Malibu Creek State Park (b)(e)
20. Sinkyone Wilderness State Park (b)(c)(e)
21. Mendocino Headlands State Park (b)(c)(e)
22. Pacheco State Park (b)
23. Calaveras Big Trees State Park (b)(d)
24. Mount Tamalpais State Park (b)(e)
25. Robert Louis Stevenson State Park (b)
26. Ahjumawi Lava Springs State Park (a)
27. Salt Point State Park (e)
28. Manchester State Park (b)(c)
29. Castle Rock State Park (e)
30. Annadel State Park (d)(b)

white fir
Abies concolor

09. THE COUNTIES

Raven
Corvus corax

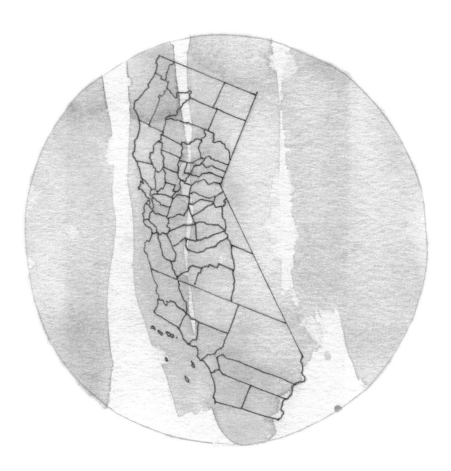

The counties of California were invented only as a convenient structure to overlay on top of human ecology. These lines in the dirt are no more than an arbitrary political effort, influenced by centuries of land trusts and assumptions of property and basic resources. Such divisions are how humans organize one another, and they have no bearing on or deference to nodes of wilderness or biome distribution. These divisions enable us to tell a different kind of story, though. Each county can be understood as a character study, and together their stories give us a new perspective on California as a whole.

Map 09.00 The Counties of California

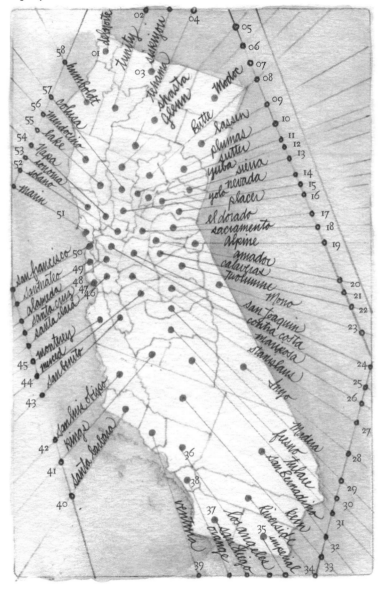

american painted lady
Vanessa virginiesia

Where Is the Nature?

The annotations that accompany each point of interest are field notes that describe local ecological features, themes, and patterns in the most general way, by offering only the highlights—superlative examples evenly spread across the whole map. The notes at each key point indicate places, and places inside of places, that not only offer sanctuary to the wildlife that require that particular habitat to survive, but also a kind of psychic sanctuary for us humans. The mere fact of these places' existence is comforting to me. As California writer Wallace Stegner astutely observed in his book *The Sound of Mountain Water* (1946), "We simply need that wild country available to us, even if we never do more than drive to its edge and look in." This is the aim of these maps: to focus the power of access that we enjoy as citizens of this land, to plant the seeds for a rewilded future. This portfolio of county maps focuses its attention on parks and wildlife corridors, negative spaces in the urban landscape where the natural heart of California seeps through.

The letter key provides the general elevation status for each county map in feet. The key depicts a line through the horizontal axis of each county at its widest point and takes its measure three times, once in the west county (A), once in the middle of the county, called mid county (B), and once in the east county (C). These are not measurements on the border and they may represent the elevation of any kind of geographic feature.

Major land designations, like watersheds and federal wilderness areas, are measured in acres, rounded to the nearest thousand.

Annotated Key-Feature Classification

In this chapter, nine classifications have been assigned to hundreds of key ecological markers (M) across all 58 California counties. This rating system presents an access of inventory across California, based on that key feature's primary designation and purpose. Most of these key features name a sequestered piece of land, and this rating system is a convenient annotation that points to the general function of the land. That function might serve some human purpose, like camping or hiking, or it might be listed for some natural purpose, like conservation or preservation.

The spirit of this classification is first, on a practical level, to present as much information as possible about each key feature in an illuminating and easily referenced system, and second, on a more conceptual level, to present a single vision of the future of California as a working, ecological machine, with these holdfasts of deep nature in the present. How do the pieces fit together to form a model for future generations of Californians to restore and rewild their state? Where are the habitats and sanctuaries, the pockets of wildness that can be cleaned up and expanded? Where are the natural moments, whether indigenous or designed, that, having survived our voracious species until now, demand our attention and our protection?

Not every key feature has a classification assignment. Not included are agricultural or metropolitan areas with limited access to natural features, mountain peaks, ridges and ranges that are part of another classified area, and other isolated areas that might be important to point out geographically but remain unclassified under this system either because classifying them would be redundant or because they fail to exhibit the utility needed to fit into this system. National forests do not have classifications, as this system only works by classifying protected, named areas, and the national forest designation encompasses too many resource types.

The classifications are fluid. Some key features can be assigned multiple classifications because, for example, there might be a wonderful campground (M9) on a mountain river (M3) that is a useful wildlife corridor (M4) and is next to a reservoir (M5). In this case, the area would receive an (M9) classification, indicating that it is a great spot to camp; and the other three classifications would be assigned to adjacent key features.

This inventory is incomplete, as it lists only the exceptional key features as deemed in the spirit of *The California Field Atlas*. The most complete list, as far as being a comprehensive account of California's natural inventory, is the (M1) classification. The most incomplete lists are the (M9) and the (M4) classifications: not every campground (M9) by far is recorded here—only the exceptional sites and many protected areas that are essential wildlife corridors (M4) are not explicitly called as such under their key features.

(M1) – The Highest Class of Ecological Protection

An (M1) key feature is either a regional designation designed to limit human contact in a particularly sensitive locale or a large parcel of land that has been designed specifically so humans can enjoy the wildness of the place, although with stringent legal protections. (M1) designations include wildlife preserves, nature preserves, national parks, federal wilderness areas, national monuments, game preserves, game refuges, geologic areas, some state parks, and sites where significant scientific study is happening, like Forest Service research natural areas. (M1) key features often have no facilities, like campgrounds or bathrooms, and are just land designations, places for nature to be protected by being left alone. Many (M1) key features are conceived of as places for the protection of a single species of animal that may or may not be endangered, but requires large swaths of habitat to maintain its numbers. Famous animals of this type include the red-legged frog, the California tiger salamander, the western pond turtle, the Mojave tortoise, the tule elk, the pronghorn, the bighorn sheep, the spotted owl, the peregrine falcon, the California condor, and the mountain lion.

(M2) – The Highest Class of Waterfowl and Avian Protection

An (M2) key feature is a bird-focused version of the (M1) classification. These are areas, mainly in the Central Valley, that exist along what is called the Pacific Flyway. The Pacific Flyway is a stretch of land that extends from Alaska down into South America, describing the primary migration corridor for thousands of species of birds. These wildlife areas are most active in seasons when the birds are moving north to south, or the other way, or are using the space temporarily for nesting.

While the (M1) classification many have hundreds of wildlife species that use the area as lifelong habitat, the (M2) classification may be more of a temporary housing situation for its key residents. These areas might be wildlife areas and sanctuaries on rivers or wetlands, state beaches, known nesting sites in secluded places, wildlife viewing stations, or Audubon preserves. The temporary habitation of an (M2) key feature is the primary reason for its classification. Thus, areas that support high-profile birds of prey are generally given the (M1) classification, as they are permanent features of their ecosystem all year long.

The main regions that hold the most (M2) key features are the Modoc Plateaus of Shasta, Modoc, and Lassen Counties; the Sacramento River Valley of Tehama, Glenn, Butte, Colusa, Yolo, Sutter, Yuba, Sacramento, and Solano Counties; the San Joaquin River Valley of San Joaquin, Merced, Stanislaus, Fresno, Madera, Kings, Tulare, and Kern Counties; and the coastal beach communities of rare nesting shore birds including San Mateo, Santa Cruz, Monterey, San Luis Obispo, Santa Barbara, Ventura, Los Angeles, Orange, and San Diego Counties. Famous birds of the type included in the (M2) classification are the clapper rail, the snowy plover, the sandhill crane, the great blue heron, the least tern, the greebe, the wood duck, and the northern pintail.

(M3) – Rivers

An (M3) key feature is a river or a creek that, for the most part, is a perennial stream in that it has water in its bed all year long. The (M3) classification is given to rivers that run wild and are not diverted, or are only minimally diverted for irrigation or for other human needs. Many (M3) rivers course through multiple counties and are mentioned multiple times with minimal annotation. Where most of the key feature classifications are specific locales, an (M3) key feature might refer to a whole stretch of different ecosystems. Fishing may or may not be allowed on an (M3) river.

(M4) – Wildlife Corridors

An (M4) key feature is open space that provides a channel of habitat for at-risk species of wildlife to move through in a way that represents a slice of historical ecology, otherwise interrupted now by human development. The (M4) key feature might be a wildlife corridor only as a secondary function, as there aren't any spaces that are actually designated wildlife corridors. These key features might be regional parks, open space preserves, national monuments, wildlife sanctuaries, or state parks. Sand to Snow National Monument is an example of an area whose land protections were established to protect the routes of bighorn sheep on the journey from Joshua Tree National Park up the slopes of Mount Gorgonio. Famous animals of the type included in this classification, which rely on wildlife corridors to survive, are monarch butterflies, mountain lions, deer, elk, bears, rams, tortoises, and owls.

(M5) - Reservoirs

An (M5) key feature is a reservoir. A reservoir is a dammed creek or river where an artificial lake has formed for the purpose of irrigation, flood control, or water storage. With over 1,300 named reservoirs in California, they have become primary features across the landscape. (M5) key features are often recreational areas that may or may not provide campgrounds, although there are a few reservoirs in this list that are closed to public access. Where fishing is allowed, most reservoirs need to be routinely stocked with populations of fish from hatching farms as sustainable ecosystems, and native-fish populations are not able to maintain themselves in these man-made bodies of water. The few natural lakes in California—Clear Lake, Lake Tahoe, Lake Elsinore, and the alkali lakes of Modoc, Lassen, and Siskiyou Counties—do not get an (M5) classification.

(M6) – Plants

An (M6) key feature is a named area of noted botanical excellence. While an (M6) key feature might exhibit a whole range of ecological utility, the heart of its designation is some plant-based species, system, or quality including exceptional biodiversity or endangered forest habitat. These key features might be botanical areas, state forests, demonstration forests, forest reserves, natural research areas, areas of critical environmental concern, botanical preserves, or national monuments. Famous plant species and forest types that are included in this classification are redwood, rhododendron, Torrey pine, desert fan palm, old-growth forest, prairies, and wildflower preserve.

(M7) – Day Use

An (M7) key feature is a small piece of natural space that usually exists adjacent to or within human development. The origin of the (M7) key feature is most often artificially imposed on the landscape, as with city parks, or it may be a natural point of interest, defined by its extreme locality. (M7) key features are most often places of nature for humans to enjoy, although they typically offer limited hiking opportunities and no camping facilities. An (M7) classification can be a road stop, a city park, a wildlife management headquarters, a museum, a viewpoint, a state park, a recreation area, or a wildlife viewing site.

(M8) – Trail

An (M8) key feature is an established, major, named trail of note in the vicinity of another key feature. Most often the (M8) key feature represents the best access through a piece of wilderness, a natural feature, a preserve, or a sanctuary. While many trails represent wildlife corridors because they are not used solely by humans, they remain classified here only as (M8). The (M8) key feature is a constructed throughway, manufactured and maintained and rarely paved.

(M9) – Camping

An (M9) key feature is a place to camp. Legal camping in California can be tough to find unless you are way in the backcountry. Most (M9) key features are fee areas in national forests, in which case they have basic facilities like bathrooms and picnic tables. Some (M9) key features are near cities and may be privately owned and operated. Some (M9) key features exist in large clusters of half a dozen sites or more; in such cases, one site is singled out as having the best access to nature, views, and seclusion.

Snowy egret
Egretta thula

California Mule deer

Odocoileus hemionus californicus

Map 09.01 Alameda: Bay Shore and Bay Leaf

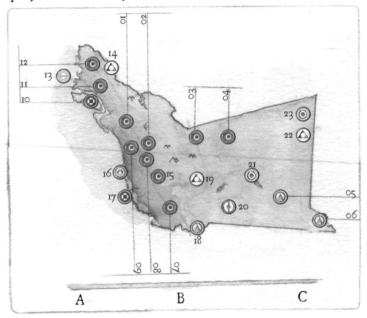

9 miles

09.01

A **West county:** Castro Valley (02) (180 feet)
B **Mid county:** Livermore (04) (480 feet)
C **East county:** Altamont Pass (22) (1,000 feet)

Speed through Alameda County in a car and the only forests you'll see are the redwood- and eucalyptus-covered ridgelines of the Oakland Hills. It is possible that the tallest coast redwood in modern times grew in the Oakland Hills until it was cut down in the 19th century. Take your time in the riparian backcountry of the Ohlone Regional Wilderness and Sunol's Little Yosemite, and you'll find acres of intact oak and bay laurel habitat where otters play with the shorebirds of the San Francisco Bay.

01. Knowland Arboretum (M4): a 450-acre arboretum in San Leandro

02. Anthony Chabot Regional Park (M8): park on Lake Chabot in Castro Valley

03. Emerald Glen Park (M7): a 40-acre park in Dublin

04. Brushy Peak Preserve (M1): a 500-acre preserve in Livermore known for its vernal pools

05. Cedar Mountain (3,675 feet): the tallest peak in the Ohlone Regional Wilderness

06. Mount Boardman (3,600 feet): the peak that divides San Joaquin, Stanislaus, and Alameda Counties

07. Mission Peak Regional Preserve (M1): 3,000 acres of scrub oak and chaparral in Fremont

08. Hayward Regional Shoreline (M2): 1,800 acres of marshland with five miles of walking trails

09. Oyster Bay Regional Shoreline (M2): a former landfill revived as a small running park and bird habitat south of Oakland airport, in San Lorenzo

10. Alameda: an island separated from Oakland by a canal; Crown State Beach (M7)

11. Oakland: city that contains Lake Merritt (M2), an estuary

12. Berkeley Marina and Strawbale Visitor and Nature Center (M2)

13. Bay Bridge: this bridge, rebuilt in 2015, connects both shores of the San Francisco Bay

14. Oakland Hills: an area of redwood- and eucalyptus-studded woodland from San Pablo Ridge in Contra Costa County to Lake Chabot (M5), whose tallest point is Round Top (1,765 feet) above the Caldecott Tunnel

15. Niles Canyon (M4): an unincorporated region with a historic train corridor through oak woodland

16. Alameda Creek (M3): this creek empties into the bay just west of the 1,000-acre Coyote Hills Regional Park (M4)

17. San Francisco Bay National Wildlife Refuge (M2): the nation's first urban wildlife refuge, this 30,000-acre oasis offers habitat to over 100 species of birds; about 9,000 acres of salt ponds within the refuge are managed by Cargill Salt, which has perpetual salt-making rights

18. Mission Peak (2,517 feet)

19. Sunol Ridge (M4): this ridge comprises three parallel ridges—Walpert Ridge, Sunol Ridge, and Pleasanton Ridge; Palomares Road bisects the entirety of the oak-lined backcountry

20. Ohlone Regional Wilderness (M1): a 10,000-acre wilderness area dominated by oak and bay woodlands; a grassy carpet of springtime wildflowers explodes in color across these hills each spring

21. Lake Del Valle (M5): a reservoir in the wine region south of Livermore best explored by the East Shore Trailhead

22. Altamont Pass: a pass through the Altamont Wind Farm, the Bay Area's oldest wind-power array of windmills

23. Bethany Reservoir (M5): a state recreation area near the ruins of the historic Byron Hot Springs Hotel

Map 09.02 Alpine: Snow and Scenery

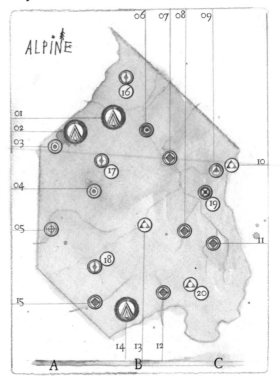

6 miles

09.02

A **West county:** Caples Lake (5) (7,798 feet)
B **Mid county:** Markleeville (6) (5,501 feet)
C **East county:** Monitor Pass (10) (8,314 feet)

Alpine County is a green gem hidden amid a pocket of mountain passes deep in the Sierra Nevada. The greatest depth of seasonal snowfall (74 feet) in California's history was recorded near Fay Canyon in Alpine County at an elevation of 8,000 feet. Carson Pass, Ebbett's Pass, and Monitor Pass offer paved passage through Alpine County from all cardinal directions. The gently sloping glacial valleys and Swiss-like forest ambiance of this region have lent it a reputation as the Alps of the Sierra.

01. Hawkins Peak (10,024 feet): the defining peak to the west of Turtle Creek County Park (M9), north of Markleeville

02. Red Lake Peak (10,063 feet): a peak north of Carson Pass (8,573 feet)

03. Caples Lake (M5) and Red Lake (M5): two lakes stocked with fish for recreation on either side of Carson Pass, up the road from the Kirkwood Ski Resort (M7)

04. Upper Blue Lake (M5)*: this lake is known for its champion brown trout fishing

05. Mokelumne River (M3): Deer Creek becomes the Mokelumne River's north fork headwaters

06. Grover Hot Springs State Park (M7): a 550-acre park in Markleeville with hot springs, open for swimming in the late summer

07. East fork of the Carson River (M3): a popular rainbow trout fishing area

08. Wolf Creek (M3): this creek is traced by the High Trail (M8), which leads to Centerville Camp (M9)* on the east fork of the Carson River

09. Highway 89: crosses Monitor Pass just up from Heenan Lake (M5)

10. Monitor Pass (8,314 feet)

11. Silver King Creek (M3): this creek is followed by the Rodriguez Flat Trail (M8)*, up to the Mono County line

12. Arnot Creek (M3): this creek runs past the Clark Flat Horse Camp (M9)* along the Clark fork of the Stanislaus River, which is also the Stanislaus County line

13. Ebbetts Pass (8,732 feet): this pass is an access point to the Pacific Crest Trail (PCT) (M8)

14. Dardanelles Cone (9,524 feet): this is the highest peak of the rocky ridgeline known as the Dardanelles*

15. Highland Creek (M3): this fishing site is best accessed by a stay at Spice Group camp (M9)*

16. Fay Canyon Wildlife Area (M1): on the Nevada border, this wildlife area is accessible by the Armstrong Pass Trail (M8), on Willow Creek (M3)

17. Mokelumne Federal Wilderness Area (M1): a 105,000-acre wilderness area

18. Carson-Iceberg Federal Wilderness Area (M1): a 160,000-acre wilderness area

19. Little Antelope Valley Wildlife Area (M1): 1,700 acres at an elevation of 7,500 feet on the border of Mono County, featuring Jeffrey pine forests and sagebrush ridges

20. Sonora Peak Ridge: this ridge is adjacent to Sonora Pass (9,625 feet), which divides Alpine, Tuolumne, and Mono Counties

* Blue Lake and the Mokelumne Rivers are in the Mokelumne Federal Wilderness Area; Wolf Creek, Silver King Creek, Arnot Creek, the Dardanelle Cone, and Highland Creek are in the Carson-Iceberg Federal Wilderness Area

Map 09.03 Amador: Red Wine and Reservoirs

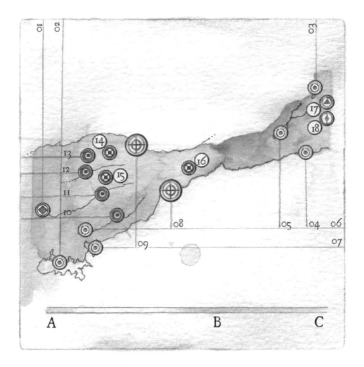

10 miles

09.03

A **West county:** Camanche Reservoir (02) (236 feet)
B **Mid county:** Plymouth (13) (1,086 feet)
C **East county:** Lower Bear Reservoir (05) (5,824 feet)

Wedged between the Cosumnes River and the Mokelumne River, Amador County has recently embraced its legacy as California's first wine region. With over a dozen reservoirs, the otherwise dry, foothill vineyards of the diminutive, narrow, and arid county are well irrigated with captured Sierra runoff.

01. Loch Lane (M5): this lake, near the town of Ione, was created by the Sutter Creek Dam

02. Camanche Reservoir (M5): this reservoir was named for the former town of Camanche, which was submerged by the reservoir's flooding

03. Silver Lake (M5): adjacent to the Mokelumne Federal Wilderness Area (M1), this lake provides access to the High Sierra

04. Salt Springs Reservoir (M5) (3,900 feet): this reservoir is accessed by the Salt Springs Trail (M8)

05. Lower Bear River Reservoir (M5): this reservoir, free of spring snow before any other lake in Amador County, is a prime recreation area

06. Lake Amador (M5): this lake was created by the Jackson Creek Dam

07. Pardee Reservoir (M5): the second of three dams on the Mokelumne River in Amador County

08. Mokelumne River (M3)

09. Cosumnes River (M3)

10. Lake Tabeaud (M5): this lake is in the Mount Zion State Forest (M7), near the city of Jackson

11. Sutter Creek (M3)

12. South fork of Dry Creek (M3), near Amador City

13. Little Indian Creek (M3), outside of Plymouth: home to the Amador Flower Gardens (M7)

14. Amador Wine Region: Italian immigrants started growing wine here in the mid-1800s; the region is home to the popular landmark Daffodil Hill (M7)

15. The Mother Lode: a massive, north–south vein (roughly following Highway 49 from Sonora up to Nevada City) of quartz deep inside the Sierra Nevada responsible for holding the gold that spurred the Gold Rush

16. Salt Springs State Game Reserve (M1): a hunting spot for quail and turkey on the Bear River (M3)

17. Plasses Trail (M8): a trail that bridges the Bear River Reservoir and Silver Lake

18. The Mokelumne Wilderness (M1): a wilderness area that protects 105,000 acres across four counties and four national forests; its tallest peak is Mokelumne Peak (9,334 feet)

Lodgepole chipmunk
Tamias speciosus

Map 09.04 Butte: Waterfalls and Water Storage

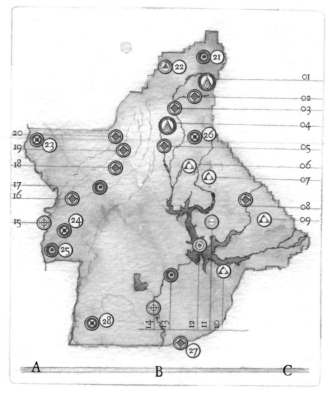

6 miles

09.04

A **West county:** Ordbend (25) (150 feet)
B **Mid county:** Oroville (13) (1,708 feet)
C **East county:** Butte Meadows (21) (4,351 feet)

Home to the state's second-largest reservoir (Lake Oroville) and the Sacramento River's largest tributary in the northern Sierra Nevada (the Feather River), Butte County is rich with water and forested natural beauty. A jagged, volcanic land-scape tumbles down from the Sierra and presents a staircase of waterfalls for a parade of summer wildflowers. Three major perennial watercourses flow through Butte County, including the Sacramento River, Butte Creek, and Feather River.

01. Snow Mountain (6,980 feet): this mountain is accessed by the Sunflower Flat Trail (M8)

02. West branch of the Philbrook Reservoir (M9)

03. West branch of the Big Kimshew (M3), whose headwaters are at Snow Mountain

04. Bald Mountain (6,980 feet): a peak between Big Kimshew Creek (M3) and the west branch of the Big Kimshew Creek (M3)

05. Paradise Lake (M5)

06. Flea Mountain (4,240 feet): a peak on the north side of the north fork of the Feather River (M3)

07. Big Bal Mountain (4,373 feet)

08. Middle fork of the Feather River (M3), accessed by the Dome Trail (M8): this is the location of Curtain Falls and Seven Falls, both part of the Feather Falls Scenic Area (M1)

09. Quartz Hill (4,350 feet), accessed by the Feather Falls National Recreation Trail (M8)

10. Stringtown Mountain (2,369 feet): headwaters of Loafer Creek (M9)

11. Brush Creek Center (M7)

12. Lake Oroville (M5)

13. Oroville Wildlife Area (M1)

14. Feather River (M3)

15. Sacramento River (M3)

16. Butte Creek (M3)

17. Chico Creek Nature Center (M7)

18. Little Chico Creek (M3)

19. Big Chico Creek (M3)

20. Mud Creek (M3)

21. Butte Meadows (M9) (4,351 feet)

22. Deer Ridge: find good camping at Soda Springs (M9) off Highway 32

23. Merrill's Landing Wildlife Area (M2): 300 acres of high-terrace riparian habitat that includes a heron rookery

24. Wildlife areas of the Sacramento River (M2): riparian habitat of oaks and cottonwoods offering shade to a thick understory of elderberry, wild grape, blackberry, wild rose, and numerous perennial flowers and plants

25. Ordbend County Park (M7), adjacent to Upper Butte Basin Wildlife Area (M2): 10,000 acres of waterfowl hunting ground

26. Upper Ridge Nature Preserve (M7): 120 acres of walking trails in Magalia, right outside of town

27. Honcut Creek (M3): a creek that divides Butte County and Yuba County

28. Butte Sink: a region of rice farmland that contains the Gray Lodge Wildlife Area (M2), 9,000 acres of wetlands that offer bird watching on the border of Sutter County

Map 09.05 Calaveras: Sequoias and Springs

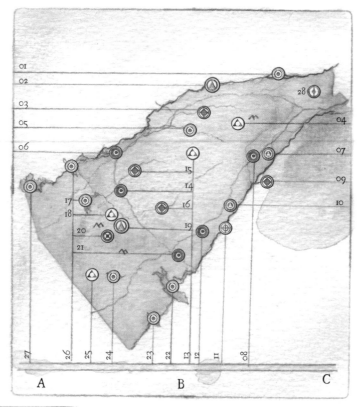

18 miles

09.05

A **West county:** Salt Spring Valley Reservoir (20) (1,120 feet)
B **Mid county:** Pine Ridge (13) (2,760 feet)
C **East county:** Salt Springs Reservoir (01) (3,949 feet)

Like many counties that climb the west slope of the Sierra Nevada, Calaveras County is defined on its north and its south by two rivers—in this case, the Mokelumne and the Stanislaus. Highway 4 is the one paved road that can take you up to the Calaveras highlands of the Sierra Nevada.

01. Salt Springs Reservoir (M5), best accessed by the Salt Springs Trail (M8)

02. Devil's Nose (4,800 feet)

03. Blue Creek (M3)

04. Bailey Ridge, along the middle fork of the Mokelumne River (M3)

05. Calaveras River (M3): this river's headwaters flow out of Red Hawk Lake (M5)

06. Mokelumne Hill: Gold Rush town in Chili Gulch

07. Calaveras Big Trees State Park (M6): home of the Big Tree Sequoia Redwood Groves

08. Hunter Reservoir (M5), Arnold

09. Middle fork of the Stanislaus River (M3)

10. Crescent Cove Park (M7): this park is located on the western border of the Stanislaus National Forest

11. Stanislaus River (M3)

12. Mercer Caves (M7), Murphys

13. Calaveras Caverns (M7), Pine Ridge

14. Jesus Maria Creek (M3): this creek has its confluence with the north fork of the Calaveras River near Mokelumne Hill

15. Calaveritas Creek (M3), San Andreas

16. San Domingo Creek: this creek runs into the south fork of the Calaveras River (M3)

17. New Hogan Reservoir (M5): this reservoir is near the confluence of the north and south forks of the Calaveras River, and fed by both

18. Bear Mountains: ranchland south of Hogback Mountain, visible from Highway 49

19. Mount Ararat (2,279 feet)

20. Old McCormick Reservoir (M5), Salt Spring Valley

21. Moaning Cavern (M7), Angels Camp

22. New Melones Lake (M5): this lake is fed by the Stanislaus River (M3)

23. Tulloch Reservoir (M5): this reservoir saddles Tuolumne County

24. Salt Spring Valley Reservoir (M5)

25. Gopher Ridge and the vista point at Boucher Mountain (1,548 feet) (M7)

26. Pardee Reservoir (M5) and the Pardee Recreation Area (M9)

27. Camanche Reservoir (M5): one of the three reservoirs of northwest Calaveras County that represent the largest concentration of water storage facilities in the Central Valley

28. Mokelumne Wilderness: 105,000 acres within the Stanislaus, Eldorado, and Toiyabe National Forests that straddle Calaveras, Alpine, and Amador Counties

Map 09.06 Colusa: Basins and Borderlands

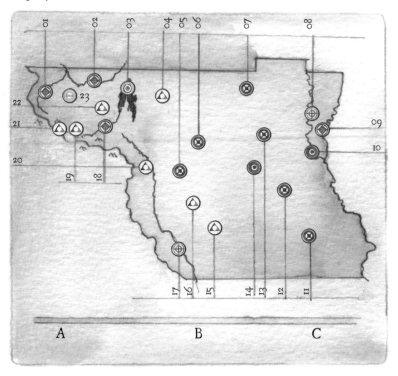

12 miles

09.06

A West county: East Park Reservoir (03) (1,198 feet)
B Mid county: Antelope Valley (06) (300 feet)
C East county: Colusa (10) (60 feet)

From the east side of the rugged, forested Berryessa Snow Mountain National Monument down through rich farmlands and the west shore of the mighty Sacramento River, Colusa County is not defined by any one kind of topography. No fewer than eight strong creeks feed this sloping wetland of different ecosystems, dotted with rich national wildlife refuges.

01. South fork of the Stony Creek (M3), Mill Creek (M7), and Dixie Glade (M8): a tangle of watercourses at the eastern border of the Snow Mountain Wilderness (M1)

02. Middle fork of the Stony Creek (M3)

03. East Park Reservoir (M5)

04. Black Mountain (1,512 feet)

05. Bear Creek (M3) and Mill Creek (M3), Bear Valley

06. Antelope Creek (M3), Antelope Valley

07. Sacramento National Wildlife Refuge (M2)

08. Sacramento River (M3): 11,000 acres of waterfowl habitat

09. Butte Sink: a riparian slough at the confluence of Butte Creek and the Sacramento River, and home to the Colusa Bypass Wildlife Area office (M7)

10. Colusa Sacramento River State Recreation Area (M7), Colusa: part of the greater Sacramento River Wildlife Area Complex, which include the Colusa and Delevan Wildlife Areas

11. Colusa Basin: an area of farmland fed by four diverted and private waterways— Salt Creek, Spring Creek, Cortina Creek, and Sand Creek

12. Colusa National Wildlife Refuge (M2)

13. Delevan National Wildlife Refuge (M2)

14. Colusa Creek (M3), Williams

15. Anderson Mountain (1,965 feet), Cortina Ridge

16. Judge Davis Trail (M8), Blue Ridge

17. Bear Creek (M3): this creek flows south following the east side of Cache Creek Ridge

18. Little Stony Creek (M3): this creek, with headwaters on the Pacific Ridge, feeds the East Park Reservoir

19. Goat Mountain (6,121 feet): this mountain is on the eastern border of the Berryessa Snow Mountain National Monument

20. Indian Valley Wildlife Area (M1): 5,000 acres near the Indian Valley Reservoir in Bear Valley and along Walker Ridge

21. Pacific Ridge: this ridge divides Colusa County from the Cache Creek watershed

22. Cedar Camp (M9) on Gilmore Peak (2,524 feet), along Trough Springs Ridge

23. Fouts Springs Campgrounds (M9)

Map 09.07 Contra Costa: Beavers and Blossoms

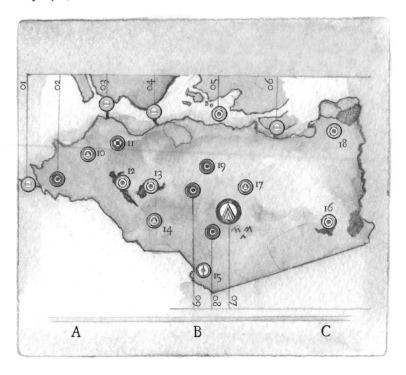

11 miles

09.07

A **West county:** Richmond Shoreline (10) (sea level)
B **Mid county:** Briones Hills (14) (500 feet)
C **East county:** Los Vaqueros (16) (25 feet)

With its rich, oak-laden grasslands and redwood-studded hills, Contra Costa County hosts a wealth of habitat for a diverse portfolio of wildlife that includes both endangered salamanders and vital populations of mountain lions. The low hills around Mount Diablo protect a host of wildflowers that take turns blooming all year long. Recently, the beaver has returned to the southern edge of the Carquinez Strait, creating new habitat by building dams inside the region's many creeks.

01. Richmond–San Rafael Bridge

02. Point Pinole Regional Park (M7), Richmond

03. Carquinez Bridge

04. Benicia–Martinez Bridge

05. Mallard Reservoir (M2), Suisun Bay

06. Antioch Bridge

07. Mount Diablo (3,849 feet)

08. San Ramon Creek (M3), Danville

09. Lafayette Reservoir (M5, M2), Lafayette

10. Wildcat Canyon Regional Park (M4), along the Richmond coastline

11. Carquinez Strait Regional Shoreline (M2): home to the John Muir National Historic Site (M7)

12. Briones Regional Park (M4): the green heart of the county, bordered by San Pablo Reservoir (M5)

13. Briones Reservoir (M5)

14. Las Trampas Regional Wilderness (M4, M6), and the Las Trampas Peak (1,827 feet)

15. Sunol Ridge (M4)

16. Los Vaqueros Reservoir (M5)

17. Mount Diablo State Park (M1): sticking out like a thumb in the middle of California, Mount Diablo catches the wildflower seeds from all over the state, making for a spectacular and unique botanical area

18. Contra Costa Delta: a watercourse that winds around Bethel Island, Bradford Island, and Jersey Island, the home of the Franks Tract State Recreation Area (M7)

19. Walnut Creek watershed (M3): home to many endangered salamander species, including the California tiger salamander

Northern Harrier
Circus cyaneus

Map 09.08 Del Norte: Rivers and Redwoods

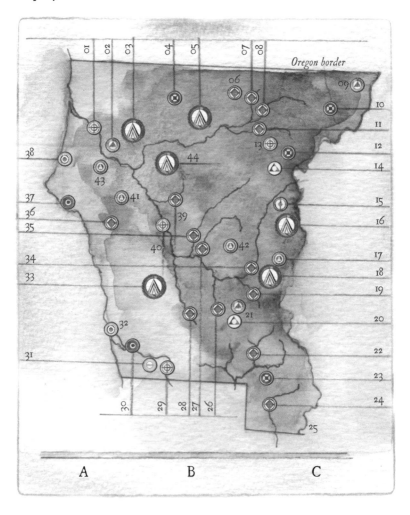

A **West county:** Smith River mouth (32) (sea level)
B **Mid county:** Lower Coon Mountain (36) (3,122 feet)
C **East county:** Bear Basin Butte (11) (5,292 feet)

6 miles

09.08

Del Norte (pronounced "dell NORT" by the locals), was settled by the Portuguese in the mid-19th century. It is the land of salmon and of the tallest trees in the world. The steep Coast Ranges that dominate Del Norte County's geography quickly climb from sea level to 6,500 feet. Amid a dense labyrinth of dark redwood forests, ferns carpet viridian rivers that endlessly lace the rural backcountry.

01. Tolowa Dunes (M9) and Smith River County Park (M7), at the mouth of the Smith River

02. Myrtle Falls Creek Botanical Area (M6): this richly forested area on a tributary of the Smith River is best accessed by the Simpson Reed Grove Trail (M8)

03. Signal Peak (2,048 feet)

04. North fork of the Smith River Botanical Area (M6): this area is accessed by the Elk Camp Ridge Trail (M8) in Peridotite Canyon, an extremely remote canyon named after the stone of its composition

05. Cold Spring Mountain (3,722 feet)

06. Shelley Creek (M9)

07. Monkey Creek (M3)

08. Patrick Creek Campground (M9), along the middle fork of the Smith River (M3)

09. Young's Valley Trail (M8): this trail follows the east fork of the Illinois River, which runs north to the Rogue River, 50 miles away

10. Broken Rib Mountain Botanical Area (M6)

11. Siskiyou fork of the Smith River (M3)*

12. Bear Basin Butte Botanical Area (M6): this area is traversed by the Doe Flat Trail (M8)*

13. Smith River headwaters (M3): this is where the south fork of the Smith River begins its 75-mile trek to the sea, past Four Brothers Peaks to the west, the tallest of which reaches 5,316 feet; Baldy Peak (6,775 feet) to the east is the tallest peak in the Siskiyou Wilderness in Del Norte County*

14. Bear Basin Butte (5,292 feet)*

15. Siskiyou Federal Wilderness Area (M1): this 153,000-acre area along the longest ridgeline in northwest California is home to a large portfolio of rare and endangered wildlife and plant species

16. Prescott Mountain (5,871 feet)*

17. Six Rivers National Forest

18. Baldy Peak (6,775 feet)*

19. Gunbarrel Trail (M8) on Eight Mile Creek*

20. Doctor's Rock (4,924 feet)

21. Boundary Trail (M8): this trail runs north–south for 57 miles*

22. Blue Creek (M3)

Spotted owl
Strix occidentalis

23. Waukell Creek Wildlife Area (M1): this area is transversed by Forks of Blue (M8)

24. Louse Camp (M9) on Bluff Creek (M3)

25. Lonesome Ridge: this ridge runs along rural Highway 13, parallel to East Fork Blue Creek Trail (M8)

26. Buck Creek (M3)

27. Jones Creek (M3)

28. Goose Creek (M3)

29. Klamath River (M3)

30. Klamath: a small town at the mouth of northwest California's biggest river

31. Yurok Reservation: runs along the Klamath River and is crisscrossed by the Coastal Trail (M8)

32. Flint Ridge (M9), at the mouth of the Klamath

33. Rattlesnake Mountain (3,658 feet)

34. South fork of the Smith River (M3), traced by the South Kelsey Trail (M8)

35. Hurdygurdy Creek (M3)

36. Mill Creek (M3): this creek in Redwood National Park is followed by the Rehim Ridge Trail (M8) and leads up to Mill Creek Camp (M9)

37. Castle Rock National Wildlife Refuge (M2), Crescent City

38. Lake Earl: this is the largest lagoon in California and the Lake Earl Wildlife Area (M2), traversed by Dead Lake Trail (M8)

39. Coon Creek (M3)

40. Smith River (M3)

41. Redwood National Park (M1): the lowlands of the tall trees region; Demartin Camp (M9) is a good place to camp, down from the scenic Damnation Creek Trail (M8)

42. Smith River National Recreation Area (M1): this 300,000-acre area defines most of Del Norte County

43. Jedediah Smith State Park (M1): this 10,000-acre park contains nearly 7 percent of the existing old-growth redwood habitat

44. Gordon Mountain (4,153 feet)

*feature within the Siskiyou Federal Wilderness Area

Short faced owl
Tyto alba

Map 09.09 El Dorado: Crystal Mountains and Emerald Lakes

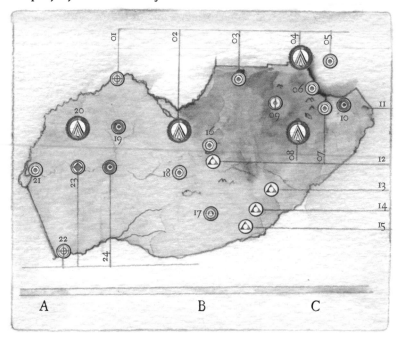

14 miles

09.09

A **West county:** Folsom Lake (21) (460 feet)
B **Mid county:** Union Valley Reservoir (16) (4,870 feet)
C **East county:** Desolation Wilderness (09) (9,000 feet)

El Dorado County is one of the many counties that run up the slope of the Sierra Nevada and are shaped such that their orientation runs west to east. The western lowlands are traced by a few deep river valleys cut by both the Cosumnes River and the middle and south forks of the American River. The western Sierra slope ends where El Dorado County does, at the shores of Lake Tahoe.

01. Middle fork of the American River (M3)

02. Lookout Mountain (5,159 feet)

03. Loon Lake (M5): this lake is on the south fork of the Rubicon River; the Loon Lake Trail (M8)* offers an entry point into the Desolation Wilderness

04. Rubicon Peak (9,183 feet)

05. Lake Tahoe: the largest and deepest alpine lake in California

06. Emerald Bay: an alcove of Lake Tahoe and place of sublime beauty; Eagle Falls Trail (M8)* is an access trail into the Desolation Wilderness

07. Fallen Leaf Lake: a lake in the Lake Tahoe Basin, under the shelf of Echo Summit and over the ridge from Washoe Meadows State Park (M7); it is accessed by the Glen Alpine Trail (M8)*

08. Pyramid Peak (9,983 feet)*

09. Desolation Wilderness (M1): this 64,000-acre wilderness exists entirely in the High Sierra; Lost Corner Mountain (8,261 feet) is its northernmost peak and Ralston Peak (9,285 feet) is its southernmost peak

10. South Lake Tahoe: this is the largest city in the Lake Tahoe Basin, filling the area between El Dorado Recreation Area (M7), the beach and the lake itself, and the Lake Tahoe Management Area; South Lake Tahoe is under Freel Peak (10,881 feet), at the border of Amador County

11. Monument Peak (10,067 feet): this peak divides the state of California from the state of Nevada

12. Big Hill (6,155 feet) and the Silver Creek camp (M9)

13. Baltic Ridge and the Capps Crossing camp (M9)

14. Plummer Ridge: this is the headwaters for the north fork of the Cosumnes River (M3)

15. Gold Note Ridge and the Pi Pi Camp (M9).

16. Union Valley Reservoir (M5): the largest reservoir in El Dorado, Union Valley fills the basin created by Silver Creek Ridge to the west and Four Cornered Peak to the east

17. El Dorado National Forest and the Iron Mountain Ridge, which runs to Jenkinson Lake (M5) and Sly Park camp (M9)

18. Stumpy Meadows Lake (M5) and the Ponderosa Creek camp (M9)

19. Coloma: this is the site of the 1848 discovery of gold and is now a historic park (M7)

20. Mount Ararat (2,012 feet): this mountain lies two miles north of the town of Lotus on the south fork of the American River, along the Dave Moore Nature Area (M7)

21. Folsom Lake (M5) State Recreation Area: Folsom Lake, fed by the south and north forks of the American River, straddles the county line with Sacramento and the Peninsula Camp (M9)

22. Cosumnes River (M3): the north, middle, and south forks of the Cosumnes River meet just east of Highway 49, near the town of River Pines

23. South fork of the American River (M3)

24. Placerville: a city once called Hang Town, named for the brutal practice of Gold Rush–era justice in early California

*feature within the Desolation Federal Wilderness Area

Map 09.10 Fresno: The High Sierra and the Great Valley

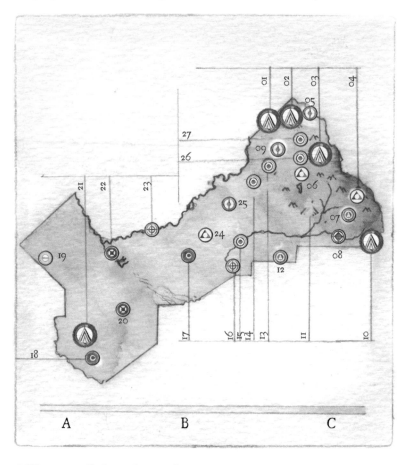

A **West county:** Coalinga (18) (1,500 feet)
B **Mid county:** Medota Wildlife Area (14) (150 feet)
C **East county:** Kings Canyon National Park (07) (7,500 feet)

Fresno County paints a large swath across the middle of California. Reaching across the San Joaquin Valley, the county rises steadily to cap out in the High Sierra in a quilt of federal wilderness areas and national parks.

22 miles

09.10

01. Kaiser Peak (10,320 feet): a peak in the Kaiser Federal Wilderness Area (M1)

02. Silver Peak (11,878 feet): a peak on the Silver Divide

03. Mount Abbot (13,715 feet): this peak on the Mono Divide divides Fresno from Mono County

04. North Palisade (14,242 feet): the first of the 14,000 peaks as they march down to the highest peak, Mount Whitney, on the border of Tulare and Inyo Counties

05. John Muir Wilderness (M1): a 500,000-acre wilderness that extends into four counties

06. Mono Divide: this divide, up from the south fork of the San Joaquin River Canyon, rides for ten miles from the west of the county line at Mount Abbot (13,715 feet)

07. Kings Canyon National Park (M1) and the Monarch Federal Wilderness Area (M1)

08. Bubbs Creek (M3): a creek on the John Muir Trail (M8)

09. Dinkey Lakes Wilderness (M1): a 30,000-acre-high divide along the Three Sisters Ridge that separates the San Joaquin watershed from the Kings River watershed

10. Mount Gould (13,005 feet)

11. Hoffman Mountain (9,622 feet)

12. Giant Sequoia National Monument (M1): this monument extends into Fresno County near Wilson

13. Huntington Lake (M5) and Potter Creek Trail (M8)

14. Shaver Lake (M5) and Camp Edison (M9)

15. Pine Flat Reservoir (M5) and Island Park (M9)

16. Kings River (M3)

17. Woodward Park (M7) and the Forestiere Underground Gardens (M7), Fresno

18. Warthan Creek (M3), Coalinga

19. Canals of the Great Valley: these four major aqueducts parallel to Highway 33 were built to water California's most productive farmland

20. Fresno County Slough

21. Black Mountain (3,640 feet)

22. Mendota Wildlife Area (M2)

23. San Joaquin River (M3)

24. Burrough Mountains: these mountains form the western border of the Sierra National Forest

25. Kaiser Federal Wilderness Area (M1): a small wilderness area of 23,000 acres, noted for its biodiverse forests and proximity to the Ansel Adams Wilderness

26. Florence Lake (M5)

27. Lake Thomas Edison (M5)

Map 09.11 Glenn: Wheat and Wildlife

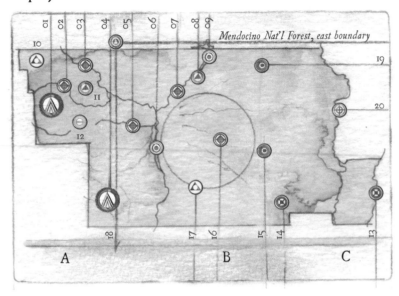

15 miles

09.11

A. **West county:** Bush Mountain (02) (6,500 feet)
B. **Mid county:** Saint John Mountain (04) (6,746 feet)
C. **East county:** Sacramento River (20) (150 feet)

Named for the most successful wheat farmer of 19th-century California, Glenn County slopes down from Mendocino National Forest to the west shore of the Sacramento River almost halfway to Mount Shasta and the capital city.

01. Brushy Mountain (6,760 feet)

02. Cold Creek (M3)

03. Grindstone Creek (M3)

04. Saint John Mountain (6,746 feet)

05. Salt Creek (M3) and the Bear Wallow Trail (M8)

06. Stony Gorge Reservoir (M5): this reservoir is adjacent to Black Butte Lake, the other dammed reservoir fed by Stony Creek in Glenn County

07. Stony Creek (M3): the predominant watershed in Glenn County

08. Big Oak Nature Trail (M8)

09. Black Butte Lake (M5, M2): home to the Burris Creek Wildlife Area (M8)

10. Black Butte (7,448 feet): the highest peak in Glenn County and headwaters of Cold Creek (M3) and the Black Butte River (M3), both of which join the west-flowing Eel River, accessible by the Black Butte Trail (M8) and the Masterson Group Camp (M9)

11. Thomas Gorge Trail (M8): this trail, whose trailhead is in Tehama County, offers access to the four peaks that define Glenn County's northwest corner

12. Grindstone Overlook (M7): this overlook on Alder Springs Road east from Shepherd Ridge offers views of Grindstone Creek to the north and the Salt Creek Valley to the south

13. Upper Butte Basin Wildlife Area (M2): this wildlife area provides fishing access (M8) on Butte Creek (M3)

14. Sacramento National Wildlife Refuge (M2): although walking access is limited, this refuge has a wildlife viewing platform (M7)

15. Willows: this city is the location of the headquarters of the Mendocino National Forest (M7)

16. Farmlands of the Tehama Colusa Canal: this area is outlined by Walker Creek, Wilson Creek, French Creek, Hayes Hollow Creek, Nye Creek, South Creek, Willow Creek, Hunters Creek, and Logan Creek

17. Gravelly Ridge and Elephant Hill (2,996 feet)

18. Eastern boundary of Mendocino National Forest

19. Orland: a farming city noted for its olive oil production

20. Sacramento River (M3)

Chipping sparrow
Spizella passerine

Starling
sturnus vulgari

Map 09.12 Humboldt: Old Growth in the Land of the Owl

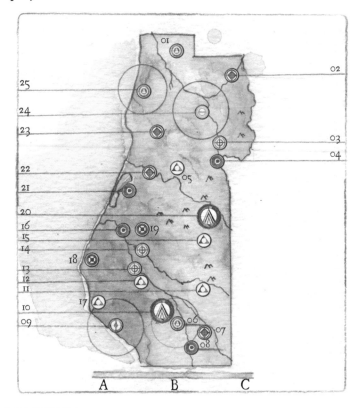

27 miles

09.12

A **West county:** Cape Ridge above Eureka (21) (1,200 feet)
B **Mid county:** Headwaters Grove (19) (2,500 feet)
C **East county:** Larabee Buttes (15) (4,196 feet)

As home to some of the most pristine old-growth forest habitat left in existence and offering refuge to the last populations of many species who depend on that habitat, including the Humboldt marten and the northern spotted owl, Humboldt County has long been home to conflict between conservationists and loggers.

01. Six Rivers National Forest: about 30 percent of this massive national forest lies in Humboldt County; the rest extends in a narrow corridor for about 150 miles from the Oregon border down into Mendocino County

02. Klamath River (M3): this river, the largest in northwest California, enters Humboldt County at Ishi Pishi Falls and runs down from Salmon Mountain, near George Geary Park (M7)

03. Trinity River (M3): this is the largest tributary of the Klamath River; it joins the Klamath down from Mill Creek Ridge, near the border of Redwood National Park and the Aikens Creek camp (M9)

04. Willow Creek and the Boise Creek camp (M9): this town is famous for being a possible home of the legendary Bigfoot

05. Tip Top Ridge and the Horse Mountain Botanical Area (M6): this area runs north–south at the intersection of Highways 299 and 101, near the Azalea State Reserve (M6)

06. Humboldt Redwoods State Park (M1): this park is home to the Rockefeller Grove (M6), the largest remaining single tract of old-growth coast redwood forest

07. Eel River: this river's two forks meet at the Avenue of the Giants (M6)

08. Benbow Lake State Recreation Area (M7), Garberville

09. Kings Range National Conservation Area (M1): this geological anomaly, a major earthquake zone, is the site where three tectonic plates meet—the Pacific Plate, the North American Plate, and the Juan de Fuca Plate; the area provides 60,000 acres of protected habitat for many endangered species, including the Chinook salmon and the brown pelican

10. Grasshopper Mountain (3,379 feet) and Burlington camp (M9)

11. Larabee Buttes (4,196 feet)

12. Mount Pierce (3,185 feet)

13. Eel River (M3): aside from the Klamath, the Eel is the major aquatic

Humboldt marten
Martes americana humboldtensis

conduit through these mountains; it is 200 miles long and has varying outflow due to localized geologic instability and potentially huge seasonal rains

14. Van Duzen River (M3): this river was named for one of the original explorers of this county; its headwaters are in the Mount Lassics Federal Wilderness Area (M1)

15. Black Buttes (4,132 feet)

16. Rohner Park (M7), Fortuna

17. Bear River Ridge: four major waterways (from north to south, the Salt River, Oil Creek, Bear River, and the Braid River) run down from both this ridge and the parallel Rainbow Ridge; the ridge is traced by the Lost Coast Headlands Trail (M8)

18. Cape Mendocino: this is the westernmost point of the mainland United States

19. Headwaters Forest Reserve (M6): this reserve, accessible by the Salmon Pass (M8) (trail by reservation only) contains the low peaks east of Eureka and down to the Van Duzen River, where many strong creeks originate, including Elk Creek, Salmon Creek, Yage Creek, Lawrence Creek, and Freshwater Creek; Headwaters was the site of forest conservation protests in the late 1990s, when the reserve was established

20. Bug Creek Butte (5,259 feet)

21. Eureka and Humboldt Bay: Eureka is home to more than half the human population of Humboldt County; Humboldt Bay (M2), the second-largest natural bay in California after San Francisco Bay, offers sanctuary to a whole host of biodiversity, including hundreds of species each of plants, invertebrate, fish, and birds

22. Mad River (M3): this river, which runs 120 miles to the coast, has its headwaters in Trinity County

23. Redwood Creek (M3): this 60-mile-long river with an approximately 190,000-acre watershed in Redwood National Park has its mouth near Orick

24. Hoopa Reservation: this is the largest Native Californian reservation in California

25. Redwood National Park (M1): one of four parks, both state and national, in Humboldt and Del Norte Counties that protect almost half of the remain old-growth redwood forest

thrasher
Toxostoma rufum

Map 09.13 Imperial: The Salton Sea and the Southern Desert

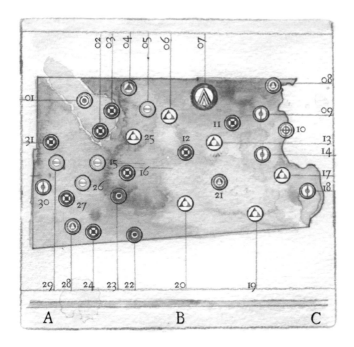

30 miles

09.13

A **West county:** Lower Borrego Valley (31) (380 feet)
B **Mid county:** Salvation Pass (06) (1,020 feet)
C **East county:** Indian Pass (17) (1,920 feet)

The southeastern corner of the state is a major agricultural area. The 8,000-square-mile Imperial Valley extends from the Salton Sea to the border of Mexico. The Salton Sink became the Salton Sea in 1902, when an intake canal along the Colorado River broke and flooded the valley.

01. The Salton Sea (M2), banked by Desert Beach Park (M7) and Bombay Beach (M9)

02. Salton Sea National Wildlife Refuge (M2) and the Red Hill Marina County Recreation Area (M9)

03. Wister Waterfowl Management Area (M2)

04. Hot Mineral Spa Road and the Seaview Spa (M7)

05. Chocolate Mountains Artillery Range: this range was closed to the public due to live bombing—only a small portion of this de facto ecological reserve is being used by the military for shelling

06. Salvation Pass (1,020 feet): this pass deep in the Chocolate Mountains Gunnery Range is now closed

07. Flat Tops (1,604 feet)

08. Palo Verde County Park (M9): a green oasis on the Colorado River

09. Palo Verde Mountains Federal Wilderness Area (M1): Clapp Spring is the only permanent water in this 30,000-acre wilderness, and it is a sanctuary for desert wildlife

10. Colorado River (M3)

11. Palo Verde: this region lies between the Chocolate Mountains and the Colorado River; here, the Milpitas Wash empties into the verdant Cibola Valley and the Cibola Valley National Wildlife Area (M1) at Three Finger Lake

12. Chocolate Mountains and Algodones Dunes: this area is accessible at the headquarters at Cahuilla Ranger Station and Visitors Center (M7), near Gecko camp (M9); North Algodones Dunes Federal Wilderness Area (M1), at 25,000 acres, is home to one of the largest dune complexes in North America

13. Mount Barrow (2,475 feet) and the Pre-Columbian Indian Trail Exhibit (M7)

14. Indian Pass Federal Wilderness Area (M1): this 32,000-acre wilderness area surrounds Quartz Peak (2,177 feet)

15. Superstition Hills: this naval bombing area is closed to the public

16. Imperial Valley: the New River (M3) occasionally flows down the middle of this agricultural area, through the Imperial State Wildlife Area (M2) and West Lake County Park (M9)

17. Indian Pass (1,020 feet) and Mica Peak (1,920 feet)

18. Picacho Peak Federal Wilderness Area (M1): a 9,000-acre wilderness area adjacent to the Picacho State Recreation Area (M9); the Little Picacho Peak Federal Wilderness Area (M1) is 38,000 acres and adjacent to the Imperial National Wildlife Refuge (M2), home to a herd of 25 bighorn sheep; Senator Wash Reservoir (M5) and Ferguson Reservoir (M5) are both reservoirs near the Colorado River

19. Cargo Muchacho Mountains and the Golden Rock Trading Post and Museum (M7)

20. East Mesa and the Tamarisk Long Term Visitor Area (M7)

21. Imperial Sand Dunes Recreational Area (M1) and Midway camp (M9)

22. Sunbeam Lake County Park (M9), El Centro

23. West Lake County Park (M9), Brawley

24. Yuha Desert: this ecological gem is home to the Crucifixion Thorn Natural Area (M6), which exemplifies Colorado Desert ecology; the Jacumba Mountains Federal Wilderness Area (M1) is 31,000 acres and home to the Valley of the Moon Trail (M8).

25. Leonard Knight's Salvation Mountain (M7)

26. United States Navy Gunnery Center at West Mesa

27. Coyote Mountains and the Yuha Desert Recreation Area (M7): this area is part of the 19,000-acre Coyote Mountains Federal Wilderness Area (M1)

28. Ocotillo Wells State Vehicular Recreation Area (M7)

29. Carrizo Impact Area (M1): closed to the public for scientific-research purposes

30. 21,000-acre Fish Creek Mountains Federal Wilderness Area (M1)

31. Lower Borrego Valley and Elephant Trees camp (M8)

california fan palm
Washingtonia filifera

Map 09.14 Inyo: The Tallest, the Lowest, and the Oldest

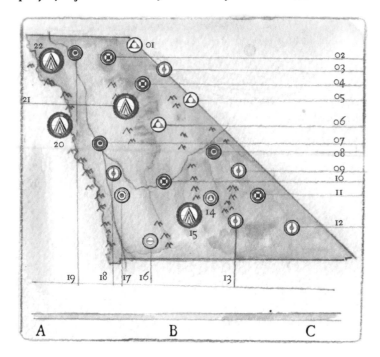

55 miles

09.14

A West county: Bishop (19) (4,147 feet)
B Mid county: Panamint Valley (10) (1,900 feet)
C East county: Pahrump Valley Wilderness (12) (2,000 feet)

Inyo County has the most disparate elevation profile in the United States, from Badwater Basin in Death Valley, the lowest point in the lower 48, to Mount Whitney, the highest. It is home to one of the oldest tree species in the world: the bristlecone pine of White Mountain. Every part of this dramatic landscape can be described by some superlative: the highest, the oldest, the lowest, etc.

01. The White Mountains: which, along with Shasta and the Whitney Range, are the only mountain ranges in the state that rise above 14,000 feet; it is home to the White Mountain Research Natural Area (M6), managed by the University of California

02. Methuselah Bristlecone Pine Forest (M6), and Grandview Camp (M9): at over 5,000 years old, this is the oldest living forest in the world

03. The Sylvania Mountains Federal Wilderness Area (M1): a 19,000-acre wilderness area; Piper Mountains Federal Wilderness Area (M1) is 72,000 acres and home to the northernmost stand of Joshua trees

Inyo mule deer
Odocoileus hemionus

04. Eureka Valley and the Eureka Dunes (M8)*

05. Cottonwood Mountains and the Panamint Range: Towne Pass (4,957 feet) is the road through this range, and is a wildflower hot spot near Emigrant camp (M9)*

06. Inyo Mountains: these mountains are composed mainly of Cambrian-age stone; the 199,000-acre Inyo Mountains Wilderness (M1) is adjacent to the 32,000-acre Malpais Mesa Federal Wilderness Area (M1)

07. The Whitney Portal (M7): the access point to Mount Whitney (M8), across the Alabama Hills to the west of the town of Lone Pine (M9)

08. Furnace Creek* (M8): home to the Salt Creek Interpretive Trail (M8)

09. Resting Spring Range Mountain Federal Wilderness Area (M1): 76,000 acres surrounding Shadow Mountain (5,071 feet); Funeral Mountains Federal Wilderness Area (M1) is 26,000 acres and surrounds Schwaub Peak (6,448 feet)

10. Panamint Valley: this valley is the twin valley to Death Valley; the west slope of Telescope Peak rises up out of the Surprise Canyon Federal Wilderness Area (M1), which covers 24,000 acres; two other wilderness areas in the vicinity include the 7,000-acre Manly Peak Federal Wilderness Area and the 66,000-acre Argus Range Wilderness (M1)

11. Chicago Valley: this valley is home to the Nopah Range Federal Wilderness Area (M1) at 107,000 acres, next to Nopah Peak (1,946 feet); the South

foothill yellow-legged frog
Rana Boylii

Nopah Range Federal Wilderness Area (M1) is 17,000 acres and adjacent to the Emigrant Pass (870 feet).

12. Pahrump Valley Federal Wilderness Area (M1)*: this 74,000-acre wilderness area is home to a large population of wild burros

13. Death Valley Federal Wilderness Area (M1)*: in this three-million-acre transition area between the Mojave Desert and the Great Basin desert, which receives only two inches of rain per year, both creosote bush and Joshua tree are found in diminishing numbers

14. Death Valley National Park (M1)*: at over 3.3 million acres, this is the largest national park in California

15. Telescope Peak (11,049 feet)*: this is the tallest peak in Death Valley National Park, and is accessible via the Telescope Peak camp (M8) and the Mahogany Flat Trail (M9)

16. China Lake Naval Weapons Center: one of the Mojave Desert's five major military bases; closed to the public

17. Coso Range: home to the 43,000-acre Coso Range Federal Wilderness Area (M1), adjacent to the Coso Peak (8,160 feet), a peak inside the China Lake basin; it shares a border with the 50,000-acre Sacatar Trail Federal Wilderness Area

18. Owens Lake: a dry lakebed, drained by the Los Angeles aqueduct, near Diaz Lake campground (M9)

19. Bishop: the largest city on Highway 395 in California; Browns Mill Pond camp (M9), Pleasant Valley camp (M9, M3), and Browns Town (M9) are all in the city limits

20. The high ridge of the Sierra Nevada: this is the western border of Inyo County and defines the 652,000-acre John Muir Wilderness (M1)

21. Waucoba Mountain (11,123 feet): the highest peak in the Inyo Mountains and home to the Whippoorwill Flat Natural Research Area (M1)

22. Mount Humphreys (13,986 feet): this peak rises over Lake Sabrina (M5) and Bishop Park camp (M9); Piute Pass Trail (M8) cuts through the Buttermilk County Wildlife Area (M1)

* feature inside Death Valley National Park

Bristlecone pine
Pinus longaeva

Map 09.15 Kern: Mountains Merging

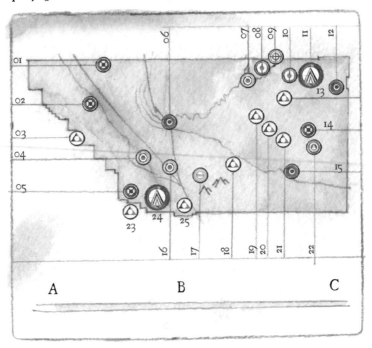

31 miles

09.15

A **West county:** Antelope Valley (02) (300 feet)
B **Mid county:** Bakersfield (16) (400 feet)
C **East county:** Tehachapi (15) (3,973 feet)

Kern County draws its borders around the bottom of the San Joaquin Valley, where the Transverse Mountain Ranges, the Sierra Nevada, and the Mojave Desert all converge. Fort Tejon, where oak trees and Joshua trees mingle, is the best spot to take in the convergence.

01. Kern National Wildlife Refuge (M2): this refuge comprises 1,300 acres of restored wetlands

02. Tule Elk State Reserve (M1, M7)

03. Temblor Range: this range, saddled by Temblor Pass (3,250 feet), runs parallel to the San Andreas Fault Zone

04. The lakes of south Kern County: these lakes, adjacent to Lake Webb (M5, M9), include Buena Vista and Kern Lake, both of which are dry, having been drained for irrigation

anna's hummingbird
Calypte anna

05. Bitter Creek National Wildlife Refuge (M1): this 15,000-acre refuge is a condor reintroduction site

06. Kern River County Park (M7), Bakersfield

07. Kern River: the upper part of this river flows into Isabella Lake (M5) and the lower Kern River flows out; camp at Pioneer Point (M9) and explore the local South Fork Wildlife Area (M1)

08. Domeland Federal Wilderness Area (M1): most of this 134,000-acre wilderness is in Inyo County and is traced by Cannell Meadow National Recreation Trail (M8), on the slopes of Pilot Knob (6,200 feet)

09. Audubon Visitor Center (M7, M2), on the banks of the south fork of the Kern River (M3)

10. Kiavah Federal Wilderness Area (M1): this 87,000-acre wilderness on the Mojave side of the Sierra is one of only two protected areas that support a pinyon-juniper forest in California, the other being the Mojave National Preserve; Black Peak (7,030 feet) is the tallest peak in the local Scodie Mountains, which are crossed by Walker Pass (M8)

11. Owens Peak (8,453 feet): this peak reigns over the 74,000-acre Owens Peak Federal Wilderness Area (M1); in May, make sure to stop at the wild-flower viewing area on Highway 395 (M7)

12. Ridgecrest Regional Wild-horse and Burro Facility (M7): this facility is located under Lone Ridge (M8), near the 24,000-acrea El Paso Mountains Federal Wilderness Area (M1)

13. Piute Mountains: these mountains harbor the Inspiration Point Botanical Area (M6), the Bright Star Trail (M8), and the 8,000-acre Bright Star Federal Wilderness Area (M1)

14. Jawbone–Butterbredt Area of Critical Environmental Concern (M1) and Pinyon Mountain (6,182 feet)

15. Tehachapi Pass (3,799 feet): the southernmost pass over the Sierra Nevada; Horse Canyon Area of Environmental Concern (M1) is near the pass and provides Pacific Crest Trail access (M8)

16. Kern Lake Bed: this lakebed has been drained for irrigation

17. Tejon Ranch: 270,000 acres of private ranchland and conservancy

18. The Tehachapi Mountains: these mountains top out at Double Mountain (7,981 feet) and can be enjoyed at the Tehachapi Mountain County Park (M9)

19. Breckenridge Mountain (7,548 feet): this is the highest peak in the Greenhorn Mountains, and home to the Breckenridge camp (M9)

20. Piute Peak (8,417 feet)

21. Weldon Peak (6,367 feet): this peak lies at the southern tip of the Sequoia National Forest

22. Red Rock Canyon State Park (M1): this state park is home to the Petrified Forest, the Last Chance Canyon Geologic Area (M1), the Red Cliffs Trail (M8), and the Ricardo camp (M9), and is near the Desert Tortoise Natural Area (M1) and the Desert Tortoise Interpretive Center (M7)

23. The San Emigdio Mountains: these mountains are home to the 38,000-acre Chumash Federal Wilderness Area (M1) and Campo Alto (M9)

24. Mount Pinos (8,831 feet): this peak in the San Emigdio Mountains is the tallest west of Tejon Pass in the South Coast Ranges

25. Tejon Pass: also called the Grapevine, this is where the Mojave Desert meets the Sierra Nevada and the coastal Transverse Ranges; it is home to Fort Tejon State Historic Park (M7)

Golden eagle
aquila chrysaetos

Map 09.16 Kings: The Ghost of California's Largest Lake

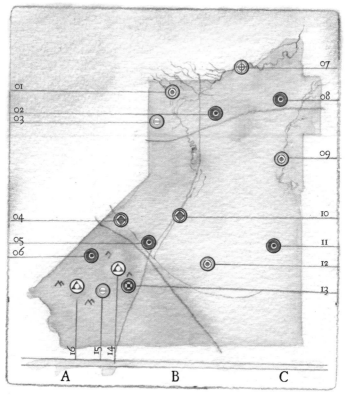

13 miles

09.13

A **West county:** Kettleman Hills (13) (700 feet)
B **Mid county:** Tulare Lake Bed (12) (200 feet)
C **East county:** Cross Creek Slough (09) (200 feet)

In 1805, on the Wise Men's Feast Day, the Spanish first mapped the river they were compelled to name Rio de los Santos Reyes: Kings River. Its mouth was once California's largest lake, Lake Tulare, drained for irrigation ditches in the latter half of the 19th century. In some particularly wet winters, the vestige flood of the lake comes back—a ghost ecology of a once-great river basin.

01. Fresno Slough and the sloughs of Tulare Lake: these sloughs line up where the Kings River empties into the wetlands, and are the historical source of Tulare Lake; the two largest sloughs are Murphy Slough and Cole Slough

02. Hickey Park (M7), Lemoore

03. Lemoore Naval Air Station

04. California Aqueduct

05. Westlake Farms (M7), Kettleman City

06. Avenal: a city named for the waist-high native oats that once dominated the landscape of this part of the Central Valley (avenal means "oats" in Spanish)

07. Kings River (M3): this river can be enjoyed at the nearby Burris Park and Museum (M7)

08. Clark Center for Japanese Art (M7), Hanford

09. Cross Creek Slough and Mill Creek Slough: both of these sloughs were diverted by a series of canals, and mark where traces of the Kaweah River still exist as it disappears on its approach to Kings County from Tulare County

10. Blakeley Canal: one of Kings County's main irrigation diversion canals

11. Corcoran: a city in the flatlands, which, in wet years, may still form vernal pools at the mouth of the Tule River

12. Tulare Lake Bed: this is the site of California's largest historical lake, now a dry lakebed

13. The Kettleman Hills, Plain, and Valley: this region is home to extensive oil fields

14. La Cima (1,326 feet)

15. Kettleman North Dome Oil Field: the largest oil and gas field in Kings County

16. Garza Peak (2,698 feet), Reef Ridge

Chukar
Alectoris chukar

377

Map 09.17 Lake: America's Oldest Lake

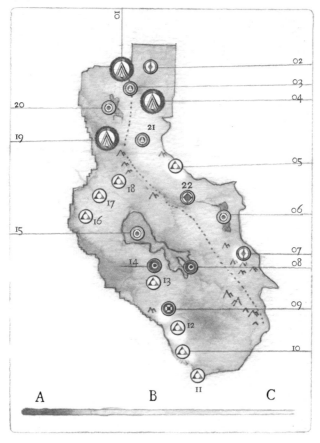

A South county: Boggs Forest (09) (2,620 feet)
B Mid county: Clear Lake (15) (1,326 feet)
C North county: Lake Pillsbury (20) (3,000 feet)

On the south shore of Clear Lake, California's oldest lake, the long-dead volcano Mount Konocti has presented archeological evidence of continued habitation by the Pomo tribe for the past 20,000 years.

8 miles

09.17

01. Hull Mountain (6,873 feet) and the Sheet Iron State Game Reserve (M1)*: access includes Bloody Rock Trail (M8)

02. Snow Mountain Federal Wilderness Area (M1)*: this 60,000-acre wilderness area has Lower Nye camp (M9) at its eastern border, with access including the North Ridge Trail (M8)

03. Berryessa Snow Mountain National Monument (M1): this monument's western border* is in Lake County; it also extends into six other counties—Napa, Yolo, Solano, Colusa, Glenn, and Mendocino

04. East Snow Mountain (7,056 feet)* and the Upper Nye Trail (M8)

05. Pacific Ridge* and the Cedar camp (M9) on the slopes of Goat Mountain (6,121 feet)

06. Indian Springs Reservoir (M5)*: this reservoir lies under Walker Ridge Road and across from Blue Oaks camp (M9) on Baldy Mountain (3,404 feet)

07. Cache Creek Federal Wilderness Area (M1)*: these 27,000 acres are home to the Cache Creek Natural Area (M6), the North Fork Trail (M8), and the Judge Davis Trail (M8)

08. Cache Creek (M3): this creek, the one outflow of Clear Lake, makes up the Anderson Marsh State Historic Park (M2)

09. Boggs Mountain State Forest (M1), along Big Canyon Creek (M3)

10. Pine Mountain (3,614 feet)

11. Mount Saint Helena (4,343 feet): the northernmost peak in the greater San Francisco Bay Area

12. Cobb Mountain (4,720 feet): this peak looms over Anderson Creek (M3)

13. Mount Konocti (4,299 feet): this peak dominates the skyline south of Clear Lake State Park (M9)

14. Lake County Visitor Center (M7), Kelseyville

15. Clear Lake: at 480,000 years old, this is the oldest natural lake in North America

16. Mayacamas Mountains and the North Cow Mountains Recreation Area (M1): this area is best accessed by the Willow Creek Trail (M8)

17. White Rock Mountain (2,690 feet): this mountain lies up from Scotts Creek (M3) and along the Glen Eden Trail (M8)

18. Pitney Ridge: this ridge tops out at Youngs Peak (3,683 feet), along the Sled Ridge National Recreation Trail (M8)

19. Elk Mountain (4,191 feet): this mountain has a view of Clear Lake Valley on Upper Deer Valley Road (M7) and can be enjoyed at Deer Valley campground (M9)

20. Lake Pillsbury (M5): this lake was formed by the Scott Dam, on the Eel River as it flows through after leaving its headwaters in Mendocino County, and is home to the Oak Flat campground (M9)

21. Mendocino National Forest: this
national forest includes the Berryessa
Snow Mountain National Monument,
in the vicinity of Bear Creek (M9)*

22. North fork of Cache Creek*: this
creek's watershed includes Little Horse
Mountain (3,420 feet)

*feature located within the Berryessa
Snow Mountain National Monument

Western Tanager
Piranga ludoviciana

Map 09.18 Lassen: Wild Horses over the Sagebrush

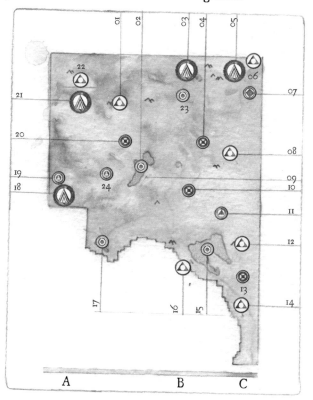

18 miles

09.18

A **West county:** Lassen Volcanic Federal Wilderness Area (19) (6,043 feet)
B **Mid county:** Eagle Lake (02) (5,800 feet)
C **East county:** Honey Lake (15) (3,986 feet)

Lassen County is home to Honey Lake, named for the sweet milk found in the wild oats that grow along its banks. The Great Basin Desert spreads into Lassen County from Nevada and brings with it an arid march of purple sagebrush prairie populated with 300-year-old herds of wild horses.

01. Dixie Valley State Game Refuge (M1): this game refuge surrounds the Silver Flat Reservoir (M5) under Snag Hill (6,072 feet), near Willow Creek (M9)

02. Eagle Lake: this is the second-largest natural lake in California, after Lake Tahoe; it is wedged between the Brockman Flat Lava Beds to the west and Mahogany Peak to the east; Eagle Lake Recreation Area (M2) is near the California State University Chico Biological Station (M1) and includes an osprey viewpoint (M7) and Aspen Grove (M9)

03. Tule Mountain (7,098 feet), up from Dry Creek (M9)

04. Madeline Plains: high plateau

05. Red Rock Mountain (8,518 feet), over Blue Lake (M5, M9)

06. Warner Mountains: Lassen County is home to the southernmost extent of this range

07. Silver Creek Wildlife Area (M1)

08. Observation Peak (7,931 feet)

09. Mahogany Peak (7,194 feet): this peak is located inside the Willow Creek Wildlife Area (M1)

10. Biscar National Wildlife Area (M1) and the Petroglyphs Trail (M8)

11. Lassen Trail (M8): this trail, a 19th-century route to California, skirts the Skedaddle Mountains and is home to the Bureau of Land Management's wild horse adoption corrals (M7)

12. Hot Springs Peak (7,680 feet)

13. Long Valley: this valley defines Doyle Wildlife Area (M1) and the Crocker Meadows Wildlife Area (M1)

14. Adams Peak (8,197 feet): the tallest peak in the Diamond Mountains

15. Honey Lake: a natural lake that is off-limits to the public and home to the Honey Lake Wildlife Area (M1); along its banks is the Sierra Army Depot

16. Laufman Camp (M9), Diamond Mountains

17. Mountain Meadows Reservoir (M5): this reservoir fills the valley between Coyote Peak and Keddle Ridge

18. Ash Butte (7,577 feet): this butte is located inside Lassen National Park and the 79,000-acre Lassen Volcanic Federal Wilderness Area (M1); the 21,000-acre Caribou Federal Wilderness Area (M1) lies near and is accessed by Triangle Lake Trail (M8)

19. Lassen National Park (M1): this park only partially extends into Lassen County from Plumas, Tehama, and Shasta Counties; just as Mount Shasta is not actually in Shasta County, Mount Lassen Peak is not in Lassen County

20. Crater Mountain (7,420 feet): this mountain lies above Crater Lake, a rich fishing area best enjoyed from Crater Lake Camp (M9).

21. Fourth Butte (4,750 feet): home to the Cinder Flats Wildlife Area (M1) on the Pit River (M3), as it dips down for 23 miles in Lassen County

22. Big Valley Mountains: Big Valley Mountain Summit (4,603 feet) is the tallest peak in the Big Valley Mountains and home to Ash Creek Wildlife Area (M1), which saddles Modoc County in Big Valley (4,125 feet); all can be surveyed from the Ash Creek wildlife viewpoint (M7)

23. Blue Deer Flat Wildlife Viewing Area (M7), Moon Lake (M5)

24. Lassen National Forest: the lonely, separated peaks of Lassen National Forest belong to the Cascade Mountains; deep valleys echo these volcanoes throughout the region, including Bogard Camp (M9) on Highway 44

Sagebrush penstemon
Penstemon speciosus

Map 09.19 Los Angeles: City and Wilderness

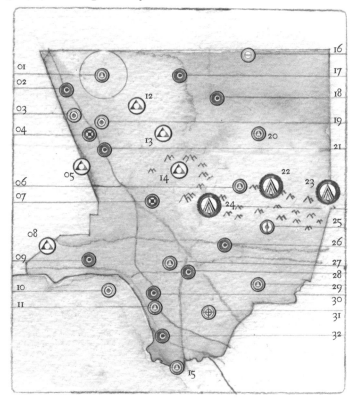

16 miles

09.19

A **West county:** Pyramid Lake (3) (2,578 feet)
B **Mid county:** San Fernando Valley (07) (1,061 feet)
C **East county:** Puente Hills (29) (900 feet)

The most populous county in the state includes some of the greatest urban access to localized wilderness of any city in California. The two generalized ecologies of urbanity and wildness collide here in a unique ecotone. Despite the present-day human environment that is the Los Angeles River Basin, wildness skirts in from all directions.

Note: This map does not include Santa Catalina Island, which is part of Los Angeles County; see map 03.37.

01. Angeles National Forest: this national forest includes the Portal Ridge, most of the Sierra Pelona, and the San Gabriel Mountains

02. Interstate 5 and Tejon Pass (4,144 feet), near Oak Flat (M9) and under Violin Summit (2,591 feet)

03. Pyramid Lake (M5) and Los Alamos (M9) at the Vista Del Lago Visitor Info Center (M7)

04. Santa Clarita Valley and Hart County Park (M7)

05. Santa Susana Mountains and Oat Mountain (3,747 feet): this area includes Ed Davis Park (M7) and Santa Clarita Woodlands Park (M7) and is connected by the Towsley Wiley Canyons Trail (M8)

06. San Gabriel National Monument (M1)

07. San Fernando Valley and the Descanso Gardens (M7)

08. Santa Monica Mountains: this region includes Castro Peak (2,824 feet), Malibu Creek State Park (M1), Topanga Canyon State Park (M1), Cold Creek Canyon Preserve (M1), the Backbone Trail (M8), and the Leo Carrillo State Beach (M9)

09. Westside cities: these cities include Calabasas, Malibu, Santa Monica, and Sullivan Canyon (M8)

10. Santa Monica Bay and the Marina Del Rey Lagoon (M2)

11. South Bay cities: these cities include Manhattan Beach, Hermosa Beach, and Redondo Beach, and are home to Manhattan State Beach (M7)

12. Portal Ridge and Liebre Mountain (5,760 feet)

13. Sierra Pelona and Mount McDill (5,187 feet)

14. San Gabriel Mountains and the 44,000-acre Sheep Mountain Wilderness

15. Palos Verdes Hills, in the city of Rolling Hills (1,000 feet), and the Royal Palms State Beach (M7)

16. Edwards Air Force Base: this air force base is closed to public

17. Apollo County Park (M9), Lancaster

18. Antelope Valley: a large, swooping land feature that is home to the Antelope Valley California Poppy State Reserve (M6)

19. Castaic Lake (M5) and the Castaic State Recreation Area (M9)

20. Saddle Back Butte State Park (M9) and the Alpine Butte Wildlife Sanctuary (M1)

21. Ed David Park (M7), Santa Clarita

22. Mount Baden-Powell (9,399 feet) and Big Rock (M9)

23. Mount San Antonio (M8), aka Old Baldy (10,064 feet), and Old Baldy Trail

24. San Gabriel Peak (6,161 feet): a peak over Valley Forge (M9), along the

Silver Moccasin National Recreation Trail (M8) up to the Mount Wilson Observatory

25. San Gabriel Federal Wilderness Area: this 36,000-acre wilderness area is crossed by the West Fork National Recreation Trail (M8)

26. Highway 210: this highway runs near the Rancho Santa Ana Botanic Garden (M7) and the LA Arboretum (M7)

27. Central Los Angeles and the Los Angeles River (M3): this area includes Elysian Park (M7), Ernest Debs Park (M7), Griffith Park (M7), Runyan Canyon Park (M7), and Franklin Canyon Reservoir (M5), and is overlooked by Cahuenga Peak (1,820 feet) in the Hollywood Hills

28. Highway 10: this highway runs near the Whittier Narrows Recreation Area Nature Center (M7) and the Bonelli Regional Park (M7)

29. Puente Hills and the Rose Hills Memorial Park (M7)

30. Highway 405: this highway runs through Sepulveda Canyon, parallel to the Stone Canyon Reservoir Trail (M8)

31. The Gateway cities: these cities include West Covina, Downey, Norwalk, and Long Beach and all lie along the San Gabriel River (M3), which empties at Alamitos Bay

32. Highway 1: this highway passes South Coast Botanic Garden (M7) in Lomita and wraps along the coast for the entirety of Los Angeles County

Map 09.20 Madera: Timber at the Center of California

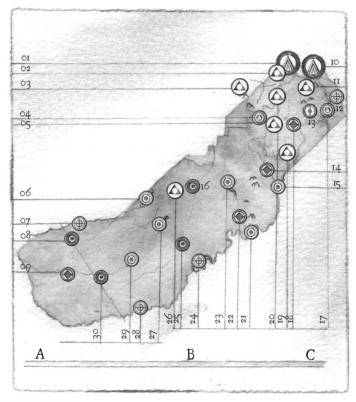

18 miles

09.20

A **West county:** Chowchilla (07) (240 feet)
B **Mid county:** Oakhurst (16) (2,289 feet)
C **East county:** Devils Postpile National Monument (17)
 (7,500 feet)

If you were able to spin California on your finger, the center point you would pick is in Madera County. Madera is Spanish for "timber." The Chowchilla River forms the county's northern border. Part of Yosemite National Park lies in Madera County, as does the Sierra National Forest, which includes Devils Postpile National Monument.

01. Mount Lyell (13,144 feet)*: this peak divides Mono, Madera, and Tuolumne Counties

02. Mount Florence (12,561 feet)*: this mountain, in the Cathedral Range, is the headwaters of the Merced River

03. Merced Peak (11,726 feet): this is the highest point in the Clark Range*

04. Yosemite National Park (M1): this park has its southern border in Madera County; it also extends into Mariposa and Tuolumne Counties

05. Madera Peak (10,509 feet): this peak is traced by the Norris Trail (M8), which leads to the Bowler Group Camp (M9)

06. Eastman Lake (M5) and the Raymond Bridge Recreation Area (M8) near Cordorniz (M9)

07. Chowchilla River (M3): from Eastman Lake, this river forms Madera County's northern border

08. Berenda Reservoir (M5) and the Berenda Slough in Chowchilla

09. Fresno River: this intermittent waterway has been diverted for irrigation

10. Banner Peak (12,945 feet): this peak was famously John Muir's favorite in the Ritter Range

11. Ritter Range: this range is defined by Mount Ritter (13,140 feet) and Banner Peak (12,945 feet) over the picturesque Thousand Island Lake and Garnet Lake, all along the John Muir Trail (M8)

12. Headwaters of the middle fork of the San Joaquin River

burrowingowl
Athene cunicularia

13. Ansel Adams Wilderness (M1): 231,533 acres

14. Chiquito Creek (M3): this creek under the Chiquito Ridge runs parallel to Boarsore Creek (M3), down from the Mile High Vista Point on Highway 81 (M7), near Soda Springs (M9)

15. Mammoth Pool Reservoir (3,330 feet) (M5): this reservoir is circled by Logan Meadow Trail (M8) and Sweet Water Trail (M8), up from Hells Half Acre Trail (M8)

16. Oakhurst: this city lies south of the Nelder Grove stand of giant sequoias (M6), traversed by the Shadow of the Giants (M8), up from the Yosemite Sierra Visitor Center (M7)

17. Devils Postpile National Monument (M1): this monument is near both Minaret Falls (M9) and Rainbow Falls (M8), near the headwaters of the middle fork of the San Joaquin River (M3).

18. Granite Creek (M3): this creek has its confluence with the San Joaquin River on the Cassidy Trail (M8)

19. Jackass Rock (7,112 feet) and Arch Rock: these rocks rise above and over Clover Meadow (M9)

20. Triple Divide Peak (11,607 feet)*: this peak is on the southern border of Yosemite Park and divides the watershed of the Merced River and the San Joaquin River

21. Redinger Lake (M5): this lake is at the geographic center of California, along the French Trail (M8)

22. Willow Creek (M3) and Wishon Point (M7)

23. Bass Lake (M5), under Lupin-Cedar Bluff (M9) and Goat Mountain Lookout (4,960 feet)

24. Millerton Lake (M5) and State Recreation Area, with the North Shore camp (M9)

25. San Joaquin Experimental Range (M1): 2,000 acres of sequestered scientific research land

26. Buford Mountain (2,066 feet)

27. Hensley Lake Recreation Area (M5) and Hidden View (M9)

28. San Joaquin River (M3)

29. Madera Lake (M5)

30. Chateau Lasgoity (M7): the largest winery in the Madera wine region

*feature inside Yosemite National Park

Map 09.21 Marin: Coastal Steppe and Cathedral Groves

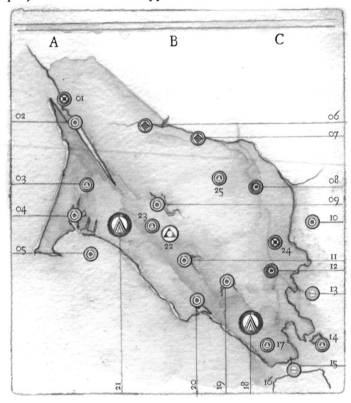

8 miles

09.21

A **West county:** Mount Wittenberg (21) (1,407 feet)
B **Mid county:** Nicasio Reservoir (09) (200 feet)
C **East county:** Novato (08) (18 feet)

A significant portion of Marin County is managed by the National Park Service at the Point Reyes National Seashore, a coastal steppe landscape with patches of native grasslands that have gone largely unchanged for a million years. The rest of it is either bucolic pastureland north of Mount Tamalpais or the mountain itself, which reigns over the Golden Gate and harbors a stand of old-growth redwood forest: a tiny jewel of well-protected wilderness.

01. Dillon Beach and Lawson's Landing (M9)

02. Tomales Bay: this bay, where the San Andreas Fault leaves California and extends into the Pacific Ocean, divides the Pacific Plate from the North American Plate; it can be enjoyed from Marshall Beach Trail (M8) near Tomales Bay State Beach (M7)

03. Point Reyes National Seashore (M1): in this segment of the Golden Gate National Seashore, Pleistocene-era coastal steppe grasslands still exist in patches beside bishop pine forests; this region is also home to the Tule Elk Reserve (M1), north of Inverness Ridge

04. Drakes Estero and Bull Point Trail (M8): this pristine estuary, a potential wilderness area, is isolated and largely roadless

05. Drakes Bay and Chimney Rock (M8) skirted by Drake's Beach (M7)

06. Walker Chileno Creek (M3)

07. San Antonio Creek (M3)

08. Mount Burdell (1,558 feet) and Mount Burdell Preserve (M1), above the city of Novato

09. Nicasio Valley and Laurel Canyon (M8), framing the Nicasio Reservoir (M5)

10. San Pablo Bay

11. Kent Lake (M5)

12. China Camp State Park (M7), San Rafael

13. Richmond–San Rafael Bridge

14. Angel Island State Park (M1)

15. Golden Gate Bridge

16. Marin Headlands: these headlands contain the steep hills and beaches of the Marin Peninsula and include the Golden Gate National Recreation Area (M1) and Redwood Creek (M3), a site of extensive salmon habitat restoration

17. Muir Woods National Monument (M1): home to 2,000-year-old groves of coast redwood forest

18. Mount Tamalpais (2,571 feet): the highest peak in Marin and home to Mount Tamalpais State Park (M1)

19. Bon Tempe Lake (M5)

20. Bolinas Lagoon (M2)

21. Mount Wittenberg (1,407 feet) and Sky Camp (M9)

22. Bolinas Ridge: this ridge is not dominated by redwood, as is the southern part of the county; its forests contain mostly Douglas fir and live oak

23. Samuel P. Taylor State Park (M9)

24. San Pablo Bay National Wildlife Refuge (M2): this bird paradise is inaccessible to the general public

25. Stafford Lake County Park (M7)

Great blue heron
Ardea herodias

Map 09.22 Mariposa: The Gateway to Yosemite

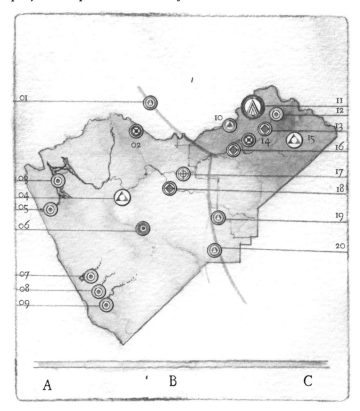

18 miles

09.22

A **West county:** Bear Lake (07) (414 feet)
B **Mid county:** Mariposa (06) (1,950 feet)
C **East county:** Yosemite Valley (14) (4,000 feet)

Within its borders, Mariposa County holds the most beautiful glacial valley in the world: the Yosemite Valley. The valley winds down the Merced River, which marks the boundary between the Stanislaus National Forest and the Sierra National Forest.

01. Eastern border of the Stanislaus National Forest

02. Lost Claim camp (M9): this camp is near the Rim of the World Viewpoint on Highway 120 (M7), near the border of Tuolumne County at Buck Meadows

03. Lake McClure (M5): this lake, also called Exchequer Reservoir, is near Horseshoe Bend (M9)

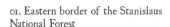
turkey vulture
Cathartes aura

04. Bullion Mountain (4,199 feet) and the Bagby Recreation Area (M9)

05. Lake McSwain (M5) and the Lake McSwain Recreation Area (M9)

06. State Mineral and Mining Museum (M7), Mariposa

07. Bear Lake (M5): this lake is fed by Bear Creek, an intermittent irrigation stream

08. Owens Lake (M5): this lake is fed by Owens Creek, an intermittent irrigation stream

09. Mariposa Lake (M5): this lake is fed by Mariposa Creek, an intermittent irrigation stream

10. The Road to Tioga Pass*, aka Highway 120: this is the road to the highest pass in the Sierra Nevada beyond the Cathedral Peaks (9,945 feet); it is closed in winter

11. Boundary Hill (8,466 feet)* on Yosemite Creek (M9)

12. Tenaya Lake (M7)*: a glacial lake of exceptional beauty

13. Tenaya Creek (M3)*: this creek runs through Tenaya Canyon, as it enters Yosemite Valley east of North Dome

14. Yosemite Valley*: The valley is eight miles in length and runs east to west from Tenaya Canyon to the Merced Gorge (M9); it is home to the natural granite monument El Capitan, which rises 3,500 feet above the valley floor

15. Mount Clark (11,522 feet): the highest peak in Mariposa County

16. Bridalveil Creek (M3): this creek runs for about 12 miles to the south of Yosemite, into where it forms Bridalveil Fall

17. Merced River (M3)

18. South fork of the Merced River (M3)

19. Yosemite National Park (M1): the west border of the park, called Yosemite West, is in Mariposa County

20. Chilnualna Creek (M3): a creek in the Sierra National Forest that runs down into Wawona, the ranger town just north of Yosemite's south entrance; the forest border runs from Clarks Valley over Footman Ridge near the town of Darrah

*feature exists in Yosemite National Park

Map 09.23 Mendocino: The Redwood Empire

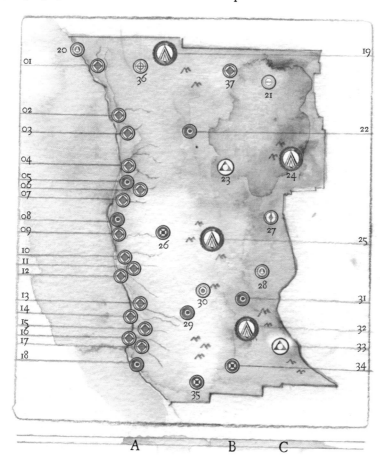

A **West county:** Sinkyone State Park (20) (1,404 feet)
B **Mid county:** Laytonville (22) (1,645 feet)
C **East county:** Bald Mountain (24) (6,212 feet)

Mendocino County is home to two major rivers, the Eel River and the headwaters of the Russian River. The Noyo, Navarro, and Albion Rivers all support ocean ports: hubs for a diminishing fishing industry. The coastal forests of redwood and Douglas fir provide habitat for about 50,000 remaining acres of old-growth forest.

01. Ursa Creek (M3) and Ursa Beach (M9)

02. Juan Creek (M3) and Westport-Union State Beach (M9)

03. Wages Creek (M3) and Wages Creek Beach (M9)

04. North fork of the Ten Mile River and MacKerricher State Park (M1)

05. Mendocino Coast Botanical Garden (M6), Fort Bragg

06. Pudding Creek (M3)

07. Novo River (M3)

08. Mendocino Headlands State Park (M7), Mendocino

09. Big River (M3) and the Montgomery Woods State Reserve (M6)

10. Little Albion River (M3) and Van Damme State Park (M9)

11. Albion River (M3) and Pygmy Forest (M6)

12. Navarro River (M3), parallel to Highway 128: along the river's path are Paul Dimmick (M9); Navarro Redwood State Park (M6), the Demonstration Forest (M6), and Hendy Woods State Park (M6)

13. Greenwood Creek (M3) and Greenwood State Beach and Visitors Center (M7)

14. Elk Creek (M3)

15. Mallow Pass Creek (M3): this creek empties into the ocean just under the vista point on Highway 1 (M7)

16. Alder Creek (M3) and Alder Creek San Andreas Fault Interpretive Center (M7)

17. Garcia River (M3) and Manchester State Park (M9)

18. Schooner Gulch State Beach (M7) and the Fish Rock Beach (M9), Point Arena

19. Red Mountain (4,095 feet)

20. Sinkyone Wilderness State Park (M1): this park is part of the Lost Coast, along with the Kings Range Conservation Area (M1) of Humboldt County; the Mattole Headwaters Ecological Reserve (M1) is traversed by Needle Rock (M8) near the Needle Rock Camp (M9)

21. Round Valley Reservation: the total resident population of this rugged land is 300

22. Standley State Recreation Area (M7), Laytonville

23. Willis Ridge: a major land feature that divides the Eel River Valley from the Cutler River Valley, near Willits

24. Yuki Federal Wilderness Area (M1): the tallest peak in this 54,000-acre wilderness area is Bald Mountain (6,212 feet)

25. Williams Peak (2,724 feet)

26. Jackson State Forest (M6): this 50,000-acre state forest is home to the pristine Ecological Staircase Nature Trail (M8)

27. Sanhedrin Federal Wilderness Area (M1): the tallest peak in this 11,000-acre wilderness area is Big Signal Peak (6,175 feet)

28. Northwestern border of the Mendocino Snow Mountain National Monument
(M1)

29. Anderson Valley, Boonville

30. Lake Mendocino (M5) and Miti (M9)

31. Mill Creek County Park (M7), Ukiah

32. Duncan Peak (2,638 feet), south of the
city of Hopland

33. The Mayacamas Mountains: these
mountains dominate the skyline east of
Highway 101 and include Red Rock
(3,277 feet), the highest peak in Mendocino County

34. Anderson Valley: an oak-dotted
region with quaint towns and ranches
that winds through the southern third of
Mendocino County

35. Maillard Redwoods State Reserve
(M6)

36. South fork of the Eel River (M3) and
the Standish-Hickey State Recreation
Area (M9) near the Smith Redwoods
Reserve (M6)

37. Eel River (M3)

Coast Redwood
Sequoia sempervirens

Map 09.24 Merced: Wildlife on the San Joaquin

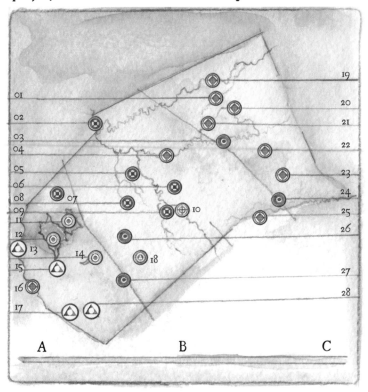

14 miles

09.24

A West county: San Luis Reservoir (12) (544 feet)
B Mid county: Los Banos (26) (120 feet)
C East county: Lingard (24) (187 feet)

Merced County is named for Nuestra Señora de la Merced (Our Lady of Mercy) and is home to the Pacheco Pass, an important 19th-century route through the Diablo Mountains. Six major wildlife refuges exist along the San Joaquin River, which runs through the center of the county.

01. Canal Creek: a diverted irrigation creek

02. West Hilmar Wildlife Area (M2): 340 acres of oaks, cottonwoods, and grasslands, adjacent to the North Grasslands Wildlife Area (M1) and the Hatfield State Recreation Area (M9)

03. Yosemite Wildlife Museum (M7), Merced

04. Bear Creek (M3)

05. San Luis Island and the Great Valley Grasslands State Park (M2): this area is near the Kesterson National Wildlife Refuge (M1), with its tule elk viewing platform (M7)

06. Merced Wildlife Area (M2): a marshland reserve in Sandy Mush Country

07. Cottonwood Creek Wildlife Area (M1): 6,000 acres on San Luis Creek (M9) near O'Neill Forebay

08. Los Banos Wildlife Area (M2): Merced County's first waterfowl refuge

09. Turner Island on the Mariposa Slough

11. O'Neill Forebay (M5)

12. San Luis Reservoir State Recreation Area (M5) and the Basalt campground (M9)

13. Pacheco Pass

14. Los Banos Creek Reservoir (M5, M9)

15. Lavedga Peak (3,801 feet): divides Merced and San Benito Counties

16. San Luis Creek: flows from Mariposa Peak (3,448 feet)

17. Ortigalita Ridge

18. California Aqueduct and the Delta Mendota Canal

19. Merced River (M3) and the McConnell State Recreation Area (M9)

20. Lake Yosemite (M5)

21. Fahrens Creek: a creek diverted for irrigation

22. Black Rascal Creek: an intermittent creek

23. Burns Creek: a creek diverted for irrigation

24. Lingard: a city in the suburbs of Merced

25. Chowchilla River (M3): divides Merced and Madera Counties

26. Volta Wildlife Area (M2), Los Baños

27. Mercy Springs Road, aka Highway 165: a paved route through wetlands

28. Sugarloaf (2,830 feet)

Map 09.25 Modoc: California's High Plateau

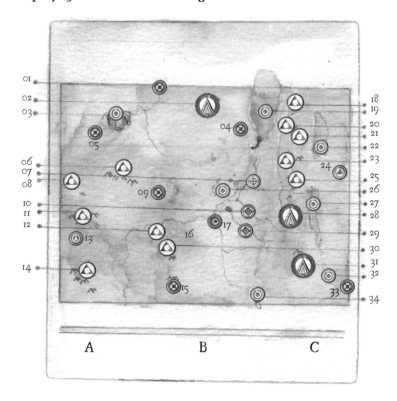

9 miles

09.25

A West county: Clear Lake Reservoir (3) (4,477 feet)
B Mid county: Big Sage Reservoir (19) (4,897 feet)
C East county: Bald Mountain (18) (8,270 feet)

Modoc County is hidden from the rest of the state by the volcanoes of the Cascade Range that rise up and form the Modoc Plateau. This volcanic region has more connection to the Great Basin Desert landscape than it does to any other part of California.

01. California's northern border with Oregon

02. Kellogg Mountain (5,467 feet): the highest point in the Fremont National Forest; Crowder Flat Fire Station (M9) is the only campground in the vicinity

03. Clear Lake Reservoir (M5) and the Clear Lake National Wildlife Refuge (M2): this reservoir is formed by the Clear Lake Dam on the Lost River

04. Devil's Garden Natural Area (M1): 400 acres of old-growth western juniper forest; logging is prohibited

05. Tule Lake Petroglyphs: this Modoc site just south of Tule Lake (M5), the Tule Lake National Wildlife Refuge (M2), and the Rim Road wildlife viewpoint (M7) is hundreds of years old and closed to the public

06. Mowitz Butte (5,128 feet)

07. Pit River (M3): this river, the largest in northeastern California, cuts through the entirety of Modoc County

08. Hollenbeck Butte (4,540 feet) and the Long Bell State Game Refuge (M1)

09. Dutch Flat Wildlife Area (M1): 160 acres of riparian and stream habitat where Jeffrey pines meet juniper sagebrush, near the Pit River Camp (M9)

10. Parker Creek (M3): home to the 100-acre Fitzhugh Creek Wildlife Area (M1) and the threatened Modoc sucker, a freshwater fish

11. Happy Camp Mountain (6,067 feet) and Cottonwood Flat (M9)

12. Schaffer Mountain (6,529 feet)

13. Modoc National Forest: in total land area, this national forest covers more than two-thirds of Modoc County

14. Splawn Mountain (4,859 feet): part of a small range of volcanic peaks called the Splawn series

15. Infernal Caves Battleground Memorial Marker near the Bayley Reservoir (M5)

16. Modoc National Wildlife Refuge (M2): more than 250 species of birds have been recorded on this 7,000-acre refuge

17. Dorris Reservoir (M5) and the Modoc National Wildlife Area Headquarters (M7), Alturas

18. Yellow Mountain (8,040 feet) and Cave Lake (M9)*

19. Goose Lake: a large alkaline lake that formed in the Pleistocene era and straddles the Oregon–California border; sometimes the basin overflows into the Pit River to the south

20. Mount Vida (8,224 feet) and the Mount Vida Trail (M8)*

21. Fandango Peak (7,792 feet) and Lassen Creek (M9)*

22. Upper Alkali Lake: one of three large lake basins in the Surprise Valley

23. Buck Mountain (7,932 feet): home to the Pink Lady rockhounding area (M7), the Obsidian Needles rockhounding area (M7), and the middle fork of Davis Creek rockhounding area (M7); camping is available at Plum Valley (M9)*

24. Cedar Creek Interpretive Trail (M8): a well-marked three-mile trail through a juniper forest that describes the transition between the Warner Mountains and the Nevada desert*

25. Bald Mountain (8,270 feet) and Cedar Pass (M9)*

26. Big Sage Reservoir (M5): this reservoir, formed by Big Lake Dam, discharges into Rattlesnake Creek near Big Sage Reservoir Camp (M9)

27. Middle Alkali Lake: one of three lakes in the Surprise Valley, all of which are remnants of the glacial lake Lahontan, which once encompassed the whole valley and is now the location of the Surprise Valley wildlife area (M1)

28. Squaw Peak (8,646 feet) and Pepperdine (M9), on the Summit Trail (M8) in the Warner Mountain State Game Reserve*

29. Pine Creek (M3) and the Pine Creek Wildlife Area (M1): Pine Creek is home to extensive riparian and prairie habitat, which attracts thousands of birds, including the greater sagebrush grouse

30. Horsehead Mountain (6,531 feet) and the Upper Rush Creek (M9)

31. Eagle Peak (9,892 feet): this peak rises up over the South Warner Federal Wilderness Area (M1) and its 70,000 acres; Patterson Camp (M9) on Eagle Peak is the southernmost camp, on the divide with Lassen County*

32. Lower Alkali Lake: this is the southernmost of the three intermittent lakes in the Surprise Valley

33. Nevada border

34. West Valley Reservoir (M5): this reservoir was formed from the south fork of the Pit River (M3), which meets the main branch near the town of Alturas, near West Valley Camp (M9)

*feature in the Warner Mountain Range, which runs the length of Modoc County from the Oregon State border in the north to the Lassen County border in the south

Greater sage grouse
Centrocercus urophasianus

Map 09.26 Mono: Limestone and Lava

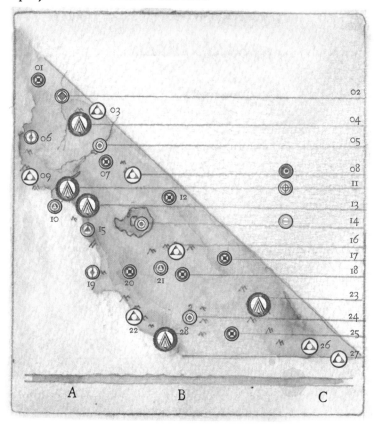

21 miles

09.26

A **West county:** Tioga Pass (15) (9,945 feet)
B. **Mid county:** Mono Lake (14) (6,402)
C. **East county:** Station Peak (27) (10,316 feet)

Exhibiting ecological allegiance to the desert of Nevada, Mono County has developed a 100-million-year-old character that is unlike any other in California. In the shadow of the Sierra Nevada, this dry land that never dips below 4,000 feet is pocked with the scars of ancient volcanoes and blanketed in sagebrush and the vanilla scent of Jeffrey pine trees.

01. Antelope Valley Wildlife Area (M1), Pickle Meadow Wildlife Area (M1), West Walker River Wildlife Area (M1), and Slinker Wildlife Area (M1): these wildlife areas are all noted fawning habitats for Inyo mule deer

02. Lost Cannon Creek (M3): this creek meets the West Walker River (M3), both fueled by Sierra snowmelt; it begins in the Sweetwater Mountains, opens into Antelope Valley, and is diverted to form Topaz Lake (M5)

Greater white-fronted goose
Anser albifrons frontalis

03. Sweetwater Mountains: a granite range formed with the Sierra Nevada

04. Mount Patterson (11,673 feet): a volcano of uncertain age

05. Bridgeport Reservoir (M5): an agriculture dam on the Walker River that

runs for 95 miles out of the Sierra, past East Walker River Wildlife Area (M1) and the Travertine Hot Springs Area of Critical Environmental Concern (M1)

06. Hoover Federal Wilderness Area (M1): these 50,000 acres of wilderness in the High Sierra northeast of Yosemite contain the Lower Twin Lakes (M9) and are crossed by the Robinson Creek Trail (M8)

07. Bodie Hills and the Green Creek Wildlife Area (M1): 2,500 acres noted for aspen-riparian habitat with strong populations of beaver and waterfowl, near the Conway Summit Area of Critical Environmental Concern (M6)

08. Potato Peak (10,296 feet): highest point in the Bodie Hills

09. High Sierra in North Yosemite: Tower Peak (11,755 feet) is the dominant peak in the line of peaks that draws the northeast border of Yosemite

10. Humboldt–Toiyabe National Forest: this national forest extends into Nevada, and about half of it reaches to the Sierra across Mono County; two threatened cut-throat trout species, the Lahotan and the Paiute, are endemic to this national forest

11. Twin Peaks (12,323 feet)

12. Mono Valley and the Mono Basin National Forest Scenic Area (M2): 300 square miles of gently inward-sloping landscape that forms a basin; Mono Valley keeps Mono Lake from draining, creating what limnologists call a endorheic system

13. Black Mountain (11,770 feet) and Trumbull Lake (M9)

14. Mono Lake (6,402 feet) and the Mono Lake Tufa State Reserve (M1): at almost a million years old, Mono Lake is one of the oldest lakes in North America; it offers respite to millions of annually migrating birds who feed on its productive brine-based ecosystem

15. Tioga Pass: the highest paved pass in the Sierra Nevada

16. Glass Mountain (11,123 feet) and the Sentinel Meadow Research Natural Area (M1)

17. Benton Valley: this valley is the launching point for hikes to Boundary Peak on the Nevada border to the east; hot springs are an attraction in its volcanic landscape

18. Long Valley Caldera and the Owens River Camp (M9): an active volcanic landscape that last erupted only 350 years ago; an eruption nearly 750,000 years ago created Mono Valley and ultimately Mono Lake

19. Kuna Crest and Koip Crest: two High Sierra divides south of Tioga Pass

20. Ansel Adams Federal Wilderness Area (M1): most of Ansel Adams's 230,000 acres lies above the tree line; lodgepole pine forest communities line alpine meadows wherever the wilderness dips under 8,500 feet or so

21. Inyo National Forest: a two-million-acre forest that extends to Nevada and down into Inyo County; principal conifer species here are the Jeffrey pine and lodgepole pine

22. Ritter Range: these metavolcanic glaciated mountains, the centerpiece of the Ansel Adams Wilderness, appear as black shark fins up from curtains of white snow across sapphire blue mountain lakes

23. White Mountain Peak (14,246 feet) and the White Mountain Research National Area

24. Lake Crowley and the South Landing Camp (M9)

25. Fish Slough Area of Critical Environmental Concern (M1): a volcanic tableland made up of delicate high-altitude ecosystems and one of the richest alkali wetlands in the Great Basin Desert

26. White Mountains: these mountains are home to the bristlecone pines, the oldest forests in the world; their range extends down to Inyo County

27. Station Peak (10,316 feet)

28. Mammoth Mountain (11,053 feet) and Coldwater Camp (M9): a recreation area north of the John Muir Federal Wilderness Area (M1)

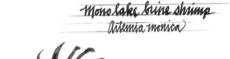

Mono Lake brine shrimp
(Artemia monica)

Map 09.27 Monterey: Peaks over the Pacific

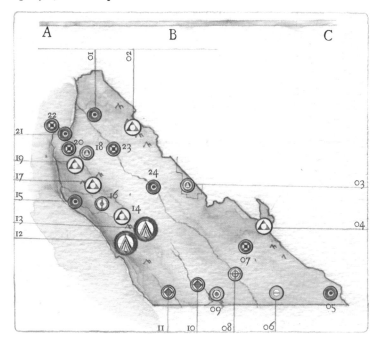

31 miles

09.27

A **West county:** Carmel Valley (20) (400 feet)
B **Mid county:** Junipero Serra Peak (13) (5,862 feet)
C **East county:** Mustang Ridge (04) (2,590 feet)

Being the oldest port in the state, the city of Monterey is the birthplace of the political entity that is California. It is where the state constitution was drafted in 1849. Monterey County is home to the Santa Lucia Mountains, which tumble down precipitous slopes to the Pacific Ocean, forming a long, port-less wall along most of Central California. The Ventana Wilderness brims with ravines full of dark coast redwood forests and chaparral-covered peaks that sing with dense blooms of springtime wildflowers.

01. Salinas: this city was the setting for John Steinbeck's novels *Of Mice and Men* and *East of Eden*

02. Gabilan Range: these low mountains have their highest peak in San Benito County; they draw their name from *gavilan*, meaning "sparrow hawk" in Spanish

03. Pinnacles National Park (M1): the western border or this national park is shown on this map; there is no direct road through the park, and there is no camping on the Monterey side of the park; the only camping access is from San Benito County

04. Mustang Ridge and the San Andreas Fault Zone

05. California juniper–dominant grass-lands, Parkfield (M7)

06. Camp Roberts: a California National Guard post

07. Cholame Hills: these hills define east Monterey County down from the Mustang Ridge

08. Salinas River and Valley: a major agricultural area approximately 100 miles long composed of alluvial soil deposited by this major river, which runs the length of Monterey County

09. San Antonio Lake: this lake was formed by San Antonio River behind the largest dam in the county

10. San Antonio River and Pleyto (M9): this 60-mile-long tributary of the Salinas River has its headwaters in the Santa Lucia Mountains

11. Nacimiento River and Nacimiento Camp (M9): over 60 miles in length, the Nacimiento River is the largest of the Salinas River tributaries; its headwaters are in Fort Hunter Liggett down from Juniper Serra Peak

12. Cone Peak (5,155 feet), the Cone Peak Gradient Research Natural Area (M1), and the Cone Peak Camp (M9): this area is home to the largest stands of Santa Lucia fir, perhaps the rarest fir tree in the world

13. Junipero Serra Peak (5,862 feet): this peak, two miles north of Fort Hunter Liggett Military base, is the highest in the Coast Ranges

14. Santa Lucia Mountains: this is the closest range to the coast in California; its west slope gets more rain than the east slopes, and the west ravines contain tall trees such as pine, redwood, and fir; the eastern slopes are dry and are covered in chaparral

15. Big Sur: a community but also a larger region that extends from south of the town of Carmel to the southernmost extent of the coast redwoods habitat near Salmon Creek for a length of about 100 miles; home to the Andrew Molera State Park (M1, M9), the California State Otter Game Reserve (M1), Julia Pfeiffer Burns State Park (M6, M9), Limekiln Creek State Park (M9), and Kirk Creek (M9)

16. Ventana Federal Wilderness Area: 236,000 acres of wilderness that are home to grassy meadows, pine-covered peaks, and virgin coastal redwood forests lining deep canyons of the fast-moving Big Sur and Little Sur Rivers

17. South Ventana Cone (4,965 feet): an ancient volcano in the Ventana Wilderness that contains the headwaters of Tassajara Creek up from Greenfield Slough

18. Toro County Park (M7): the northern tip of the Sierra de Salinas, whose highest peak, just west of Soledad along the Paloma Ridge, is Eli Peak (4,280 feet)

19. Mount Carmel and Garland Ranch Regional Park (M7): a low peak inland from the town of Carmel (4,417 feet)

20. Carmel Valley: formed by the Carmel River (M3, M8), the Carmel Valley contains both the San Clemente Reservoir (M5) and the Los Padres Reservoir (M5)

21. Fort Ord Public Lands (M1) and Garrapata State Park (M7), near Monterey Bay: this area is home to California's largest population of sea otters, which are continuing their recovery after being driven nearly to extinction in the 19th century by the fur industry

22. Monterey Peninsula and the Monarch Butterfly Grove (M7): this peninsula juts into the Monterey Bay between the Carmel River and the Monterey Bay; it is legally protected by the Pacific Grove State Marine Gardens Fish Refuge and is home to native stands of Monterey cypress

23. Gabilan Creeks: three creeks that run west down from the Gabilan Range in the northern Salinan Valley, from south to north: Johnson, Chualar, and Quail Creek

24. The towns of the Salinas Valley: these towns are home to the historic Camino Real, the Mission Nuestra Señora de Soledad, and the three, contemporary towns of the middle Salinas Valley down Highway 101—Soledad, Greenfield, and King City

Sea otter
Enhydra lutris

Map 09.28 Napa: Wine and Wildlife

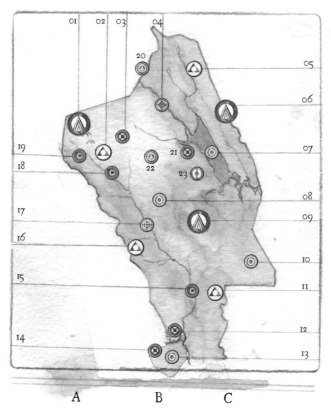

7 miles

09.28

A **West county:** Mount Veeder (16) (2,680 feet)
B **Mid county:** Hennessey Lake (08) (365 feet)
C **East county:** Lake Curry (10) (384 feet)

Napa County is home to the 40-mile-long valley through which the Napa River runs. It is also home to chaparral-clad Mount Saint Helena and wildflower-ringed Lake Berryessa. The author Robert Louis Stevenson moved here in the 1860s, when the fertile agricultural region was already gaining a reputation for quality wine.

01. Mount Saint Helena (4,343 feet) and Robert Louis Stevenson State Park (M7): the border point between Napa, Lake, and Sonoma Counties

02. The Palisades: low mountains covered in vines, except for their rocky tops; the Palisades separate Napa Valley to the west and Pope Valley to the east

03. Pope Valley: this valley is north of Las Posadas State Forest (M6), Maxwell Creek, and the Rector Valley Wildlife Area (M1)

04. Putah Creek: this creek is the main water feed to Lake Berryessa, near Cedar Roughs Wildlife Area (M1), an adjunct portion of the Berryessa Snow Mountain National Monument (M1)

05. Blue Ridge: this ridge lies up from Eticuera Creek on the border with Yolo County

06. Berryessa Peak (3,057 feet) and Lake Berryessa Wildlife Area (M1): a potential wilderness area

07. Lake Berryessa and Lake Berryessa Camp (M9): a reservoir defined by the Blue Ridge Basin and the damming of Putah Creek

08. Hennessey Lake (M5): a city recreation area on Highway 128

09. Atlas Peak (2,663 feet)

10. Lake Curry: this lake is located between Wooden Valley Road and Mount Vaca (2,819 feet), on the border of Solano County

11. Sugarloaf (1,630 feet): just east of Skyline Wilderness Park Campground (M9)

12. Napa–Sonoma Marshes Wildlife Area (M1): 15,200 acres of baylands, tidal sloughs, and wetland habitat

13. San Pablo Bay: a bay at the mouth of the Napa River; Napa County does not have a bay shoreline that is not in the Napa River

14. San Pablo Bay National Wildlife Refuge (M1)

15. Skyline Wilderness Park (M9), Napa

16. Mount Veeder (2,680 feet)

17. Napa River: the mouth of the river is at Vallejo, where the intertidal zone of fresh and salt waters flow into the Carquinez Straits on San Pablo Bay

18. Saint Helena

19. Napa Camp (M9), Calistoga

20. Southern border of Berryessa Snow Mountain National Monument

21. Rector Reservoir Wildlife Area (M1): 433 acres of oak woodland and mixed chaparral vegetation

22. Las Posadas State Forest (M6): a 70,000-acre demonstration forest; demonstration forests are about land and resource management and are not open to the public; Las Posadas is solely for research

23. Cedar Roughs Federal Wilderness Area (M1): 6,000 acres of serpentine soil supporting communities of Sargent cypress trees; Cedar Roughs is also a known black bear breeding area

Map 09.29 Nevada: Mining Scars and Cedar Forests

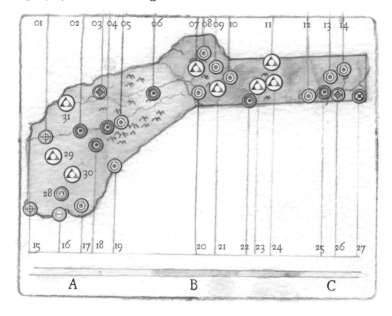

13 miles

09.29

A **West county:** Grass Valley (18) (2,411 feet)
B **Mid county:** Washington (06) (2,640 feet)
C **East county:** Truckee (26) (5,920 feet)

Nevada County was ground zero for the most devastating hydraulic mining in the 19th century, a process that altered the landscape with scars that are still visible. Much of the eastern part of the county lies in Tahoe National Forest. From Grass Valley, the cedar forests of Yuba County open to the ponderosa and sugar pine forests of the northern Sierra Nevada.

01. Lake Wildwood (M5): a lake on Deer Creek (M3)

02. Rough and Ready: a town across the Yuba River from the Kentucky Ridge

03. Shady Creek: a tributary of the south fork of the Yuba River

04. Nevada City: a former Gold Rush town that is now a cultural hub

05. Scotts Flat Reservoir (M5) (3,069 feet) and Scotts Flat (M9), near Deer Creek (M3)

06. Washington: a Gold Rush town and river sports hub on the Yuba River

American kestral
Falco sparverius

07. Fall Creek Mountain (7,485 feet) and the Black Buttes on Lindsey Lake (M9)

08. French Lake: a lake lined with a grand tableau of 1,000-year-old petroglyphs

09. Meadow Lake (M5): a quiet reservoir with rustic camp (M9)

10. Fordyce Lake (M5): a lake with good backpacking campsites down from Eagle Lakes

11. Mount Lola (9,143 feet)

12. Donner Lake (5,933 feet) and Donner State Park (M91): a glacial lake under Donner Summit (7,240 feet)

13. Prosser Creek Reservoir (M5): a sprawling reservoir fed by the Truckee River (M3); this is a good spot to see bald eagles nesting in the summer

14. Boca Reservoir (M5): a reservoir downstream from Stampede Dam

15. Bear River (M3): this river feeds Camp Far West Reservoir, south of Spenceville Wildlife Management and Recreation Area (M1)

16. Border with Placer County at Lucas Hill

17. Lake of the Pines near Higgins Corner: a housing development surrounded by incense cedar and Douglas fir

18. Grass Valley: a Gold Rush town and primary location in Wallace Stegner's novel *Angle of Repose*

19. Rollins Reservoir (M5): a fish-stocked reservoir known for trout fishing in spring and largemouth bass in summer; one of ten reservoirs in Nevada County

20. Fordyce Creek (M3): up from the reservoir called Lake Spaulding (M5), Fordyce Creek is renowned for its idyllic river rafting through the granite landscape

21. Red Mountain (7,841 feet): the big peak you can see from east Highway 80 at Emigrant Gap

22. Kingvale: a small town near Donner Summit on Highway 80

23. Andesite Peak (8,219 feet): a peak bound by Hole in the Ground Trail (M8), which winds through this part of the High Sierra near Donner Pass

24. Castle Peak (9,103 feet): a peak on the Pacific Crest Trail (M8)

25. Truckee: a resort town known for its bear population

26. Truckee River (M3): Lake Tahoe's only outlet; its rocky shores provide habitat for marmots

27. Truckee River Wildlife Area (M1): 5,300 acres of gentle riverbanks and uplands scattered with lodgepole and Jeffrey pines

28. Spenceville Wildlife Management and Recreation Area (M1): 12,000 acres of blue oak and gray pine woodlands, characteristic of this 1,200-foot elevation in the Sierra Foothills

29. Vandervere Mountain (1,846 feet): a peak in rural Nevada County surrounded by small farms

30. Wolf Mountain (2,632 feet): the highest peak along Wolf Creek between Auburn and Grass Valley

31. San Juan Ridge: thick cedar forest from the tiny town of North San Juan over to Malakoff Diggins State Historic Park (M7); this region was the most extensive hydraulic mining site of the 19th century, and scars of this terrible, destructive 19th-century mining technique are still visible

Sacramento pikeminnow
Ptychocheilus grandis

Map 09.30 Orange: The Santa Ana and the Sycamore

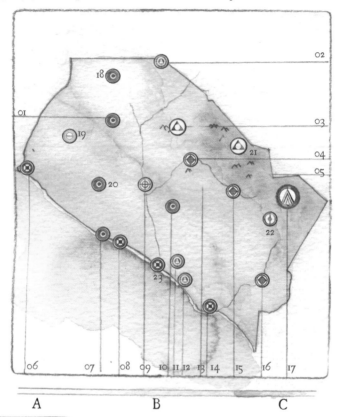

7 miles

09.30

A. **West county:** Seal Beach (06) (15 feet)
B. **Mid county:** Santiago Reservoir (04) (789 feet)
C. **East county:** Santa Ana Mountains (03) (3,500 feet)

Early in the 20th century, the pastured wetlands of Orange County, watered by the Santa Ana River, became the world's foremost producer of the fruit the county is named for. The county is now the second-most populous county in California, after Los Angeles, and it is known for Disneyland as much as anything. The Santa Ana Mountains and the Cleveland National Forest represent stalwart wild lands despite incessant development.

01. Anaheim: a major city and early 20th-century epicenter of agricultural citrus production

02. Chino Hills State Park (M4): this park, which provides critical wildlife habitat, is currently working on acquiring the land between the Chino Hills and the Puente Hills to secure a necessary wildlife corridor for these grasslands

03. Santa Ana Mountains: a 61-mile-long range containing knobcone pine, bigcone Douglas fir, and the southernmost stands of madrone forest

04. Santiago Reservoir (M5): this reservoir on Irvine Lake is the largest body of water in Orange County

05. Santiago Peak, aka Old Saddleback (5,687 feet)

06. Seal Beach National Wildlife Refuge (M1): Seal Beach is threatened by rising sea levels; in 2016, the U.S. Fish and Wildlife Service applied a thin layer of sediment over ten acres of existing low-salt marsh habitat here to protect the flooding of shore-nesting birds

07. Huntington Beach

08. Huntington State Beach (M1): this protected beach is a nesting site for California least terns, also called sea sparrows, and snowy plovers

09. Santa Ana River (M3, M4): this river historically provided rich habitat for steelhead trout; now, years go by when only a few dozen make their way up the broken and polluted river, which is now finally getting vital assistance in the form of organized habitat restoration efforts

10. Orange County Great Park: 1,300 acres in the city of Irvine

11. Crystal Cove State Park (M7, M4): a 4,000-acre beachside state park that is home to thousands of acres of canyon, where dozens of reptile species dwell

12. Aliso Wood Canyon Regional Park (M7, M4): 4,500 acres surrounded by a larger complex called the South Coast Wilderness, a chain of wildlife areas along Aliso Creek and into the Santa Ana Mountains; rare forests of white alder are common here

13. Loma Ridge and the East Loma Ridge Trail (M8): this area is accessible via the Irvine Ranch Conservancy Wilderness (M1), home to Limestone Canyon Regional Park (M7)

14. Dana Point: one of the few harbors in Orange County and home to Capistrano Beach (M7)

15. Santiago Creek: this 34-mile-long creek, a tributary of the Santa Ana River, drains most of the Santa Ana Mountains; it is dammed at Irvine Lake

16. Arroyo Trabuco (M4): a 22-mile creek through semiarid scrubland and chaparral; a salmon ladder in its lower reaches has been approved by voters to restore the salmon run, but work has yet to begin

17. Los Pinos Peak (4,510 feet): a summit whose viewshed includes all of the Cleveland National Forest

18. Fullerton: a city south of the Puente Hills and west of the Peralta Hills

19. Knott's Berry Farm: a working citrus farm 100 years ago, now an amusement park; no major tracts of citrus still exist in Orange County

20. Garden Grove: an urbanized enclave north of the Los Alamos Naval Station

21. Cleveland National Forest covers the Santa Ana Mountains

22. Ronald W. Caspers Wilderness Park (M1): an 8,000-acre rural park with noted sycamore-riparian habitat that borders Riverside County and the San Mateo Canyon Wilderness

California least tern
Sternula antillarum browni

Map 09.31 Placer: The Trail through the Trees of Tahoe

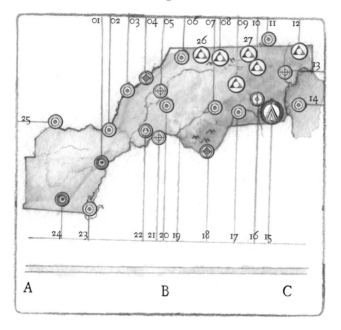

18 miles

09.31

A. **West county:** Roseville (24) (1,160 feet)
B. **Mid county:** Rollins Reservoir (03) (1,700 feet)
C. **East county:** French Meadows Reservoir (07) (5,221 feet)

Placer County is home to Donner Pass and Emigrant Gap, two land features that made the Gold Rush, and modern California, possible. Today, this route across the Sierra Nevada is the most used and most accessible. A drive down Highway 80 from Lake Tahoe over Donner Pass and down to Auburn is a tour through the strata of forest across the northern Sierra Nevada.
Jeffrey pines and sugar pines move through ponderosa pine forest, which then give way to incense cedar and gray pine corridors in the foothill woodlands.

01. Auburn: a city near the Auburn State Recreation Area (M7), which follows the deep river canyon and is traced by the Indian Creek Trail (M8) through valley oak riparian forests, running for 40 miles along the American River, the border of Placer and El Dorado Counties

02. Lake Combie (M5): a reservoir on the Bear River in the foothills that is known for fishing and provides habitat for the Sacramento pikeminnow

03. Rollins Reservoir (M5): a reservoir on the border with Nevada County

04. Bear River (M3): a 73-mile-long tributary of the Feather River with its headwaters in the Emigrant Gap; there are currently plans for a new dam to be installed just upriver from Lake Combie to store over 100,000 acre-feet of water

05. North fork of the American River (M3): this 88-mile-long fork joins the other branches of the American River at Folsom Lake; it has its headwaters in the Granite Chief at Granite Chief Peak (9,008 feet)

06. Lake Valley Reservoir (M5): a fisherman's lake where brown bullhead catfish are stocked and currently outcompeting the trout

07. French Meadows Reservoir (M5): a hydroelectric dam on the middle fork of the American River, within the state game refuge; no guns are allowed

08. Snow Mountain (8,014 feet) and Big Bend (M9): a rocky dominant peak crowned with Jeffrey pine forest

09. Red Star Ridge: above French Meadows Reservoir, this is one of several east–west ridgelines cut from a million years of snowmelt

10. Tinker Knob (8,949 feet)

11. The Cascade Lakes: these lakes comprise Lake Van Norden, Ice Lakes, and Kidd Lake (M9)

12. Lookout Mountain (8,104 feet)

13. Truckee River (M3): this is the outlet for Lake Tahoe; crystal water over smooth stones flows out of the lake to the northwest and then turns northeast, cutting a deep ditch down into Nevada

Gray pine
Pinus sabiana

14. Lake Tahoe: California's highest and deepest all-natural alpine lake

15. Twin Peaks (8,878 feet)

16. Granite Chief Federal Wilderness Area: 20,000 acres of extensively glaciated forest replete with black cottonwood, alder, and quaking aspen; Granite Chief provides habitat for the rare three-bracted onion

17. Hell Hole Reservoir (4,700 feet) (M5): a dammed reservoir with 15 campsites on the Rubicon River

18. Rubicon River (M3): a river under the Nevada Point Ridge

19. Forest Hill Divide (M4), near the Placer County Big Trees, which harbors the northernmost grove of giant sequoias (M6) along Forest Road 96

20. Sugar Pine Reservoir (M5): this reservoir was built in the 1980s to supply rural residents with water; just down from Mumford Bar Trail, it has great views of the north fork of the American River Canyon

21. Middle fork of the American River (M3): this fork runs for 62 miles and joins the north fork near Auburn; the American River has been promoted as America's favorite whitewater river

22. Auburn State Recreation Area (M7)

23. Folsom Lake (M5) and Folsom Lake State Recreation Area (M7): a 20,000-acre park with blue oak, interior live oak, and gray pine communities; many blue oaks living here date to 500 years old

24. Roseville

25. Camp Far West Reservoir (M5): this reservoir is at the meeting place of Placer, Nevada, and Yuba Counties; it is surrounded by free-range cattle land

26. Emigrant Gap: a high-mountain pass near present-day Interstate 80 and the North Fork Camp (M9)

27. Donner Pass: this highway, where the Pacific Crest Trail crosses Interstate 80, used to be difficult to pass in winter snowstorms but rarely closes these days

Valley Carpenter bee
Xylocopa varipuncta

Map 09.32 Plumas: One Thousand Miles of Mountain Rivers

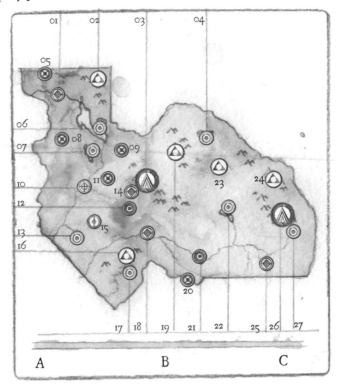

18 miles

09.32

A **West county:** Lake Almanor (o6) (4,100 feet)
B **Mid county:** Indian Valley (o9) (3,100 feet)
C **East county:** Sierra Valley (25) (4,945 feet)

The uplands of Plumas County are where the Sierra Nevada finds its northern terminus and begins to acquiesce before the southern Cascade volcanoes. This rural country of reservoirs and ponderosa fir forests is bookended by the Diamond Mountains to the east and the Feather River to the west. All three forks of the Feather River pass through Plumas County.

01. Feather River (M3): this 220-mile-long river is the principal tributary of the Sacramento River; its watershed is spread across nearly four million acres, and both the north fork and the middle fork trace their headwaters to the Diamond Mountains

02. Swain Mountain (7,054 feet): home to the Swain Mountain Experimental Forest (M6), where forest service research with the seeding of white and red fir is conducted

06. Lake Almanor (M5): one of California's largest reservoirs, the lake is held by a 130-foot hydroelectric dam; wetlands to the north serve as breeding grounds for Canada geese; the lake itself is noted duck habitat, and includes significant populations of green-winged teal

07. Butt Valley Reservoir (M5): a scenic artificial lake, Butt Creek is a tributary of the north fork of the Feather River; currently there are three bald eagle and two osprey nesting territories on the banks of the lake monitored by the Forest Service

Green-winged teal
Anas carolinensis

03. Grizzly Peak (7,704 feet): a fire look-out peak east of the town of Portola

04. Antelope Lake (M5) and Boulder Creek (M9): Antelope Lake dams Indian Creek (M3); it is tributary of the north fork of the Plumas River, stocked with trout and channel catfish for recreational fishing

05. Warner Valley Wildlife Area (M1): a picturesque 700-acre drainage from Lassen Volcanic National Park with steep and narrow streams for rich beaver habitat

08. Coon Hollow Wildlife Area (M1): a 731-acre area at just about 6,000 feet of elevation, featuring wet meadow and riparian vegetation, timbered uplands, and over a dozen mountain streams

09. Indian Valley: an alluvial valley that is home to the small town of Greenville in the Plumas National Forest; historic copper mines dot the valley, and Elephant's Playground (M7), a huge complex of granite boulders, lies just east of the valley

10. North fork of the Feather River (M3): this fork of the river flows for 70 miles from Lassen National Park, traveling through several hydroelectric dams

11. Mount Hough State Game Refuge (M1): in this game refuge with significant populations of mule deer, black bear, mountain lions, and bobcat, hunting is not permitted at any time

12. Quincy: a mountain town that is home to the Butterfly Valley Botanical Area (M6)

13. Bucks Lake (M5): a ghost town on a reservoir

14. East branch of the north fork of the Feather River: throughout this watershed, fir-dominant forests are most common; this area grows mostly from volcanic soil deposited by Mount Lassen

15. Bucks Lake Federal Wilderness Area (M1): this 24,000-acre wilderness is the northernmost in the Sierra Nevada; the rare little willow flycatcher makes its home throughout its creek-side habitats

16. Bald Mountain (6,255 feet)

17. Little Grass Valley Reservoir (M5) and Running Deer camp (M9)

18. Middle fork of the Feather River (M1): a 100-mile-long stretch of which nearly 77 miles are designated as wild and scenic; receives nearly 40 inches of rain per year

19. Kettle Rock (7,820 feet)

20. Lakes Basin Recreation Area (M7): this extensive network of glacial lakes high on a plateau near the Pacific Crest Trail extends south from the town of Graeagle to the Sierra Buttes in Nevada County

21. Graeagle: this mountain town, the site of California's first ski resort, is now closed

22. Lake Davis (M5), north of Sierra Valley

23. Dixie Mountain Game Refuge (M1): this game refuge in the Diamond Mountains near Conklin Park camp (M9) on Willow Creek (M3) is blanketed in summertime wildflowers, including lupine, gentian, and Labrador tea

24. Diamond Mountains: this rural mountain range divides Plumas and Lassen Counties

25. Sierra Valley: California's largest alpine valley; wetlands and livestock happen here at 5,000 feet

26. Dixie Mountain (8,327 feet): this peak features a now-abandoned lookout called Nomad's Place

27. Frenchman Lake (M5): a recreation area known for fishing in the summer and ice fishing in the winter; below the dam, Little Last Chance Creek campground (M9) is quiet and secluded and part of a Forest Service experimental area of interest

Map 09.33 Riverside: A Low Desert and a High Desert

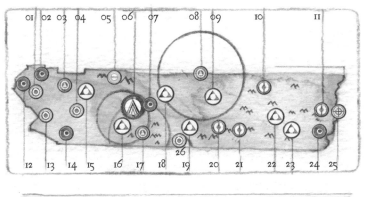

48 miles

09.33

A **West county**: Lake Mathews (01) (1,390 feet)
B **Mid county**: Little San Bernardino Mountains (18) (906 feet)
C **East county**: McCoy Peak (23) (2,054 feet)

The wide Riverside County cuts a broad swath through Southern California, extending for nearly 200 miles from east to west. From the Inland Empire of the town of Riverside, the county rolls over the desert gateway of San Jacinto and up into Joshua Tree National Park. Parts of the low and hot Colorado Desert climb up to the high and cooler Mojave Desert at the county's midway point. The eastern half of the county is made up of a patchwork of public wilderness areas across the heart of the Mojave.

01. Lake Mathews (M5): this lake, in Cajalco Canyon up in the Temescal Mountains, is the end of the Colorado River Aqueduct; the 9,000-acre Lake Mathews Estelle Mountain Reserve (M1) and Prado Regional Park (M9) are together one of the last strongholds for the endangered Stephens' kangaroo rat

02. Rancho Jurupa Park (M9), Riverside

03. Lake Perris State Recreation Area (M5, M9) and the San Jacinto Wildlife Area (M1): these areas in the Russell Mountains and across the Bernasconi Hills exhibit many riparian habitats dominated by willow and elderberry

04. Diamond Valley Lake (M5): a Paleolithic excavation site between the Domenigoni Mountains and the Rawson Mountains

05. Morongo Reservation and the White-water River (M3), accessed via Raywood Flat Trail (M8)

06. San Jacinto Peak (10,804 feet): the highest peak in the county and home to the 32,000-acre San Jacinto Federal Wilderness Area, Black Mountain Scenic Area (M7), and Marion Mountain (M9)

Mountain yellow-legged frog
(Rana muscosa)

07. Palm Springs: home to Tahquitz Canyon, continually inhabited by humans for 2,000 years, and reintroduction site for the endangered mountain yellow-legged frog (M7)

08. Joshua Tree National Park (M1): this park is named for the distinctive Joshua trees whose distribution is a good border indication of the Mojave desert; the park, an ecosystem unlike any other, geographically fills most of central Riverside County; across the region, monzogranite boulders are arranged like giant marbles

scattered across a desert shrub forest of prickly cholla cactus and twisting yucca

09. Pinto Basin: a landscape barren and beautiful, scenic and serene, within the 595,000-acre Joshua Tree Federal Wilderness Area (M1) located across the eastern half of Joshua Tree National Park

10. Palen-McCoy Federal Wilderness Area (M1) and Rice Valley Federal Wilderness Area (M1): these two wilderness acres, totaling 282,000 acres, contain five distinct ranges—the Palen, McCoy, Granite, Little Maria, and Arica; they are home to the ironwood shrub, a rare, heavy-wood, flowering plant that supports and lives with a whole forest of plants and animals

11. Black Hill (1,225 feet): the highest point in the 45,000-acre Big Maria Mountains Federal Wilderness Area (M1)

12. Corona: city on Temescal Creek

13. Lake Elsinore: the largest natural lake in Southern California; fed by the San Jacinto River, it is the lowest point in the river's watershed; on occasionally wet years the lake will spill, making the San Jacinto a tributary of the Santa Ana

14. Temecula: city adjacent to the 38,000-acre San Mateo Canyon Federal Wilderness Area (M1), the Santa Rosa Plateau Ecological Reserve (M1), and the 18,000-acre Aqua Tibia Federal Wilderness Area (M1)

15. The Badlands: a mountain range also called the San Timoteo Badlands and home to San Timoteo Canyon State Park

(M7), known for its horse trails through the sage scrub and its rich fossil beds

16. Santa Rosa Mountains: a range approximately 30 miles long on the west side of the Coachella Valley that is home to the Santa Rosa and San Jacinto National Monument (M1) and the Coachella Valley Mountains Conservancy (M1, M4); the 79,000-acre Santa Rosa Mountains Federal Wilderness Area provides habitat for bighorn sheep

17. Anza Borrego State Park (M1): the largest state park in California; features Sonoran-Colorado Desert ecology

18. Little San Bernardino Mountains: these mountains form the dividing line between the Sonoran-Colorado "Low Desert" to the west and the cooler Mojave "High Desert" to the east

19. Orocopia Mountains: a range approximately 18 miles in length southeast of the Mecca Hills; the Orocopia Mountains Wilderness (M1) is 51,000 acres

20. Chuckwalla Mountains Federal Wilderness Area (M1): a 100,000-acre, 40-mile range named for the region's biggest native lizard; in this area, Colorado and Mojave Desert ecologies mix

21. Black Butte (4,504 feet): a butte in the 28,000-acre Little Chuckwalla Federal Wilderness Area (M1)

22. Little Maria Mountains: during the Cretaceous period, these mountains rose as part of the Maria Fold and Thrust Belt along faults that don't exist anymore, in proximity to what geologists call the Colorado River Extension Corridor

23. McCoy Mountains: an 18-mile-long range whose highest point is McCoy Peak (2,054 feet)

24. Blythe

25. Colorado River: eight parks in Riverside County lie on this river, among which is a park named for an ancient lake, Lake Cahuilla (M5); modern Lake Cahuilla is a reservoir; the Colorado River is part of the 24,000-acre Riverside Mountain Federal Wilderness Area (M1)

26. Salton Sea (M2)

Ring-necked duck)
aythya collaris

Map 09.34 Sacramento: Where the Great Rivers Meet

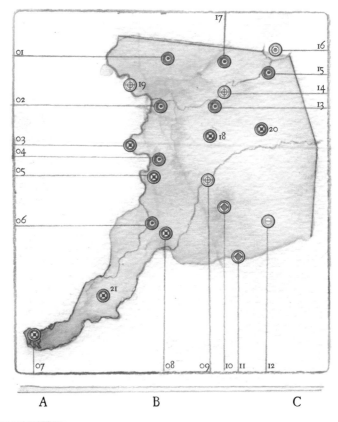

9 miles

09.34

A **West county:** Locke (06) (5 feet)
B **Mid county:** Florin (04) (34 feet)
C **East county:** Folsom Lake (16) (460 feet)

Sacramento County is the political heart of the state and the lowland confluence of all the major ecological systems of Northern California. The Sacramento and the San Joaquin Rivers meet in this region across a fertile network of wetlands, carrying fresh water into the Delta and, beyond that, into San Francisco Bay. The state capital is at the confluence of the American and the Sacramento Rivers.

01. Rio Linda: a rural town on the much-diverted Dry Creek water channel adjacent to the Gibson Ranch County Park (M7), which offers horse trails through the lowland prairie

02. Sacramento: the state capital, located on the Sacramento floodplain; the original city was built on stilts because of flooding

03. Yolo Bypass Wildlife Area (M2): a wildlife area created with the intent of restoring and managing the greater ecology of the Sacramento–San Joaquin River Delta; from the expansive wetlands you can easily see the skyscrapers of the state capital

04. Florin: a small rural city that was a Japanese American hub in the early 20th century, before internment; Florin is now making a comeback economically with the advent of wine culture in Sacramento County

05. Stone Lakes National Wildlife Area (M1): a throughway destination for thousands of migrating birds and colonial nesting species, including the sandhill crane

06. Locke: a 19th-century Chinese migrant town whose original architecture still exists, having miraculously survived being destroyed by fire or development for over 125 years

07. Sherman Island: the tip of the county where the two major rivers of California, the San Joaquin and the Sacramento, meet; the Delta marsh ecosystems here support large populations of fish, including sturgeon and perch
08. Cosumnes River Preserve (M1): this

46,000-acre preserve once contained the largest expanses of oak tree savanna, mostly gone now due to the unwavering march of agriculture; three species of oak mix with black walnut to support hundreds of visiting species of migratory birds

09. Cosumnes River (M3): this 52-mile-long river empties into the Mokelumne River at the Cosumnes River Preserve, along what ornithologists call the Pacific Flyway, the major route for migratory birds along California's vertical axis

10. Badger Creek (M3): small fishing creek

11. Dry Creek: the southern border of Sacramento County, where it meets San Joaquin County

12. Rancho Seco Nuclear Power Plant: a nuclear power plant that was closed in 1989 after a near meltdown; in the early 1970s, Rancho Seco Regional Park (M7) and Rancho Seco Lake (M5) were built; the Amanda Blake Wildlife Refuge (M7) stands here now across 74 acres that include rescued animals like, strangely enough, ostrich; with the cooling towers

nearby, and all the abandoned air raid sirens, this landscape carries an almost surreal quality

13. Rancho Cordova: an urban area that was once a wine region

14. American River (M3): this 119-mile-long river is the main source of drinking water for the county; below the Folsom Dam is the American River Parkway, a 30-mile park that runs to the river's confluence with the Sacramento

15. Folsom

16. Folsom Lake (M5): located 25 miles from downtown Sacramento, this is the largest regional dammed lake on the American River; it is surrounded by buckeye, gray pine, and oak communities

17. Citrus Heights: a suburban area containing the Rusch Botanical Gardens (M7), which feature displays designed to represent seven different biomes from California's landscape

18. Stone Lakes National Wildlife Refuge (M1): this refuge includes the Upper Beach Lake Wildlife Area (M1), where Laguna Creek and Morrison Creek meet the Sacramento River

19. The Hub of All Rivers: from all directions, rivers meet here, where today stands the state capital of California—from the west, Putah Creek comes in from Yolo County; from the north, Sacramento River; from the east, the American River; then downriver on the Sacramento, the Cosumnes and the San Joaquin River run into the Delta

20. Prairie City, Mather Regional Park (M7), and Effie Yeaw Nature Center (M7)

21. The Islands of the Delta: here, wine regions and Gold Rush–era riverfront towns wind down to the Brannan Island State Recreation Area (M7)

Sandhill crane
Grus canadensis

Map 09.35 San Benito: Faults and Flowers

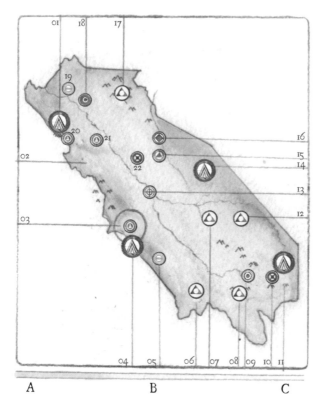

A B C

13 miles

09.35

A **West county:** Gabilan Range (02) (3,000 feet)
B **Mid county:** San Andreas Fault Zone (22) (1,340 feet)
C **East county:** Cerro Colorado (14) (3,656 feet)

Home to Pinnacles National Park, San Benito County is an undiscovered paradise of
coastal ranges, blanketed in chaparral and patrolled overhead by a tenacious population
of California condors intent on not going extinct. The San Andreas Fault bisects the whole county down the entire length of the San Benito River, separating the Diablo Mountains to the east and the Gabilan Mountains to the west.

01. Fremont Peak (3,171 feet): the highest peak in the Gabilan Mountains

02. Gabilan Mountains: this range, part of California's southern inner Coast Ranges, reaches its highest point at Mount Johnson (3,456 feet); these chaparral-blanketed peaks are governed by a dramatic climate that oscillates in the same day between chilling coastal fog and baking sunshine

03. Pinnacles National Park (M1): a park named for the peaks of eroded volcanoes that make up its topography; these peaks have migrated hundreds of miles northward since their creation along the shifting San Andreas Fault, and have fallen, broken, and become weathered, creating caves and cracks that serve as habitat for a wide variety of wildlife; among Pinnacles's uncommon residents are California condors and Townsend's big-eared bats

04. North Chalome Peak (3,304 feet): the highest point in Pinnacles National Park, eight miles up the trail from the Bear Gulch visitor's center; hit the trail around dawn to avoid the midday heat

05. La Laguna Vieja Ranch: in a rural residential area, these hills, full of thistle and cows, turn bright green for only three months beginning in February, turning then to gold, and finally to silver after autumn hits

06. Eagle Mountain (2,494 feet)

07. Cerro Bonito: this area near Panoche Pass, deep in the Diablo Mountain Range (2,250 feet) and the headwaters of Panoche Creek, which is a tributary of the San Benito River, features grassland habitat for wildflowers including the endangered yellow mariposa lily

08. Hepsedam Peak (4,487 feet): a prominent peak

09. Hernandez Reservoir (M5): this reservoir was formed by a dam along the San Benito River and Laguna Creek

yellow Mariposa lily
Calochortus luteus

10. Clear Creek Management Area (M1): this area, which includes San Benito Mountain, has been closed to the public for 20 years because of asbestos contamination due to mining in the first half of the 20th century; because of its isolation from the human world, most ecologists believe this whole area will restore itself to a pristine ecology

11. San Benito Mountain (5,241 feet) and the San Benito Mountain Research Natural Area (M1): because of the metallic makeup of the soil on this mountain, there is not a lot of vegetation, and the whole mountain is a Superfund site that has been closed to the public since 2008; big stands of incense cedar and ponderosa pine crowd its peaks

12. Griswold Hills: a low range of hills that runs along the southern Panoche Valley

13. San Benito River (M3): a 110-mile river that runs the length of the county, with headwaters near San Benito Peak; the river is usually dry during the summer

14. Cerro Colorado (3,656 feet)

15. Santa Ana Valley Road: suburban landscape under Cibo Peak (2,845 feet)

16. Quien Sabe Creek: this creek feeds the Pacines River

17. Henrietta Peak (3,626 feet)

18. The Calaveras Fault: this creeping fragment of the San Andreas Fault runs right through the town of Hollister and is notorious for tearing roads and breaking houses

19. San Juan Bautista Mission and State Historic Park: San Juan Bautista is a historic mission surrounded by olive trees only feet from the San Andreas Fault

20. Fremont Peak State Park and Observatory (M1, M9): a 160-acre park containing pine and oak woodlands; the astronomical observatory houses what is called the Challenger Telescope, managed by the state park system

21. Hollister Hills State Vehicle Recreation Area (M7)

22. San Andreas Fault Zone

three bracted onion
allium tribracteatum

Map 09.36 San Bernardino: The Mojave and the Military

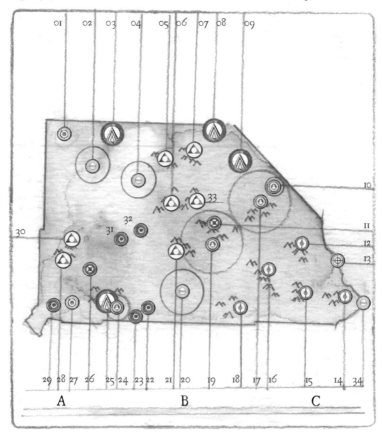

A **West county:** Lucerne Valley (26) (2,946 feet)
B **Mid county:** Soda Mountains (33) (1,200 feet)
C **East county:** Piute Mountains (12) (2,770 feet)

The forested southwest corner of this, California's largest county, is defined by lots of people and a giant peak. The rest of the county is rural desert: delicate ecosystems including Joshua Tree National Park and the Mojave National Preserve. The military calls San Bernardino home as well, with three major installations (Twentynine Palms Marine Base, Fort Irwin National Training Center, and China Lake Naval Weapons Center) making the military the number-one steward of the Mojave Desert.

42 miles

09.36

01. Golden Valley Federal Wilderness Area (M1): within this 37,000-acre wilderness area, Searles Dry Lake and the Trona Pinnacles Recreation Lands (M7) exist across a series of barren flats 12 miles long and 8 miles wide; over the past several hundred thousand years, Searles Lake has gone through many cycles of desiccation and hydration

02. Naval Weapons Center China Lake: this center dominates the northern border of San Bernardino County near the Panamint Valley; at over one million acres, China Lake is the navy's single largest landholding and is adjacent to the 30,000-acre Grass Valley Federal Wilderness Area (M1) and the 21,000-acre Black Mountain Federal Wilderness Area

03. Brown Mountain (5,125 feet)

04. Fort Irwin National Training Center: an army base adjacent to China Lake that surrounds the Avawatz, Granite, and Tiefort Mountains; because the area is largely roadless and the army only uses a small portion of the land itself for artillery testing, it is generally believed among ecologists that this million acres or so remains largely a pristine wilderness

05. Granite Mountains: inside the Fort Irwin Army Base, these mountains are the location for the massive Fort Irwin Solar Project, which is currently being built; once completed, it will be the largest renewable energy project the government has ever invested in

06. The Tiefort Mountains: a mountain range inside Fort Irwin, whose highest peak is Tiefort Peak (5,063 feet)

07. The Avawatz Mountains: a mountain range whose highest peak is Avawatz Peak (6,144 feet); on the mountains' eastern slope, the Salt Creek Hills Area of Critical Environmental Concern (M1) protects delicate salt cedar ecosystems.

08. Kingston Peak (7,323 feet): this peak, the northernmost in San Bernardino County, harbors a remnant alpine forest; the 200,000-acre Kingston Range Federal Wilderness Area (M1) surrounds the mountains and extends to the Amargosa Canyon Dumont Dunes Natural Area (M7); dotted with federally protected areas, the 29,000-acre North Mesquite Mountains Federal Wilderness Area (M1) and the 45,000-acre Mesquite Mountains Federal Wilderness Area flank the Kingston Range

09. Clark Mountain (7,929 feet): this peak rises at the northern end of the Mojave National Preserve (M1)

Joshua tree moth
Tegeticula yucca stella

10. Castle Mountains National Monument (M1): designated in 2016, this 21,000-acre monument, surrounded by the Mojave Preserve on the border of Nevada, has no paved roads; it features desert grassland that blooms in March

11. Kelso Dunes: a unique dune field in the heart of the Mojave Preserve featuring 650-foot-tall sand dunes, stabilized by grass and creosote shrub; the list of endemic species mainly includes insects

12. Piute Mountains Federal Wilderness Area: a 50,000-acre area of alluvial fans that supports creosote communities of desert wildlife and provides excellent desert tortoise habitat, as does the adjacent 15,000-acre Bigelow Cholla Garden Wilderness (M1)

13. Colorado River: Lake Havasu (M5), as constructed on the Colorado by the Parker Dam, is the single largest feature of the river in San Bernardino County; Lake Havasu is continually stocked with fish, as sustainable populations regularly fail

14. Whipple Mountain Federal Wilderness Area (M1): most of these 76,000 acres are either bright red with iron deposits or ruddy brown, as is typical of the Colorado desert; to the area's south, the Chemehuevi Mountains Federal Wilderness Area (M1) extends for 86,000 acres

15. The Turtle Mountains Federal Wilderness Area (M1): this 180,000-acre wilderness area and the 83,000-acre Stepladder Mountains Federal Wilderness Area (M1) are a boundary range for many species, what ecologists call a "delimiter of occurrence"; the region provides the northernmost extent of the desert fan palm, signaling the transition from the Colorado desert to the Mojave

16. Old Woman Mountains Federal Wilderness Area (M1): a 165,000-acre, 15-mile-long range with deep canyons that harbor a few dozen springs, which is very unusual for the Mojave; there are many communities of songbirds at the springs

17. Mojave National Preserve (M1): this almost 2.5-million-acre preserve features over two dozen distinct desert ecologies unique to these mountains and valleys, from the Cima Dome—a low granite formation that covers most of the northern end of the park—to the high wall of the Providence Mountains to the south; among the ecologies included are alkali salt scrub, juniper-pinyon forest, and the Kelso sand dunes

18. Sheephole Valley Wilderness (M1): these 190,000 acres are known for large communities of particularly salt-resistant plants, including pickleweed and inkweed; the endangered Borrego milkvetch is a small plant that lives in the Sheephole dunes

19. Mojave Trails National Monument: this newly designated national monument encompasses several mountain ranges and federal wilderness areas; the historic Route 66 runs through this area, near the 145,000-acre Kelso Dunes Federal Wilderness Area (M1) and the 71,000-acre Bristol Federal Wilderness Area (M1)

20. Twentynine Palms Marine Air Ground Combat Center

21. The Cady Mountains: these mountains are part of the Mojave Trails National Monument (M1) and rise near the elusive Mojave River (M3), which flows mostly underground and surfaces at only a few

points as it runs its course through these mountains; within these mountains are the 27,000-acre Newberry Mountains Federal Wilderness Area (M1) and the 34,000-acre Rodman Mountains Federal Wilderness Area (M1)

Joshua tree
Yucca brevifolia

22. Joshua Tree: a town just north of Joshua Tree National Monument

23. Yucca Valley: this whole area is covered with Joshua trees, a unique yucca that takes a tree-like form and is pollinated by the Joshua tree moth

24. Sand to Snow National Monument (M1, M4): this newly designated national monument links Joshua Tree National Park with Mount San Gorgonio and encompasses the 39,000-acre Bighorn Mountains Federal Wilderness Area (M1)

25. San Gorgonio (11,502 feet): the tallest peak in Southern California

26. Lucerne Valley: this valley contains the Grapevine Canyon National Recreation Lands (M7) at the southern section of the Antelope Valley

27. Big Bear Lake (M5) and Serrano (M9)

28. Shadow Mountains: a low range near Saddleback Butte State Park (M9)

29. San Bernardino

30. Silver Peak (4,043 feet): the highest peak in the Shadow Mountains of Antelope Valley

31. Helendale

32. Rainbow Basin National Natural Landmark (M7): this landmark near Barstow lies near Owl Canyon (M9), Coon Canyon (M8), and Calico Ghost Town Regional Park (M9)

33. Soda Mountains: site of a 2,000-acre solar array project that is being fought in order to conserve dwindling bighorn sheep populations in the area

34. Parker Dam: bordering Arizona on the Colorado River, this dam creates Lake Havasu (M5)

Map 09.37 San Diego: Coastal Forests and Mountain Deserts

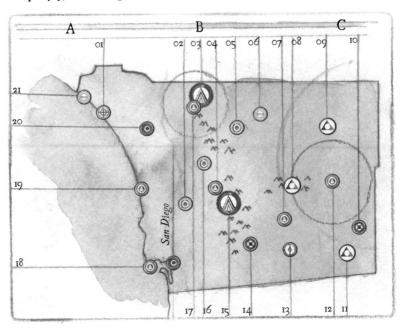

22 miles

09.37

A **West county:** Lake Hodges (02) (275 feet)
B **Mid county:** San Diego Audubon Wildlife Sanctuary (14)
(1,300 feet)
C **East county:** Borrego Springs (12) (590 feet)

Home to the Torrey pine—one of the rarest pine species in the world, which exists only on a few sand dunes south of Del Mar—San Diego County holds many fine ecological examples of habitat that exist nowhere else in California. The forests of the Volcan Mountains, Cuyamaca Rancho State Park, and California's largest state park, Anza Borrego, all exhibit unique systems of wildlife that, having crept up from Mexico, end their northward march here.

01. Santa Margarita River (M3) and the Audubon Nature Center (M1): a 220-acre preserve that is part of the county's Multiple Species Conservation Program

02. Lake Hodges, also called the San Vicente Reservoir (M3): up from the Sycamore Canyon Reserve (M4), the Oak Oasis Preserve (M4), and El Capitan Preserve (M4), this area is defined by its coastal sage scrub and willow riparian habitats, with thorny berry bushes making up the understory

03. Palomar Mountain (6,140 feet): the highest peak in the Aguanga Mountains, Palomar Mountain is named after the wild band-tailed pigeon

04. Mount Gower Preserve (M1): a 1,500-acre preserve that closes in August due to extreme heat; the adjacent Volcan Mountains Wilderness Preserve (M6) presents mixed conifer forest

05. Lake Henshaw (M5): a lake in the Mesa Grande Reservation, near the Santa Ysabel Reservation

06. Los Coyotes Reservation: a reservation near Warner Springs amid sagebrush and yucca-covered rolling hills

07. Cuyamaca Rancho State Park (M7): 26,000 acres of pine, fir, and oak forests

08. Laguna Mountain Recreation Area (M7): this recreation area is located in the Laguna Mountains, which find their highest point at Sheephead Mountain (5,896 feet); these mountains are dominated by peninsular chaparral in the Colorado Desert and are home to the headwaters of Noble Creek, Cottonwood Creek, and Kitchen Creek

band-tailed pigeon
Ectopistes migratorius

09. Borrego Springs in the San Ysidro Mountains: most of this range is included in the Otay Mountain Wilderness Area (M1) and is the gateway to Anza Borrego State Park from the east; the highest point of the range is Otay Mountain (3,566 feet)

10. McCain Valley National Cooperative Land and Wildlife Management Area (M7) and the Yuha Desert Recreation Area (M7) near the Crucifixion Thorn Natural Area (M6): this area supplies habitat for the endangered flat-tailed horned lizard

11. Tecate Divide in the Campo Reservation: this divide is traversed by the Shepard Mountain Trail (M8), a wind-farm location

12. Anza Borrego State Park (M1): a 600,000-acre California montane chaparral and woodlands ecoregion in the Colorado desert, which is the Sonoran desert in California

13. Pine Creek Federal Wilderness Area (M1): this and the adjacent Hauser Federal Wilderness Area (M1) are the state's southernmost designated wilderness areas

14. San Diego Audubon Wildlife Sanctuary (M1): an 800-acre sanctuary that protects over 300 native plant species and over 100 bird species

15. Cuyamaca Peak (6,512 feet) and the William Heise County Park (M7): this park, at 4,000 feet, is one of the only parks in San Diego County to get snow

16. Lake Wohlford inside Hellhole Canyon Preserve (M1): a 400-acre wilderness preserve, covered in chaparral and located near the Guejito Gateway in the foothills of Palomar Mountain

17. Palomar Mountain State Park (M7): on the top of Palomar Mountain, this 1,800-acre state park is an alpine forest of pine, fir, and cedar

18. Point Loma and the Cabrillo National Monument (M1): this area is in the intertidal zone, with rich tide pools beside native coastal sage scrub

19. Torrey Pines State Reserve (M1), near Los Penasquitos Canyon: Torrey pine is one of the rarest pine tree species in the world, with only a few acres here of the bluff-dwelling pines

20. Elfin Forest Reserve (M4) near Escondido: this reserve contains one of the largest areas of virgin coastal scrub in Southern California

21. San Onofre Nuclear Power Plant (closed), San Clemente

Map 09.38 San Joaquin: The Gathering of the Rivers

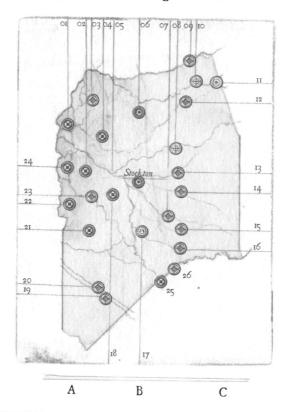

13 miles

09.38

A West county: Union Island (20) (48 feet)
B Mid county: Stockton (15 feet)
C East county: Bear Creek (12) (104 feet)

The brackish waters of the San Francisco Delta reach, with delicate fingers, up into the low wetlands of San Joaquin County, tracing dozens of islands and feeding canals for expansive agriculture projects. The people of San Joaquin County have a complicated relationship with the environment; although the valley's largest riparian restoration project is under way on the San Joaquin River, a tire fire south of Tracy in 1998 burned through seven million acres for over two years before it was finally extinguished.

01. The Islands of the Delta in San Joaquin County: these include Staten Island and Bouldin Island, both home to the critically endangered Delta smelt and a key migration corridor for millions of birds

02. Stockton Deep Water Channel, McDonald Tract

03. The Isenberg Sandhill Crane Reserve (M1) on Hog Slough: the largest freshwater wintering habitat in the state

04. White Slough Wildlife Area (M1): 880 acres of canals, freshwater marshes, grassland, and riparian habitat adjacent to the Woodbridge Ecological Reserve (M2)

05. Oak Grove Regional Park (M7) in the Port of Stockton: this park harbors a few groves of old valley oaks

06. Micke Grove Regional Park (M7): this park is located in Lodi, alongside Wortley Lake (M7), a popular 3-acre lake

07. Oakwood Creek: location of the San Joaquin landfill

08. The Calaveras River (M3): this river runs beside Highway 26, down from New Hogan Lake Reservoir (M5), and meets the San Joaquin River south of Stockton

09. Dry Creek: this creek forms northern border of San Joaquin County

10. The Mokelumne River (M3): this river near the Woodbridge Wilderness Area (M1) is best known for fishing of largemouth bass and catfish

11. Camanche Reservoir (M5): located at the junction of Amador, Calaveras, and San Joaquin Counties, this reservoir is home to Chinook salmon and steelhead trout, and is surrounded by savanna oak woodland

12. Bear Creek: the creek is accessed here at the heron habitat Stillman Magee Park (M7)

13. Mormon Slough: this region is dominated by loamy soil, a combination of sand, silt, and clay

14. Duck Creek (M3): this creek features bass fishing holes near Linden

15. Lone Tree Creek (M3): this creek's entire length has been altered for irrigation; Lone Tree joins the French Camp Slough and Little John Creek

16. Ripon Creek: this creek near the city of Ripon features cottonwood groves

17. Mossdale Crossing Regional Park (M7), Manteca

18. Roberts Island: one of the low island networks that regularly floods; a controversy boils as small farms are saved by very expensive levees

19. California Aqueduct: this aqueduct begins its state-long run to carry water from the San Francisco Delta to Southern California here

20. Delta Mendota Canal: this canal brings water to the Central Valley agriculture areas

21. Union Island: home to Dos Reis County Park (M7) along the San Joaquin River as it runs through the park behind a large levee; Mount Diablo in Contra Costa County is viewable to the west

22. Victoria Island: a 7,000-acre island, where in 2007 a three-mile-wide meteorite impact crater created 40 million years ago was discovered

23. Middle River: the Middle River County Park (M7) lies across a ubiquitous steel bridge indicative of roadways across these wetlands, amid farmland dotted with live oaks and cottonwoods

24. Bacon Island: a 5,400-acre peat-soil island inside a maze of canals and rerouted rivers

25. San Joaquin River National Wildlife Refuge (M1): this 7,000-acre wildlife refuge lies at the junction of the San Joaquin River (M3) with the Stanislaus River, and is where one of the world's largest riparian forest restoration projects is underway, with the replanting of half a million native trees supplying essential habitat for many birds, including the great blue heron

26. The Stanislaus River: a 95-mile river that enters San Joaquin County at Riverbank, near Jacob Myers Park and the Caswell Memorial State Park (M7), both located along the Pacific Flyway for migratory birds

Delta smelt
Hypomesus transpacificus

Map 09.39 San Francisco: Seven Hills and Seven Ecologies

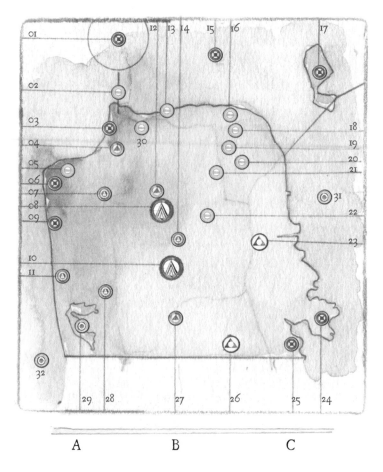

A **West county:** Lake Merced (29) (21 feet)
B **Mid county:** Mount Sutro (10) (908 feet)
C **East county:** Visitacion Knob (26) (525 feet)

2 miles

09.39

The city of San Francisco and the county of San Francisco are co-terminous: an area of land roughly seven miles by seven miles sometimes referred to as the Seven Hills of San Francisco. The ecological foundation of California's first major city contains seven major ecosystem types: chaparral, coastal scrub, dunes, grassland, riparian, wetland, and oak woodland. Sixty primary native plants that have historically done well and continue to do well here are known as the "Super 60": a list of hardy plants that are being planted and fostered in wildlife habitat reclamation projects across the city.

01. Marin County: from San Francisco, the arching peak of Mount Tamalpais in Marin, home to Muir Woods National Monument, dominates the skyline above the Golden Gate Bridge

02. The Golden Gate Bridge: it is hard to imagine a piece of architecture more in harmony with and in proportion to its setting

03. Baker Beach: part of the Golden Gate National Recreation Area (M1), Baker Beach is known for being the birthplace of the Burning Man festival; it also provides habitat for the snowy plover and salt marsh harvest mouse

04. Highway 1: on the stretch of Highway 1 in San Francisco, watch out for coyote near the Presidio Bridge

05. Legion of Honor: this art museum is surrounded by American dune grass, which provides habitat for Anna's hummingbird

06. The Esplanade: this length of open space along Ocean Beach is known for its coyote bush and coastal prairie

07. Golden Gate Park (M7): home to the San Francisco Botanical Garden and California Academy of Sciences, and habitat for the cedar waxwing, one of the few North American birds that specializes in eating fresh fruit

08. Mount Sutro (908 feet): San Francisco's tallest hill, east of the green hairstreak butterfly wildlife corridor (M4)

09. Ocean Beach: a popular surf spot that extends for miles, from the Esplanade to the zoo

10. Mount Davidson (925 feet) and Glen Canyon Park (M7): habitat for the Nuttall's white-crowned sparrow, coastal live oak, and California buckeye

11. San Francisco Zoo: this zoo is surrounded by acres of coastal dune scrub

12. Haight Street: on Haight Street near Buena Vista Park (M7) is Adah's Stairway, a manicured habitat for songbirds, pollinating insects, and local wildlife

13. Palace of Fine Arts (M7): the woodlands surrounding this art museum provide nesting habitat for red-winged blackbirds

14. Glen Canyon Park (M7): this provides bird habitat for the American bushtit and

the anise swallowtail

15. Alcatraz: a premier nesting site for colonial seabirds

16. Fisherman's Wharf: a tourist site with local nature that includes sea lions relaxing off the pier, tidal ecologies, and monarch butterfly habitat

17. Treasure Island and Yerba Buena Island: Treasure Island is an artificial island that supports small forests of pygmy oak; the dune gilia, a rare native herb, has recently found its niche on Yerba Buena Island

18. North Beach: urban habitat for the western tiger swallowtail

19. Chinatown: Portsmouth Square (M7) in Chinatown is a tree-lined park, a historic hub, and a community centerpiece

20. Union Center: provides habitat for urbanized red-tailed hawks and peregrine falcons

21. Civic Center and the Yerba Buena Gardens: home to pollinator-rooftop restoration projects and near the small Redwood Park (M7) at Transamerica Pyramid Center

22. Mission Dolores: this Spanish-style mission was built on top of Lago de Los Dolores (Lake of the Sorrows), a filled lagoon

23. Potrero Hill: home to the Starr King Open Space (M4) which consists of four acres of wildflower grassland near the Dogpatch's Esprit Park, a large local green space

24. Hunters Point: a decommissioned naval shipyard that still requires massive ecological remediation; its redevelopment plan calls for the establishment of a 400-acre waterfront park (M7)

25. Candlestick Point State Recreation Area (M7): before World War II, Candlestick Point was a 170-acre landfill area; now it is known for its views of the bay

26. Visitacion Knob (525 feet): San Francisco's second-tallest peak and home to John McLaren Park (M7), which holds seven miles of trails that meander through meadows, grasslands, and wetlands

27. Ocean Avenue: this avenue forms a corridor from Stearn Grove to Visitacion Knob

28. Stearn Grove (M7): the 33-acre park is home to Pine Lake, one of just three natural lakes in the city

29. Lake Merced (M5) in Harding Park: a natural lake fed by an underground spring

30. The Presidio: a trail area (M7, M8) and reclaimed military site that is part of the Golden Gate National Recreation Area

31. San Francisco Bay

32. The Pacific Coast: part of the Monterey Bay National Marine Sanctuary (M1)

Map 09.40 San Luis Obispo: Marine Reserves and Mountain Reaches

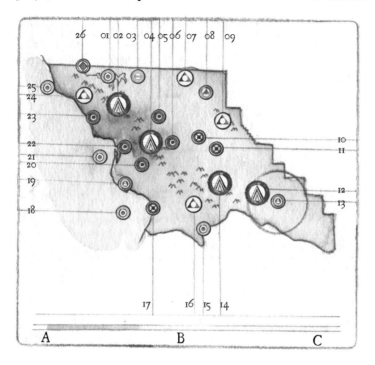

18 miles

09.40

A **West county:** Lake Nacimiento (01) (800 feet)
B **Mid county:** Templeton (06) (800 feet)
C **East County:** Carrizo Plain (13) (1,970 feet)

The Santa Lucia Mountains—and with them, the rest of the
Coast Ranges—end their march down the coast in San Luis
Obispo County. The Santa Lucias divide the coastal sage steppe
from the hot inland wildflower ranges. To the south, the Trans-
verse Ranges of the Santa Ynez and the Sierra Madres push
inland. Over the La Panza Range from across the Cuesta Grade
Summit, the county descends to the Carrizo Valley National
Monument.

01. Lake Nacimiento (M5): around the lake, native grass habitats abound; the lake has a low fish population due to mercury mining contamination

02. Black Mountain (2,933 feet): near Dover Canyon, this mountain is covered by private ranches and vineyards on the boundary between the coastal grassland steppe and the oak-dappled forests and chaparral-covered hills of the Santa Lucia Mountains

03. Camp Roberts Military Reservation

04. Frog Pond Mountain (2,436 feet): this mountain, on the other side of Cuesta Grade from the Santa Lucia Federal Wilderness Area (M1), is the northernmost point in the Los Padres National Forest

05. The Paso Robles wine region: this is the third-largest wine-producing region in California, surpassed only by Sonoma and Napa Counties

06. Templeton: a city on the Salinas River

07. Cholame Hills: part of the Cholame Creek watershed, which contains about 50,000 acres of grazing land

08. Shandon on Highway 41 in the San Luis Creek watershed: this area, down the ridge from the San Andreas Fault, is known for wildflowers in March and April

09. The Temblor Range: these mountains receive occasional snow in the winter and were formed by the San Andreas Fault; broken creek beds, dead-end channels, and ridgeline escarpments tell the geologic tale of the fault—the name Temblor means "earthquake"

10. Camatta Canyon: this canyon is home to sometimes very localized species of flowers, including the Camatta Canyon amole

11. San Juan Valley: this roadless 18-mile-long creek bed cuts through the wildflower lowlands of the Temblor Range

12. Painted Rock (2,221 feet): an enormous marine sandstone rock covered with ancient pictographs inside the Carrizo National Monument

elephant seal
Mirounga angustirostris

13. Carrizo Plain National Monument (M1): this 50-mile-long national monument is the largest single native grassland left in California; the San Andreas Fault runs down its length and is home to dozens of endangered species of plants and animals

14. Machesna Mountain (4,063 feet): this is the highest point in the La Panza Range and sits among the pine-crowned peaks of the Machesna Federal Wilderness Area (M1); rocky crags provide habitat for prairie falcons and tule elk, and it is conjectured that the local Coulter pine may be its own species

15. Twitchell Reservoir (M5): fed by the Cuyama and the Sisquoc rivers, this reservoir is filling with sediment; no public access

16. Newsom Ridge: this ridge runs east of Pismo Beach and is covered by pristine sagebrush grasslands and streambed vegetation

17. Nipomo-Guadalupe Dunes (M1): this 2,500-acre national wildlife refuge and natural landmark has nesting sites for birds who need coastal sage scrub and isolated populations of local species of rare amphibians, including the California tiger salamander and the red-legged frog

18. Pismo Beach (M7): this beach rings the San Luis Obispo Bay and is accessed by the Butterfly Trail (M8)

19. Montaña de Oro State Park (M4): near Point San Luis and Pismo Beach, this park is the site of the Monarch Butterfly Grove (M1)

20. San Luis Obispo: this city is home to El Chorro Regional Park (M7), Laguna Lake Park (M5), Cuesta Canyon County Park (M7), and the sycamore and big-leaf maple riparian habitat of the Reservoir Canyon Trail (M8)

21. Estero Bay: home to many endemic species on the shoreline near Morro Bay, including the Morro Bay kangaroo rat, which lives in the fine sand habitats in Montaña de Oro

22. Morro Bay: a state marine reserve (M1) noted for its oyster farms, and an important nesting site on the Pacific Flyway for migrating birds

23. The Cambria State Marine Conservation Area (M1): this area lies near the White Rock State Marine Conservation Area (M1), along seven miles of protected coastline that prohibits private fishing in the rocky intertidal zone

24. Santa Lucia Mountains: the Santa Lucias form the spine of the county; in the north, the Santa Rosa Creek Natural Preserve (M1), part of Hearst San Simeon State Park (M7), provides habitat for the tiny and endangered northern tidewater goby

25. Piedras Blancas State Marine Reserve: an important elephant seal breeding site and marine conservation area (M1) next to the California Sea Otter Game Refuge (M1)

26. Nacimiento River (M3): this river passes through San Luis Obispo on its way north to the Salinas River; it provides habitat for the rare arroyo toad, and would provide habitat for steelhead trout if the Nacimiento Dam had been constructed with fish passage in mind

Map 09.41 San Mateo: Open Space and Endangered Species

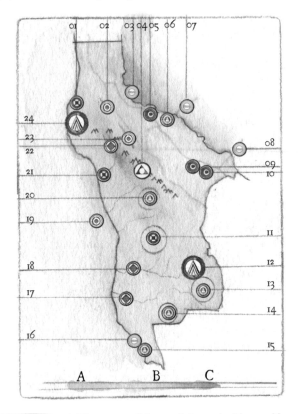

8 miles

09.41

A **West county:** Pilarcitos Lake, under Montara Mountain (01) (699 feet)
B **Mid county:** Morena Sierra (20) (2,417 feet)
C **East county:** Portola Valley (13) (455 feet)

San Mateo County exists on the San Francisco Peninsula south of the city. After the airport, the peninsula changes character as the Santa Cruz Mountains rise beyond Montara Mountain. In this isolated forest ecosystem, north of Butano and west of Santa Clara County, habitat for a number of endangered species finds small purchase in a shrinking forest. The Midpeninsula Regional Open Space District has permanently preserved over 62,000 acres over 26 open space preserves across the county.

01. Pacifica State Beach (M7), Montara State Beach (M7), and McNee Ranch State Park (M4): these are known as the only spots where a number of rare wildflowers grow, including the endemic San Mateo thornmint and Hickman's potentilla

04. The Santa Cruz Mountains: these mountains run the length of the county under Skyline Boulevard and have been designated as an American Viticultural Area, with over 30 local wineries

05. Foster City: a city built on a landfill in the San Francisco Bay

San Francisco Garter snake
Thammophis tetrataenia

06. Coyote Point Park (M7), Bair Island

07. San Mateo Bridge: this bridge is located near Redwood Creek and the Arroyo de Ojo Agua tributary, which is home to the endangered fountain thistle

02. Lower Crystal Springs Reservoir (M5), Pilarcitos Lake (M5), and Crystal Springs Park (M5): these long and narrow reservoirs follow the seam of the Earth created by the San Andreas Fault

03. San Francisco International Airport

08. Dumbarton Bridge: the Ridgway's clapper rail, also called California clapper rail, nests here on both sides of the bridge in the Don Edwards San Francisco Bay Wildlife Refuge (M2)

09. Redwood Shores Ecological Reserve (M2) in Redwood City: these 268 acres of cordgrass and pickleweed provide nesting habitat for song sparrows, rails, white-tailed kites, and short-eared owls

10. Bedwell Bayfront Park (M2) in Menlo Park: this park has a network of trails that are part of the Bay Rim Trail that circumambulates the entire Bay Area (M8)

11. El Corte Madera Redwoods Preserve (M6): the preserve contains 36 miles of trails through mixed evergreen and redwood forest; it is closed to all off-trail use

12. Mindego Hill (2,143 feet): home to the Russian Ridge Open Space (M7), with rare American kestrel and northern harrier nesting sites

13. Portola Redwoods State Park (M6): 2,800 acres, some of which is old-growth forest

14. Butano State Park (M9): a 5,000-acre oak woodland and redwood riparian forest that provides habitat for the calypso orchid

15. Año Nuevo State Park (M1): this park contains many different coastal ecologies, including old-growth redwood forest, freshwater marsh, red alder riparian forest, and knobcone pine forest; it provides habitat for the endangered San Francisco garter snake and is an important marine mammal breeding site

16. Pigeon Point State Historic Park (M7): this park is home to the Pigeon Point lighthouse, as well as tide pools of great variety

17. Pescadero Creek: home to Pescadero State Beach (M7) and the Pescadero Marsh Natural Preserve (M2) and near Pomponio State Beach (M7), a blue heron nesting site

18. San Gregorio Creek and San Gregorio State Beach (M7): this beach is ranked one of the cleanest in the state and is a wintering locale for the endangered western snowy plover

19. Monterey Bay National Marine Sanctuary (M1): 300 miles of protected coast all the way to San Luis Obispo County

20. Purisima Creek Redwoods Preserve (M6): Purisima Creek and several of its tributaries flow through this 3,360-acre preserve, featuring coastal scrub with hardwood forests that include large stands of tanoak and madrone

21. Half Moon Bay State Beach (M7), Half Moon Bay

22. Pilarcitos Creek: a 13-mile-long creek through Pilarcitos Canyon that serves as a drinking water source, steelhead trout run, and arroyo willow and coastal Douglas fir riparian forest

23. San Mateo Creek (M3): this creek feeds and flows from Crystal Springs Reservoir (M5), and is fed in large part by fog drip over Montara Mountain; the mudflat mouth of the creek provides critical nesting habitat for the endangered clapper rail

24. Montara Mountain (1,813 feet): one of the five primary peaks of the Bay Area, and the highest peak on the peninsula

Map 09.42 Santa Barbara: Three Rivers and Three Ranges

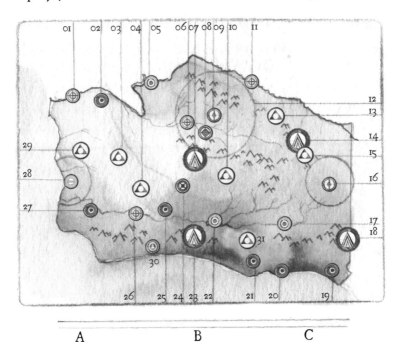

13 miles

09.42

A **West county:** Santa Maria (02) (216 feet)
B **Mid county:** Lake Cachuma (22) (750 feet)
C **East county:** Divide Peak (18) (4,707 feet)

Santa Barbara is a mostly rural county, with a belt of urban activity along its coast. The sharp Santa Ynez Mountains rise quickly over the coastal steppe and shine pink in the Pacific sunset. Two other ranges, the San Rafael and the Sierra Madre, dictate the paths of the Santa Ynez, the Sisquoc, and the Cuyama River valleys that run the entire width of the county.

01. Santa Maria River: this river begins following the confluence of the Sisquoc and the Cuyama Rivers at the Twitchell Reservoir

02. Santa Maria: this city has 230 public acres of open space within its borders

03. Solomon Hills: a low range south of Santa Maria that is rich in oil; the Orcutt Oil Field in these hills has been pumped for oil for over 125 years

04. Purisima Hills: these low hills divide the Santa Ynez watershed and Los Alamos Valley, and feature the southernmost distribution of the coast Douglas fir

05. Twitchell Reservoir (M5): the Cuyama and Sisquoc Rivers meet at this reservoir; no public access

California condor
Gymnogyps californianus

06. Sisquoc River (M3): along with the Santa Ynez and the Cuyama, this 57-mile-long river with its headwaters at Big Pine Mountain is one of the three main rivers in Santa Barbara County

07. Figueroa Mountain (4,528 feet): this mountain's springtime wildflower bloom is an epicenter for lupine and poppy flowers

08. Manzana Creek (M3): this wilderness river, a popular backpacking destination, runs from San Rafael Mountain down the north side of Figueroa Mountain to join the Sisquoc River at the ruins of a 19th-century schoolhouse

09. San Rafael Federal Wilderness Area (M1): this wilderness area includes the Sisquoc Condor Sanctuary, the first such sanctuary, despite the fact that this doesn't seem to be a current nesting site for the struggling condor population

10. The San Rafael Mountains: these mountains run parallel to the Sierra Madre Mountains in Los Padres National Forest, a woodland ecosystem where fire cycles occur in a 25-year regime

11. Cuyama River (M3): a 118-mile-long river that traces the north border of the county; Cuyama is a Chumash word that means "freshwater mollusk"

12. Peak Mountain (5,843 feet)

13. The Sierra Madre Mountains: a mountain range largely uninhabited by humans and dominated by a thick carpet of California interior chaparral

14. Samon Peak (6,227 feet)

15. Big Pine Mountain (6,828 feet)

16. Dick Smith Federal Wilderness Area (M1): one of two large designated wilderness areas in Santa Barbara County; contains a relict population of Sierra sagebrush, the closest distribution of this shrub to the coast in California; almost all the wilderness was scorched in the 2007 Zaca fire

17. Gibraltar Reservoir (M5): this reservoir on the Santa Ynez River (M3) provides the drinking water for Santa Barbara and, like many dammed waterways across California and the West, is slowly filling with sediment

18. Divide Peak (4,707 feet)

19. Montecito: a coastal city

20. Santa Barbara: home to the Santa Barbara Mission and Rose Garden

21. Goleta County Beach (M7), Goleta

22. Lake Cachuma (M5): this lake sits over San Marcos Pass from Santa Barbara and contains extensive fields of many species of sage—black sage, white sage, purple sage, and hummingbird sage

turkey vulture
Cathartes aura

23. Santa Ynez Peak (4,298 feet)

24. Los Olivos: this town is known for its wineries on the Foxen Canyon Wine Trail (M8)

25. Buellton

26. Santa Ynez River (M3): this 92-mile-long river drains the steep and coastal Santa Ynez mountains; it can become a raging torrent in December and dry to a trickle in August

27. Lompoc: site of La Purisima Mission on the Santa Ynez River

28. Vandenberg Air Force Base: an air force base surrounding Lompoc and the mouth of Santa Ynez River

29. Casmalia Hills and the Point Sal State Beach (M2): this is an important bird-roosting site among the coastal sage communities

30. Gaviota State Beach (M9): this beach is located under the hot springs up on the pass off Highway 1

31. Santa Ynez Mountains: home to the Painted Cave State Historic Landmark, a native Chumash painting site that dates back 500 years; there are hundreds of pre-Columbian painting sites in this range

Horned owl
Bubo virginianus

Map 09.43 Santa Clara: Watersheds and Wildflowers

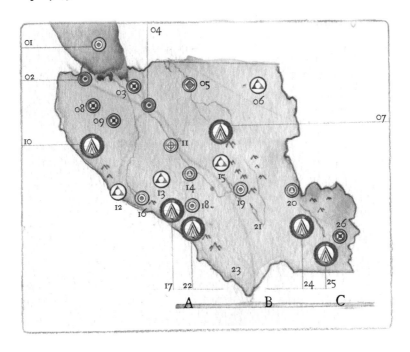

15 miles

09.43

A **West county:** Santa Cruz Mountains (12) (2,200 feet)
B **Mid county:** Santa Clara Valley (14) (250 feet)
C **East county:** Henry W. Coe State Park (20) (2,400 feet)

Santa Clara County is geographically dominated by the Santa Clara Valley, home to the city of San Jose. Coyote Creek runs down the middle of the valley and forms an enormous watershed that drains Mount Hamilton, the Bay Area's tallest peak. To the east of the valley are the oak- and wildflower-covered peaks of the Diablo Mountains, and to the west is Loma Prieta, the highest peak in the Santa Cruz Mountains.

01. San Francisco Bay: the largest estuary in North America

02. Palo Alto Bayland Nature Preserve (M2): these 2,000 acres of protected land that hide several gray fox dens make up the largest tract of wetlands left on the San Francisco Bay

03. Don Edwards San Francisco Bay National Wildlife Refuge (M2): this 30,000-acre wildlife refuge extends along the shoreline from one side of the bay to the other and hosts 280 species of birds

04. Los Gatos Creek (M3): this creek is enjoying the return of the beavers along its banks near downtown San Jose after their absence for the past 150 years

05. Arroyo Hondo (M3) along Alameda Creek: this water-course is seeing steel-head salmon return for the first time in decades, emptying into the bay, north of the county line

06. Mount Mocho in the Burnt Hills

07. Mount Hamilton (4,213 feet) and Mount Isabel: both of these mountains rise here, making the tallest ridgeline in the Bay Area

08. Silicon Valley: the ten towns of Silicon Valley—Stanford, Palo Alto, Los Altos, Mountain View, Sunnyvale, Milpitas, San Jose, Santa Clara, Los Gatos, and Cupertino—sit at the foot of Black Mountain (2,800 feet), the top of the Lower Peninsula Watershed

09. San Andreas Fault Zone: California's most definitive fault follows the western border of Santa Clara County on the east slope of the Santa Cruz Mountains

10. Black Mountain (2,800 feet) along Monte Bello Ridge: this mountain is up the trail and across Highway 9 from Villa Montalvo Arboretum County Park (M7), a 75-acre private park that is home to many rare and exotic trees

11. Coyote Creek (M3): this creek is the main drainage in Santa Clara Valley and offers a home for many species of fish, including the rare tule perch

12. Santa Cruz Mountains: a long ridgeline that extends into many counties; these mountains were formed by compressive

acorn woodpecker
Melanerpes formicivorus

uplift against the San Andreas Fault that parallels the mountains throughout the region

13. Santa Teresa Hills (M4): these hills surround the county park, which contains 1,700 acres of mixed oak woodland on serpentine soil

14. Almaden Quicksilver County Park (M7): this park was built around the 19th-century mercury mine featured in Wallace Stegner's novel *Angle of Repose*

15. Pine Ridge and the eastern ridge that runs the length of Santa Clara Valley up from the reservoirs: this area includes the San Felipe Hills and Palassou Ridge, which opens into oak savanna that forms the bucolic entrance to Henry W. Coe State Park

16. Lake Eisman (M5) and Lexington Reservoir (M5): these are the two dams on Los Gatos Creek; at the 1,000-acre Lexington Reservoir County Park (M7), fishermen angle for largemouth bass and bluegill surrounded by redwood-madrone forest

17. Mount Umunhum (3,486 feet)

18. Calero Reservoir (M5): this reservoir sits in the Guadalupe Watershed, where the Santa Clara Valley rapidly rises to the top of Loma Prieta—climbing almost 4,000 feet in only four miles

19. Anderson Lake (M5): this is the largest reservoir in Santa Clara County and home to a 3,000-acre county park

20. Henry W. Coe State Park (M1): at nearly 90,000 acres, this is the largest state park in Northern California

21. Coyote Lake (M5): this lake, at the center of a 5,000-acre regional park, is stocked with many species of fish

22. Loma Prieta (3,806 feet)

23. Mount Madonna (1,896 feet): this mountain lies just to the north of Highway 152, west of Gilroy and one mile from Santa Cruz County

24. Burra Burra Peak (2,281 feet): this peak, on the north fork of Pacheco Creek, is one of the remote peaks on the east side of Henry W. Coe State Park, deep in the wildflower veld of the Diablo Peaks

25. Pacheco Peak (2,770 feet)

26. Pacheco Pass: In 1868, when John Muir arrived in California, he went straight away to exploring California, walking through Santa Clara Valley and up over this pass, noting Pacheco Peak along the way

Signal crayfish
Pacifastacus leniusculus

Map 09.44 Santa Cruz: Otters and Old Growth

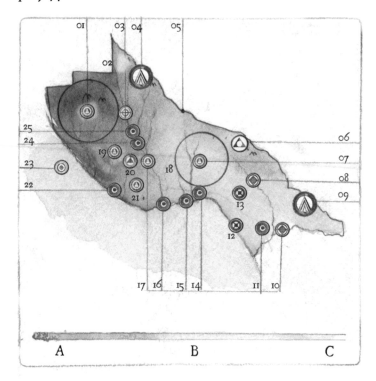

10 miles

09.44

A **West county:** Ben Lomond (25) (364 feet)
B **Mid county:** Patchen Pass (05) (1,800 feet)
C **East county:** Atherton Peak (09) (1,616 feet)

Five state parks roll down the redwood-blanketed ravines of
Santa Cruz County toward Monterey Bay, claiming a significant
portion of the county's land area. The largest park, Big Basin,
which was California's first state park, protects the largest
old-growth forest south of San Francisco. On the other side of
the county, at the mouth of the Pajaro River, record numbers of
river otters are returning to feast on recovering fish populations.

long-toed salamander
Ambystoma macrodactylum croceum

01. Big Basin Redwoods State Park (M6): this park preserves 11,000 acres of old-growth redwood forest in the Waddell Creek watershed

02. Castle Rock State Park (M6): a 5,000-acre park containing unique rock formations over redwood-madrone forest; this is the starting point of the 30-mile Skyline-to-the-Sea Trail

03. San Lorenzo River (M3): this was once one of the most productive salmon rivers in California; due to pollution, most of the salmon were expatriated, but the populations are beginning to recover

04. Mount Bielawski (3,231 feet)

05. Patchen Pass on Highway 17 (1,800 feet)

06. Santa Cruz Mountains: this ridgeline contains the headwaters of Waddell Creek, Soquel Creek, and the San Lorenzo River

07. The Forest of Nisene Marks State Park (M7): this 10,000-acre park features 40 miles of hiking trails through Douglas fir and redwood forest, as well as cottonwood and alder riparian creeks and waterfalls

08. Corralitos River (M3): this tributary, the lowermost of the Pajaro River, is home to a distinct population segment of steelhead trout

09. Atherton Peak (1,616 feet)

10. Pajaro River (M4): this river borders four counties and empties into the middle of the moon-shaped Monterey Bay coast; it is home to the largest population of river otters on the California coast

11. The Nature Center at Ramsey Park (M7), Watsonville: this is the headquarters for fun and scientific engagement with the Central Coast wetlands environment

12. Manresa State Beach (M7) and Moss Landing at the Elkhorn Slough National Estuary Research Preserve (M1) near the mouth of the Pajaro River

13. Corralitos Basin (M1): among the ephemeral ponds in this ecological reserve is the perfect habitat for the long-toed salamander

14. Seacliff State Beach (M7), Aptos

15. Capitola State Beach (M7) and the New Brighton State Beach (M7), Soquel Cove

16. Monarch Butterfly Natural Preserve (M1), Santa Cruz: this preserve, next to the 65-acre Natural Bridges State Beach (M7), is visited by a quarter of a million monarch butterflies each year between October and February

17. Felton: home to Henry Cowell Redwoods State Park

18. Soquel Creek: this creek runs along the old San Jose Road and opens to the sea at Capitola State Beach (M7)

19. Henry Cowell Redwoods State Park (M6): this 4,600-acre park contains one old-growth redwood grove

20. Swanton Road: up from the hamlet of Bonny Doon, this section of Highway 1 is called the Cabrillo Highway, named for the 16th-century explorer

21. Wilder Ranch State Park (M7): this historic dairy ranch, adjacent to the University of California, was newly added to the California Coast National Monument

22. Davenport: a coastal community and hub of local wine culture

23. Point Año Nuevo in San Mateo County, Año Nuevo Bay

24. Highland County Park (M7) on the San Lorenzo River, Ben Lomond

25. Boulder Creek: this 175-acre reservoir north of Lompico in the Loch Lomond Recreation Area (M5) supplies Santa Cruz's drinking water

River otter
Lontra canadensis

Map 09.45 Shasta: Lava and Lumber

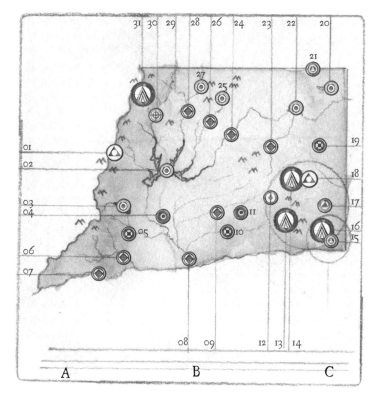

21 miles

09.45

A. **West county:** Rattlesnake Hill (01) (6,154 feet)
B. **Mid county:** Shasta Lake (02) (1,067 feet)
C. **East county:** Hat Creek Valley (19) (3,199 feet)

Shasta County is home to six major reservoirs and one major national park. Mount Shasta is not in Shasta County, but in Siskiyou County, although Mount Lassen, the southernmost volcano in the Cascade mountain range, is in Shasta County. The largest dam in California, Shasta Dam, is ten miles north of Redding on the Sacramento River. Half the land area of the county is covered in timber-industry forest.

01. Trinity Mountains: these mountains are within the Shasta-Trinity National Forest and make up the western border of Shasta County; the Shasta-Trinity National Forest, which forms a horseshoe around Shasta Lake, defines the larger watershed, which informs the headwaters of California's largest river: the Sacramento (M3)

02. Shasta Lake (M5): California's largest reservoir

03. Whiskeytown Lake (M5): a reservoir noted for its visibility of 30 feet

04. Redding: with a prominent view of Mount Shasta to the north, Redding is the northernmost city in the Sacramento Valley

05. Little Bally Mountain (5,360 feet): this mountain separates the Whiskeytown-Shasta-Trinity National Recreation Area (M9) from the majority of southeastern Shasta County

06. North fork of Cottonwood Creek (M3): all forks of Cottonwood Creek support fall-run salmon

07. Middle fork of Cottonwood Creek (M3): this fork provides riparian habitat for many forest creatures, including the rare valley elderberry longhorn beetle

08. Sacramento River (M3): at the point where the Sacramento emerges from Shasta Dam, it is the largest river by volume in the state

09. Oak Run Creek (M3): in this region of ridges and creeks, black oak mixes with Douglas fir

10. Battle Creek Wildlife Area (M1): this 600-acre area of riparian habitat saddles Shasta and Tehama Counties and is home to strong populations of bald eagle and osprey

11. Shingletown: a small community approximately 15 miles west of Lassen National Park that is home to a large wild horse sanctuary (M1) and the historic Bear Creek Trading Post; this region also provides habitat to the rare Shasta clarkia, a beautiful wildflower in the primrose family

12. Thousand Lakes Federal Wilderness Area (M1): 17,000 acres of volcanic and glaciated ranges with approximately 21 miles of trails and, contrary to its name, only seven major lakes

13. Lassen Peak (10,457 feet): a volcano

14. Table Mountain (6,919 feet): this is the peak nearest to the Loomis Museum and the Manzanita Lake Trail (M8)

15. Lassen Volcanic National Park (M1): inside Lassen National Forest, this park is rich with hydrothermal sites including Bumpass Hill, with acres of bubbling mud

16. Crater Butte (7,267 feet): this butte is covered by a white fir–dominant forest

17. Devastated Area Trail (M8): this trail provides evidence of Lassen's last eruption among acres of pink and gray lava rocks, evidence that continues across the Hat Lake Trail

18. Badger Mountain (7,127 feet)

19. Hat Creek Valley: this valley between the Pit River and Highway 299 sits under Hatchet Mountain (5,487 feet); nearby, on Hat Creek Rim, is the massive University of California Radio Astronomy Observatory

20. Horr Pond (M5): this pond sits in the heart of this rangeland north of McArthur, an area paved by a thick layer of volcanic basalt 3,000 years ago

21. Ahjumawi Lava Springs State Park (M2): a 6,000-acre state park at the northern edge of Big Lake, which feeds the Fall River, a major tributary of the Pit River; this pine and juniper forest provides excellent birding on the lake, which includes geese, pelican, owls, and osprey

22. Lake Britton (M5): located within the McArthur-Burney Falls Memorial State Park (M7), this lake is near the paradisiacal Burney Falls on Lake Britton, a dammed reservoir on the Pit River

23. Burney Falls Loop Trail (M8), Burney Creek

24. Pit River (M3): at 300 miles, the Pit is the longest tributary of the Sacramento River

25. Iron Canyon Reservoir (M8): one of seven reservoirs fed by the Pit River on the border ridge of Shasta Lake and the larger watershed of the Pit, all of which are in various stages of disrepair

26. Squaw Creek

27. Lake McCloud (M5): this lake feeds the McCloud River, which in turn feeds Shasta Lake to the west; the lake is also headwaters for Hawkins Creek to the east, which in turn feeds the Iron Canyon Reservoir

28. McCloud River (M3)

29. Tombstone Mountain (5,613 feet): this is the tallest peak in the series of ridges that defines the boundary between the Sacramento River, traced by Interstate 5, and the McCloud River arm of Shasta Lake

30. Sacramento River north of Shasta Lake: this section of the river runs past Castle Crags Federal Wilderness Area (M1), down from Mount Shasta in Siskiyou County

31. Rattlesnake Hill (6,154 feet)

Pronghorn
Antilocapra americana

Map 09.46 Sierra: Buttes, Birds, and Blooms

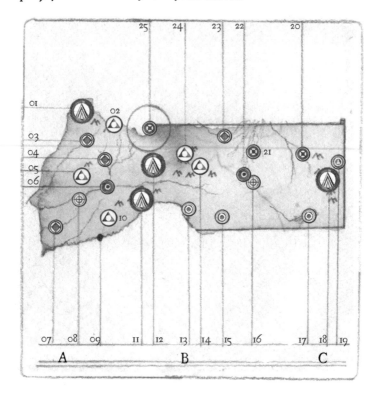

9 miles

09.46

A **West county:** Downieville (06) (2,899 feet)
B **Mid county:** Yuba Pass (14) (6,701 feet)
C **East county:** Sierraville (22) (4,950 feet)

Incense cedar forests give way to red fir up over the northern-most extent of the Sierra Nevada, the Sierra Buttes: an ancient, exposed volcano that crowns the terminus of the Gold Rush Mother Lode. Fragrant forests that shade gnarled volcanic ridges harbor cold enough temperatures to keep snow through June, only to let the blanket of wildflowers cover the region's meadows in color in July. Swollen with snowmelt, the Yuba and Feather Rivers begin their charge from this remote and rural county.

01. Democrat Peak (6,779 feet): this peak is accessed by the Chimney Rock Trail

02. Cray Croft Ridge: this ridge rises between the Downie River and Lavezzola Creek (M3); north of Downieville, Second Divide Creek leads out of where the Lavezzola meets Pauley Creek

03. Canyon Creek (M3): a tributary of the North Yuba River; Devils Postpile basalt geological feature sits near its headwaters

04. Downie River (M3): this river's ecosystem was deeply wounded by hydraulic mining in the mid-19th century, and scars are still evident

05. Bald Mountain (5,534 feet)

06. Downieville: a Gold Rush town

07. Oregon Creek (M3): this creek runs parallel to the Table Mountain Trail (M8)

08. North fork of the Yuba River (M3): this fork of the river runs among the dogwood blooms and patches of monkey flowers that crowd the wet seeps of canyon walls of the precipitously steep river valley

09. Middle fork of the Yuba River (M3): in the marshy areas, spring blooms of marigolds and kitkitdizze crowd the swollen river full of shad and bass

10. Lafayette Ridge: this ridge is traced by Pliocene Ridge Road (M8), named for fossils found here that date back four million years

11. Granite Mountain (6,481 feet)

12. Sierra Buttes (8,591 feet): from here north, the Sierra begins to taper off and give way to the Cascade Mountains of Lassen and Shasta

13. Jackson Meadows Reservoir (M5): a nesting site for Canada geese, mergansers, mallards, and green-winged teal

14. Yuba Pass (6,701 feet): the northernmost pass over the Sierra Nevada, and also the lowest

15. Webber Lake (M5) (8,092 feet): this lake is close to Jackson Meadows Reservoir and home to nearly ten Forest Service campgrounds

16. Headwaters of the Feather River (M3)

17. Stampede Reservoir (M5): flanked by the Verdi Range to the east and the Kyburz Flat meadow to the north, this reservoir feeds the Little Truckee River and Sagehen Creek

18. Crystal Peak (8,089 feet)

19. Toiyabe National Forest: this forest spreads out along the Bald Mountain Range and down into the Sierra Valley, providing extensive sites for the wildlife viewing of waterfowl, shorebirds, songbirds, numerous species of hawks, osprey, and bald eagles

20. Smithneck Creek Wildlife Area (M2)

21. Sierra Valley: an alpine meadow and the largest of its kind in the Sierra Nevada, the Sierra Valley extends north into Plumas County and is home to two major wildlife areas: the Antelope Valley and the Smithneck Creek (M3)

22. Sierraville: site of the county's only traffic light

23. Carman Creek (M3): this creek's birding includes Canadian geese, great blue herons, sandhill cranes, numerous ducks, and songbirds

24. Deadman Peak (7,494 feet)

25. Lakes Basin Recreation Area (M9): 40 lakes dot the glacial landscapes of this recreation area; after the snow melts, look to the creeks for lilies, azaleas, penstemon, and yampa flowers

Common merganser
Mergus merganser

Map 09.47 Siskiyou: Rare Trees in the Land of Glass

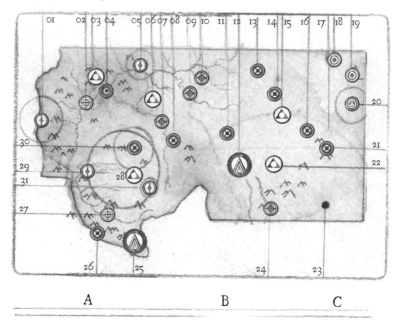

38 miles

09.47

A **West county:** Happy Camp (04) (1,085 feet)
B **Mid county:** Mount Shasta (12) (14,162 feet)
C **East county:** Tule Lake (19) (4,035 feet)

Mount Shasta dominates the view from most of Siskiyou County. From the Siskiyou Mountains, defined by the Klamath River Valley, to the county's east side, defined by ancient lava flows, fire and water have shaped this landscape like no other corner of California. Fir, pine, and cedar mingle and reinvent themselves in river valleys deep in the Klamath watershed; on the other side of the hub that is Shasta, the Great Basin desert creeps in over thin-soiled volcanic mountains made of glass.

01. Siskiyou Federal Wilderness Area (M1): this wilderness area protects 182,000 acres; the Siskiyou Mountains are the longest single mountain chain in the Klamath Mountains region; rare conifer trees include the southernmost distribution of Alaskan cedar and also the endemic Brewer spruce

02. Klamath River (M3) dams: the three major dams along the Klamath as it enters California that are scheduled for removal are Iron Gate Reservoir (M5) and Copco Lake dams number one and number two (M5)

03. Thompson Ridge: this ridge divides the Red Buttes Federal Wilderness Area and the Siskiyou Federal Wilderness Area

04. Happy Camp: a rural town on the Klamath River

05. Red Buttes Federal Wilderness Area (M1): this wilderness area is surrounded by three national forests—the Siskiyou, the Rogue River, and the Klamath—and contains the Seiad Baker Cypress Botanical Area

06. Scott Bar Mountain: a long ridge north of Scott Valley, mainly now a ponderosa pine tree forest plantation

07. Scott River (M3): this is the largest tributary on the Klamath River; mining in the early 20th century did terrible mercury damage here, but remediation is underway and the beavers have recently returned to build ponds

08. Scott Valley: a valley surrounded by botanical areas and conservation areas, including Scott Mountain Botanical Area (M6), Cement Banks Geologic Area (M1), Duck Lakes Botanical Area (M6), and, up on the Scott Bar Mountain, Deadwood Conservation Camp (M6)

09. Mill Creek and the Mill Creek Trail (M8): the creek and trail run through tree plantations and exhibit many Forest Service remediation projects from 20th-century mining operations

10. Humbug Creek (M3): a tributary of the Klamath; where the two meet, the popular Tree of Heaven Campground (M9) attracts fishermen from afar

11. The Shasta River: this river runs north from Mount Shasta, through the Shasta-Trinity National Forest, and up to

Peregrine falcon
Falco peregrinus

the Klamath River; Shasta Valley is 4,700 acres of Great Basin Juniper woodland

12. Mount Shasta: from anywhere in Shasta Valley, the profile of Mount Shasta, the largest active volcano in California, dominates

13. Butte Valley National Grassland (M6): these 400 acres of grassland provide habitat for marsh wrens and are the site of a long-term study on the Swainson's hawk; the adjacent Butte Valley Wildlife Area (M2) comprises 13,000 acres of wetlands, sage flats, and farmlands

14. Red Rock Valley: a major land feature, full of farmlands, just north of the Shasta-Trinity National Forest

15. Sharp Mountain (6,251 feet)

16. Pumice Crater Geologic Area (M1): one of the geologic areas of interest caused by the volcanic activity of the former volcano at Medicine Lake

17. Medicine Lake (M5): a lake in the center of a large, ancient volcano known as Medicine Crater, which has been active for half a million years (its last eruption was 900 years ago)

18. Lower Klamath Lake (M5, M2): one of two large reservoirs, both national wildlife refuges, that dominate the northeast county

19. Tule Lake (M2): the other large reservoir that dominates the northeast county, Tule Lake is part of the Klamath Basin National Wildlife Refuge Complex and a major hub of waterfowl habitat, including

Wood duck
aix sponsa

Ring necked pheasant
Phasianus colchicus

hundreds of species of migratory ducks
and geese

20. Lava Beds National Monument (M1):
this monument, in the eastern part of the
county, is defined by ancient lava flows
and the dramatic landscapes they left
behind; the four main geologic areas in the
monument are Callahan Lava, Pumice-
Crate, Glass Mountain, and Burnt Lava

21. Glass Mountain Geologic Area (M1):
this area, a major site of obsidian finds,
was named for the quality of the lava
flow that still covers many acres

22. Alder Creek Divide: a major ridgeline
at over 8,000 feet to the northeast of
Mount Shasta that traces a line of small
volcanoes

23. Giant Crater Lava Flow: an area of
devastation that runs for nearly 20 miles
up against the Whitehorse Mountains

24. McCloud River (M3): this 78-mile-
long river contains the McCloud Falls,
which are renowned for their wild beauty;
the McCloud River was once a habitat for
the rare bull trout, but the last one was
caught in the 1980s

25. Russian Peak (8,196 feet)

26. Gray Pine Botanical Area (M6): this
area sits at the northern edge of the Trinity Alps and contains the northernmost
distribution of the gray pine species

27. Salmon River (M3): there are no
dams or diversions on this 20-mile-long
tributary of the Klamath, which provides
habitat for the largest spring Chinook
salmon run in the watershed

28. Russian Federal Wilderness Area
(M1): this area is known for its high conifer diversity and harbors the most tree
species per mile of any area in California

29. Marble Mountains: this range has
peaks averaging around 7,500 feet and
contains 89 lakes stocked with trout

30. Klamath National Forest: this forest
covers one-third of the county and protects 170,000 acres of old-growth mixed
conifer forest

31. Marble Mountain Federal Wilderness
Area (M1): this 240,000-acre area draws
its name from the swirling limestone
that shines across many local peaks; rare
conifers include subalpine fir, Shasta fir,
and Pacific silver fir

Map 09.48 Solano: Watefowl and Wetlands

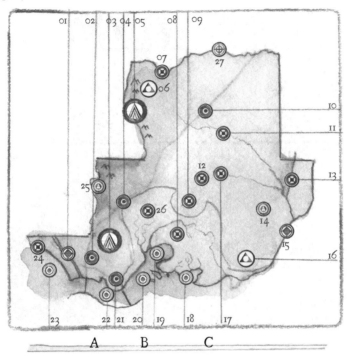

8 miles

09.48

A **West county:** Sulphur Springs Mountain (03) (1,112 feet)
B **Mid county:** Vaca Mountain (05) (2,819 feet)
C **East county:** Dixon (10) (60 feet)

The richest living wetlands of San Francisco Bay exist here, north of Suisun Bay. The Grizzly Island Wildlife Area, so named for the rich bear habitat that it supported for thousands of years before the twentieth century, is the last bastion of a brackish ecosystem where a relatively great number of endangered fish, birds, and amphibians make their last stand. Every year, hundreds of thousands of ducks and waterfowl make their way through this important stop on the Pacific Flyway, and 150 duck-hunting clubs gather here to do what they do.

01. Napa River (M3): this river is currently undergoing habitat restoration efforts up and down its length; lost wetlands near its mouth in the San Pablo Bay are returning to life from recovered salt ponds

02. Glen Cove Natural Area (M2): this natural area near Vallejo along the Carquinez Straight preserves 15 acres of riverside, riparian habitat with mature eucalyptus groves

03. Sulphur Springs Mountain (1,112 feet)

04. Dunnell Nature Park (M7): this six-acre parcel of land near Fairfield is currently being transformed into an urban park of oaks and grassland; near this park is a historical park called Lagoon Valley Park (M7), site of the Peña Adobe

05. Mount Vaca (2,819 feet)

06. Vaca Mountains: this range forms the county's western border with Napa County; Manuel Vaca, for whom the region and the town of Vacaville are named, moved here from Mexico in 1841

Dowitcher
Limnodromus griseus

07. Putah Creek Wildlife Area (M1): a single corner of the new Berryessa Snow Mountain National Monument that runs down Pleasants Ridge in the northwest corner of Solano County

08. Grizzly Island Wildlife Area (M2): these 100,000 acres of marshland in the Suisun Slu (the local spelling of "slough"), also called the Suisun Marsh, are subject to the tides of San Pablo Bay and managed for waterfowl, providing enough recreation for over 150 hunting clubs

09. Peytonia Slough Ecological Reserve (M1): this 117-acre brackish salt marsh contains large stands of tule reed and cattail and provides habitat for river otters

10. Dixon: home to the world's record for largest corn maze

11. Haas Slu: this 1,200-acre valley riparian and vernal pools ecosystem network, accessible by boat only, is home to the Calhoun Cut Ecological Reserve (M1)

12. Jepson Prairie Preserve (M6): east of the town of Fairfield and Travis Air Force Base, this preserve is a pristine example of vernal pool ecology, a once common and now rare Central Valley ecosystem

13. Miner Slough Wildlife Area (M2): this 37-acre wildlife area has willows and nesting grounds for night herons

14. Grasslands Regional Park (M7): this park, home to the Liberty Island Bird Club, sits on the Solano County's eastern border; the 4,450-acre Liberty Island Ecological Reserve (M2) sits next to Yolo County's Bypass Wildlife Area,

providing key habitats for thousands of migratory birds

15. The Deep River Canal: this canal, which runs parallel to the Sacramento River and past the port town of Rio Vista, is a major artery by which the agriculture of the region, including sugar beets, tomatoes, fruits and nuts, and field crops, goes out for distribution

16. Montezuma Hills: home to the Solano Wind Project

17. Hill Slough Wildlife Area (M2): 1,700 acres of salt tidal marsh

18. Honker Bay

19. Grizzly Bay

20. Suisun Bay

21. Benicia: this city on the Carquinez Strait is home to the Lake Herman Recreational Area, a reservoir that provides Benicia's drinking water

22. Carquinez Strait: this strait between Solano and Contra Costa County is spanned by two bridges—the Carquinez and the Benicia

23. San Pablo Bay Wildlife Area (M2): this area on Mare Island provides bird habitat for over four dozen bird species, including the dowitcher

24. Mare Island, across from Vallejo: this factory landscape and historic naval shipyard is home to the 215-acre Mare Island Shoreline Heritage Preserve (M1), a remediation project

25. Rockville Hills Park (M7): 650 acres over the Sugarloaf Ridge from Napa County; these oak woodlands lie along the Bay Area Ridge Trail

26. North Bay Wetlands: these 90,000 acres of prime California wetland ecosystem provide habitat to some endangered animals, including the California clapper rail and the Suisun shrew, who live only in this tidal habitat

27. Putah Creek (M3): this creek along the northern border of Solano County runs through Stebbins Cold Canyon Reserve (M1), a private nature reserve

Map 09.49 Sonoma: The Madrone and the Mayacamas

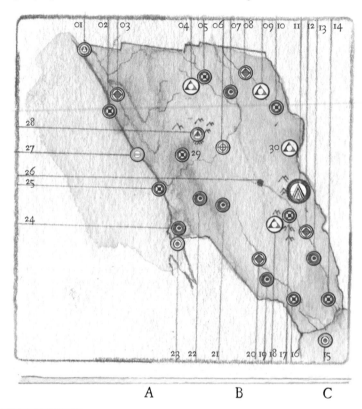

18 miles

09.49

A **West county:** Irish Hill (24) (882 feet)
B **Mid county:** Santa Rosa (26) (160 feet)
C **East county:** Sonoma Mountain (18) (2,295 feet)

In every forest across Sonoma County, the flame-red bark of the Pacific madrone stands out against the gray-green of the live oak, or up under the thick pillars of the shadowed redwoods. It doesn't form pure stands with itself; it prefers mixed company and the precise climate that Sonoma County has to offer: wet, cool winters and hot, dry summers. The Mayacamas Mountains slope down from the east to cover most of Sonoma County, up to the wide Russian River, which drains them. Across vineyards and forested ranchland and the Petaluma salt marsh on the county's east side, Sonoma Mountain rises as the land's highest peak.

01. Gualala Point Regional Park (M9): 100 acres of cypress coast forests at the mouth of the Gualala River; legal camping is rare along the coast south of here

02. Kruse Rhododendron State Preserve (M6): in this preserve, rhododendrons flash unusual color across the dark second-growth redwood forest each May

03. Gualala River (M3): this 40-mile-long river runs in three forks parallel to the coast across timberland in a watershed that receives up to 70 inches a year of rain

04. Big Mountain (2,675 feet)

05. Dry Creek Valley: this valley extends down from Lake Sonoma and into the town of Healdsburg, just north of Laguna Wildlife Area (M1) and just south of Lake Sonoma Recreational Area (M9)

06. Russian River (M3): this 110-mile-long river carries more water than any other coastal river; white sturgeon over eight feet long call the river home

07. Healdsburg: a city famous for local wine; Healdsburg Ridge Open Space Preserve (M4) is a 150-acre park of oak woodlands and chaparral

08. Little Sulphur Creek (M3): this creek provides recreational opportunities for whitewater rafting and steelhead trout fishing

09. Bradford Mountain (1,220 feet)

10. Knights Valley: an American Viticultural Area in the Mayacamas Mountains; Knights Valley's microclimate makes it the warmest wine region in Sonoma

Black-crowned night heron
Nycticorax nycticorax

11. Mount Hood (2,730 feet)

12. Sonoma Creek (M3): this 35-mile-long creek runs from Sugarloaf Ridge State Park (M1) through Sonoma Valley to the San Pablo Bay and supports the winter Chinook salmon run

13. Sonoma: a historically rich town and mission location, located south of Jack London State Historic Park (M7)

14. San Pablo Bay National Wildlife Refuge (M2): this refuge lies north of Skaggs Island, on an abandoned naval site, and extends out into the bay; the best wildlife viewing is on the Cullinan Ranch Trail (M8)

15. San Pablo Bay

16. Petaluma Marsh Wildlife Area (M2): at 4,200 acres, this is the largest remaining tidal brackish marsh in California

17. Valley of the Moon: this valley surrounds Mount Hood; Sugarloaf Ridge State Park (M9) rises from the valley and is just up from the Bouverie Wildflower Preserve (M6), a 535-acre mixed evergreen, oak, and chaparral nature reserve

18. Sonoma Mountain (2,295 feet)

19. Petaluma: a town on the Petaluma River

20. Petaluma River (M3): this river, fed by many salmon-supporting creeks, flows in a southeasterly direction through to Petaluma Marsh Wildlife Area

21. Sebastopol: a city near the Laguna Wildlife Area (M2) that contains 520 acres of waterfowl habitat and freshwater wetland

22. Occidental: a town in the redwoods on the Bohemian Highway

23. Bodega Harbor: this harbor is where the south jetty meets the mainland at Doran Regional Park (M2); a bird walk trail surrounding the harbor enables visitors to watch the array of birds that use Bodega Bay, including the ruddy duck

24. Bodega Bay and the Sonoma Coast State Park (M7), extending from the town of Bodega Bay north to Jenner: a long beach, with crags and natural arches, pocks this enchanting, often fog-shrouded stretch of about five miles between both ends of the park

25. The mouth of the Russian River at the small town of Jenner, across from Peaked Hill (376 feet), on the south shore of the river as it enters the Pacific

26. Annadel State Park (M7), Santa Rosa

27. Fort Ross State Historic Park (M7): this is where the Russians were the first to establish a settlement on the Sonoma Coast at Fort Ross in 1821

28. Austin Creek State Recreation Area (M7): this area offers 20 miles of trails through oak-topped knolls above the redwood forest; it shares its entrance with Armstrong Redwoods State Reserve

29. Armstrong Redwoods State Reserve (M6): this 800-acre preserve near Guerneville, the largest town this far down on the Russian River, is the largest remaining old-growth forest in Sonoma County

30. Mayacamas Mountains: in the northeast part of the county, this range extends north to Clear Lake and then into Mendocino County; Mount Saint Helena (4,343 feet) is the tallest peak in the county

black-crowned night heron
Nycticorax nycticorax

Map 09.50 Stanislaus: Rivers and Rangeland

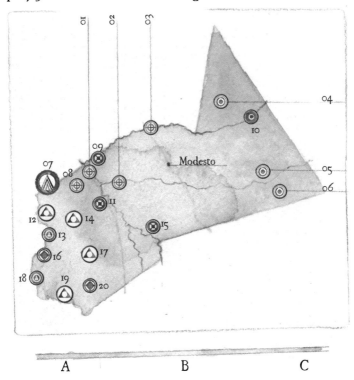

A **West county:** Mount Oso (07) (3,347 feet)
B **Mid county:** West Hilmar Wildlife Area (15) (100 feet)
C **East county:** Knights Ferry (10) (200 feet)

The farmland surrounding the modest urban center of Modesto extends over all of Stanislaus County except for a few segments of preserved riparian habitat. Heavy grazing has homogenized the grassland of the gentle east slope of the Diablo Mountains as they bow down to meet the San Joaquin River. From the eastern half of the county, the Tuolumne and the Stanislaus Rivers end their long journeys, unloading themselves among the vast, quiet, reeded riverlands.

18 miles

09.50

01. San Joaquin River (M3): this is the main artery of the Great Valley of California, the conduit that brings all the snow and rain of the South Sierra to the San Francisco Bay and the Pacific beyond

02. Tuolumne River (M3): by this river, south of the San Joaquin County border, the water of Yosemite reaches the San Joaquin River at the San Joaquin River Wildlife Area (M2)

03. Stanislaus River (M2): by this river, which defines Stanislaus County's northern border, the water under the Calaveras sequoia trees is brought to the San Joaquin River, past Knights Ferry

04. Woodward Reservoir (M5): a 3,000-acre lake stocked with catfish, bass, and crappie and surrounded by a 4,000-acre regional park

05. Modesto Reservoir (M5): this regional park is equivalent in size to Woodward Reservoir

06. Turlock Lake State Recreation Area (M2): these 26 miles of shoreline exhibit a diverse portfolio of ecologies, including Central Valley grassland mix and Delta button-celery habitat for the endangered vernal pool fairy shrimp and the signal crayfish

07. Mount Oso (3,347 feet)

08. California Aqueduct

09. San Joaquin National Wildlife Area (M2): this 7,000-acre wetland area where the Tuolomne, the Stanislaus, and the San Joaquin Rivers meet offers essential nesting grounds for the Aleutian cackling geese's population recovery over the past 40 years

10. Knights Ferry Recreation Area (M2): this riparian grassland on the Stanislaus River offers songbird habitat

11. Laird Park: a two-acre regional park (M7); winter fishing is prohibited in order to protect the winter salmon run

12. Diablo Range: the longest of the Coast Ranges, the Diablos slope down across the west side of Stanislaus County to form the Wilcox Ridge and a few low peaks

13. Deer Creek Park (M9): this park is up Del Puerto Canyon, toward Mount Hamilton in Santa Clara County

14. Copper Mountain (2,678 feet)

15. West Hilmar Wildlife Area (M2): 340 acres of cottonwoods and grasslands providing nesting sites for the big fishing birds, the egret and the heron

16. Crow Creek: an intermittent rangeland creek

17. Orestimba Peak (2,074 feet)

18. Henry W. Coe State Park (M1): the largest state park in Northern California; there is no direct access by road or trail to the de facto wilderness of Robinson Mountain from Stanislaus County

19. Robinson Mountain (2,657 feet): the highest peak in Henry W. Coe State Park in Stanislaus County

20. Orestimba Creek (M3): the largest creek in the west county; when it rains enough the creek reaches the San Joaquin River

Map 09.51 Sutter: Restoration and Ringtails

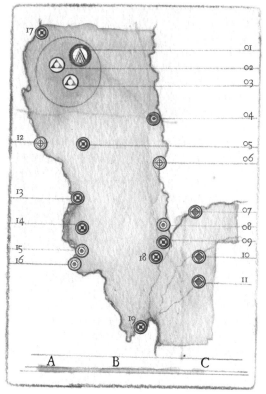

10 miles

09.51

A **West county:** Bullock Bend (15) (35 feet)
B **Mid county:** West Butte (02) (1,685 feet)
C **East county:** Yuba City (04) (59 feet)

Sutter County is drawn between the two largest rivers in Northern California: the Sacramento and the Feather. Those river lines,
along with the Sutter Buttes, form the three geographic features
that define the county. The Sutter Buttes, a tiny mountain
range in the middle of the Sacramento Valley that consists of the
remnants of ancient volcanoes, provide habitat to many isolated
populations of endangered animals, including the rare ringtail
cat.

01. Sutter Buttes, Peak 1: North Butte (1,863 feet)

02. Sutter Buttes, Peak 2: West Butte (1,685 feet)

03. Sutter Buttes, Peak 3: South Butte (2,117 feet)

04. Yuba City: twin city with Marysville across the Feather River; peaches are the number-one farmed crop of the immediate region

05. Sutter National Wildlife Refuge (M2): the Sutter Bypass is a floodwater bypass from the Sacramento River that floods about once a year, and the 2,600-acre Sutter National Wildlife Refuge supports wintering populations of more than 175,000 ducks and 50,000 geese

06. Feather River (M3): the Sacramento's largest tributary picks up the waters of the Yuba River and the Bear River as it makes its way to join the biggest of all Northern California rivers at the southernmost terminus of Sutter County

07. Bear River (M3): the smallest main tributary of the Feather River

08. Abbott Lake (M5): a riparian restoration site inside the Feather River Wildlife Area

09. Bobelaine Audubon Sanctuary (M2)

10. Coon Creek (M3): an intermittent creek that provides habitat for songbirds, including Bullock's oriole

11. Sutter Canal: agricultural redirectment of the Sacramento River

12. Sacramento River (M3): the largest and most unruly of Northern California's rivers; because of Sacramento's tendency to flood, rice, with its need for wet farmland, has become a common crop

13. Steiner Bend: major levee project site

14. Collins Eddy Wildlife Area (M1): 25 acres of scrub willow and oak woodland

15. Bullock Bend: this post-agricultural remediation site consists of 100 acres of restored floodplain; it is closed to the public

Ringtail
Bassariscus astutus

16. Mystic Lake (M5): a lake cut off from the Sacramento, one of many like this in the low, flat area of the county; Mystic Lake is dry in the summer, but open to fishing in winter

17. Butte Sink (M2): these 18,000 acres along the Pacific Flyway stretch into three counties; not open to the public

18. Feather River Wildlife Area (M2): 3,000 acres of thick riparian ecosystems at the confluence of the Feather and the Bear Rivers, providing habitat for river otters and a large portfolio of songbirds and water birds

19. Fremont Weir Wildlife Area (M1)

Map 09.52 Tehama: Black Peaks and Black-Tailed Deer

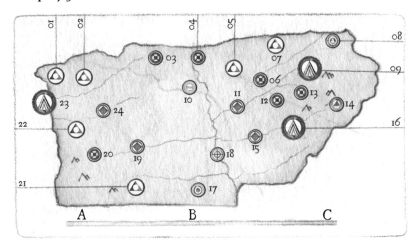

16 miles

09.52

A. **West county:** North Yolla Bolly (23) (7,863 feet)
B **Mid county:** Red Bluff (10) (500 feet)
C **East county:** Blue Ridge (07) (6,200 feet)

Tehama County exists as a massive valley across the top of the Sacramento Valley. On the west side of the county, the rocky peaks of the Yolla Bolly Wilderness in Mendocino National Forest form long ridgelines that follow a maze of steep-sloped river gulches. On the east side of the county, the volcanic lands of Mount Lassen extend down into the Ishi Wilderness to provide habitat for the state's largest existing herd of migratory animals, black-tailed deer. Across the county, the rampaging effects of millions of years of geologic activity have left oddly shaped and often jagged peaks, whose dark basalt compositions create ominous silhouettes against either the rising or the setting sun.

01. Round Mountain (5,831 feet): a mountain at the western border of the Mendocino National Forest

02. Tedoc Mountain (1,614 feet)

03. Long Gulch and the Cottonwood Creek Basin: this area winds through farm country and runs into the Sacramento River at the town of Cottonwood on the Shasta County line

Black-tailed deer
Odocoileus columbianus

08. Lassen Volcanic National Park (M1): this park's southwest entrance sits under Brokenoff Mountain (9,253 feet); only the southwest border of the park dips down into Tehama County

09. Turner Mountain (6,893 feet)

10. Red Bluff Diversion Dam (M5): this dam directs water to the Corning Canal and the Colusa Canal

11. Antelope Creek (M3): a scenic creek capable of supporting boats and rafts

12. Ishi Federal Wilderness Area (M1): this 41,000-acre federal wilderness area is home to the state's largest herd of black-tailed deer

04. Mouth of Cottonwood Creek Wildlife Area (M1): 1,100 acres of cottonwood and Oregon ash with willow riparian valley habitats

05. Inskip Hill (3,100 feet)

06. Tehama Wildlife Area (M1): these 45,000 acres of rugged canyons and chaparral are home to wild pigs and black-tailed deer

07. Blue Ridge: from the peaks of Lanes Valley Road, the Blue Ridge runs up past the south fork of Ash Creek toward Lassen Volcanic National Park

13. Tehama State Game Reserve (M1): this deer-hunting reserve above Tehama Wildlife Area runs along the Mill Creek Rim and up the Mill Creek Trail, which leads through the Mill Creek Conservancy (M2); Mill Creek is home to a number of endangered species, including a spring run of Chinook salmon, and the creek itself cuts through the area's ubiquitous black rock geology

14. Deer Creek Highway: this highway runs near Humboldt Peak in Plumas County, where, at the Tehama County line, there is an access point on the Pacific Crest Trail

15. Mill Creek Park (M7): 33 acres of cottonwood and oak grassland in Los Molinos

16. Pinnacle Peak (3,293 feet)
17. Black Butte Lake (M5) (474 feet): a reservoir that saddles Glenn County; Black Butte itself rises on the reservoir's north shore

18. Sacramento River (M3): Northern California's largest river draws a thick blue line on the north-south axis through the middle of Tehama County

19. Elder Creek (M3): the south and north forks of Elder Creek meet just south of Gleason Peak (1,165 feet); the creek runs underground for much of the year on its eastward crawl to the Sacramento River

20. Yolla Bolly–Middle Eel Federal Wilderness Area (M1): the mountainous western part of Tehama County lies largely

in this federal wilderness area; many trails head into the rugged Yolla Bolly Mountains from many points, including the newly developed Bigfoot Trail, the Ides Cove Trail, and the Sugarfoot Glade Trail (M8)

21. Round Mountain (4,287 feet)

22. South Yolla Bolly (8,092 feet): these remote, high ridges are lined with old-growth Jeffrey pine forests

23. North Yolla Bolly (7,863 feet)

24. Cottonwood Creek (M3): this creek, with headwaters near Yolla Bolly, runs half the county to the Sacramento

striped skunk
Mephitis mephitis

Map 09.53 Trinity: Remote Ridges and Complex Conifers

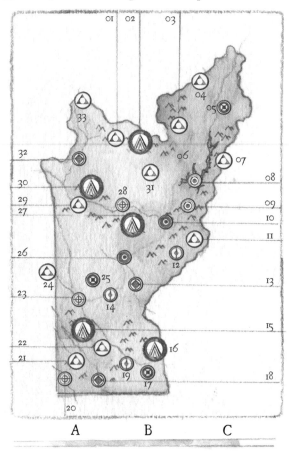

A **West county:** South Fork Mountain (24) (4,077 feet)
B **Mid county:** Hayfork (26) (2,327 feet)
C **East county:** Trinity Lake (08) (2,387 feet)

The few parts of Trinity County that aren't covered by thick forest are covered by either northwest California's only glaciated mountain range or by cold, swollen rivers populated with salmon populations that struggle to navigate their way back up to the headwaters of their birth.

21 miles

09.53

01. Cabin Peak (6,866 feet)

02. Thompson Peak (9,002 feet)

03. Sugar Pine Butte (7,861 feet)

04. Scott Mountains: a 20-mile ridgeline shared with Siskiyou County; Scott Mountain Summit (5,400 feet), covered in mixed forests of cedar, hemlock, and Douglas fir, is the highest peak

05. Upper Trinity River Valley: the upper, northeastern corner of Trinity County is the headwaters of the wild Trinity River, near Mount Eddy (9,025 feet)

06. Trinity Alps Federal Wilderness Area (M1): only 60 miles from the Pacific, this 525,000-acre wilderness presents plant types that are unexpected here, as they are more common in inland, alpine forests like the Sierra Nevada

07. Trinity Mountains: the only glaciated area in the Klamath system of mountain rivers; there are three ranges—the White, the Red, and the Green Trinities—named for the generalized color of their ultramafic bedrock

08. Trinity Lake (M5): a massive reservoir and recreation area

09. Lewiston Lake (M5): the second dam on the Trinity River, past Trinity Lake on the same river

10. Weaverville

11. Bully Choop Mountain (6,974 feet)

12. Chanchelulla Federal Wilderness Area (M1): this 8,000-acre wilderness area harbors known populations of rare fishers, tiny carnivorous members of the marten family; Chanchelulla Peak (6,399 feet) is the wilderness area's tallest peak

13. Hayfork Creek (M3): home of the Hall City Cave, a limestone cavern with Permian-age fossils in its walls

14. Yolla Bolly–Middle Eel Federal Wilderness Area (M1): 14 different species of conifer can be found in these 170,000 acres of rugged backcountry

15. Pickett Peak (5,916 feet)

ithuriel's spear
triteleria laxa

16. North Yolla Bolly (7,863 feet)

17. Mendocino National Forest: this national forest in Trinity County contains approximately 35,000 acres of old-growth forest, most of which is Douglas fir

18. North fork of the Eel River (M3)

19. North Fork Federal Wilderness Area (M1): a very remote 8,000-acre forest wilderness area

20. Eel River (M3): this river cuts a small track of just a few miles inside Trinity County; its watershed is home to the ghost town of Island Mountain, previously home to a sulphur mine

21. Kettlehorn Peak (4,089 feet)

22. Chinquapin Butte (5,870 feet)

23. South fork of the Trinity River (M3): this fork has its headwaters at North Yolla Bolly, and meets the main fork of the Trinity at the county's western border

24. South Fork Mountain (4,077 feet): a long, low ridge that frames Trinity's west border

25. Shasta–Trinity National Forest: this enormous forest reaches from the Sacramento Valley to the border of Oregon; in the canyons of the Trinity River, bigleaf maples mix with dogwood and alder

26. Hayfork

27. Hayfork Bolly (6,277 feet)

28. Trinity River (M3): this river begins its 165-mile trek to join the Klamath River north of Trinity Lake and defines a path for the main road all the way through Trinity County

29. Chaparral Mountain (5,382 feet)

30. Eagle Rock (4,741 feet)

31. Trinity Alps: this remote alpine forest is home to a huge variety of conifer species, including subalpine fir, Pacific silver fir, Engelmann spruce, incense cedar, ponderosa pine, white fir, northern foxtail pine, and weeping spruce

32. New River (M3): the New River Trail up from the small town of Denny has been the site of major restoration and offers an excellent entry point into the Trinity Alps Wilderness

33. Salmon Mountains: as with the Scott Mountains, the main ridgeline of the Salmon Mountains is shared with Siskiyou County

Map 09.54 Tulare: Stairway of the Sierra

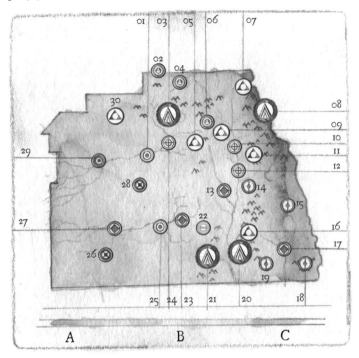

24 miles

09.54

A **West county:** Visalia (29) (288 feet)
B **Mid county:** Moro Rock in Sequoia National Park (04) (6,725 feet)
C **East county:** Ball Mountain in the Sacatar Wilderness (15) (9,256 feet)

Tulare County's east side is dominated by the steep rise of the southwestern slope of the Sierra Nevada. Although the west-side rise of California's mountain range is not comparable to the precipitous rise of the mountain's east-side wall, which includes Mount Whitney, the Tulare Foothills do rise to the Giant Sequoia Forest 11,000 feet in only ten miles. There are no roads up in these light, bowl-shaped valleys, whose pine and fir forests rise up to touch the timberline.

01. Lake Kaweah (M5): this lake's primary purpose is flood control in May and June for the cities and farmlands below

02. Giant Sequoia National Park (M1): this giant forest is up the windy Highway 198, a grove of giant sequoia trees that contains the most massive tree in the world; there are five, major trails that find their beginning along this road

03. Yucca Mountain (4,927 feet)

04. Sequoia National Park (M1): the entirety of this 400,000-acre park is in Tulare County; on the park's west side is the largest tree in the world, the General Sherman Sequoia, and on the east side is the tallest peak in the lower 48, Mount Whitney

swallowtail
Papilio multicandata

05. Castle Rocks (9,180 feet)

06. Kings Canyon National Park (M1): Kings Canyon saddles Tulare and Fresno Counties; the Jennie Lakes Wilderness, on the south end of the park, shares a border with the Giant Sequoia National Monument

07. Kings–Kern Divide

08. Mount Whitney (14,494 feet): on the border of Inyo County, Mount Whitney is the tallest peak in the lower 48; the peak and its adjacent ridgeline all top out higher than 14,000 feet

09. Picket Guard Peak (12,302 feet): the tallest peak in the Kaweah Peaks Range

10. Kern River (M3): cold, clear, and deep, the Kern River claims the Whitney Ridge in its watershed, where it begins its 165-mile march to the San Joaquin Valley

11. Kern Peak (11,510 feet)

12. Golden Trout Creek (M3): in this high mountain tributary of the Kern, rare trout species hybridize and fight to maintain their populations

13. Little Kern River (M3)

14. Golden Trout Federal Wilderness Area (M1): this 300,000-acre wilderness area includes pristine sequoia forests and provides habitat for numerous rare and endemic species, including the Kaweah fawn lily

15. Sacatar Trail Federal Wilderness Area (M1): home to Kennedy Meadows, a convenient resupply point on the Pacific Crest Trail

16. Bald Mountain (9,382 feet)

17. South fork of the Kern River (M3)

18. Chimney Peak (7,990 feet): the highest peak in the Chimney Peak Federal Wilderness Area (M1)

Cackling goose
Branta hutchinsii leucoparcia

19. Domeland Federal Wilderness Area (M1)

20. Tobias Peak (8,284 feet)

21. Hatchet Peak (6,385 feet)

22. Tule River Reservation: on nearly 56,000 acres, this reservation is currently home to about 600 people from many different tribes from the eastern Sierra foothills

23. Tule River (M3)

24. Kaweah River (M3)

25. Lake Success (M5)

26. Pixley National Wildlife Refuge (M1): this refuge provides 7,000 acres of sandhill crane nesting grounds along the Pacific Flyway

27. Friant-Kern Canal

28. Elk Bayou

29. Visalia

30. Sequoia Foothills: many water canals bisect this region, where the elevation begins to climb out of the San Joaquin Valley and finally up to the Whitney Ridge

Map 09.55 Tuolumne: In the Yosemite Highlands

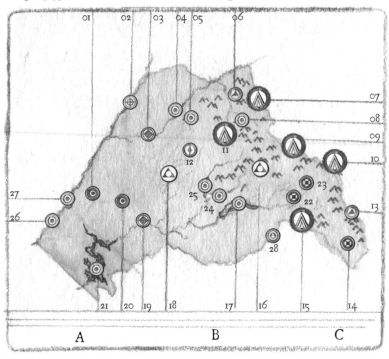

16 miles

09.55

A **West county:** Don Pedro Reservoir (20) (800 feet)
B **Mid county:** Lake Eleanor (24) (4,657 feet)
C **East county:** Tioga Pass (13) (9,945 feet)

Tuolumne County lifts suddenly off the Central Valley floor, rising several thousand feet through narrow canyon in just a few miles. Steep, old river courses gouge this glaciated landscape—rivers that are now dammed and flooded. The most famous of these reservoirs is Hetch Hetchy, which has been hailed many times as a second Yosemite Valley. It is likely that in the next 100 years we will see a free Hetch Hetchy Valley once again, as many believe the antiquated dam is obsolete and ready to be removed.

01. Dragoon Gulch Trail (M8): a three-mile trail through oak woodlands preserve in Sonora City

02. North fork of the Stanislaus River (M3): a 30-mile tributary of the Stanislaus River that has its headwaters near Ebbett's Pass

03. Middle fork of the Stanislaus River (M3): in this fork, brown and rainbow trout spawn above Beardsley Lake

04. Beardsley Lake (M5): this mountain reservoir features good fishing because its insect populations are thriving off of nutrient-rich soils under the water

05. Pinecrest Lake (M5): this lake is fed by the south fork of the Stanislaus River

06. Sonora Pass: this pass divides Alpine and Mono Counties on Highway 108

07. Leavitt Peak (11,569 feet): a peak on the Pacific Crest Trail (M8)

08. Relief Reservoir (M5): a reservoir on Kennedy Creek, near Kennedy Meadows

09. Tower Peak (11,755 feet)

10. Twin Peaks (12,323 feet)

11. Granite Dome (10,322 feet)

12. Emigrant Federal Wilderness Area (M1): in these 113,000 acres of glaciated landscape, snow lingers through June; livestock are permitted to graze here in the summer

13. Tioga Pass: the highest paved pass in the Sierra Nevada

14. Lyell Canyon: this canyon is traced by the trail from Tuolomne Meadows to Donahue Pass; it has a similar ecology to Tuolomne Meadows under Cathedral Peak—a high mountain meadow thick with summertime grasses

15. Cathedral Peak (10,940 feet)

California quail
Callipepla californica

16. Piute Mountain (10,541 feet)

17. Hetch Hetchy Reservoir (M5): this reservoir is deemed by many experts to be outdated, and a movement to restore the valley is growing

18. Dodge Ridge: the snow on this ridge is the closest snow to the Central Valley

19. Tuolumne River (M3): this 150-mile-long river feeds Hetch Hetchy and Don Pedro Reservoir; with these two major reservoirs, the amount of water that now flows into the San Joaquin River is half of its historic amount, a disaster for fish populations

20. Twain Hartey

21. Don Pedro Reservoir (M5): a major dam on the Tuolomne River

22. Tuolumne Meadows

23. Moraine Flat

24. Lake Eleanor (M5): this lake inside Yosemite Park is part of the Hetch Hetchy Reservoir system

25. Cherry Lake (M5): this reservoir 25 miles east of Sonora is another part of the Hetch Hetchy system and forms a dam for three branches of Cherry Creek

26. Tulloch Reservoir (M5): an irrigation reservoir on the Stanislaus River

27. New Melones Reservoir (M5): one of California's largest dams, built in a steep canyon in 1983; the dam destroyed many scenic areas and is another reservoir in Tuolumne County that is deemed unnecessary and whose removal has been called for

pipevine swallowtail
Battus philenor

green hairstreak butterfly
Callophrys rubi

Map 09.56 Ventura: Sage of the Sespe

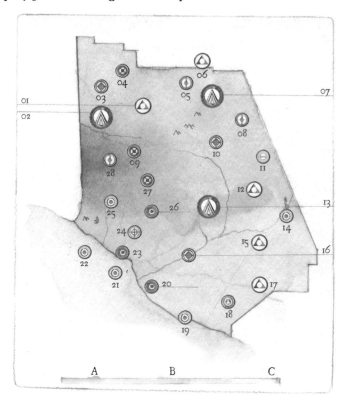

A West county: Lake Casitas (25) (510 feet)
B Mid county: Topatopa Peak (12) (6,210 feet)
C East county: Lake Piru (14) (1,055 feet)

Ventura County is a land of majestic variety. From the sage- and pinyon-covered slopes of the Sespe to the wildflower-blanketed grasslands of the Santa Monica Mountains, the wild and rugged land lies mostly inside Los Padres National Forest.

15 miles

09.56

01. Reyes Peak (7,510 feet)

02. Pine Mountain (5,080 feet): this pinyon-covered ridgeline is three miles to Reyes Peak, both on Pine Mountain

03. Cuyama River (M3): this river, which runs all the way to the sea, has its headwaters on the border of Ventura and Kern Counties in the San Emigdio Mountains

04. Los Padres National Forest: Los Padres extends down the west border of the county to Lake Casitas; the national forest designation covers nearly 80 percent of Ventura County

05. Chumash Federal Wilderness Area (M1): the tallest peak in this 38,000-acre wilderness area in the Los Padres National Forest is Mount Pinos (8,830 feet)

06. Mount Pinos: deep in the San Emigdio Mountains, this peak divides Ventura and Kern Counties

07. Alamo Mountain (7,362 feet): this is the highest peak in the northern Sespe Wilderness and part of a larger cluster of mountains above Aqua Blanca Creek between San Rafael Peak (6,666 feet) and Cobblestone Mountain (6,730 feet)

08. Sespe Federal Wilderness Area (M1): this 220,000-acre wilderness contains two major landforms, the Topatopa Mountains and Sespe Creek

09. Sespe Gorge: this steep, sedimentary river valley is filled at dawn with songbirds over acres of native sage and buckwheat

10. Sespe Creek: this creek winds east around the Topotopa Mountains to meet the Santa Clara River near Kenney Grove County Park

11. Sespe Condor Sanctuary (M1): this 53,000-acre wildlife refuge was the release site for a breeding pair of California condors in 1992; the population of California condors has recovered here to 150 individuals

12. Topatopa Mountains: from Nordhoff Peak (4,495 feet), the Topatopa Mountains run east to Devil's Heart Peak (5,203 feet), deep in the Sespe Wilderness.

13. Hines Peak (6,704 feet)

14. Lake Piru (M5): this lake is the source of Piru Creek, which is the same water that makes Pyramid Lake in Los Angeles County; the lake continues to be infested with quagga mussels, an aggressive, invasive species that destroys native fish habitat by eating all the phytoplankton and collapsing the food chain

15. Santa Susana Mountains and the Oak Ridge

16. Santa Clara River (M3)

17. Simi Hills, east of the Santa Monica Mountains

18. Point Mugu State Park (M9): this beachside park is home to Sycamore Canyon, a springtime wildflower epicenter; its tallest peak is the pinnacle of Boney Mountain (2,880 feet)

19. Mugu Lagoon: this salt marsh offers habitat for harbor seals

20. Oxnard: coastal city

21. Pierpont Bay

22. Santa Barbara Channel

23. Ventura: a coastal city

24. Ventura River (M3): this is the smallest of the three rivers in Ventura County; its steelhead habitat is threatened by Spanish cane, an invasive and thirsty reed

25. Lake Casitas (M5): this lake provides Ventura's drinking water

26. Ojai

27. Wheeler Gorge: this is the sycamore-lined riparian home to the small town of Wheeler Springs, just down from Matilija Reservoir

28. Matilija Federal Wilderness Area (M1): the highest point in this 30,000-acre wilderness area, bisected by Matilija Creek, is Ortega Hill (5,317 feet)

Southern mule deer
Odocoileus hemionus fuliginatus

Map 09.57 Yolo: A Land of Birds

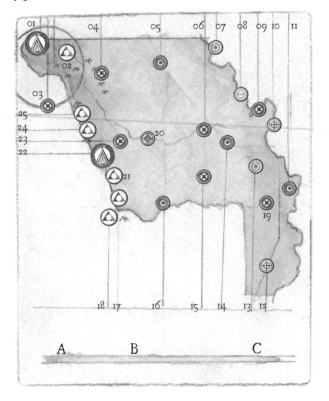

8 miles

09.57

A **West county:** Berryessa Peak (24) (3,057 feet)
B **Mid county:** Capay Valley (04) (204 feet)
C **East county:** Knights Landing (08) (33 feet)

The western edge of Yolo County is defined by the Berryessa Snow Mountain National Monument. The eastern edge, just west of Sacramento, is home to Yolo Bypass Wildlife Area, one of the state's great wetland sanctuaries for migratory birds.

01. Langs Peak (2,640 feet)

02. Berryessa Snow Mountain National Monument (M1): this monument skirts the western border of Yolo County

03. Little Blue Ridge and the Knoxville Wildlife Area (M1): these are both part of a 300,000-acre designated natural area inside the Berryessa Snow Mountain National Monument

04. Capay Valley and Nichols County Park (M7): 22 acres in the town of Guida

05. Dunnigan: a town on the Buckeye Creek

06. Cache Creek Nature Preserve (M1): a riverine habitat and wildlife sanctuary for songbirds and waterfowl

07. Mystic Lake (M5) and China Bend, near Kirkville

08. Knights Landing: a boat launch on the Sacramento River

09. Fremont Weir Wildlife Area (M1): 1,500 acres of valley oaks, willows, sycamores, otter, and quail

10. Sacramento River (M3)

11. West Sacramento and the Grasslands Regional Park (M1): a restored vernal pool habitat just outside of the state's capital city

12. Sacramento Deep Water Channel

13. Tule Canal: one of two major irrigation canals in the county; the other is the Colusa Basin Canal

yellowheaded blackbird
Xanthocephalus xanthocephalus

14. Woodland: city on the Willow Slough

15. Willow Slough: slough on the Sacramento River Floodplain

16. Winters: city

17. Edgar Peak (2,256 feet)

18. Rocky Ridge: this ridge on Cache Creek, inside the Putah Creek Wildlife Area (M1), draws the southern border of Yolo County

19. Yolo Bypass Wildlife Area (M2): one of the Great Valley's largest bird sanctuaries; major populations of hundreds of migrating species of birds nest in these wetlands

20. Cache Creek (M3): this creek runs from Clear Lake County to the Sacramento River

21. Edgar Peak (2,256 feet)

22. Canterbury Mountain (2,474 feet)

23. Brooks: a farming community

24. Berryessa Peak (3,057 feet)

25. Blue Ridge: this ridge forms the eastern basin of Lake Berryessa in adjacent Napa County

white-crowned sparrow
Zonotrichia leucophrys

Map 09.58 Yuba: Water and Gold

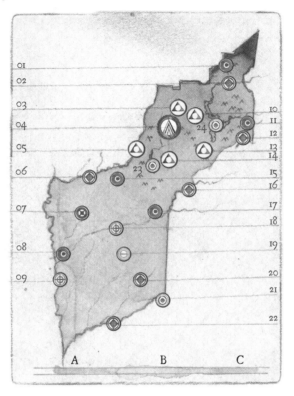

6 miles

09.58

A West county: Marysville (08) (63 feet)
B Mid county: Collins Lake (23) (1,183 feet)
C East county: Bullards Bar Reservoir (24) (1,903 feet)

This small county was the center of northern Sierra Nevada culture during the Gold Rush. Using massive hoses to divert an incredible amount of water, miners washed away hills and mountainsides, looking for gold in a process called hydraulic mining. Elsewhere in the county, cedar and oak mix on hilltop forests across foothill wildlife sanctuaries under significant mountain reservoirs.

01. Strawberry Village: a mountain village

02. Canyon Creek: this creek has its head-waters in Nevada County; it is dammed by Bullards Bar Reservoir

03. Chitterden Ridge

04. Clark Hill (2,346 feet)

05. Donovan Hill (1,650 feet)

06. South Huncut Creek (M3)

07. Jack Slough: a fishing creek down from Browns Valley Ridge

08. Marysville

09. Feather River (M3): the largest tributary of the Sacramento River that comes down from the Sierra

10. Oregon Hills (M7)

11. Camptonville: a city on Oregon Creek

12. Oregon Creek (M7)

13. Dixon Hill (2,304 feet)

14. Flanly Peak (2,099 feet)

15. Loma Rica and Honcut Creek: two tributaries of the Feather River

16. South Yuba River (M3): this river runs past the Point Defiance Camp (M9) and the South Yuba State Park (M7) at Bridgeport

17. Timbuctoo: a Gold Rush ghost town

18. Yuba River (M3): for the last 13 miles of its run, the Yuba River goes through Yuba County to meet the Feather River at Marysville

19. Beale Air Force Base

20. Dry Creek: a creek in the Best Slough on Beale Air Force Base

21. Camp Far West Reservoir (M5): this reservoir is surrounded by the Spenceville Wildlife Management and Recreation Area (M1), where the oaks meet the cedars of the Sierra

22. Bear River (M3): at the southern border of the county, this river is at the confluence of the Feather River with the Bobelaine Audubon Sanctuary and the Feather River Wildlife Area

23. Collins Lake (M5) and the Daugherty Hill Wildlife Area (M1)

24. Bullards Bar Reservoir (M5): this is the largest reservoir in county, and is formed by Canyon Creek, Fiddle Creek, and Slate Creek

10. A REWILDED FUTURE

Grizzly bear
Ursus arctos

One way or another, California will eventually rewild itself, and all humanity can do is get in front of that rewilding and attempt to direct it. For all our control and all our technology, the great living machine that is California will roll on forever. California will experience a warming trend over the next century that will see the swelling of desert-like temperatures in the Central Valley and the northward retreat of cooler temperature averages.

If we dig our heels in and refuse to listen to what the science is telling us, if we continue to go the way we are going, our society will not survive in its current form. The burning and the consumption of fossil fuels as our primary energy source is not a plan for the future. Fortunately, however, we are excellent problem solvers. With the right information and the right spirit, and a bit of ingenuity, we can ensure that the natural California that our grandchildren and their grandchildren know is in even better condition than it is in today.

Natural California is under attack now, and always has been. The California Floristic Province has lost an estimated 70 percent of its primary, original habitat over the 120 years since the Gold Rush. That means that only about 30 percent of California's original vegetation remains in relatively pristine condition today. The ever-growing human population, unsustainable resource extraction, and continued march of invasive species eat at its breadth of diversity. Over the next 100 years, as greenhouse gas emissions increase to levels not seen since the advent of humanity, the global climate

Spotted owl
Strix occidentalis

will shift in ways that are very difficult to predict. Across the California Floristic Province, the generally accepted model suggests that a drying effect will shrink current zones of extreme biodiversity in plant communities to 60 percent of current levels.

Map 10.01 Natural Landscapes Now

Natural landscape blocks (shown in blue in the map) represent about 30 percent of California's total land area. This fractured diagram of so-called blocks include parks, open spaces, mountain peaks, rugged valleys, wilderness, and undeveloped landscape.

47 percent of the state's land area enjoys some measure of protection; protected lands include national forest and public land protected by the Bureau of Land Management and often utilized for resource extraction, timber, and industry. California has more federally designated wilderness areas than any other state besides Alaska, and it rivals Alaska for percentage of total land area protected by federal wilderness; 14 percent of California's land area is wilderness.

There are those who believe that our human society would not suffer if we were to continue to eat away at that 30 percent of California's original landscapes and even at that 14 percent of California's remaining wilderness. There are those who do not mind if the dwindling and isolated, disparate islands of natural landscape become islands of extinction for 10,000 species of plants and animals that call this land home. There are those who do not believe in the rights of wild landscape to be left to live.

However, there are also those—and in fact, we are the majority—who do not believe that the resources of California can be extracted into perpetuity. A strengthening chorus among the people of California believes plainly that what we do to the natural world we do to ourselves, and that if we are not careful to adopt immediate wisdom about how the natural systems of California should be governed in the 21st century and beyond, the sustainability of our state may suffer in the long term. There are many among us who believe in the ethics of conservation and stewardship and who foster an active respect for all living things. We believe that living things are not things at all, but neighbors. We are beginning to realize that all of nature's work in California is part of one dynamic organism and that we, too, are part of it. This perspective, this mindset, is the tool that will become humanity's greatest ally in the challenges that lie ahead.

Piñon pine
Pinus edulis

Map 10.02 Identifying the Rewildling Bridges

What if we sincerely reinvested in California? What if we altered rangeland policy enough to allow wildlife to gain a foothold? What if we mandated that municipalities plan for wildlife corridors? What if we redefined wealthy as meaning "able to do the most common good," the common good being defined as leaving the most intact, optimized system of biodiverse resources and ecologies for many generations of human society to come?

If we were to establish new land protections and rearrange our current land rights uses in uninhabited areas, we could build a network of habitats for wildlife. It would not be easy—renegotiating would take a massive collaboration between private and public agencies—but it is possible. Anything is possible in California; just add political will and a sound vision and the seed will grow. We could redevelop our housing code to rely solely on reusable energy; we could mandate cities to include as much zoning for wild space as for any other use; we could develop systems of transportation beyond the wasteful world of the automobile. It is fun to think about such things, but, alas, such things do not happen overnight. They happen only with concerted, everyday efforts: consider how rivers cut through mountains, or how glaciers are carved in Yosemite. These, of course, are geological processes that take a very long time, and a very long time is what we don't have. What we do have are agile minds and the extraordinary ability to change our environment like no other species in the nearly four billion years of life on this planet.

We've got a strategy, we've got a vision, and we've got a growing plan. Like all plans, it is designed to face challenges, and we've got many of those, too, including 1) the challenge of climate change affecting where the forests are and where they will be; 2) the challenge of dams and the diminishing of salmonid eco-viability; 3) the challenge of water to meet the agricultural needs of a human population that is projected to reach 60 million people in the next 25 years (currently we stand at about 35 million); 4) the challenge of supplying energy to those 60 million people. Attempting to address all of these challenges, our plan calls for a drastic course of action in the rewilding of California that may go against intuition: a reintroduction of big animals to massive wild tracts of land across the state.

mountain lion
Puma concolor

Map 10.03 A Rewilded California

Imagine California as a fully integrated eco-circuit where all living systems can thrive. Imagine a California where not only is the natural quality of life for humans better but we are all the richer for it as well. By repairing connectivity among essential habitats with stringent conservation policies aimed at building new wildlife bridges, we would be doing a favor for ourselves, at least as much as for "nature." As part of this repair, we would need to reintroduce big animals, like grizzly bears and wolves, to these massive wildlife corridors. We would need to do this in conjunction with dismantling as many dams as possible, in order to bring back the salmon, and we would need to eat less beef. A lot less. Unless we figure out how to 1) desalinate ocean water, cheaply and on an industrial scale, and 2) solve our energy demands with a combination of sources that does not include fossil fuels, the beef industry must change.

This plan of rewilding by reintroducing big animals and changing the beef industry comes with many significant challenges. There will never be peace between cowboys and natural predators, and California is a land of cowboys. Thus, California is a land of beef. Raising cattle is something that humans have done since the agricultural revolution 5,000 ago. It is also a wasteful source of food production. In a rewilded California, the role of beef is diminished and large carnivores are reintroduced. Large carnivores hold wild ecologies together by strengthening the fitness of deer herds and fish populations, which, in turn, help to stabilize river courses, mitigate erosion, and normalize wildfire regimes. This model of a balanced ecosystem what is called a top-down model: it holds that predators influence every aspect of a well-rounded, localized natural system, and that without big predators, the conservation movement will not achieve its ultimate goal: the restoration of pristine, healthy, and balanced wild lands.

We know that we are facing an increased tendency toward desertification in California, and the fact that we know this offers us an incredible advantage in our ability to mitigate it. The general public and certain energy interests, in particular, may be leery of pie-in-the-sky environmental solutions, so instead let's consider it a goal to focus on a conservation ethic, a savings account of environmental health, putting as much as we possibly can in a vault and letting it sit there to gain interest. Framing the implementation of the conservation ethic in economic terms is an apt way of imagining how humanity can reward itself in the long run.

Gray wolf.
Canis lupis

Afterword: Wilderness Talking

The human species is both the most beastly and the most divine of all of nature's creations. More than all other lifeforms in the Earth's long history, humans have demonstrated the capacity to rapidly alter our own environment. On a global scale, we are learning that this ability to manipulate, if not tempered with real humility and wisdom, may work to our own detriment. Is it possible that we, the most impactful megafauna in history, can't help but be carried by our own momentum to our potentially awful end? What will ultimately "save" us from this momentum may be not our own cleverness, but rather a different kind of thinking altogether. Different thinking doesn't mean that something radical inside ourselves needs to fundamentally change and that we should all sit around waiting for that to happen. Different thinking may simply entail learning a new skill, and, like all new skills, it will take practice to develop.

Let's start by naming this new skill. For our purposes, let's call it wilderness talking. It would be just as appropriate to call it wilderness listening, as this skill relies on identifying relationships and reading situations in a context that is not about me and you, but rather about us. We begin to practice wilderness talking by modifying our language. We begin by understanding that words are symbols of intent and opportunities for respect. English is, in many ways, a language bereft of words to describe humanity's relationship with nature. In some ways, English is anti-nature. For example, if a small mammal has gotten into my compost bin and scattered apple cores everywhere, and I report it to my family, I am likely to say, "Something got into the compost." I don't say, "Someone got into the compost." In so doing, I have objectified—made a thing out of—nature. I have killed my relationship with nature simply through my choice of words.

Information needs to flow in two directions, a back-and-forth between the subtle and the obvious, the fluidly intuitive and the rigorously academic, the vulnerable and the strong, both locally concerned and globally aware. Language, as it serves communication, is only a piece of this conceptual puzzle; wilderness talking also involves both abstract analysis and poetic synthesis. Take a walk. Take a long walk. See the patterns around you. Use all of your senses. Note your observations. Stoke your curiosity. Ask questions. These are the tenants of wilderness talking.

The foundation for wilderness talking is geographic literacy. Geographic literacy involves a basic knowledge of one's place: its systems of ecology, its historic narrative, and its political trajectory. Geographic literacy is the baseline for any plan of collective sustainability. What a joy it is to conceive of one's place in the world on many different levels of scale. What a joy and indeed a power it is to be able to expand one's thinking and name the systems at work, from the very small to the very large. What a joy it is to know the workings of your bioregion and be counted among its honored and productive citizens. What a joy it is to begin to understand the workings of this, our most wild and cherished home: our California.

California condor
Gymnogyps californianus

Appendix

Coho salmon, *Oncorhynchus kisutch* (03.23)

Columbian mammoth,
Mammuthus columbi (01.10)

Common green darnel,
Anax Junius (03.09)

Common merganser,
Mergus Merganser (09.46)

Common yellowthroat,
Geothlypis trichas (08.13)

Costa's hummingbird, *Calypte costae* (07.14)

Coyote, *Canis latrans* (02.36)

Delta smelt, *Hypomesus
transpacificus* (09.38)

Desert Pupfish, *Cyprinodon
macularius* (07.11)

Digger bee, *Anthophora plumipes* (08.11)

Double-crested cormorant,
Phalacrocorax auritus (08.09)

Douglas iris, *Iris douglasiana* (07.00)

Dowitcher, *Limnodromus
scolopaceus* (09.48)

Elephant seal, *Mirounga
angustirostris* (09.40)

Fawn lily, *Erythronium pusaterii* (03.06)

Foothill yellow-legged frog,
Rana Boylii (09.14)

Foxtail pine, *Pinus balfouriana* (04.07)

Giant sequoia, *Sequoiadendron
giganteum* (04.17)

Gila Woodpecker, *Melanerpes
uropygialis* (06.11)

Golden eagle, *Aquila chrysaetos* (09.15)

Golden-crowned kinglet,
Regulus satrapa (08.07)

Goldenstone shuck, *Calineuria
californica* (03.13)

Gray pine, *Pinus Sabiniana* (09.31)

Gray whale, *Eschrichtius robustus* (03.35)

Gray wolf, *Canis lupus* (10.03)

Great blue heron, *Ardea herodias* (03.05)

Greater sage grouse,
Centrocercus urophasianus (09.25)

Greater white-fronted goose,
Anser albifrons frontalis (09.26)

Green hairstreak butterfly,
Callophrys rubi (09.55)

Green-winged teal,
Anas Carolinensis (09.32)

Grizzly bear, *Ursus arctos* (10.00)

Horned lizard, *Phrynosoma
platyrhinos* (06.15)

Horned owl, *Bubo virginianus* (09.42)

Humboldt marten,
Martes americana (09.12)

Hummingbird sage,
Salvia spathacea (07.18)

Incense cedar, *Calocedrus decurrens* (04.14)

Inyo mule deer, *Odocoileus hemionus* (09.14)

Ithuriel's spear, *Triteleia laxa* (09.53)

Jackrabbit, *Lepus californicus* (06.15)

Joshua tree moth, *Tegeticula
yuccasella* (09.36)

Joshua tree, *Yucca brevifolia* (09.36)

Kern River golden trout,
Oncorhynchus aguabonita (03.00)

King salmon, *Oncorhynchus
tshawytscha* (08.14)

Largemouth bass, *Micropterus
salmoides* (03.31)

Lark sparrow, *Chondestes
grammacus* (05.03)

Little willow flycatcher,
Empidonax brewsteri (02.31)

Lodgepole chipmunk, *Tamias
speciosus* (09.03)

Long-toed salamander, *Ambystoma
macrodactylum creoceum* (09.44)

Meadowlark, *Sturnella neglecta* (05.16)

Mojave roadrunner, *Geococcyx
californianus* (06.00)

Mojave tortoise, *Gopherus agassizii* (06.09)

Mono Lake brine shrimp,
Artemia monica (09.26)

Monterey cypress, *Cupressus
macrocarpa* (04.10)

Mountain hemlock, *Tsuga
mertensiana* (04.00)

Mountain kingsnake, *Lampropeltis
zonata* (07.10)

Mountain Lion, *Puma concolor* (07.06)

Mountain yellow-legged frog,
Rana muscosa (09.33)

Northern flicker, *Colaptes auratus* (02.08)

Northern goshawk, *Accipiter gentilis* (07.01)
Northern harrier, *Circus cyaneus* (09.07)
Northern pintail, *Anas acuta* (07.00)
Osprey, *Pandion haliaetus* (03.03)
Our Lord's candle yucca,
    Hesperoyucca whipplei (03.30)
Peregrine falcon, *Falco peregrinus* (09.47)
Pipevine swallowtail butterfly,
    Baitus philenon (09.55)
Ponderosa pine, *Pinus Ponderosa* (04.12)
Pronghorn, *Antilocapra Americana* (06.16)
Pygmy nuthatch, *Sitta pygmaea* (05.03)
Raccoon, *Procyon lotor* (03.10)
Raven, *Corvus corax* (03.32)
Red fir, *Abies magnifica* (04.00)
Red paintbrush, *Castilleja affinis* (07.17)
Red-tailed hawk, *Buteo jamaicensis* (03.29)
Red-bellied newt, *Taricha rivularis* (03.18)
Ridgway's clapper, *Rallus obsoletus* (03.25)
Ring-necked duck, *Aythya collaris* (09.33)
Ring-necked pheasant,
    Phasianus colchicus (09.47)
Ringtail, *Bassariscus astutus* (09.51)
River otter, *Loutra Canadensis* (09.44)
Ruby-crowned kinglet, *Regulus*
    calendula (04.08)
Ruddy duck, *Oxyura jamaicensis* (03.08)
Sacramento perch, *Archoplites*
    interruptus (08.05)
Sacramento pikeminnow,
    Ptychocheilus grandis (09.29)
Sagebrush penstemon, *Penstemon*
    speciosus (09.18)
San Joaquin rat, *Dipodomys nitratoides* (07.13)
San Francisco garter snake,
    Thamnophis tetrataenia (09.41)
Sandhill crane, *Grus canadensis* (09.34)
Sea otter, *Enhydra lutris* (09.27)
Short-faced bear, *Arctodus simus* (01.00)
Short-faced owl, *Tyto alba* (09.08)
Signal crayfish, *Pacifastacus*
    leniusculus (09.43)
Snowy egret, *Egretta thula* (09.00)
Song sparrow, *Melospiza melodia* (02.27)
Southern mule deer,
    Odocoileus hemionus
    fuliginatus (09.56)

Spotted owl, *Strix occidentalis* (09.08)
Starling, *Sturnus vulgaris* (09.00)
Steelhead trout, *Oncorhynchus*
    mykiss (07.04)
Steller's jay, *Cyanocritta stelleri* (02.22)
Striped skunk, *Mephitis mephitis* (09.52)
Swallowtail, *Papilio multicaudata* (09.54)
Tarantula, *Aphonopelma smithi* (06.12)
Thrasher, *Toxostoma rufum* (09.12)
Threebract onion, *Allium*
    tribracteatum (09.35)
Torrey pine, *Pinus torreyana* (04.13)
Townsends' big-eared bat,
    Corynorhinus townsendii (08.12)
Trillium, *Trillium ovatum* (04.09)
Tule elk, *Cervus canadensis ssp.*
    nannodes (introduction)
Tule perch, *Hysterocarpus traskii* (03.04)
Tule, *Schoenoplectus acutus* (03.20)
Turkey vulture, *Cathartes aura* (09.22)
Valley elderberry longhorn beetle,
    Desmocerus californicus (03.24)
Valley oak, *Quercus lobate* (03.16)
Vermillion flycatcher, *Pyrocephalus*
    rubinus (02.27)
Vermillion rockfish, *Sebastes*
    miniatus (03.33)
Western rattlesnake, *Crotalus Oreganus* (03.19)
Western tanager, *Piranga*
    ludoviciana (09.17)
White fir, *Abies concolor* (08.14)
White sturgeon, *Acipenser trans*
    montanus (03.07)
White-crowned sparrow,
    Zonotrichia leucophrys (09.57)
Wild horse, *Equus ferra* (07.16)
Wild pig, *Sus sciofa linnaeus* (07.15)
Wood duck, *Aix sponsa* (09.47)
Yellow mariposa lily, *Calochortus*
    luteus (09.35)
Yellow-headed blackbird,
    Xanthocephalus
    xanthocephalus (09.57)
Yellow-headed bumblebee,
    Bombus vosnesenskii (08.11)

A Glossary of Ecological Definitions

Acre-foot. One acre-foot is the standard of measurement for water storage. It is equivalent to one acre in surface area by one foot in depth.

Alpine zone. A region that occurs above the tree line and below the snow line on the tops of mountains; in California, the alpine zone ranges from as high as 9,000 feet in southern ranges and as low as 6,000 in northern ranges.

Anadromous. The behavior of fish that spend most of their lives at sea but come to fresh water to spawn, characteristic particularly of salmon.

Anthropogeomorphology. The study of landforms and processes that are a direct result of human activity, including accelerated erosion, channelized rivers, the melting of permafrost, and ground subsidence caused by the extraction of water or minerals.

Aquifer. A body of permeable rock that is capable of storing significant amounts of water.

Bajada. A broad slope of alluvial material at the foot of an escarpment or mountain.

Biodiversity. The variety of life as measured by the quantity of differentiated speciation in a particular area, habitat, or ecosystem. The term biodiversity is used to describe all aspects of biological diversity, including species richness, ecosystem complexity, and genetic variation.

Bioregion. A region defined by characteristics of the natural environment rather than by man-made divisions.

Chaparral. An herbaceous, woody ecosystem that covers approximately 5 percent of California's total land area.

Conifer. A tree that bears cones and evergreen needle-like or scale-like leaves.

Conservation. The maintenance of environmental quality and resources or a particular balance among the species in a given area.

Distinct population segment. The smallest division of a taxonomic species protected under the U.S. Endangered Species Act.

Ecology. The study of the relationship of organisms to one another and to their physical surroundings.

Ecoregion. A major ecosystem defined by distinctive geography and receiving uniform solar radiation and moisture.

Endemic. Native or restricted to a certain area.

Evolutionary significant unit. A population of organisms that is considered distinct for purposes of conservation. Delineating these populations is important when considering conservation action. This term can apply to any species, subspecies, geographic race, or population.

Fire regime. The pattern, frequency, and intensity of the scheduled, periodic occurrence of wildfire in any given ecosystem based on a balance of factors including fuel load, drought, and plant invasiveness.

Geography. The study of the physical features of the Earth and its atmosphere, and of human activity as it affects and is affected by these, including the distribution of populations, resources, and land use.

Habitat. Where a plant or animal meets its requirements for survival.

Herbaceous. Of, denoting, or relating to herbs in the botanical sense

Human ecology. The study of the quality of interhuman systems and how those systems interact with the natural world.

Human society. The social structure and infrastructure invented by humans, regardless of consequence to natural systems.

Hybridization. Refers to the crossbreeding of two animals or plants of different species.

Indicator species. A species whose abundance in an ecosystem is believed to be a measure of environmental conditions in that ecosystem.

Invasive. An introduced species which spreads rapidly once established and disrupts patterns in an existing ecological locality.

Isothermal. Of or relating to a change in a system, where the temperature remains constant, as in when a snowpack begins to melt once its temperature from top to bottom is 32°F.

Keystone species. A species on which other species in an ecosystem largely depend, such that if it were removed the ecosystem would change drastically.

Migratory. Refers to animals that travel seasonally.

Native. Naturally occurring species in a specified geographic region.

Natural community. General term often used as a synonym with habitat.

Pacific Flyway. The westernmost migratory bird route in North America—most often used in connection with the Central Valley.

Range. Maximum geographic extent of taxon or habitat.

Riparian. Of or relating to rivers or streams.

Scale. The relationship between distance on a map and distance on the surface of the Earth.

Speciation. The process by which new species evolve.

Species. The highest level of biological classification from which organisms can breed and produce fertile offspring.

Tectonic plate. One of the many large plates that make up the crust of the Earth.

Temperate. A climate that is neither extremely hot nor extremely cold.

Topography. The shape of the surface of the Earth.

Vernal pools. Seasonal wetlands.

Watershed. Stream or river basin and the adjacent hills and peaks that drain water.

Wildlands. Collective term for largely undeveloped public and private lands.

Noted Sources

Map 01.09 Northern Arizona University, nau.edu (2009)
Map 01.09 University of California Museum of Paleontology, ucmp.berkeley.edu (2010)
Map 01.11 Parrish, California Geologic Survey; 2005
Map 02.02 Jennings, Strand, and Rogers (1977)
Map 02.03 Alt and Hyndman (2000); Durrenberger and Johnson (1976)
Map 02.06 Maizlish (2004)
Map 02.18 College of the Siskiyous, siskiyous.edu (2002)
Map 03.04 Fire Resources and Assessment Program, frap.fire.ca.gov (2015)
Map 03.32 the Los Angeles Aqueduct; by Miguel Abalos (1971)
Map 04.02 Firescience.gov project 09-2-01-9, Chapter 3: Fire Regimes (2010)
Map 04.03 Fire Resources and Assessment Program, calfire.gov (2015)
Map 04.04 Carle (2008)
Map 04.05 Carle (2008)
Map 04.06 Gonzalez, Battles, Collins, Robards, and Saah (2015)
Map 04.13–04.16 Kauffman (2003)
Map 04.17 Pavlik et al. (1991)
Map 05.02 FRAP, precipitation (2015); cagarden.edu (2016)
Map 05.03 California Energy Commission, report (2013)
Map 05.04 California Department of Conservation, conservation.ca.gov (2010)
Map 05.05 National Oceanic and Atmospheric Administration, climate.gov (2013)
Map 05.06 California Data Exchange Center, Department of Water Resources (2012)
Map 05.07 National Hydrologic Remote Sensing Center, noaa.gov (2015)
Map 05.08 California Environmental Protection Agency, Air Resources Board (2010)
Map 05.09 California Air Pollution Control Officers Association (2014)
Map 05.10 Pacific Institute, californiadrought.org (2014)
Map 05.11 U.S. Geological Survey, usgs.gov (2016)
Map 05.12 American Electric Power, aep.com (2013)
Map 05.13 California Energy Commission (2016)
Map 05.14 Independant Statistics, U.S. Energy Administration (2016)
Map 05.15 Defense Meteorological Satellite Program (1995)
Map 05.16 Fws.gov (2012)
Map 06.03 USGS Publications Warehouse, pubs.usgs.gov (2004)
Map 06.05 University of Montana, wilderness.net
Map 07.01 Center for Biological Diversity, biologicaldiversity.org (2014)
Map 07.02–7.04 California Department of Fish and Wildlife, wildlife.ca.gov (2001)
Map 07.05–07.12 Nature Mapping Foundation, naturemappingfoundation.org, UW (2010)
Map 07.08 Conservation Biology Institute, consbio.org (2014)
Map 07.09 UC Davis Information Center for the Environment, ice.ucdavis.edu (2012)
Map 07.14–07.15 Bureau of Land Management, blm.gov (2001)
Map 07.16 environmentalsciencesite.weekly.com (2001)
Map 07.19 Faber (1997)
Map 07.20 Petersen (1993)
Map 10.01 Federal Highway Administration, environment.fhwa.dot.gov (2015)

*Author's Note: Noted sources were referenced peripherally; all the maps in this book are creatively original; reference for scale and accuracy are only made to known and common public borders without infringement on intellectual property in any known form.

Bibliography

Ackerman, Diane. 1990. *A Natural History of the Senses*. New York: Random House.

Alden, Peter, and Fred Heath. 1998. *National Audubon Society Field Guide to California*. New York: Knopf.

Allaby, Michael. 1994. *The Concise Oxford Dictionary of Ecology*. New York: Oxford University Press.

Alt, David, and Donald W. Hyndman. 2000. *Roadside Geology of Northern and Central California*. Missoula, MT: Mountain Press.

Anderson, M. Kat. 2005. *Tending the Wild: Native American Knowledge and the Management of California's Natural Resources*. Berkeley: University of California Press.

Arnold, Daniel. 2009. *Early Days in the Range of Light: Encounters with Legendary Mountaineers*. Berkeley: Counterpoint.

Bakker, Elna. 1971. *An Island Called California: An Ecological Introduction to Its Natural Communities*. Berkeley: University of California Press.

Barbour, Michael, Bruce Pavlik, Frank Drysdale, and Susan Lindstrom. 1993. *California's Changing Landscapes: Diversity and Conservation of California Vegetation*. Sacramento: California Native Plant Society.

Beck, Warren A., and Ynez D. Haase. 1974. *Historical Atlas of California*. Norman: University of Oklahoma Press.

Beesley, David. 2004. *Crow's Range: An Environmental History of the Sierra Nevada*. Reno: University of Nevada Press.

Behrensmeyer, A. K., et al. 1992. *Terrestrial Ecosystems through Time: Evolutionary Paleoecology of Terrestrial Plants and Animals*. Chicago: University of Chicago Press.

Beidleman, Richard G. 2006. *California's Frontier Naturalists*. Berkeley: University of California Press.

Bishop, Greg, Joe Oesterle, and Mike Marinacci. 2006. *Weird California: Your Travel Guide to California's Local Legends and Best Kept Secrets*. New York: Sterling.

Blackburn, Chet. ed. 2014. *Trees and Shrubs of Nevada and Placer Counties, California*. Nevada City: Redbud Chapter and California Native Plant Society Press.

Blackwelder, E. 1931. "Pleistocene Glaciation in the Sierra Nevada and Basin Ranges." Geologic Society of America Bulletin 42 (4): 865–922.

Blackwell, Laird. 1999. *Wildflowers of the Sierra Nevada and the Central Valley*. Edmonton, AB: Lone Pine Publishing.

Boeck, Raynell. 2011. *Peaceful Places: San Francisco: 110 Tranquil Sites in The City and the Greater Bay Area*. Birmingham, AL: Menasha Ridge Press.

Brower, Kenneth. 2013. *Hetch Hetchy: Undoing a Great American Mistake*. Berkeley: Heyday.

Brown, Ann Marie. 1997. *California Waterfalls: Where to Hike, Bike, Backpack, Walk, and Drive to 200 of the Golden State's Most Spectacular Falls*. San Francisco: Foghorn Press.

Browning, Peter. 1986. *Place Names of the Sierra Nevada: From Abbot to Zumwalt*. Berkeley, CA: Wilderness Press.

Buchmann, Stephen. 2015. *The Reason for Flowers: Their History, Culture, Biology, and How They Change Our Lives*. New York: Scribner.

Carle, David. 2004. *Introduction to Water in California*. California Natural History Guides. Berkeley: University of California Press.

———. 2008. *Introduction to Fire in California*. California Natural History Guides. Berkeley: University of California Press.

———. 2010. *Introduction to Earth, Soil, and Land in California*. California Natural History Guides. Berkeley: University of California Press.

Caruthers, William. 1951. *Loafing along Death Valley Trails: A Personal Narrative of People and Places*. Ontario, CA: Death Valley Publishing Co.

Chase, J. Smeaton. 1911. *Cone-Bearing Trees of the California Mountains*. Chicago: A. C. McClurg & Co.

Childs, Craig. 2000. *The Secret Knowledge of Water: Discovering the Essence of the American Desert*. Seattle: Sasquatch Books.

Cooper, Daniel S. 2004. *Important Bird Areas of California*. Pasadena: Audubon California.

Crampton, Beecher. 1974. *Grasses in California*. Berkeley: University of California Press.

Critser, Greg. 2000. *National Geographic Traveler: California*. Washington, DC: National Geographic.

Cunningham, Laura. 2010. *A State of Change: Forgotten Landscapes of California*. Berkeley: Heyday.

Curtis, Molly. 2013. *Lela Rhoades, Pit River Woman*. Berkeley: Heyday.

Dale, Nancy. 1986. *Flowering Plants: The Santa Monica Mountains, Coastal and Chaparral Regions of Southern California*. California Native Plant Society. Santa Barbara: Capra Press.

Darlington, David. 1996. *The Mojave: A Portrait of the Definitive American Desert*. New York: Henry Holt.

De Vries, Carolyn. 1978. *Grand and Ancient Forest: The Story of Andrew P. Hill and Big Basin Redwood State Park*. Fresno, CA: Valley Publishers.

Didion, Joan. 2003. *Where I Was From*. New York: Knopf.

Dirke-Edmunds, Jane Claire. 1999. *Not Just Trees: The Legacy of a Douglas-Fir Forest*. Pullman: Washington State University Press.

Durrenberger, Robert W., and Robert B. Johnson. 1976. *California, Patterns on the Land*. A California Council for Geographic Education Publication. Palo Alto: Mayfield Publishing Co.

Faber, Phyllis M., ed. 1997. *California's Wild Gardens: A Guide to Favorite Botanical Sites*. Berkeley: University of California Press.

Fauver, Toni. 1992. *Wildflower Walking in Lakes Basin of the Northern Sierra*. Orinda, CA: Fauver and Steinbach.

Finson, Bruce, ed. 1983. *Discovering California: A Selection of Article and Photographs from Pacific Discovery Magazine in Facsimile Reprint*. San Francisco: California Academy of Sciences.

Fleischner, Thomas Lowe, ed. 2011. *The Way of Natural History*. San Antonio, TX: Trinity University Press.

Fradkin, Philip L. 1997. *The Seven States of California, A Natural and Human History.* Berkeley: University of California Press.

Gell, Lachlan, Harry Glass, and Ezekiel Morgan, eds. 2014. *Pollen, Issue #01: The Idea of Natural History.* Sydney: Modem-Verlag.

Grillos, Steve J. 1966. *Ferns and Fern Allies of California.* Berkeley: University of California Press.

Gudde, Erwin G. 1949. *California Place Names: The Origin and Etymology of Current Geographical Names.* Berkeley: University of California Press.

Hanson, Mary. 2014. *A Species Guide to the Berryessa Snow Mountain Region.* Woodland: Tuleyome Books.

Harden, Deborah. 1992. *California Geology.* New York: Pearson.

Hart, James D. 1987. *A Companion to California.* Berkeley: University of California Press.

Hart, John. 1975. *Hiking the Bigfoot Country, The Wildlands of Northern California and Southern Oregon.* A Sierra Club Totebook. San Francisco: Sierra Club Books.

———. 1978. *San Francisco's Wilderness Next Door.* San Rafael: Presidio Press.

Heffernan, Helen, Irmagarde Richars, and Alice Salisbury. 1948. *Desert Treasure: A Story of Adventure and The Mohave Desert.* San Francisco: Harr Wagner Publishing Co.

Henson, Paul, and Donald J. Usner. 1993. *The Natural History of Big Sur.* Berkeley: University of California Press.

Holing, Dwight. 1988. California *Wild Lands: A Guide to the Nature Conservancy Preserves.* San Francisco: Chronicle Books.

Hornbeck, David. 1983. *California Patterns: A Geographical and Historical Atlas.* Palo Alto, CA: Mayfield Publishing Co.

Huntsinger, Linda. 2002. *Sierra Nevada Grazing in Transition: The Role of Forest Service Grazing in the Foothill Ranches of California.* CA: Sierra Nevada Alliance.

Irwin, Sue. 1991. *California's Eastern Sierra: A Visitor's Guide.* Los Olivos, CA: Cachuma Press.

Jaeger, Edmund C. 1933. *The California Deserts.* Stanford, CA: Stanford University Press.

———. 1940. *Desert Wildflowers.* Stanford, CA: Stanford University Press.

Jennings, C. W., R. G. Strand, and T. H. Rogers. 1977. *Geologic Map of California.* San Francisco: California Division of Mines and Geology.

Johnson, Paul. 1970. *Pictorial History of California.* Garden City, NY: Doubleday.

Johnston, Verna R. 1998. *Sierra Nevada: The Naturalist's Companion.* Berkeley: University of California Press.

Kauffman, Eric. 2003. *Altas of Biodiversity of California.* Sacramento: State of California, Resources Agency Department of Fish and Game.

Kaufmann, Michael E. 2013. *Conifers of the Pacific Slope: A Field Guide to the Conifers of California, Oregon and Washington.* Kneeland, CA: Backcountry Press.

Keator, Glenn. 2009. *California Plant Families: West of the Sierran Crest and Deserts.* Berkeley: University of California Press.

Kimmerer, Robin Wall. 2013. *Braiding Sweetgrass.* Minneapolis: Milkweed Editions.

Koford, Carl B. 1953. *The California Condor.* Museum of Vertebrate Zoology of the University of California. New York: Dover Publications.

Kroeber, Theodora. 1961. *Ishi in Two Worlds: A Biography of the Last Wild Indian in North America.* Berkeley: University of California Press.

Lanner, Ronald. 1999. *Conifers of California.* Los Olivos, CA: Cachuma Press.

Laws, John Muir. 2007. *The Laws Field Guide to the Sierra Nevada.* California Academy of Sciences. Berkeley: Heyday.

Lee, W. Storrs. 1968. *California, a Literary Chronicle.* New York: Funk & Wagnalls.

Lentz, Joan Easton. 2013. *A Naturalist's Guide to the Santa Barbara Region.* Berkeley: Heyday.

Leopold, A. Starker. 1985. *Wild California: Vanishing Lands, Vanishing Wildlife.* Berkeley: University of California Press.

Lightfoot, Kent G., and Otis Parish. 2009. *California Indians and Their Environment: An Introduction.* Berkeley: University of California Press.

Lindsay, Lowell, and Diana Linday. 1978. *The Anza-Borrego Desert Region: A Guide to the State Park and Adjacent Areas of the Western Colorado Desert.* Berkeley: Wilderness Press.

Locklin, Linda, ed. 1981. *California Coastal Access Guide.* California Coastal Commission. Berkeley: University of California Press.

Lopez, Barry, and Debra Gwartney. 2006. *Home Ground: A Guide to the American Landscape.* San Antonio, TX: Trinity University Press.

Lyons, Kathleen, and Mary Beth Cuneo-Lazaneo. 1988. *Plants of the Coast Redwood Region.* Soquel: Shoreline Press.

Maizlish, Aaron. *Lineage Groups.* 2004. Peaklist.org.

Margolin, Malcolm. 1974. *The East Bay Out: A Personal Guide to the East Bay Regional Parks.* Berkeley: Heyday.

———. 1978. *The Ohlone Way: Indian Life in the San Francisco-Monterey Bay Area.* Berkeley: Heyday.

Marianchild, Kate. 2014. *Secrets of the Oak Woodlands: Plants and Animals Among California's Oaks.* Berkeley: Heyday.

McAuley, Milt. 1985. *Wildflowers of the Santa Monica Mountains.* Canoga Park: Canyon Publishing Co.

McKinney, John. 2011. *Dayhiker's Guide to California State Parks.* Santa Barbara: Trailmaster.

McPhee, John. 1993. *Assembling California.* New York: Farrar, Straus and Giroux.

Miller, Crane S., and Richard S. Hyslop. 1983. *California: The Geography of Diversity.* Mountain View: Mayfield Publishing Co.

Miller, Henry. 1957. *Big Sur and the Oranges of Hieronymus Bosch.* New York: New Directions Books.

Montanarelli, Lisa, and Ann Harrison. 2005. *Strange but True, San Francisco.* London: PRC Publishing.

Morgan, Neil. 1969. *The California Syndrome.* Englewood Cliffs, NY: Prentice Hall.

Mott, William Penn, Jr. 1960. *California Historical Landmarks.* Sacramento: California Landmarks Advisory Committee.

Muir, John. 1988. *The Mountains of California.* San Francisco: Sierra Club Books. First published 1894.

———. 1984. *Summering in the Sierra.* Edited by Robert Engberg. Madison: University of Wisconsin Press.

Nixon, Stuart. 1966. *Redwood Empire.* New York City: Galahad Books.

Nolan, Ruth, ed. 2009. *No Place for a Puritan: The Literature of the California Deserts.* Berkeley: Heyday.

Noy, Gary, and Rick Heide, eds. 2010. *The Illuminated Landscape: A Sierra Nevada Anthology.* Rocklin: Sierra College Press; Berkeley: Heyday.

Ornduff, Robert, Phyllis M. Faber, and Todd Keeler-Wolf. 2003. *An Introduction to California Plant Life.* California Natural History Guides. Berkeley: University of California Press.

Pavlik, Bruce M, Pamela C. Muick, Sharon G. Johnson, and Marjorie Popper. 1991. *Oaks of California.* Los Olivos: Cachuma Press.

Pavlik, Bruce M. 2008. *The California Deserts: An Ecological Rediscovery.* Berkeley: University of California Press.

Peterson, B. "Moose." 1993. *California, Vanishing Habitats and Wildlife.* Wilsonville, OR: Beautiful American Publishing Co.

Pickett, Edwin R. 1971. *Birds of Central California.* Sacramento: Sacramento Bee.

Pratt-Bergstrom, Beth. 2016. *When Mountain Lions Are Neighbors: People and Wildlife Working It Out in California.* Berkeley: Heyday.

Press, Daniel. 2002. *Saving Open Space: The Politics of Local Preservation in California.* Berkeley: University of California Press.

Preston, Richard. 2008. *The Wild Trees: A Story of Passion and Daring.* New York: Random House.

Quinn, Ronald D., and Sterling C. Keeley. 2006. *Introduction to California Chaparral.* California Natural History Guides. Berkeley: University of California Press.

Rasmussen, Cecilia. 1996. *Curbside L.A.: An Offbeat Guide to the City of Angels, from the Pages of the Los Angeles Times.* Los Angeles: Los Angeles Times.

Reisner, Marc. 1986. *Cadillac Desert: The American West and Its Disappearing Water.* New York: Penguin Books.

Riegert, Ray. 1988. *Hidden Coast of California: Including San Diego, Los Angeles, Santa Barbara, Monterey, San Francisco, and Mendocino.* Berkeley: Ulysses Press.

———. 1990. *California: The Ultimate Guidebook.* Berkeley: Ulysses Press.

Robinson, John W. 1972. *San Bernardino Mountain Trails: 100 Wilderness Hikes in Southern California.* Berkeley: Wilderness Press.

Sanford, Bill. 1994. *The San Joaquin, the Sierra, and Beyond.* Santa Cruz: Western Tanager Press.

Schoenherr, Allan A. 1992. *A Natural History of California.* Berkeley: University of California Press.

Schoffstall, Patricia. 2010. *Mojave Desert Dictionary.* Barstow: Mojave River Valley Museum.

Scott, Commander. 1945. *Romance on the Highways of California: Unusual and Interesting Facts About the Golden State.* Pasadena: Commander Scott Productions.

Sharp, R. P., C. R. Allen, and M. F. Meier. 1959. "Pleistocene Glaciers on Southern California Mountains." American Journal of Science 257 (2): 81–94.

Showers, Mary Ann. 1981. *A Field Guide to The Flowers of Lassen Volcanic National Park.* CA: Loomis Museum Association for Lassen Volcanic National Park.

Snyder, Gary. 1995. *A Place in Space: Ethics, Aesthetics, and Watersheds.* Berkeley: Counterpoint.

Sowaal, Marguerite. 1985. *Naming the Eastern Sierra: Dirty Sock to Bloody Canyon.* Bishop, CA: Chalfant Press.

Starr, Kevin. 2005. *California: A History.* New York: Modern Library.

Starr, Walter A., Jr. 1964. *Starr's Guide to the John Muir Trail and the High Sierra Region.* San Francisco: Sierra Club Books.

Stegner, Wallace. 1946. *The Sound of Mountain Water.* New York: Dutton Books.

———. 1971. *Angle of Repose.* New York: Penguin Books.

Stienstra, Tom. 2000. *California Wildlife: A Practical Guide.* Emeryville: Foghorn Outdoors.

Storer, Tracy I., and Robert L. Usinger. 2004. *Sierra Nevada Natural History.* California Natural History Guides. Rev. ed. Berkeley: University of California Press.

Telander, Todd. 2012. *Birds of California: A Falcon Field Guide.* Helena, MT: Rowman & Littlefield.

Timbrook, Jan. 2007. *Chumash Ethnobotany: Plant Knowledge Among the Chumash People of Southern California.* Santa Barbara: Santa Barbara Museum of Natural History; Berkeley: Heyday.

Tweed, William C. 2016. *King Sequoia: The Tree That Inspired a Nation, Created Our National Park System, and Changed the Way We Think about Nature.* Berkeley: Heyday.

U.S. Geological Survey. 2006. Quaternary Fault and Fold Database for the United States. https://earthquake.usgs.gov.

Waite, Heather. 1999. *Calling California Home: A Lively Look at What It Means to Be a Californian.* Berkeley: Wildcat Canyon Press.

Wallace, David Rains. 1983. *The Klamath Knot: Explorations of Myth and Evolution.* Berkeley: University of California Press.

———. 2014. *Articulate Earth: Adventures in Ecocriticism.* Kneeland, CA: Backcountry Press.

———. 2015. *Mountains and Marshes: Exploring the Bay Area's Natural History.* Berkeley: Counterpoint.

Watkins, T. H. 1973. *California: An Illustrated History.* The Great West Series. Palo Alto, CA: American West Publishing Co.

Wheat, Frank. 1999. *California Desert Miracle: The Fight for Desert Parks and Wilderness.* San Diego, CA: Sunbelt Publications.

White, Mike. 1983. *Trinity Alps and Vicinity: A Hiking and Backpacking Guide.* Berkeley, CA: Wilderness Press.

Wiese, Karen. 2013. *Sierra Nevada Wildflowers: A Field Guide.* A Falcon Guide. Guilford, CT: Guilford Falcon Guides.

Williams, T. B., H. M. Kelsey, and J. T. Freymueller. 2002. *Escape of Sierra Nevada–Great Valley Block Motion Contributes to Upper-Plate Contraction Within the Southern Cascadia Margin Near Humboldt Bay, CA.* Washington, DC: American Geophysical Union.

Winnett, Thomas. 1971. *Mt. Whitney. High Sierra Hiking Series no. 5.* Berkeley: Wilderness Press.

Wohl, Ellen. 2009. *Of Rocks and Rivers: Seeking a Sense of Place in the American West.* Berkeley: University of California Press.

Wright, Bank. 1973. *Surfing California: A Complete Guide to the California Coast.* Manhattan, MT: Mountain and Sea.

Zwinger, Ann Haymond. 1989. *The Mysterious Lands: An Award-Winning Naturalist Explores the Four Great Deserts of the Southwest.* New York: Truman Talley Book/Plume.

Acknowledgments

As I compiled a list of all of those without whom this compendium would not have happened, I was shocked at the wealth of creative and radiant humans who I am so privileged to call friends. This list is global in scope and spans the past several decades. I must begin with my love, Alli, and her family: Rhonda, Frank, Max, and Francisca. Rounding out my immediate circle, I must include my mother, Dr. Jeffre Talltrees; her loving husband, Somraj Pokras; and my sister, Kristine, and her beautiful daughters, Bryanna and Sophia. As the circles of influence radiate out, I think of all the professional advice I've gotten and am so very grateful for. Lindsie Bear, Ashley Ingram, and Diane Lee at Heyday have collectively represented for me a sail, an anchor, and a compass throughout the creative ordeal. Malcolm Margolin, a man of massive generosity and the founder of Heyday, has straightened my course at many points in this journey. I am grateful to Steve Wasserman for coming on with Heyday and championing this book endeavor. I also need to call out in grand appreciation my fellow Heyday heroes and favorite artists—Gary Snyder, Tom Killion, and John Muir Laws—who inspire me day in and day out.

I would never have come to the city if it weren't for my immediate circle of friends and the love of Matt and Hilary Decker, Finn and Olive too; Robert Porter and Carrissa Bowman, Vander and Olivia too; John Casey and Mary Kalin-Casey; Seth and Ahna Wright; Leb Borgerson and Lauren Finbraaten.

I would like to also tap in appreciation for their impressive, intellectual magnanimity toward this project Hall Newbegin of Juniper Ridge; Jordan Vouga of Vouga Designs; Juniper Ridge; Tobias Hayduk; Desert & Denim; Mats Andersson of Indigo Fera Jeans; Jeff Thrope of Cold Splinters; Lindsey Shiflett Smith with Makers Workshop; Bob Schneider, Sara Husby, and Charlotte Orr with Tuleyome; Andrea Alday with the Wilderness Society; Victoria Schlesinger at *Bay Nature* magazine; Sam Goldman of the Bureau of Land Management; Mike and Jenn Smith with the Los Padres Forest Association; John Sterling with the Conservation Alliance; Mike Splain with the Ventana Wilderness Alliance; Seth Shteir and Ron Sundergill of the National Parks Conservation Association; Matt Dolkas of the Peninsula Open Space Trust; Stephen Goldblatt of Mill Valley Walking Stick Company; Bridget Muscat of Allet; Steve Rogerson; Michael Friedes; Julie Atherton; Jordan Phillips; Lulu and Micha... of the wolves; Nikiya, Kitkitdizzi, and Nevada City; and, of course, Ciel Bergman and April Funke for turning me on to paint at all.

I am so privileged to have spent long days and nights on the trail with many of the greatest, most open-hearted people on the planet, who surely helped with campfires and whiskey sipping after a long day on the trail: Minoo Hamilton, Matt Fisher, Michael Hamilton, Marty Caplan, Elliot Fredericksen, Travis Luther, Ben Borgman, Lexa

Walsh, Brett Baumgart, David Lyle, Mike Bullas, Greg Migdale, Dan Nelson, Tim Bohr, Joanne Gillespie, Tori Willis, Rob Doser, August Varlack, Laura Sweitzer, Vicki Kuskowski, Amy and Darby Flook, Zoe and Owen too; Telisa Swan, Tyler Evans, Gus Elg, Scott Hayden, Steven Schaaf, Forest Stearns, Kevin Carney, Kari Salmela, Pontus Rogbring, Jessica Arkenstone, Mike Flaherty, Tanya Grimes, and Tom Accettola.

Lastly a special thank you to my father, Dr. William John Kaufmann III, for sharing with me his wonder at the universe.

About the Author

The son of an astrophysicist and a psychologist, Obi Kaufmann grew up in the East Bay. He spent most of high school studying calculus and breaking away on weekends to scramble around Mount Diablo, mapping and naming the creeks, oak forests, and sage mazes he found there. Into adulthood he would regularly journey into the mountains, spending more summer nights without a roof than with one, as his identity as a wilderness naturalist took hold. For Obi, the epic narrative of the California backcountry holds enough art, science, mythology, and language for a hundred Field Atlases to come. When not backpacking, Obi can be found at his desk in Oakland, posting @coyotethunder #trailpaintings on social media. His website is www.coyoteandthunder.com.

HEYDAY
into California

About Heyday

Heyday is an independent, nonprofit publisher and unique cultural institution. We promote widespread awareness and celebration of California's many cultures, landscapes, and boundary-breaking ideas. Through our well-crafted books, public events, and innovative outreach programs we are building a vibrant community of readers, writers, and thinkers.

Thank You

It takes the collective effort of many to create a thriving literary culture. We are thankful to all the thoughtful people we have the privilege to engage with. Cheers to our writers, artists, editors, storytellers, designers, printers, bookstores, critics, cultural organizations, readers, and book lovers everywhere!

We are especially grateful for the generous funding we've received for our publications and programs during the past year from foundations and hundreds of individual donors. Major supporters include:

Anonymous; Arkay Foundation; Judith and Phillip Auth; Judy Avery; Richard and Rickie Ann Baum; Randy Bayard; BayTree Fund; Jean and Fred Berensmeier; Nancy Bertelsen; Edwin Blue; Philip and Jamie Bowles; Beatrice Bowles; Peter Boyer and Terry Gamble Boyer; Brandt-Hawley Law Group; John Briscoe; California Humanities; The Campbell Foundation; John and Nancy Cassidy; The Christensen Fund; Lawrence Crooks; Chris Desser and Kirk Marckwald; Steven Dinkelspiel; Frances Dinkelspiel and Gary Wayne; The Roy and Patricia Disney Family Foundation; Tim Disney; Patricia Dixon; Gayle Embrey; Richard and Gretchen Evans; Megan Fletcher, in honor of J.K. Dineen; Patrick Golden and Susan Overhauser; Wanda Lee Graves and Stephen Duscha; Whitney Green; Walter & Elise Haas Fund; Penelope Hlavac; Nettie Hoge; Michael Horn, in memory of Gary Horn; Humboldt Area Foundation; JiJi Foundation; Claudia Jurmain; Kalliopeia Foundation; Marty Krasney; Abigail Kreiss; Guy Lampard and Suzanne Badenhoop; Thomas Lockard and Alix Marduel; David Loeb; Judith Lowry-Croul and Brad Croul;

About the Author

The son of an astrophysicist and a psychologist, Obi Kaufmann grew up in the East Bay. He spent most of high school studying calculus and breaking away on weekends to scramble around Mount Diablo, mapping and naming the creeks, oak forests, and sage mazes he found there. Into adulthood he would regularly journey into the mountains, spending more summer nights without a roof than with one, as his identity as a wilderness naturalist took hold. For Obi, the epic narrative of the California backcountry holds enough art, science, mythology, and language for a hundred Field Atlases to come. When not backpacking, Obi can be found at his desk in Oakland, posting @coyotethunder #trailpaintings on social media. His website is www.coyoteandthunder.com.

HEYDAY
into California

About Heyday

Heyday is an independent, nonprofit publisher and unique cultural institution. We promote widespread awareness and celebration of California's many cultures, landscapes, and boundary-breaking ideas. Through our well-crafted books, public events, and innovative outreach programs we are building a vibrant community of readers, writers, and thinkers.

Thank You

It takes the collective effort of many to create a thriving literary culture. We are thankful to all the thoughtful people we have the privilege to engage with. Cheers to our writers, artists, editors, storytellers, designers, printers, bookstores, critics, cultural organizations, readers, and book lovers everywhere!

We are especially grateful for the generous funding we've received for our publications and programs during the past year from foundations and hundreds of individual donors. Major supporters include:

Anonymous; Arkay Foundation; Judith and Phillip Auth; Judy Avery; Richard and Rickie Ann Baum; Randy Bayard; BayTree Fund; Jean and Fred Berensmeier; Nancy Bertelsen; Edwin Blue; Philip and Jamie Bowles; Beatrice Bowles; Peter Boyer and Terry Gamble Boyer; Brandt-Hawley Law Group; John Briscoe; California Humanities; The Campbell Foundation; John and Nancy Cassidy; The Christensen Fund; Lawrence Crooks; Chris Desser and Kirk Marckwald; Steven Dinkelspiel; Frances Dinkelspiel and Gary Wayne; The Roy and Patricia Disney Family Foundation; Tim Disney; Patricia Dixon; Gayle Embrey; Richard and Gretchen Evans; Megan Fletcher, in honor of J.K. Dineen; Patrick Golden and Susan Overhauser; Wanda Lee Graves and Stephen Duscha; Whitney Green; Walter & Elise Haas Fund; Penelope Hlavac; Nettie Hoge; Michael Horn, in memory of Gary Horn; Humboldt Area Foundation; JiJi Foundation; Claudia Jurmain; Kalliopeia Foundation; Marty Krasney; Abigail Kreiss; Guy Lampard and Suzanne Badenhoop; Thomas Lockard and Alix Marduel; David Loeb; Judith Lowry-Croul and Brad Croul;

Praveen Madan and Christin Evans; Joel Marcus; Malcolm and Rina Margolin; William, Karen, and John McClung; Michael McCone; Nion McEvoy and Leslie Berriman, in honor of Malcolm Margolin; Judy Mistelske-Anklam and William Anklam; Karen and Tom Mulvaney; National Wildlife Federation; The Nature Conservancy; Eddie Orton; The Ralph M. Parsons Foundation; Alan Rosenus; The San Francisco Foundation; San Manuel Band of Mission Indians; Greg Sarris; Save the Redwoods League; Stanley Smith Horticultural Trust; Roselyne Swig; Tappan Foundation; Thendara Foundation; Michael and Shirley Traynor, in honor of Malcolm Margolin; The Roger J. and Madeleine Traynor Foundation; Al and Ann Wasserman; Sherry Wasserman and Clayton F. Johnson; Lucinda Watson; Peter Wiley and Valerie Barth; Mina Witteman; and Yocha Dehe Wintun Nation.

Board of Directors

Getting Involved

To learn more about our publications, events, and other ways you can participate, please visit www.heydaybooks.com.

Hartweg's Iris
Iris hartwegii